Doing a
Literature
Review

Sara Miller McCune founded SAGE Publishing in 1965 to support the dissemination of usable knowledge and educate a global community. SAGE publishes more than 1000 journals and over 800 new books each year, spanning a wide range of subject areas. Our growing selection of library products includes archives, data, case studies and video. SAGE remains majority owned by our founder and after her lifetime will become owned by a charitable trust that secures the company's continued independence.

Los Angeles | London | New Delhi | Singapore | Washington DC | Melbourne

→SAGE Study Skills

Doing a Literature Review

Releasing the Research Imagination

Chris Hart

2nd Edition

SAGE

Los Angeles | London | New Delhi
Singapore | Washington DC | Melbourne

Los Angeles | London | New Delhi
Singapore | Washington DC | Melbourne

SAGE Publications Ltd
1 Oliver's Yard
55 City Road
London EC1Y 1SP

SAGE Publications Inc.
2455 Teller Road
Thousand Oaks, California 91320

SAGE Publications India Pvt Ltd
B 1/I 1 Mohan Cooperative Industrial Area
Mathura Road
New Delhi 110 044

SAGE Publications Asia-Pacific Pte Ltd
3 Church Street
#10-04 Samsung Hub
Singapore 049483

Editor: Mila Steele
Editorial assistant: John Nightingale
Production editor: Tom Bedford
Marketing manager: Ben Sherwood
Cover design: Jennifer Crisp
Typeset by: C&M Digitals (P) Ltd, Chennai, India
Printed in the UK

First edition published 2003. Reprinted 2003, 2005 (twice),
2006, 2007, 2008, 2009, 2010, 2011, 2013, 2014 (twice),
2015, 2016

This second edition first published 2018

Library of Congress Control Number: 2017944145

British Library Cataloguing in Publication data

A catalogue record for this book is available from the
British Library

ISBN 978-1-5264-1920-0
ISBN 978-1-5264-1921-7 (pbk)

At SAGE we take sustainability seriously. Most of our products are printed in the UK using FSC papers and boards.
When we print overseas we ensure sustainable papers are used as measured by the PREPS grading system.
We undertake an annual audit to monitor our sustainability.

Contents

List of Figures and Tables

Figures

Tables

Acknowledgements

This second edition would not have been possible without Beverley, who with an extremely busy schedule, found the time and effort to keep this project alive. Her dedication and input to this book are is equal to my own.

Preface

Undertaking research for a thesis or dissertation is an experience that most people never forget. Worries about what topic to investigate, how to go about doing the research and writing at length, are common concerns raised by research students. No one can do the research for you; the responsibility is yours and yours alone. This often leads to feelings of isolation and sometimes to a loss of confidence. But with a little planning, careful thought and the adoption of the right attitude, you will be able to set realistic objectives and find that the stress and anxiety of doing the research can be managed and even enjoyable! Few experiences match the sense of achievement and exhilaration that result from finishing your thesis or dissertation.

This book has been written for postgraduate research students and tutors as well as anyone with an interest in the use of research as evidence for an intervention or argument.

This book is not a manual nor is it prescriptive. It is an introduction, aimed at postgraduates, on what it means and what is involved in reviewing research literature. It looks at explaining as well as describing the ideas on which the methods and techniques for analysing a literature are based.

Skills and capabilities for research

Various frameworks have been developed to guide researchers, from all disciplines, through the complexities of the skills and abilities they need to acquire and demonstrate. The proposition underpinning these frameworks is that the national economy will be partly dependent on producing competent world-class researchers. Research will, it is assumed, drive innovation, wealth creation and lead the way to a better world for all. Not all of this will be achieved with great leaps; the small incremental contributions will also have a role to play. In the UK, the Vitae Researcher Development Framework (RDF) is an example of a guide that has been developed to be used by all sectors – education, business, government and charities – for individual and teams of researchers, their supervisors and employers to adopt regardless of the subject discipline or purpose of the research.

The RDF is a framework specifying a range of skills, knowledge, capabilities and activities that are divided into four broad domains. From the standpoint of a researcher it shows what is expected from them and provides a guide to what you (as that researcher) should be doing to develop your competences. Figure 0.1 shows the four domains and how each has sub-divisions. Throughout this book indications are given as to which domain is being looked at and which core skills it relates to.

The RDF is downloadable from the Vitae website (www.vitae.ac.uk/rdf) as a professional development tool. You can use it to identify your training needs, create action plans and record evidence of your progress. The RDF is not for any one discipline; all disciplines and types of research activity are encompassed within the framework. These include the traditional higher degree as well as research done for professional practice. The four main domains are:

> *Knowledge and intellectual abilities.* Acquiring the knowledge, cognitive abilities and capacity to do competent research.
>
> *Personal effectiveness.* Developing the personal qualities and attitudes to be an effective researcher.
>
> *Research governance and organisation.* Understanding the standards and requirements of professional, scholarly research.
>
> *Engagement and impact.* Working and networking with others, sharing ideas and disseminating research.

Domain A, *Knowledge and intellectual abilities*, is relevant to searching and reviewing a literature and all that this involves. This domain is built on the SCONUL Seven Pillars of Information Literacy (SCONUL, 2011). This scheme places a primacy on citizens, including researchers, having a sound understanding of the ways in which information is generated, stored, categorised, disseminated and can be applied.

> In the 21st century, information literacy is a key attribute for everyone, irrespective of age or experience ... it is evidenced through understanding the ways in which information and data is created and handled, developing skills in its management and use and modifying attitudes, habits and behaviours to appreciate the role of information literacy in learning and research. (SCONUL, 2011:13)

The Seven Pillars of Information Literacy is not only about skills but includes – and this is important – statements relating to the need for developing ways of evaluating and understanding information and data. This is not a linear scheme but one that reflects real world researcher experience by being iterative.

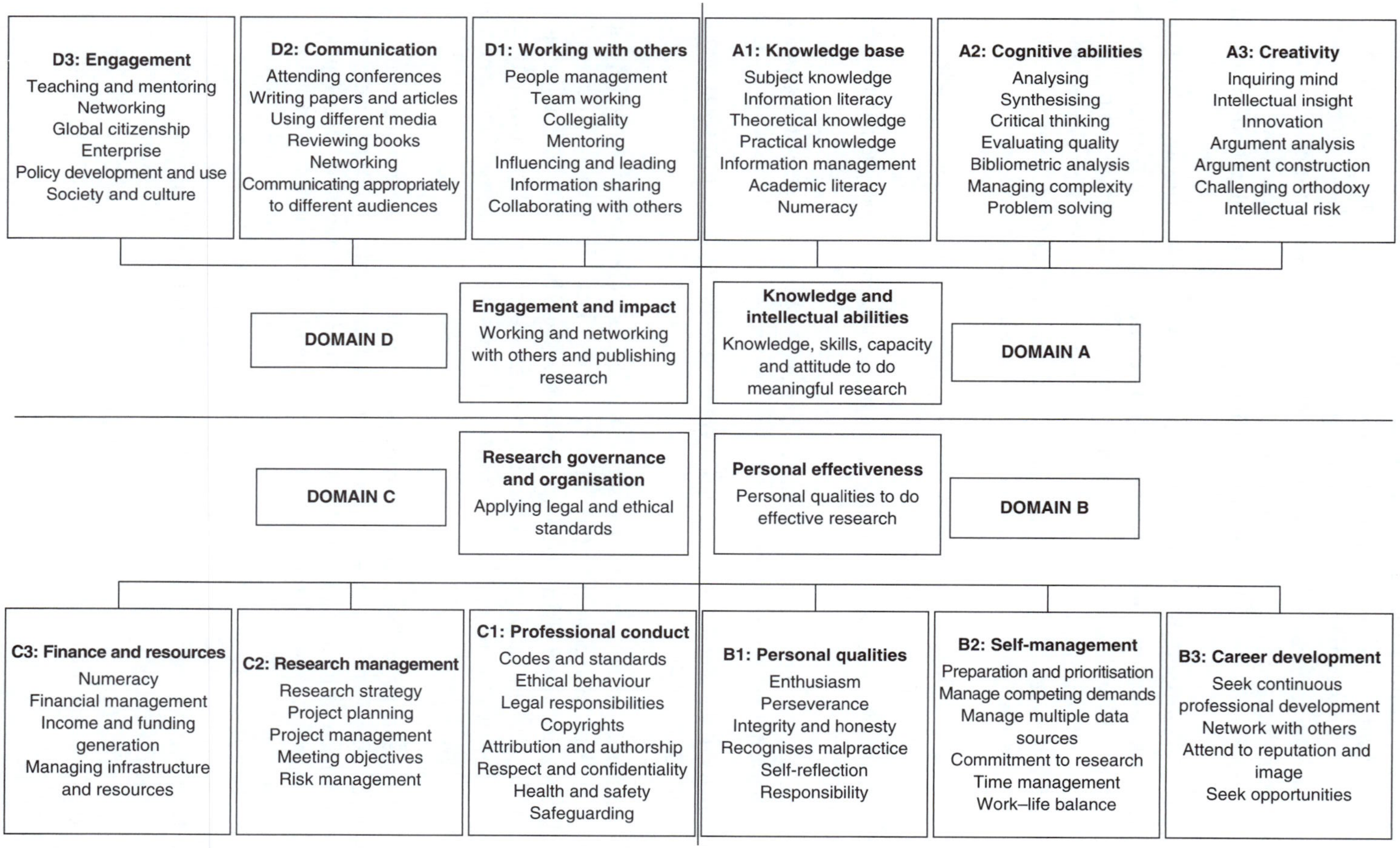

A3: Creativity
Inquiring mind
Intellectual insight
Innovation
Argument analysis
Argument construction
Challenging orthodoxy
Intellectual risk

A2: Cognitive abilities
Analysing
Synthesising
Critical thinking
Evaluating quality
Bibliometric analysis
Managing complexity
Problem solving

A1: Knowledge base
Subject knowledge
Information literacy
Theoretical knowledge
Practical knowledge
Information management
Academic literacy
Numeracy

DOMAIN A

Knowledge and intellectual abilities
Knowledge, skills, capacity and attitude to do meaningful research

D1: Working with others
People management
Team working
Collegiality
Mentoring
Influencing and leading
Information sharing
Collaborating with others

D2: Communication
Attending conferences
Writing papers and articles
Using different media
Reviewing books
Networking
Communicating appropriately to different audiences

D3: Engagement
Teaching and mentoring
Networking
Global citizenship
Enterprise
Policy development and use
Society and culture

DOMAIN D

Engagement and impact
Working and networking with others and publishing research

B3: Career development
Seek continuous professional development
Network with others
Attend to reputation and image
Seek opportunities

B2: Self-management
Preparation and prioritisation
Manage competing demands
Manage multiple data sources
Commitment to research
Time management
Work–life balance

B1: Personal qualities
Enthusiasm
Perseverance
Integrity and honesty
Recognises malpractice
Self-reflection
Responsibility

DOMAIN B

Personal effectiveness
Personal qualities to do effective research

C1: Professional conduct
Codes and standards
Ethical behaviour
Legal responsibilities
Copyrights
Attribution and authorship
Respect and confidentiality
Health and safety
Safeguarding

C2: Research management
Research strategy
Project planning
Project management
Meeting objectives
Risk management

C3: Finance and resources
Numeracy
Financial management
Income and funding generation
Managing infrastructure and resources

DOMAIN C

Research governance and organisation
Applying legal and ethical standards

FIGURE 0.1 The Vitae Researcher Development Framework

The seven pillars are:

- identifying information needs
- scoping information available
- planning a logical search for information
- gathering relevant information
- evaluating information sources
- managing the process
- presenting findings.

There are examples you will find in each chapter that can be used as a guide to the literature review, but the main purpose is to help you, as the reader, to understand what it means to be a research student and engaged in using evidence. On a practical level, a number of references are provided that may be useful sources to more information on a particular topic or issue. The examples are chosen to illustrate particular methods and techniques, rather than for their content, and hence the citations in the examples and quotations have not been given, for these refer to the original source. This assumes that if you can work out how the ideas, techniques and methods found in the literature can be adapted and used in your own research, then you will have taught yourself some very useful skills that no manual can provide. One of these skills is to learn *how* to learn. In reading this book you will be forced, in some places, to think seriously about the meaning of literature reviewing, the implications of methodology and the role of argument in research. You will, therefore, be encouraged to avoid copying what others have done and, instead, teach yourself how to analyse, evaluate and synthesise ideas and so produce work that is distinctively yours.

This edition differs from the first in many ways. The key point to note is that since the publication of the first edition there have been many books published on literature reviewing. Some are good and others not so good. It is heartening to note just how important literature reviewing, across all disciplines, has become since the late 1990s. Many of the developments, in using the literature as evidence, have been incorporated into this new edition. Chapter 4 is new. It looks at different kinds of review from across the social sciences and evidence-based professions. Chapter 6, another new chapter, looks at synthesising different kinds of review using a realist approach. This edition also takes into account changes in postgraduate education, paying attention to the quality standards that have been introduced in the past five to eight years, which have meant institutions are assessed and ranked. Part of this assessment is on the quality of teaching and supervision and this includes evidencing the intellectual and technical skills sets of all postgraduate students.

This second edition takes into account the quality assessment of postgraduate teaching by incorporating the Vitae Researcher Development Framework

(RDF) to show which intellectual capabilities are required and the reasons for this and how these relate to the competency of a researcher (this is also linked to employability – a major measure of postgraduate courses). You may also note that the language (parole) used in this book is based on ideas from design-based research (see Design-based Research Collective, 2003), in which complex information, ideas and theories are discussed in different ways using different methods of communication. This is done to encourage Sophistic ways of critically evaluating and thinking about the place of theory and evidence in understanding the world around us and making recommendations for interventions.

If you are looking at this book for a 'how to do your literature review in so many easy steps' then look elsewhere. This book will not be for you. This is because the skills sets used here go beyond the mere technical level to encourage, through examples and further inquiry, the acquisition and use of an existential andragogical attitude to epistemological matters – this shows researchers from all disciplines that they are capable of developing a cognate capacity to engage at the highest levels of intellectual life.

1

The Research Imagination

Key questions

- What is a literature review and what does a literature review look like?
- What is the place of the literature review in a research project?
- What kinds of skills and capabilities will undertaking a review give you?
- What do we mean by the 'research imagination'? Why is this important?
- What are the essential skills and attitudes for doing a literature review?
- What is a core text and how do you locate them?
- Why are argument and debate important for the development of research?

Core skills

- Seek information, data and ideas on your topic
- Identify trends, research traditions and interesting ideas
- Develop ways to question orthodoxy in order to create research opportunities
- Acquire and apply an attitude that develops your creative, imaginative and interpretative capacity.

Introduction

It has become an annual ritual for graduate researchers embarking on their projects to ask about the literature review. They usually want to know what a review of the literature *looks like* and *how* to do one. The main problem is that neither I nor anyone else can tell you what *your* review of the literature for your research should look like. Your review will be unique. This is because no research project is ever the same as another and the literature on any given topic is an evolving resource.

The aims of this book

This book is not a step-by-step manual to producing a literature review. It is much more than this. It aims to help you develop your critical thinking skills and capabilities, so that you can apply them to all kinds of debates, interpretations and issues beyond the academic realm.

This book looks at a range of techniques that can be used to analyse ideas, find relationships between different ideas and understand the nature and use of argument in research. You can expect to look at and be asked to think about what it means to provide an explanation, participate in scholarly discussion and to analyse the worth of other people's ideas and research; it is other people's work that constitutes the body of knowledge on the topic. Your work will either make a contribution to the existing body of knowledge or attempt to challenge some aspect of it.

Undertaking a review of a body of literature is often seen as something obvious and as a task easily done. In practice, although research students do produce what are called reviews of the literature, the quality of these varies considerably. Many reviews, in fact, are only thinly disguised annotated bibliographies. Quality means appropriate breadth and depth, rigour and consistency, clarity and brevity, and effective analysis and synthesis. In other words, the literature is a key resource. It will provide the materials to justify a particular approach to the topic, the selection of methods, and demonstrate that this research contributes something new to our understanding of the world.

What is a literature review?

Initially, before saying what a review is, we can say that a review of the literature is important because without it you will not acquire an understanding of your topic, know what has already been done on it, understand how it has been researched or grasp what the key issues are that need addressing.

In your written project, you are expected to show that you understand previous research on your topic. You need to demonstrate that you understand the main theories used in your subject area, as well as how they have been applied and developed, and know what the main criticisms are of the research and methods used in your field.

The review is a part of your academic and professional development of becoming a capable researcher and critical user of research knowledge. However, the importance of the literature review is not matched by a common understanding of how a review of related literature can be done, how it can be used in the research, or why it needs to be done in the first place.

The product of most research is some form of written account. This can take various forms including an article, report, dissertation or conference paper. The dissemination of findings is important. This is because the purpose of research is to contribute in some way to our understanding of the world. This cannot be done if research findings are not shared. The public availability of research ensures that accounts of research are reconstructed 'stories'. That is, the serendipitous, often chaotic, fragmented and contingent nature of most research (the very things that make research challenging!) is not described in the formal account. We, therefore, need to get an initial understanding of what a literature review is and where it fits in the research project. Figure 1.1 shows the four main stages involved in searching and reviewing a body of literature.

Figure 1.1 shows a two-phase, four-stage process. These are not always linear, with one neatly following the other. The process is iterative. Within the *searching stage* (Phase One) you will move from trying to find everything to focusing on what is relevant to your own work. This could be prior findings, arguments, interpretations, methodological assumptions and the methods used to collect data. In short, you will move from a review *of* the literature to a review *for* your research.

Some working definitions

A *literature search* (Phase One in Figure 1.1) is a systematic search of the accredited sources and resources. It involves identifying paper and electronic sources relevant to *your* topic and method(s) by preparing a clear plan for the search that includes a justifiable vocabulary that defines what will and will not be included in the search. The search will include establishing a robust scheme for the management of what will be a massive amount of information and paper.

A *literature review* (Phase Two in Figure 1.1) is the analysis, critical evaluation and synthesis of existing knowledge relevant to your research problem,

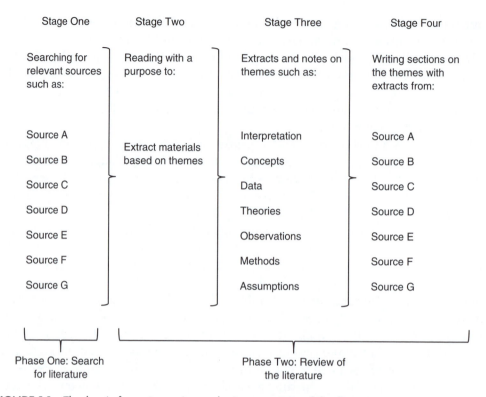

FIGURE 1.1   The basic four stages in producing a review of the literature

thesis or the issue you are aiming to say something about. In your analysis, you are selecting from different texts, concepts, theories, arguments and interpretations that seem relevant to the development of *your* particular theoretical frame of reference and/or use of a particular methodology. It involves classifying these parts into schemes that enable you to critically evaluate those concepts, arguments and different interpretations. In critically evaluating, you interrogate the work of others (regardless of their standing in the academic community). You are scrutinising the chain of reasoning another has used and the evidence they have offered to support their argument. You are aiming to follow the use of a seminal work by successive authors; to evaluate their assessments and use of that work; to evaluate the synthesis that has been developed with other keynote scholars. Your reason for doing this is to identify fallacies in arguments, methodological assumptions and theories or to show how an issue and problem could benefit from the application of an existing theory and/or methodology and/or practice. This is 'finding the gap' for your research or finding in the literature what could be proposed as best practice.

What a search and review of the literature is not

A search and review of the literature is not a copy and paste job. It is not a search of the Internet, Amazon or the local bookshop. It is not something that can be done in an afternoon or a week. The following, for example, is not a review of the literature. It is part of a bibliography.

Beck, U. (1999). 'Introduction: The cosmopolitan manifesto', in U. Beck, *World Risk Society*. Cambridge: Polity Press.

Beck, U. (2000). *What is Globalization?* Cambridge: Polity Press.

Beck, U. (2000). 'The cosmopolitan perspective: Sociology in the second age of modernity'. *British Journal of Sociology*, 151: 79–106.

Beck, U. (2002). 'The cosmopolitan society and its enemies', *Theory, Culture and Society*, 191(2): 17–44.

Beck, U. (2004). 'The truth of others: A cosmopolitan approach', *Common Knowledge*, 10: 430–49,

Boehm, M.H. (1931). 'Cosmopolitanism': *Encyclopedia of the Social Sciences 4*. New York: MacMillan.

Cohen, R. and Fine, R. (2002). 'Four cosmopolitan moments', in S. Vertovec and R. Cohen (eds), *Conceiving Cosmopolitanism: Theory, Context, and Practice*. Oxford: Oxford University Press.

Featherstone, M. (2002). 'Cosmopolis: An introduction', *Theory, Culture, and Society*, 19(1-2): 1–16.

Beck, U. and Sznaider, N. (2006). 'A literature on cosmopolitanism: An overview', *British Journal of Sociology*, 57(1): 154.

A bibliography is essentially a list of sources that share a common theme. This may be a topic, method, language or some other criteria. You will need to construct lists of sources that look useful for your research. Bibliographies, even with annotations, are not a substitute for a proper review of the contents of the sources on your lists. Nonetheless, bibliographies are useful starting points for identifying useful sources.

What a review of a literature looks like

Throughout this book you will find extracts from a range of different reviews. To get us started we are now going to look at extracts from two literature reviews. The first will give you an idea of what a review can look like. The second is longer and shows how a review can be developed using themes.

Extract 1: Political participation

The following is a section taken from a review of the literature into a decline in voting behaviour among young adults. In this short extract, we see how the author, Helena Catt displays her utter familiarity with the literature. The extract shows she has worked her way through the different phases of the review – from searching for relevant sources, reading with a purpose and extracting materials based around themes, to writing up her review.

Questions a review can help answer

What have other researchers found on my topic?

What are the core concepts?

Are there findings from different countries?

A strong finding from Franklin's (2004) study was the persistence of early behaviour: those who voted when they first could were more likely to repeat the behaviour and those who did not vote were likely to not vote again. Surveys of non-voters consistently find that many are repeat non-voters. In the New Zealand 2002 post-election survey a third of Mori and a fifth of non-Mori non-voters said that they had not voted in the past either (Vowles et al., 2004). Some writers suggest that political participation leaves a psychological imprint on those who act (Green & Shachar, 2000). More pragmatically, those who have voted are familiar with the process whilst for some who have not, there may be apprehension at what it entails (Horwitt, 1999) and embarrassment at admitting this lack of knowledge. Like internal efficacy, this orientation concerns one's self-confidence in a political environment (Green & Shachar, 2000). In contrast, participation by providing familiarity with the process increases confidence and thus internal efficacy (Finkel, 1985). The idea that repetition creates familiarity and confidence is commonplace. There is also evidence that the practice of voting or not is passed across generations. Surveys in the UK and USA (Nestle, 2003; Horwitt, 1999) have found that non-voters are more likely to come from families of non-voters and that those who vote at their first election have memories of their parents voting.

What are some of the variables?

Discussion of politics at home also had an impact: "half of those who often talk to their parents about politics said they voted in 1998, compared to one quarter of those who talk to their parents about politics infrequently or never" (Horwitt, 1999). This study concludes that voting is developed as a habit. Some young people may start voting primarily out of the idealistic sense that their vote makes a difference; after an election or two, they begin to view voting as a duty and are much more likely to turn out to vote primarily because they feel it is something they *should do*. In this way, "young people come to voting as a personal norm."

(Helena Catt (2005). *Now or Never - Electoral Participation Literature Review.*)

Catt's (2005) review is not perfect. For example, where possible attribution should include page numbers in the citation.

Extract 2: Stereotyping

The following extracts are from Oakes et al. (1994), who in their study of stereotyping dedicate two chapters of their book (based on their research) to outlining the nature and scope of the literature on stereotyping. Oakes et al. (1994) provide a detailed description of the origins of academic interest in the topic and explicate the main points from the *landmark* studies – they take a whole chapter to do this. In a second chapter, they critically analyse previous approaches on stereotyping to show how their work differs from previous work. At the same time, they aim to show how their work is a development in our understanding of stereotyping. In the following series of extracts, we can see many of the things that we have just been discussing. See if you can identify the ways in which the authors achieve the following:

- place the topic into an historical perspective
- identify key landmark studies
- select what they consider to be the key sources and authors
- establish a context for their own interest and research
- distinguish what has been done in order to identify a space for their own work.

Extract from Oakes et al., 1994: 2–3	Observations
Lippman (1922) initiated formal enquiry into stereotyping with the publication of his book *Public Opinion*. The attraction of this work has been enduring, primarily because it identifies a number of features of stereotypes and stereotyping that were to form the basis of subsequent understanding.	*Key landmark study.* *Indication of Lippman's influence on stereotyping research.*
In *Public Opinion* stereotypes were characterised as being selective, self-fulfilling and ethnocentric, ideas summed up in the claim that they 'constitute a very partial and inadequate way of representing the world', the word 'partial' here conveying the double sense of incomplete and biased (p. 72). Other apparent shortcomings were noted. Stereotypes were understood as defences, which justify individuals' own positions and blind spots, which preclude objective, balanced reasoning. They were seen to be rigid in the sense of being both 'obdurate to education or criticism' and insensitive to changes in reality (p. 65). They presented over generalised, exaggerated images, which overlooked variability and denied individuality.	*Summary of* Public Opinion. *Some key concepts and phrases.* *Quote to show core propositions.* *Page number verification.* *Summary of Lippman's view of the stereotype.*

In any study of stereotyping reference to Lippman (1922) is essential. This is because it was his initial work that set a foundation for the study of the topic. Oakes et al. (1994) show the relevance of Lippman by describing some of the main points he made. In later sections of their review they pick up many of these points and show how they were used by different authors to develop a broader understanding of the topic. In this next extract it can be seen how Oakes et al. (1994) bring their reader to a watershed in the research on stereotyping.

Extract from Oakes et al., 1994: 2–3	Observations
In the 1950s two distinct trends are discernible in stereotyping research, each elaborating one aspect of the Kernel of Truth Debate [already mentioned by the authors in a section preceding this extract]. The majority of researchers continued to concentrate on the deficiencies of stereotyping (e.g. Bogardus, 1950; Hayakawa, 1950; Klineberg, 1950, 1951) while others began to question the assumptions which underpinned this traditional position (e.g. Laviolette and Silvert, 1951).	*Chronological development of research shown with a framework for making distinctions between perspectives. Reference to a major debate among social psychologists.* *Key references to be followed up indicate a critical position is to be developed towards traditional assumptions.*
Related ideas were presented by Fishman (1956) and Vinacke (1956, 1957). Fishman argued that stereotypes were valid to the extent that they served to reflect the nature of interaction between stereotyped and stereotyping groups (1956: 60), while Vinacke suggested that stereotypes were representations of authentic high-level conceptual relationships between individuals (i.e. social groupings; 1957: 329). The radical implication of all of this work was that stereotypes were by nature neither irrational nor 'bad'.	*Shows a shift in understanding of the rationality of stereotypes. Inversion of Lippman's original view of stereotypes points out implications of the inversion.*

What the reader is given here are some directions for categorising the literature on stereotyping. Two trends are identified with indicative but key references that could be followed up. Added to this, works on ideas related to these two trends are indicated, for example in the work of Fishman (1956) that Oakes et al. (1994) cite. Again, what can be seen here is a setting of the context of the topic through a chronological presentation of landmark and related studies into stereotyping. One may also observe in this extract related works as an example of the convention to cite relevant references. This is in the last sentence that identifies the implications of Vinacke's work. Later in the review, exceptions to conventional approaches to stereotyping are discussed. These are mentioned not merely to provide a full coverage of the literature, but to introduce key developments and research insights that can be picked up and developed at a later stage of their review, especially in justifying their own study (i.e., Oakes et al.'s work).

Extract from Oakes et al., 1994: 5–6	Observations
... not all research which approached stereotyping as an aspect of prejudice followed this line. Notably ... Allport (1954) discussed the extent to which the *categorisation process* (i.e. cognitive grouping of individual objects as identical, interchangeable) was involved in prejudice. Whilst he emphasised that categorisation was essential to 'orderly living' (in particular, its general flexibility and responsiveness to the	*Introduces exceptions to the norm and provides an initial claim to the psychological basis of stereotyping.* *Establishes a continuity from previous work.*

changing definition of ingroups and outgroups), he continued to regard stereotypes as deficient because they exaggerated the properties of the categories with which they were associated and stood in the way of differentiated thinking. Moreover, in his discussion of these issues Allport maintained a clear distinction between the rational and irrational use of categories as associated with the behaviour of tolerant and prejudiced people respectively. Allport took a crucial theoretical step forward in suggesting that prejudice might be a product of *normal* processes, but his analysis contained an inherent contradiction. It suggested that the processes of categorisation implicated in stereotyping were essentially rational (cf. Asch, 1952; Vinacke, 1957) but that their rationality was nonetheless contingent upon the character of the individual stereotype (cf. Adorno et al., 1950; see Billing, 1985).

Shows how even the exception maintained the distinction between rational and irrational – a major claim that is the basis of Oakes et al.'s study.

Shows how this major claim has not hitherto been explored.

Traditional focus on the individual and character in traditional work.

In this final extract it can be seen how Oakes et al., having established the context and history of the topic from the perspective of *social psychology*, provide a summary of the main points of their initial review of the literature. This is usefully done in a table that is reproduced in a later chapter. But their reason for doing this is to make their claim for the relevance of their study and claim this approach is distinctive from what has been done before.

Extract from Oakes et al., 1994: 9

Observations

Table 1.1 [not included here] summarises what we see as the major milestones in the study of social stereotyping up to Tajfel (1981). While personality theories of the type advanced by Adorno et al. have now more or less disappeared from the stereotyping scene, research into both intergroup relations (following Sherif and Tajfel) and individual cognition (following Allport and Tajfel) is still active and crucial. In the 1981 paper Tajfel tried to begin a process of rapprochement between the hitherto rather disparate cognitive (individual) and intergroup (social) traditions in the area, having himself been closely involved in both. In some ways this book can be seen as a continuation of that effort.

Broadly speaking, we aim to elaborate the argument that in order to understand the psychology of group phenomena (like stereotyping) it is necessary to examine the ways in which cognition both mediates and *is mediated* by individuals' group memberships and social relations (see Tajfel, 1979, 1981; Turner and Oakes, 1986). In these terms, processes of perception and cognition are *social* psychological, not merely because they involve the processing of information about people, but because they are the psychological products of an interaction

The scope of the study is narrowed down by the exclusion of early personality theories (e.g. Adorno, etc.). Table 1.1 that Oakes et al. refer to can be seen in their book.

Re-emphasis of what they consider relevant to the topic. Mentions previous attempts at what they are attempting to do.

Emphasises the focus they intend to take and claim it is different from but related to what others have looked at, i.e. justification is provided.

Focus on cognition between social groups based in information processing.

(Continued)

Extract from Oakes et al., 1994: 9	Observations
between mind and society. In this ... we focus these ideas on the issue of stereotyping, and in so doing aim to achieve a better understanding of the role of this fascinating process in the individual's adaptation to the social environment.	*Initial warrant for their claim to have a different research focus than previous studies based on 'individuals', i.e. the social psychological in the context of the broader social environment.*

Different subject disciplines tend to have differing ways of framing their approach to a given problem. Some disciplines have specific issues and debates that are particular to them alone. In the examples given above, we can see the social psychological approach and explication of a key area that is of concern to social psychologists.

A researcher can only become sufficiently familiar with disciplinary debates and perspectives through an investigative search and analytical reading of the literature. Knowledge of the perspectives distinct to the discipline or topic will be required in order to establish the significance of the topic. This needs to be done in order to be able to justify a research topic from within the conventions and intellectual tradition of the most relevant discipline.

As a consequence, familiarity with subject knowledge will enable gaps to be identified and anomalies in previous research. Questions can then be asked that have significance, and which can be turned into a viable research topic. The literature is, therefore, an essential resource – it can help to find an appropriate and valid topic. The same materials are nearly always useful in defining the parameters, dimensions and scope of what is to be investigated.

Looking at the extracts from the two reviews, we can now see the processes described in Figure 1.1. Once the search and selection of sources has been done, ideas, concepts, arguments and findings will have been extracted and categorised. These are the materials that the authors have used to construct their reviews. Citations show the sources and the grouping of those citations shows the use of categories to do that grouping. Stages One and Two in Figure 1.1 are largely technical while Stages Three and Four are interpretive.

The literature review in the research project

The formal report of most research relies for its recognisability on standardised arrangements. Many of the sections found in a report are also found in a proposal for research. Parts that are normally common to both are shown below. Within this arrangement the author of the account usually employs a range of stylistic conventions to demonstrate the 'authority' and 'legitimacy' of their research. They also try to show that they, as researchers, have undertaken their project in a way that is rigorous and competent.

TABLE 1.1 Some sections in a research proposal

Sections	Intent of the section
Introduction	To show the aims, objectives, scope, rationale and design features of the research. The rationale is usually supported by references to other works, which have already identified the broad nature of the problem
Literature review	To demonstrate skills in library searching, show command of the subject area and understanding of the problem; to justify the research topic, design and methodology
Methodology	To show the appropriateness of the techniques used to gather data and the methodological approaches employed. Relevant references from the literature are often used to show an understanding of data collection techniques, the methodological implication, and to justify their use over other, alternative techniques
And in the research dissertation or report, you will have the following:	
Findings	To show the place (and contribution) of your findings, within the general and specific literature – the very literature you sourced and evaluated at the beginning of your research.

The review of related literature is, therefore, an essential part of the *research process* and the *research report*. It is more than a stage to be undertaken or a hurdle to get over.

What the literature review amounts to is a factor in the success of academic and applied research. The benefits of a comprehensive review are also *purposes* that the review can fulfil. The main one is the need to ensure the researchability of the topic before research commences. All too often the scholar new to research equates the breadth of their research with its value. Initial enthusiasm, combined with this common misconception, often result in broad, generalised and ambitious proposals from a student. It is the progressive narrowing of the topic, through the literature review, that makes most research a practical consideration.

Narrowing down a topic can be difficult and can take several weeks or even months. But it is a part of the process that makes the research more likely to be successfully completed. It also contributes to the development of your intellectual capacity and practical skills. This is because it engenders a *research attitude* and will encourage you to think rigorously about your topic and what research you can do on it, in the time you have available. Time and effort carefully expanded at this stage can save a great deal of effort and vague searching later in the research. Therefore, we have two tasks. One is to search for relevant sources and the second is to critically evaluate the sources identified.

Effort and thought are needed

If all of this looks like a lot of work, well it is. But it is also, say many researchers, one of the most enjoyable parts of doing research. The main thing is to see the search and review as a series of stages. Each stage successively builds on the previous ones to construct the review for the thesis.

Reading advice: A guide to literature searching

For a guide on how to conduct a literature search, see Hart (2001) *Doing a Literature Search*, which works well as a companion to this book.

There are two main kinds of search and review for most research; the initial (or indicative) search and review and the comprehensive search and review. The initial search is like a reconnaissance of the landscape of the literature. You are looking to get an idea of what literature is 'out there' and readily obtainable, what databases exist and where and how they can be accessed. Your academic librarian can be an indispensable source of information and guidance at this stage. It is worth making an appointment to discuss your research with them. From what literature is readily available a short review can be constructed that 'indicates' the key ideas, concepts, authors, works and arguments of the broader literature. At this stage the Internet, library catalogues and online book suppliers can be helpful – but only as indications of the themes. The indicative review is often used for research proposals. If the indicative review has been done competently then the skills and knowledge acquired can be rapidly developed. A more comprehensive search can be planned on the basis of the databases selected, articles and books ordered which are not in the library, and more time given to 'mining' the literature.

The research apprenticeship

Frameworks such as the RDF and The Seven Pillars of Information Literacy invoke two images for researchers at different stages in their professional development. The first, for the new or early career researcher, is that of the research apprentice.

The responsibility to read widely

As a student researcher, it is your responsibility to read as much as you can across a range of subject disciplines to acquire a broad general knowledge. This should include making yourself familiar with issues in the natural sciences as well as the social sciences, humanities and arts.

The second, for the experienced researcher, is that of a set of reference points for their own continuing professional development and for the training and education of their supervisees. There is a third idea here and this is cross-disciplinarity.

Cross-disciplinarity

There has been a move in higher education and research to learn from other disciplines – to be cross-disciplinary. Many students now have the opportunity to study ideas from other disciplines. Added to this is the trend towards combined degrees. A consequence is that students and researchers need to be more flexible in their attitude to knowledge. To do this, they need a much broader range of skills and knowledge bases to take full advantage of the availability of sources and resources.

Understanding how research is done and how data are created and disseminated is an essential part of information literacy. Figure 1.2 provides an overview of these areas, showing the main sources of knowledge and tools by which data are organised for retrieval.

Undergraduate, postgraduate and practitioner research is an ideal opportunity for such personal transferable skills to be acquired and developed. Searching and reviewing a literature involves all of the Seven Pillars (mentioned above). The acquisition of core skills has to be for a purpose. It is not merely a formal matter to display the kinds of skills and abilities expected of a competent researcher in the report of the research.

Although these general skills are important they are not core components of the curriculum across the disciplines of human studies. It is not unusual to find that education, in the general nature and character of research, predominates over, and often displaces, formal skills acquisition. Most disciplines socialise their students into the theoretical and historical traditions that give shape and distinctiveness to the subject knowledge. But in so doing, the methodological bias, disciplinary boundaries and misunderstanding about other subjects are perpetuated. This often creates barriers to cross-disciplinary studies and a lack of appreciation of alternative ways of researching and understanding the world. This book aims to show ways in which these kinds of barriers can be overcome. This begins with a reminder of the practice that is scholarship.

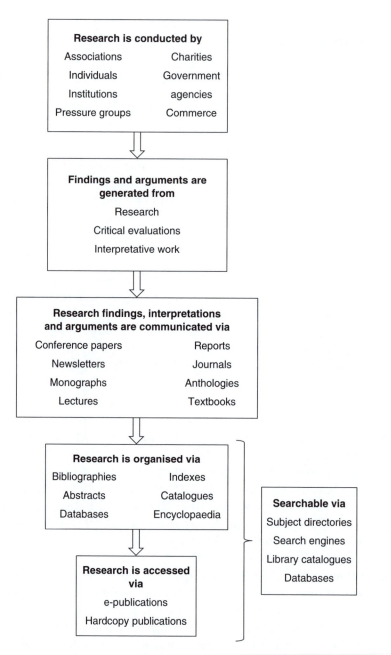

FIGURE 1.2 The generation and communication of research knowledge and information

Intellectual craftship

Technically speaking, most people are capable of doing a piece of research. That capability has, however, to be acquired; you cannot simply write a questionnaire, as if writing a shopping list. A sound knowledge of the whole research process is required; you need to understand where data collection fits into the global picture of what you are doing.

> ## Scholarship is an activity
>
> Scholarship is an activity; it is something most people can do. It does not require you to be of a certain social class, gender, ethnic origin or to have successfully jumped over formal educational hurdles.

This means knowing how to state the aims and objectives of the research, define your major concepts and methodological assumptions, operationalise those concepts and assumptions by choosing an appropriate technique to collect data, know how you are going to collate results and so on. Competent research, therefore, requires technical knowledge. There is, however, a difference between producing a piece of competent research and a piece of research that demonstrates *scholarship*.

Intellectual craftship and scholarship

The main question is, what is scholarship? This is a very difficult question to answer because there are differences of opinion between academics, and between disciplines, as well as universities, as to what counts as scholarly activity. Without summarising this debate, there are a number of statements about scholarship that can be added to those just made. Firstly, it is not very useful to create simple dichotomies between teaching and research or between knowledge and information or between theory and practice. Scholarly activity encompasses all of these and more.

Secondly, scholarly activity is about knowing how to do competent research, read, interpret and analyse arguments, synthesise ideas and make connections across disciplines, write and present ideas clearly and systematically, and use your imagination. Underpinning these activities are a number of basic attitudes to research and doing research. These are discussed below in the next section. But what they amount to is an attitude of mind that is open to ideas, different styles and types of research, and is free of prejudices about what counts as useful research or what type of person should be allowed to do research.

Scholarship and integration

A key element that makes for good scholarship is *integration*. Integration is about making connections between ideas, theories and experience. It is about applying a method or methodology from one area to another new context. Integration is therefore about making connections; about placing some episode into a larger theoretical framework, thereby providing a new way of looking at that phenomenon. This may mean drawing elements from different theories to form a new synthesis or to provide a new insight. It may also mean re-examining an existing corpus of knowledge in the light of a new development.

The activity of scholarship is, therefore, about thinking systematically. It may mean forcing new typologies in the structure of knowledge or onto a perspective that is taken-for-granted. Either way, the scholar endeavours to interpret and understand. The intent is to make others think about and possibly re-evaluate what they have hitherto taken to be unquestionable knowledge. Therefore, systematic questioning, inquiring and a scrutinising attitude are features of scholarly activity.

Integration and re-configuration

The aim of scholarship is to systematically examine what it is that others take as a body of knowledge. At Master's degree level this may mean looking at the application of a methodology; to look at applying a methodology in ways not tried before. At doctoral level it may mean attempting to *re-figure* or *re-specify* the way in which some puzzle or problem has traditionally been defined. The anthropologist Clifford Geertz (1980: 165–6) suggested that re-configuration was more than merely tampering with the details of how we go about understanding the world around us. He says re-configuration is not about redrawing the cultural map or changing some of the disputed borders, it is about altering the very principles by which we map the social world.

From the history of science Nicolaus Copernicus (1473–1543) re-examined theories about the cosmos and the place of the Earth within it. Traditional theory held the view that the Earth was motionless and stood at the centre of the universe; the Sun, other planets and stars were believed to revolve around the Earth. Copernicus asked himself if there was another way of interpreting this belief. What if, he asked, the Sun was motionless and the Earth, planets and stars revolved around it? In 1541, he outlined his ideas and there began a re-configuration of how the cosmos was mapped. In the recent history of social science, the work of Harold Garfinkel is a classic example of re-configuration. Garfinkel re-specified the phenomenon of the social sciences, especially sociology (see Button, 1991). He undertook a thorough-going scrutiny of traditional sociological theory and found that social science ignored what real people do in real situations. So radical was his re-specification that traditional social science took several decades to incorporate his ideas into their work.

Centrality of argument

Scholarship and integration often involves analysing arguments and constructing an argument (rationale) for your own research. Argument over the meaning of data, how these were collected and what can be done with them, related to some of the most interesting philosophical questions. These include questions about how we know what we think we know, what we can take as real is and why we do what we do in the ways we do it. All subject fields in the social and human sciences are based on argument. Research is always done from some standpoint, often being influenced by paradigmatic beliefs and assumptions about what constitutes the best way to finding things out. Argument is about attempting to persuade others about something you think is important. For example, is the MMR vaccine really dangerous? Does social isolation lead to mental health problems? Is *Doctor Who* the best show on television? Are some computer games too violent? Was greed the cause of the 2008 recession? Is intelligence genetic? These are questions that lead to debate and argument in all disciplines.

As researchers, we need to appreciate that argument and argumentative analysis is a core activity in all research. A review of a literature is an ideal opportunity to develop advanced skills and knowledge of how different arguments are made and how they can be critiqued.

The need for clarity

Most authors attempt to make their writing clear, consistent and coherent. But these are very difficult to achieve in any work, regardless of its length or topic. Nevertheless, clarity, consistency and coherence are essential because without them a text can be unintelligible. As a consequence, it may be misunderstood, dismissed or used in ways not intended by the author. More importantly, the main idea, no matter how interesting, may be lost.

Conversely, what seems clear and coherent to the writer can, as we all know, be utterly frustrating to the reader. Unfamiliarity with the style, the format, presentation or language use is nearly always a cause of frustration to the reader. The easy way out is to dismiss a text one finds difficult. To do so is not only to admit defeat but also to fail to invest the necessary effort required for intellectual research.

From both the writer and reader, effort is required. The basis of that effort is accepting that clarity, consistency and coherence are not mysterious qualities able to be practised only by the few. They can be achieved through explicit expression in writing and explicit commitment in reading. A problem for the academic author, however, is the time readers allocate to their reading and the level of effort they are willing to invest in order to grasp the ideas in a text. Similarly, some authors seem to neglect the needs of their potential readers and manage to make a relatively simple idea confusing.

In terms of reviewing a body of literature, made up of dozens of articles, conference papers and monographs, a problem is the diversity of materials needing to be read. Originating from several disciplines and writing in different styles engender the need for a flexible and charitable attitude from the reviewer. Added to this is the lack of explicitness often found in many accounts of research. That is, it is rare to find an account of a piece of research that systematically lays out what was done and why it was done, and discusses the various implications of those choices.

The reviewer needs to appreciate some of the reasons for the lack of explicitness. Firstly, it takes considerable effort and time to express ideas in writing. Secondly, limitations placed on space or word counts often result in editing not deemed ideal by the author. Also, being explicit exposes the research (and researcher) to critical inspection. Presumably, many able researchers do not publish widely so as to avoid criticism.

Charity in understanding

Competence in reading research is not, as has already been indicated, something easily acquired. It is a part of the process of research training and education. As such it takes time and a willingness to face challenges, acquire new understandings and have sufficient openness of mind to appreciate that there are other views of the world.

This begins by recognising that the reviewer undertakes a review for a purpose and as such an author writes for a purpose. While an author may not always make their ideas clear, consistent and coherent the reviewer is required to exercise patience when reading. The reviewer needs to assume, no matter how difficult an article is to read, that the author has something to contribute. It is a matter of making the effort to tease out the main ideas from the text under consideration. It also means making the effort to understand why you are having difficulty in comprehending the text. This means not categorising the text using prejudicial perceptions of the subject discipline. It means therefore making the effort to place the research in the context of the norms of the discipline and not judging it by the practices of the discipline, with which you are most familiar.

The literature review, therefore, is not something to be 'gotten over'. It is not a chore or ritual in a research project. It is an integral part of a piece of research in that it enables the researcher to cross disciplinary boundaries, encounter new ideas and styles, and enhance the quality of their work. The review of the literature is, therefore, much more than a chapter in a thesis.

This means reading to review is about making connections between what are often diverse and contrasting ideas. In thesis-based research, this is a crucial criterion for assessment of its worthiness. In the next chapter, this activity is outlined in the context of what it means to be original. This involves making the assumption that there are no prescriptions about what ideas can be related or how they can be analysed and synthesised. Techniques to analyse and synthesise are available but how they are used is a matter for the user to decide.

As a part of this attitude, all researchers need to exercise a willingness to understand philosophical (or methodological) traditions. The choice of a particular topic, the decision to research it using a specific strategy rather than others and to present it in a certain style, are design decisions often based on prior commitments to a view of research. An individual piece of research therefore can be placed, in general terms, into an intellectual tradition such as *positivism* or *phenomenology*. But the reviewer needs to take care not to criticise that research purely on general terms and especially from the standpoint of one approach to another. The different intellectual traditions need to be appreciated for what they are and not for what they are assumed to lack from the view of another standpoint.

These assumptions, although briefly stated, are the basis for the following chapters. Collectively what they amount to is an operationalisation (putting into practice) of scholarship and good manners in research. They also signpost the need for reviewers of research to be informed about and able to demonstrate their awareness of the different styles and traditions of research.

The research imagination

At the end of his short book, *The Sociological Imagination* (1978[1959]), C. Wright-Mills provides the would-be-researcher with some guides on how to think, how to manage large amounts of information and how to generate an attitude conducive to a research imagination. In his definition of the sociological imagination, Wright-Mills provides us with a starting point for understanding the need for a research imagination.

> The sociological imagination, I remind you, in considerable part consists of the capacity to shift from one perspective to another, and in the process to build up an adequate view of a total society and of its components. It is this imagination, of course, that sets off the social scientist from the mere technician. (Wright-Mills, 1978[1959]: 211)

A researcher, therefore, needs to have the basic skills to do competent research. Some of these have already been mentioned, such as being able to use a library. However, what Wright-Mills is saying is that the effective use of these skills involves the development of an *imaginative* approach to research. It is not something easily acquired. A research imagination takes time to develop; it is something that is part of the research apprenticeship. For Wright-Mills the research imagination is about: having a broad view of a topic; being open to ideas regardless of how or where they originated; questioning and scrutinising ideas, methods and arguments regardless of who proposed them; playing with different ideas in order to see if links can be made; following ideas to see where they may lead; and being scholarly in your work. What better examples of the research imagination, claims Wright-Mills, than the work of some of the founding theorists. It is thinkers like Marx, Weber, Spencer, Mannheim and Durkheim, according to Wright-Mills, who can provide illustrations of what a research imagination can promise.

> The sociological imagination enables us to grasp history and biography and the relations between the two within society. That is its task and its promise. To recognise the task and its promise is the mark of the classical social analyst. It is characteristic of Herbert Spencer – turgid, polysyllabic, comprehension of E.A. Ross – graceful, muckraking, upright; of August Comte and Emile Durkheim; of the intricate and subtle Karl Mannheim. It is the quality of all that is intellectually excellent in Karl Marx; it is the clue to Thorstein Veblen's brilliant and ironic insight; to Joseph Schumpeter's many-sided constructions of reality; it is the basis of the psychological sweep of W. E. Lecky no less than of the profundity and clarity of Max Weber. (Wright-Mills, 1978[1959]: 12)

These and other social theorists may be dead and some long forgotten but Wright-Mills emphasises the usefulness of reading their work. This is because contemporary society is dominated by information rather than knowledge. Many academic libraries have embraced the concept of *just in time* rather than *just in case*. They have become access points to information. It is for these reasons that the researcher faced with this force needs to acquire the searching skills to exploit the technology and develop an intellect that enables them to think their way through the information maze; to be able to construct summations of what is going on in the world (Wright-Mills, 1978[1959]: 11).

Questions and the research imagination

Wright-Mills suggests that the researcher adapt a questioning and critical attitude. Figure 1.3 lists some of the questions that can be useful when beginning a journey into the literature of a topic; they can lead one back to those social theorists whose names and works are forgotten or have become vague, but who laid the foundations on which contemporary ideas, views and standpoints have been built.

But how does one use such a diverse and seemingly ambiguous set of questions? This is where an example may help. The following case study on advertising is intended to show some of the essential skills required to analyse and think through the methodological implications of different assumptions.

Basic questions: RDF Domain A: A1: Knowledge base. Subject knowledge. Information searching. Understanding how information and data are created and organised. Managing findings.

What are the databases I can use to search for relevant information?

What is the language (vocabulary) of my topic and how is it used?

What are the key sources (books, articles, reports) on my topic?

What research, methods and theory are there on my topic?

Who are the main researchers in this area?

What is the history, the chronological development, of the topic or problem?

Intermediate questions: RDF Domain A: A2. Cognitive abilities. Analysing. Evaluating. Critical thinking. Mapping ideas. Bibliometrics.

How has the topic or problem been defined?

What are the different frames of reference for researching and discussing the topic?

How has theory been related to practice or empirical research?

What methodological assumptions and approaches have been used?

What key concepts, variables or factors have been identified?

What are the main debates on my topic?

What gaps in knowledge, theory or application of a methodology are there in my topic area?

More advanced questions: RDF Domain A: A3: Creativity. Intellectual insight. Finding connections. Analysing arguments. Seeking alternatives.

What inconsistencies, shortcomings or contradictions are there in our knowledge of the topic?

What evidence is lacking, inconclusive or too limited?

What alternate approaches are there for understanding the topic, which have not been used?

FIGURE 1.3   The hierarchy of questions when reviewing

Source: Adapted from Wright-Mills, 1978[1959]: 13

It illustrates how it is possible to use a search of the literature to construct the parameters that make up the paradigm of a topic. It shows how the kinds of questions suggested by Wright-Mills can be used to bring about a shift from a traditional perspective on a topic to another that is more imaginative and contentious. Do not get concerned about any of the terms or references to technology. The main things are the use of the literature to provide the following:

- the construction of a map of the literature
- a demonstration of familiarity with the subject area
- the acquisition of a knowledge base, from which previous research could be critically analysed
- a justification for a new approach to a well-worn topic area
- the development of various skills such as information handling and classification
- the operation of a non-partisan stance (*methodological indifference*).

Extended example: Social science and advertising

The following case study is a partial reconstruction of a comprehensive and time-consuming search and evaluation of the literature about advertising. It was undertaken as part of doctorate research into advertising (Hart, 1993). The case study begins with a description of a research situation and reports on the process by which the research problem was identified, defined and alternative approaches to a topic generated. An essential part of the process was the classification and categorisation of information. The importance of this can be seen in the 'subject relevance tree' presented in Chapter 8. Wright-Mills may not have used the phrase *subject relevance tree* but he certainly had something like it in mind when he said:

> Many of the general notions you come upon, as you think about them, will be cast into types. A new classification is the usual beginning of fruitful developments. The skill to make up types and then search for the conditions and consequences of each type will ... become an automatic procedure ... Rather than rest content with existing classifications ... search for their common denominators and for differentiating factors within and between them ... To make them so you must develop the habit of cross-classification. (Wright-Mills, 1978[1959]: 213)

The research problem was the common one faced by postgraduate students: identifying the specific aspects of the topic to study and defining, in clear terms, the problem to be investigated. The topic chosen was advertising. The starting point for the research was a search and analysis of what had already been done. There were a number of reasons for this. Without a comprehensive, painstaking and critical analysis of the literature the topic and problem definition would not have had the clarity it had. Nor would it have had the purposeful justification and rationale as a topic for serious sociological study. The review of the literature provided a focus for the research that was specific, and which was fully justified in terms of meeting the criteria of uniqueness and creativity.

Finding too much stuff

The research began by planning a search of the literature. Information on previous and current works on the topic of advertising was identified using hardcopy and electronic data-bases. The general sweep of the databases threw up thousands of records or hits. The problem was one of too much data, i.e. too many records to be looked at in the time available and cost in terms of ordering inter-library loans. The advice from Wright-Mills was, 'to know when you ought to read, and when you ought not to' (1978[1959]: 214). The requirement was to identify the books and articles considered by the sociological community to be 'key' works on the study of advertising. Narrowing the search was, therefore, important. The problem was: how could the search be narrowed? The answer to this problem emerged from the records already located. There are some ways to identify the core literature through what is called bibliographic analysis. Figure 1.4 shows a typical process, through which publications and authors that have had an influence on a topic can be identified.

There were still hundreds of potentially relevant items on the list. Various tactics could have been employed at this point to reduce the list even further. All records could have been looked at in their full version. This however would have been too time consuming. Alternatively, looking at abstracts of all the records was possible. This would have given a good idea of the contents of the articles. A particular concern in the records, for example, advertising and children, may have been specified. This would have prohibited a full map of the topic to be drawn. Finally, a language or data limit could have been used to narrow down the number of records. Some of these were chosen. The search was narrowed by specifying items were to be in English. However, the main tactic employed consisted of using citation indexes and common sense, applying a systematic approach to bibliometrics.

The library catalogues of academic libraries from around the world were scanned to find out what items they had in their collections. Simple comparison of lists showed what were the items stocked by most libraries. The result, after a relatively short time, was a list of monographs in the sociology of advertising held by most academic libraries in the UK, North America and Australia. It was a straightforward job to subject the list (bibliography) to what is called *citation analysis*. This amounted to looking in special indexes (Web of Science, citation indexes) to find out which authors and works were most frequently cited by other authors in their work. The procedure employed for this was chronologically based. Starting with the oldest book on the list and working through to the most recent, the frequency of citation for each work was obtained. The individual frequencies of citation were then plotted onto a chart showing the increase and decrease of citations of a work over time. The starting point for the chart was the earliest published reference.

Identifying core works

However, citation frequencies need to be treated with some care. It is not the case that the most cited work is necessarily the most important. A frequently cited work merely stands for reference to that work by other authors in the field and nothing more. A citation is not a judgement of quality or importance. It is a nominal count of use by others. Citation frequencies have, however, a number of uses. Firstly, the citations provide a

(Continued)

useful picture of current knowledge in the field and what techniques to collect evidence have been used. They also allowed for the construction of a 'citation map' extending forwards in time. These trees show which books, and subsequently which articles, disseminated the core questions and assumptions of the literature. Core works are those that have had a major influence methodologically and politically, and which had fostered cross-disciplinary work. Figure 1.4 shows the general flow of stages involved in finding relevant items.

The following three criteria were developed for identifying core works on the topic:

1. An item, published or unpublished, that had an important effect on subsequent work on the topic as a whole and on the development of sub-areas within the main topic. An example here was the work of Raymond Williams (1980). His short essay, *The Magic System,* was the most frequently cited reference in most works published from 1980, across all social science disciplines. The methodological assumptions he stated about advertising, including the moral stance he took against advertising, were explicated through a large part of the literature.
2. An application of a technique or methodology that others had replicated, and which was consistent with the methodological assumptions of how the topic had been traditionally defined. An example here was the semiology of Roland Barthes (1967). This was found to have been a technique of analysis commonly employed across disciplines to reveal the hidden structures of coded messages in advertisements.
3. An item that had been used across several disciplines and movements, so that the topic became a research topic in those disciplines and movements. An example here was the work of Judith Williamson (1979). She brought semiological and psychoanalytical analysis to analyse advertising from a feminist standpoint.

Knowing which works were most cited also identified the articles and books in which they were cited, thus focusing the search towards more relevant materials. The resulting 'tree' showed how different ideas and studies had contributed to different lines of inquiry, and importantly the way in which advertising had been approached as a research topic by sociology. The identification of key authors and works was an important step. It provided the basic materials for the construction of subject relevance trees. This consisted of mapping out on large pieces of paper the relevances (i.e. concerns and arguments) in the literature on advertising.

Mapping the concerns in the core works

Articles and books tended to fall into one of three main categories: there were those items concerned with the *role* and *reason* for advertising; those concerned with *how* advertising worked; and those concerned with the *effects* of advertising. Within each main category individual works were placed and listed according to their major concerns. This allowed for the extended development of this tree in combination with the citation tree. Naturally these trees do get a little messy due to cross-referencing but their value is incalculable for analysis of a topic.

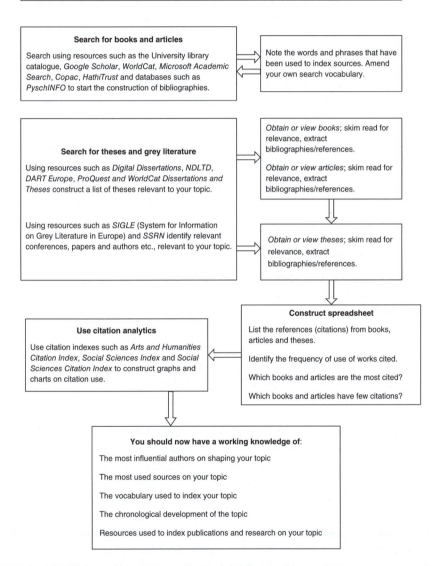

FIGURE 1.4   Identifying relevant items through bibliographic analysis

(Continued)

The map of the concerns of the literature produced the parameters around the methodological foundations of studies about advertising. It also made visible the inter-relationships between differing concerns and the use of common views. In short, the sociological paradigm of advertising was mapped out. This showed a number of interesting and problematic findings. Firstly, advertising was generally regarded as something 'bad'. A variety of moral and ethical judgements were being used as starting points for research into advertising. Secondly, advertising was seen as a modern phenomenon that was essential to the maintenance of capitalist social relations and social structures. Thirdly, advertising was seen to use various psychological or referent methods to influence people such as subliminal messages. Fourthly, various analytical methods, such as *semiological* and *content analysis*, were assumed appropriate to study an advertisement and for revealing the real meaning of an advertisement such as maintaining capitalism. Finally, the effects of advertising were often cast in terms of 'bad' things in everyday life in a *deductivistic* application of certain concepts. For example, advertising was blamed for creating and maintaining sexism, racism, age-ism, and alienation. At this stage, it may have been logical to undertake a study of advertising using these assumptions. One could have, for example, looked at a batch of advertisements aimed at children, to show how sex role stereotyping reinforces gender categories and expectations. One could have, in other words, done much of what had already been done. However, this strategy was not followed. This is the choice between adding some bricks to an existing intellectual building or beginning a new building of your own.

Looking for the assumptions in the core works

The subject relevance tree demonstrated the circular feedback analysis in current approaches to the topic of advertising. It showed how initial assumptions about the role, place and effects of advertising were often the starting point for studies of advertising. It also showed the need for a sound knowledge of the history of sociological thought:

> Some knowledge of world history is indispensable to the sociologist; without such knowledge, no matter what else she or he knows, he or she is simply crippled. (Wright-Mills, 1978[1959]: 215)

These assumptions about the dysfunctional nature of advertising provided a general methodological framework and common research problem. The methodological framework was characterised by *holism* and *contrast*. The holistic approach of *conflict structuralism* (see Cuff and Payne, 1984, for a description of the sociological development of this approach) was used to relate advertising to capitalism and locate advertising as a product of the great transformation (see Francis, 1987, for a description of the great transformation debate). Advertising was seen as a product of industrial society. Therefore, a contrast was made between pre-industrial and industrial society. Contrast and holism provided ground on which other concepts could be utilised. For example, *rationality* was a common concept in the literature. It was used to make a contrast between the irrationality or non-rationality of advertising and what might be if advertising did not exist in association with capitalism. Advertising was generally seen as an irrational phenomenon of modern society. The effects it had on people were consequently regarded as generally irrational.

In the traditional literature the research problem of advertising was almost wholly conceived of in the following terms: How may the real character of advertising be revealed? The puzzle for the bulk of the sociological literature about advertising was, How does advertising work? Why don't people see it for what it is? What are the effects of advertising? How can these effects be shown? The literature on advertising is, therefore, replete with semiological and content analysis of advertisements. These are techniques of analysis and synthesis that are thought to be capable of revealing hidden structures and patterns not directly observable in isolated instances of any phenomenon.

The analysis of the literature had, therefore, provided a description of the assumptions that had been deemed necessary for sociological accounts of advertising. This analysis would not have had the breadth and depth it had without the use of the tools by which information is stored, organised and made retrievable. But having found out what assumptions had been made and mapped them out, it was a short step to asking: What assumptions *need* we make in order to study an advertisement? In other words, What if we subjected the assumptions making up the sociological paradigm on advertising to a thorough-going *phenomenological* scrutiny? Where may this lead? This was not an original tactic but was advocated by Wright-Mills:

> Often you get the best insights by considering extremes – by thinking of the opposites of that which you are directly concerned ... when you try to contrast objects, you get a better grip on the materials and you can sort out the dimensions in terms of which the comparisons are made ... shuttling between attention to these dimensions and to concrete types is very illuminating. (Wright-Mills, 1978[1959]: 214)

In a previous work, the *phenomenological scrutiny* of the methodological assumptions of sociological studies to date on advertising was followed through. It took one, not surprisingly, to some of the works of major social theorists such as Husserl, Schutz and Garfinkel. This scrutiny demonstrated that there was something missing in the sociological study of advertising. That something was the topic: advertisements themselves as a pre-theoretical experience. The relevance trees showed that studies of advertising to date had been solely concerned with 'cause and consequence' and had used an *explanatory* and not a *descriptive* framework. This pre-occupation with the external reality of advertising was augmented by additional preconceptions about the morality of advertising. Advertising was therefore a topic not only approached in terms of external theorising but also its characteristics and features were defined in advance. The general conclusion was that a large corpus of material in the sociological literature on advertising showed advertising to be an important topic. But analysis of the literature also showed studies of advertising to have hitherto only theorised about it as a topic. Advertising had been talked about only in reference to power, ideology, control, alienation and hidden meanings. None of this work could have any purchase if

(Continued)

it were not for what we call the 'mundane reality' of advertisements; the ways in which ordinary people read advertisements and the ways people in advertising agencies put together advertisements to be read by ordinary people.

Using the analysis to make a recommendation for research

Therefore, the question was set – What if one placed to one side all assumptions hitherto made about advertising, where may this lead? What types of research problems may this approach throw up? A research topic was now, therefore, in the making. This was possible because the analysis of the literature had shown there to be a 'hole' at the centre of conventional theorising about advertising. That hole consisted of a disregard for the taken-for-granted aspects of advertisements as a serious topic for sociological description. The outcome was that methodological assumptions, moral judgements and methods hitherto used to study advertising were placed to one side. In short, the analysis of the literature had identified the need for a completely different approach to advertisements. The task, therefore, was now to think about the methodological policies and assumptions for the research. The criteria for that approach were that it should be free from the constraints and limitations of looking for hidden structures and free from moral pre-judgements. Finding an approach that would be able to describe the experience of an advertisement was not going to be easy. The readymade, off-the-peg approach had already been rejected. However, some leads had already been identified, rooted in the tradition of phenomenology and *methodological indifference*. This is the practice of placing to one side existing approaches and views about a phenomenon. These leads had definite intellectual traditions of their own, which may form the starting point for what was required. The task now was to see how the assumptions in these traditions could be applied to produce research. Suffice to say, it was done and formed a part of the methodological story making up a rationalisation for a piece of research – a project that would not have been possible without a search and review of the literature.

Conclusions

The forgoing introduction should lead you to be aware that a review of the literature is not a task that can be done in a few weeks by applying a series of discrete steps. The review is an integral part of any research project and will, depending on your needs, provide the justification for your research question, as well as evidence for recommendations, and give you the opportunity to develop your transferable skills. If doing a literature review seems daunting then see it as a challenge and an opportunity. For whatever type of research you are doing, for whatever purpose, the challenge is to develop and apply your technical skills and cognitive capacity to become the practical and intellectual expert in the field. All research is an opportunity to immerse yourself into a world of intellectual endeavour that has been millennia in the making.

In summary

- A review of the literature for research requires many skills and capabilities – a combination of technical skills in literature searching and knowledge of sources is the starting point to searching for relevant materials.
- Being able to organise and find the methodological and conceptual connections between different pieces of research requires higher capabilities, and in particular an ever-increasing capacity to amalgamate information and arguments – hence, a review of the literature can make demands on the technical and intellectual abilities of the researcher.
- The review is not something that can be 'done by numbers', over a few weeks. All research problems have different ways of being framed, and as a result every review is unique.
- When doing a review there is a set of questions that can be asked, which is common to most reviews. Using these questions with an enquiring, questioning and critical approach, you will teach yourself, through experience, how to become a competent user of the research literature.

2

The Purpose of Literature Reviewing

Key questions

- Why do a review of the literature? What are the benefits?
- What does a review look like? Are there different types of review?
- Where does the review of the literature fit into a piece of research?
- What do we define as originality and the role of the literature review in scholarship?
- How can information for the literature review be managed?
- What are the do's and don'ts when doing a review?

Core skills

- Critically analyse and evaluate complex information and argument from different sources
- Compare and contrast theories and concepts from different approaches to research
- Map and locate gaps in knowledge
- Construct different types of literature review.

Introduction

In academic and applied research the review of the *single work* can be important. This is because it can be the impetus for a research programme or alter the way we see and do things. However, for the research student and practitioner a review of a *body of literature* is, normally, much more important than the single review. This is because the focus, methodological particulars and originality of a topic often depend on a critical reading of a wide-ranging literature (topic, methodological, historical sources). The nature of this concerns, on the one hand, immersing oneself in the topic to avoid the shallowness of quick and shallow research. On the other hand, there is the need to identify the key ideas and methodologies that may be relevant to your research.

Without a systematic search, selection and critical reading of the literature, it would be very difficult to see how academic research could make a new application of a methodology or contribute in some way, no matter how small, to the knowledge of a problem. In other words, knowledge generation and understanding is an emergent process and not a universal product. In order to know the implications of a development, you need to know the intellectual context in which that development took place.

The purpose of the review

If research is about generating understanding and possible courses of action, then the review of relevant literatures has a range of purposes. There are at least 12 and these are:

1. distinguishing what has been done from what needs to be done
2. discovering important variables relevant to the topic
3. synthesising and gaining a new perspective
4. identifying relationships between ideas and practice
5. establishing the context of the topic or problem
6. rationalising the theoretical or practical significance of the problem
7. enhancing and gaining the subject vocabulary
8. understanding the origins and structure of the subject
9. relating ideas and theory to problems and questions
10. identifying the main methodologies and data collection tools that have been used
11. placing the research into an historical context to show familiarity with state-of-the-art developments
12. having a body of knowledge to which you can relate your own research findings.

No one purpose is of greater significance than any other. They are all equally important in a review of relevant literature. In many cases the individual purposes merge into one another and manifest themselves in numerous places and in various ways in a review. There are some good reasons, therefore, to take the time on a search of the literature. Of course, no matter how good a review may be, it does not mean any subsequent research will be equally as good.

At a very simplistic level, would it not be a waste to find on completing a piece of research that it had been done before? A thesis that duplicates what has already been done is of very little use and is a waste of resources. It may even be invalidated and rejected by the university. A search of the literature may help to eliminate this possibility from happening.

Reading advice: Methodological traditions

If you're interested in a more extensive outline and discussion of methodological traditions and their consequences, see Chapters 7 and 8 of my guide to postgraduate dissertations, Hart (2005) *Doing Your Masters Dissertation*.

That same search will show not only what has been done but also what has not been done. An initial search will help the researcher become more familiar with the topic, help to identify the major theorists and ideas and generally provide a cognitive map of the subject knowledge. This is a picture of the current leading concepts and topics attracting attention. It will enable the researcher to identify the matters and topics that feature most significantly in current debates. In doing this, you will become familiar with those people and organisations that are working in the area you intend to study. By getting to know who is doing what and where they are doing it, you will be able to evaluate and get involved in that research community. Getting to know other researchers in your field, through conferences and correspondence, is an ideal way to network. They may be able to suggest sources and ideas that will help in the research.

One of the most important outcomes of the search and review will be the identification of *methodological traditions*. These are the methodological assumptions and research strategies that they have employed by other researchers. In evaluating the relative merits of current methodologies, you will soon become acquainted with thinking about the importance of methodology. This will assist you in deciding on the methodological assumptions for your own work, while helping you to make decisions on the design features of your research strategy.

This latter dimension embodies both the design features of the research and the educational purposes of carrying out a piece of independent research. If we take the Master's dissertation as being a significant piece of investigative work then the following opportunities (or educational aims) are embodied in that investigation.

- To design and carry out a substantial piece of investigative work in a subject specific discipline. Whether field based or desk based the review of related and relevant literature will be important to contextualise the research, to provide a rationale and to justify the methodology.
- To take a topic and through a search and analysis of the literature focus that topic into a researchable question or hypothesis. This puts to the test the researcher's ability to search for and manage relevant texts and materials and to analytically interpret ideas and data.
- To recognise the structure of various arguments, to provide coherent, reasoned and objective evaluative analysis. This puts to the test the ability of the researcher to integrate and evaluate ideas.

Reviewing the literature on a topic can, therefore, provide an academically enriching experience, and if directed towards making changes to some situation, a plan for a course of action. But this is only the case if it is done properly.

Selecting relevant works

From the available literature you need to select relevant works that have something that can be used in your own research. This may be in its design, the framing of the hypothesis, refining the research question, aiding interpretation, providing key concepts and theoretical frameworks.

The review should be regarded as a process that is fundamental to any worthwhile research or development work in any subject matter in whatever discipline. The researcher and practitioner have the responsibility to find out what already exists in the area they propose research, before doing the research itself. The review forms the foundation for the 'research proper'. This is because the researcher needs to know about the contributions others have made to the *knowledge pool* in their topic. In a meta-review, it is the review of prior data that is the goal. When the goal is to do primary research then it is the ideas and work of others that will provide the researcher with the framework for their own work; this includes identifying methodological assumptions, data collection techniques, core concepts and ideas on how to structure the research into a format that is suited to a particular audience.

Understanding the history of the topic and methodologies

A basic requirement for the research scholar is that they should understand the history of the subject they intend to study. This means acquiring sufficient knowledge of the subject area along with comprehending the significance of work already done in the field. This knowledge serves the purpose of providing a perspective on how the subject has developed, become established, and assists in the development and acquisition of the appropriate vocabulary.

> **A good literature review**
>
> A good literature review does not include everything that has been found; it is selective, only presenting in discussion work that is relevant to the research itself. It is, therefore, important to justify the inclusion and exclusion criteria.

By becoming familiar with the history of the subject the researcher will also become acquainted with the current research and debate on their topic. This will make it possible to identify the general areas of concern that may give pointers to specific matters worth studying. Areas of concentrated, current interest and, possibly, areas of relative neglect will become apparent. The review will also help the research scholar to gain an understanding of the relationships between the subject being considered and other subject areas. Thus, they will be better placed to recognise or establish a context in which the subject for study exists. The overall result is that the researcher will become thoroughly knowledgeable about a topic, and they will be ready to do research that advances knowledge on that topic.

In the examples that follow, we can see that there are two basic reviews, the categorical and the generative. The categorical aims to categorise the literature according to sets of concerns or categories. The generative review uses the literature to make a case for the research; it generates a position and argument that extends the literature.

The difference between a review of and review for the research

The National Centre for Research Methods (NCRM), in the UK, has produced many reviews of the literature on a number of research methods. The general purpose of these reviews falls into two types. The first introduces the methods and related issues through a review *of* the relevant literature. The second type discusses the issues and problems of using these methods *for* research. Some, of course, do both.

Extended example: A review *of* the research

In this extract from Corinne Squire's (2008) review of narrative method, is an example of a summative description of the literature. The summative description of a literature is intended to provide a survey of the sources. This is done by organising the sources according to various categories. These categories often start with the most general ones that give outlines of the method or topic. Squire (2008) goes on to give citations which discuss specific issues and applications.

The citations are the main content, organised using simple categories

No need for page numbers unless quoting.

Narrative is a popular portmanteau term in contemporary western social research. The crowd of much-used summary and outline texts about narrative research (Clandinin and Connelly, 2004; Elliot, 2005; Freeman, 1993; Holstein and Gubrium, 1999; Langellier and Peterson, 2004; Mishler, 1986; Ochs and Capps, 2001; Personal Narratives Group, 1989; Plummer, 2001; Polkinghorne, 1988; Riessman, 1993a, 2007; Roberts, 2002; Sarbin, 1986; Wengraf, 1999) **exemplifies its popularity. So do the recent burst of empirically-based texts focused on specific studies** (Andrews, 2007; Emerson and Frosh, 2004; McAdams, 2006; Mishler, 1999; Squire, 2007; Tamboukou, 2003), **the rich crop of narratively-themed collections of essays** (Andrews et al., 2004; Bamberg and Andrews, 2004; Brockmeier and Carbaugh, 2001; Chamberlayne et al., 2000; Clandinin, 2006; Patterson, 2002; Rosenwald and Ochberg, 1992) **and the increasing number of books addressing narrative in specific domains such as development, health, sexuality and social work** (Daiute and Lightfoot, 2004; Greenhalgh and Hurwitz, 1998; Hall, 1997; Mattingley, 1988; Plummer, 1995; Riessman, 1993b).

Source: Adapted from Squire, 2008: 5. Bold emphasis is mine; it shows the categories used to organise the literature.

Some of the key features of the basic review of research include:

- the use of general categories to group the citations
- emphasis on the author and date of publication
- broad set of criteria for what to include and exclude
- emphasis on inclusion

Extended example: A review *for* the research

In this second extract, Squire (2008) takes a selection from the sources found to focus on what is useful *for* designing and implementing narrative research. Squire's review is aimed at the knowledgeable reader, readers who already have advanced understanding of the

(Continued)

general literature within the social sciences. Therefore, she has no reason to give definitions or explications of key concepts and approaches. Squire can assume the reader will be familiar with these and that she is free to talk about what matters for doing narrative research.

Many approaches and concepts are not given attribution. This is because the author assumes the reader will have sufficient knowledge to infer them.	A 'cultural' approach… does not necessarily avoid relativism, guarantee political engagement or provide a clear concept of the relationship between narrative representations and their effects. It is difficult to say anything definitive about narrative genres, given the multiplicity and incompleteness just described. Focusing on 'cultural stories' can lead to narrow particularism about specific stories; or to reifying them, for instance by collapsing them into categories, such as 'women's stories', from which politics is evacuated (Stanley, 1992). The political shapes of narratives are larger than a 'cultural' analysis can indicate (Parker, 2003); a move towards broader understandings of them is becoming more common in narrative researchers' work, as work like that of Molly Andrews (2007), demonstrates. From an opposed perspective, some critics also accuse culturally oriented approaches of losing sight of the individual stories, on which experience-centred research rests.
Generic references to Labovian and Ricoeurian need no explanation. *There is no need to add in all the citations especially for ones everyone knows.* *The focus is on the problems and necessary compromises that have to be addressed when using narrative research.*	Some problems, however, remain. For instance, what is left out of these brave new self-disclosure stories, or indeed, any culturally described set of stories? Here, what is not said assumes an importance, it lacks within Labovian and Ricoeurian perspectives, according to which the 'unsaid' can often be derived, albeit with difficulty, from the syntactic or semantic substructures of a story. The rich interlinkings that a notion of cultural narrative generates, between individuals and across social and historical moments, often seem to leave no space, however, for an unconscious. When you tell a 'coming out' story, for example, you may produce an account that despite its meaningfulness necessarily omits some difficult and important emotions that fall outside words (Frosh, 2002: 127–8; see also Craib, 2004). When a woman testifies to her acceptance of her HIV positive status and tells of her commitment to living long and healthily and spreading the truth about HIV to her family and friends, what happens to sexual shame, loss and grief in the story? A partial solution to such questions is to borrow from literary and cultural theory a notion of the unconscious that sees it as constitutive of cultural representations, infiltrating even the most conventional of them. Parker (2003), for instance, describes a 'self' spread across stories and storytelling in his consideration of psychoanalytic, and specifically Lacanian stories of subjectivity.
The key features of the approach are summarised	In addition, in looking at the genre structure of for instance conversion narratives, we miss out, inevitably, on smaller, co-occurring structures, the co-construction of narratives between speakers and hearers, and the limits of such co-construction.

A focus on 'genre' allows us to understand narratives as contextual cultural genres that are always in contest, compromising between redemptive closure and unrepresentable openness (Bersani, 1990). The fluidity of the coming out genre for instance (Sedgwick, 1990) involves this kind of perpetual instability – you are never fully 'out' to everyone, even yourself – as does the conversion genre, in which faith is a process, not an end point. Thus, cultural genres do not leave out the unsayability and ambiguity that makes 'telling the whole story' impossible, so much as negotiate across them.

Source: Adapted from Squire, 2008: 48–50

Some of the key features of the generative review for research include:

- there is no need to explain every approach, perspective and method
- you can make references to positions such as Lacan without the need to reference Lacan or secondary works on him
- you can assume that the reader will have at least your level of knowledge on the general and some specific literature within the social sciences.

The problem from the authors' standpoint is writing clearly, knowing what can reasonably be assumed on behalf of the reader and what cannot. Squire (2008) shows that she can write clearly and where examples are required she gives one or two. She does not populate her text with numerous citations to show her knowledge of the sources. She has no need to do this. This is because her readership is doctoral and post-doctoral researchers.

Ways of making a contribution to existing research

The American Education Research Association (2006) explains some of the ways new research can contribute to existing research. This can be adapted to state the purpose of the literature review within your research. This four-part scheme shows the differences and inter-connections between the summative review based on categorising the literature and the generative review that aims to make something new from the literature.

The role of reviewing in different research outputs

The outcome of most research is a document of some kind. This document can be a single report on the research or a summative formulation of prior findings from several research studies or a dissertation (or thesis). Research is also found in conference papers and essays.

TABLE 2.1 Purpose of a review in different types of research

Research orientation	Role of the literature review
If the study is **a contribution to an established line of theory and empirical research**, it should make clear what the contributions are and how the study contributes to testing, elaborating or enriching that theoretical perspective.	The literature should categorise the main theories and empirical studies according to their particular concerns or research questions/problems. The need to make additional contributions is done by identifying extensions to existing research and/or theory.
If a study is intended to **establish a new line of theory**, it should make clear what that new theory is, how it relates to existing theories and evidence, why the new theory is needed, and the intended scope of its application.	The literature on the problem needs to be examined critically and shown to be inadequate, insufficient or applicable to a new kind of problem. The objective is to create new lines of inquiry.
If the study is **motivated by practical concerns**, it should make clear what those concerns are, why they are important, and how this investigation can address those concerns.	The literature is from primary research studies that have generated results having investigated same or similar problems, conditions or happenings to show, where possible, the best available evidence for a recommendation.
If the study is **motivated by a lack of information about a problem or issue**, the problem formation should make clear what information is lacking, why it is important, and how this investigation will address the need for information.	The importance of the problem needs to be shown with examples of its impact as documented in the literature. Then based on the evidence taken from the literature a course of action can be recommended to address the problem, i.e. further research.

Source: Adapted from Justus, 2009:13.

Understanding the role the literature review can play in any publication and how they have been written can be useful. This is because it will guide efforts to produce what is required for a particular audience. Table 2.2 summarises the place of a review in four publications, while the next section looks at publications such as the dissertation for different degree qualifications.

A major product of academic programmes in postgraduate education is the dissertation (or what is sometimes called the thesis). This section will look at the place of the literature review in relation to the thesis. It will attempt to outline some of the dimensions and elements that provide evidence for assessing the *worthiness* of a thesis. Whereas undergraduate projects are often assessed according to proforma marking schedules a Master's thesis is assessed for its 'Master's worthiness'. In either case and in the case of other types of thesis, the literature review plays a major role in the assessment. A problem, however, is saying just what constitutes an undergraduate dissertation or project and how this differs from, say, a Master's research project. Although this is not the platform to look closely at this problem Table 2.3 provides a summary.

TABLE 2.2 The role of the review in different kinds of publication

Type of publication	Role of the literature in the document	Arrangement of the document
Conference paper	20 minutes at 9–10 pages double-spaced in Ariel 12 point at 250 words per page gives 2500 words. Therefore, time is very short and content should attend to this limiting factor. Refer sparingly to the literature to: • place your study in the context – a *thin slice* – of other work that has already been done in the field • inform your listeners about the theories your paper is based on • state the significance of your argument or methodology • quote from your sources sparingly.	It will normally have the following sections: • brief introduction to the argument or the research that has been done • the reason the research was done, referring to selected items from the literature • how the research was done; the how, where, with who, using what data collection tools • findings and key arguments. Discussion and 'argument based' papers will differ but will normally invoke literature as backing for the case being made.
Research report	The length varies but many exceed 30 pages, which include chapters dealing with previous research and methodologies. A research report focuses on a single topic, aiming to make a deliberate attempt to find out what experts know in order to find the best possible information in that field that can inform your own research design and allow you to place your findings into the context of what is already known. Therefore, the sources used are an important part of the structure, and are used to place the problem into a detailed context. Refer extensively to the literature to: • establish the need for your investigation, typically by identifying how it fills a gap in the knowledge accumulated about the subject area	It will normally have the following sections or chapters: • introduction that places the research into context • literature review of selected sources to show the ways in which the topic has been researched and theorised about • methodology that explains how the research was done, using which methods, and assumptions justified by reference to the methodological literature • findings presented as a result of the research • discussion of the relevance of the findings showing how they fit with other research on the topic • conclusion that summarises the research • recommendations of what now needs to be done as a result of your research justified by reference to your research and that of others.

(Continued)

Type of publication	Role of the literature in the document	Arrangement of the document
	• look for patterns in methods, subjects tested, results, conclusions and assumptions researchers have made about the topic • emphasise the main arguments or findings made in each source • aggregate findings • justify recommendations and conclusions.	
Essay	Usually from 2500 words to 5000 words with the intent being to discuss, compare, contrast and evaluate. An essay generally addresses one central question and develops a thesis, your approach or position to the question. Usually you explain or defend your thesis with reasons and evidence gained from your own thinking gained from your reading or research. Therefore, the sources used are an important part of the assessment of your knowledge. Refer extensively to the literature to: • show the nature of the topic and debates about it • highlight which textbooks and articles may be referred to alongside original sources • show the history of the debate • examine the opposing positions citing the core sources • quote and cite extensively from the sources to provide backing or materials for source criticism.	It will normally have the following sections: • *introduction*: a thematic overview of the topic and introduction of the debate • *narration*: a review of the background literature, often using a recognised structure, to orient the reader to the debate • *affirmation*: the evidence and arguments in favour of the preferred position • *negation*: the evidence and arguments against the preferred position; these also require either 'refutation' or 'concession' • *conclusion*: summary of the argument, and placing it in the larger context or issues • references of texts referred to in the essay.

TABLE 2.3   Degrees and the nature of the literature review

Types of degree	Function and format of the literature review in research at these levels
Bachelor of Art and Science (BA/BSc) Research project	Essentially descriptive, topic focused; mostly indicative of the core and current sources on the topic. Analysis of the topic to write a justification, research question or hypothesis. Reading of the research literature to identify a workable methodology.
Master of Arts and Science (MA/MSc) Dissertation, thesis or project	Analytical summative, covering methodological issues, research techniques and topic. Possibly two literature-based chapters, one on methodological issues that demonstrate knowledge of the advantages and disadvantages of different approaches, and another on theoretical issues relevant to the topic/problem.
Doctor of Philosophy (PhD) Thesis	Analytical synthesis, covering all known literature, including other languages, on the problem. High level of conceptual linking within and across theories. Summative and formative evaluation of previous work on the problem. Depth and breadth discussion on relevant philosophical traditions and ways in which they relate to the problem.

Note that, at the outset, the main concern is not only to satisfy assessors but also to produce a competent review of a body of literature. An understanding of what all this means can be obtained by looking at what we mean by a doctorate and then looking at the Master's dissertation. This is because if we start at what most people regard as the 'top' and work down we may be able to pick out some of the main distinctions between the different levels of academic research and see more clearly just what is expected from the student-researcher.

Criteria of a doctorate

The Doctor of Professional Studies (DProf) normally requires reviews of the research literature and literature on the problem. Boote and Beile's (2005) criteria for assessing a dissertation can still be applied.

You will find this summarised later in the chapter.

The two descriptions that follow are not intended to be read as separate criteria for a doctorate and those for a Master's research. Rather read them as guides to what may be expected from postgraduate research. We spend more time describing the criteria common to doctorate work than those of the Master's simply to show that a Master's can provide the necessary prerequisite skills for a doctorate.

What is a doctorate?

The recent expansion of higher degrees research in the UK has rekindled the debate about just what constitutes a doctorate. As yet there is no definitive answer to this question, which may be for the good of research. This is because it will allow for the current flexible and divergent approach to higher degrees research to continue. However, what we have are a number of statements from across the academic profession about the key elements that are common to postgraduate research. There are at least seven main *requirements* that cover the content, process and product of a doctorate thesis. These are:

1. a requirement for specificity in scholarship
2. a requirement for making a new contribution to an area of knowledge
3. a vehicle for demonstrating one has developed a high level of scholarship
4. to demonstrate originality
5. the ability to write a coherent volume of intellectually demanding work of a significant length
6. to have been able to develop the capacity and personal character to intellectually manage the research including the writing of the thesis
7. to have in-depth understanding of the topic area and work related to your research.

We may also add an eighth one more common to the doctoral viva:

8. to be able to defend orally what was produced in terms of the reason for doing the research and choices over the way it was done.

These requirements do not capture the scope and depth of all doctoral research. They do, however, provide a set of requirements that show the crucial importance of the literature review in the process, product and content of doctoral research. The first four of these requirements show the input that can be made by a thorough search and reading of related literature. It is those four that will now be discussed. This is because it is these requirements that mostly concern students undertaking research. The substance of the other requirements will be picked up throughout the remainder of this and the next chapter.

On the requirement for specificity of scholarship

Although some universities allow candidates to enrol for higher degrees without a first degree the model used here assumes an *academic career*, in which scholarship is developmental and not conveyed through a title. This career normally consists of a first degree followed by postgraduate work, both of which can be via full-time or part-time modes of study. Through the academic career, the individual gradually acquires a cumulative range of skills and abilities and focuses their learning around a subject specific knowledge. Through choice of degree and options within degrees subject specialisation of some form is inevitable. In terms of skills and ability, most undergraduates are expected to acquire and develop a wide range of personal transferable skills. Figure 2.1 shows the relation of these skills to the information management task involved in reviewing a literature. The RDF (Researcher Development Framework) specifies these essential skills in being competent with information technology, especially online searching, being able to manage information and manage priorities to meet deadlines.

The major form in which information is to be managed, is as text and numbers. Most commonly in the form of articles from journals, periodicals, anthologies and monographs, the raw material for undergraduate work is the ideas of other people.

Core skills in managing information

Relevant core skills for managing information from a literature review are:

- self-management
- research management.

Depending on the subject discipline these others are usually the 'founding theorists' and 'current notables' of the discipline. In order to understand what the specifics of the subject are about it is essential that the undergraduate comes to terms with the ideas of the founding theorists and current notables. Only when they have done this will they have sufficient *subject knowledge* to be able to talk coherently about and begin to analyse critically the ideas of the subject. This means demonstrating *comprehension* of the topic and the alternative methodologies that can be used for its investigation.

While it may be possible to reach a level of advanced standing without an appropriate intellectual apprenticeship, the academic career is a more reliable method of acquiring the depth and breadth of knowledge demanded from a doctoral scholar. There are sound academic reasons for the academic career as preparation for higher degrees research. Some of these are not only about skills. The acquisition of the ability and capacity to cognitively manage massive amounts of information, play with abstract ideas and theorems and see insights cannot be gained through short-term, drop-in programmes. In short, the academic game is very different from vocational pragmatism – both demand a different attitude. Whereas vocational life tends to be dominated by a pragmatic mentality, the academic game is more altruistic in terms of being an end in itself and personalised.

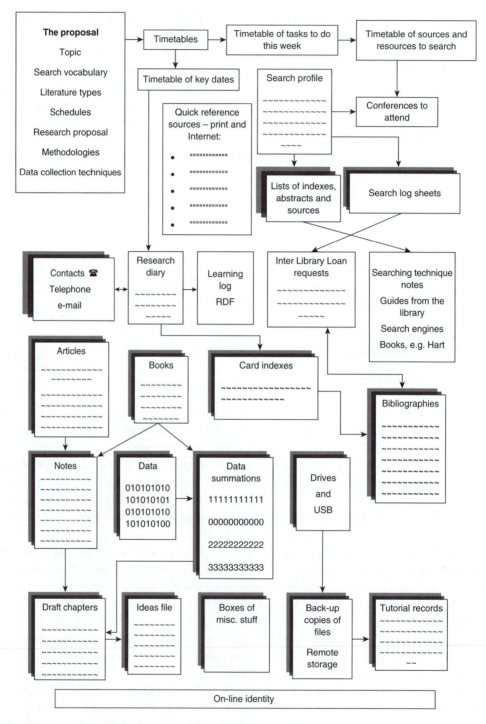

FIGURE 2.1 Managing information from a literature review

On the requirement for making a new contribution

In a section below what is meant by creativity and innovation is discussed and relates to what is said here. In terms of a subject the requirement that postgraduate research advances understanding through making a new contribution is directly dependent on knowledge of the subject. Knowledge can only be obtained through the work and effort of reading and seeking out ways in which general ideas have been developed through theory or application. This process requires from the researcher the kinds of skills already mentioned in relation to using sources. It also requires a spirit of adventure (a willingness to explore new areas); an attitude of charity (not to pre-judge an idea); and tenacity (to invest the time and effort even when the going gets hard).

This can be illustrated with a brief example. Many social science students will have come across ethnomethodology. Except for a few notable exceptions ethnomethodology is quickly passed over in most programmes of study. This, from experience, we have found, is often due to the extreme difficulty of coming to terms with what *ethnomethodology* is about and how one does an ethnomethodological study. The following is the *title* from an article by Garfinkel:

> Respecification: evidence for the locally produced, naturally accountable phenomena of order, logic, reason, meaning, method, etc. in and as of the essential haecceity of immortal ordinary society - and announcement of studies. (Garfinkel, 1991: 10)

Those unfamiliar with ethnomethodology may now appreciate the difficulties in merely understanding what Garfinkel is trying to say. There are two very relevant points here. The first is tenacity is required to understand an approach such as ethnomethodology. Simply because Garfinkel's work is not instantly recognisable as sociology is not sufficient reason to dismiss it. Secondly, Garfinkel's ideas may be important. If they are dismissed because one was less willing to invest the effort then an important opportunity for learning may have been missed.

It is important to note that what we are talking about here is the attitude of charity. This attitude requires more than just making an effort, though this is important. It involves resisting the temptation to make prior assumptions about any idea or theory until one is knowledgeable about that idea or theory. The only way one can become competent to comment on complex ideas such as those proposed by Garfinkel is to read the works of the theorist and follow through what that person has said. This involves the spirit of research: this is looking for leads to other works cited by the author, which have led her or him to their position. It also means looking for ways in which, say, Garfinkel's ideas were developed by others. In short, the spirit of research involves a large amount of detective work and close attention to detail.

Scholarship is many dimensions. For a typology of these see Figure 2.2 below.

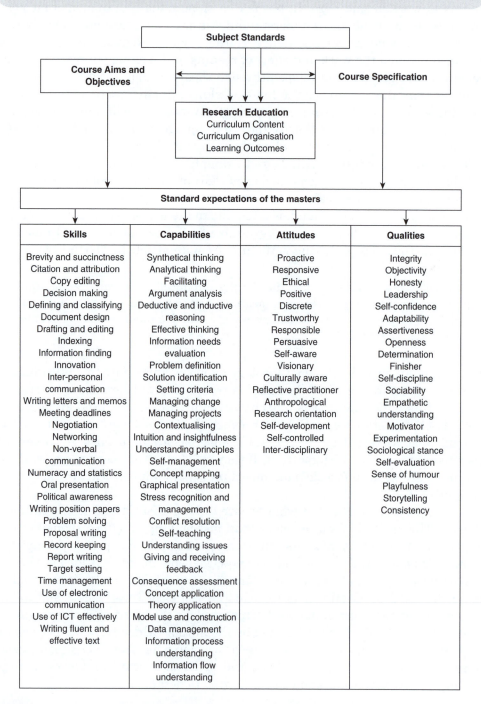

FIGURE 2.2   Skills, capabilities, attitudes and qualities of the masters

The third point is that Garfinkel's ethnomethodology, like many other interesting developments in all subject fields, did not appear from where there was once nothing. It was a development from an existing set of theories and ideas. Garfinkel systematically worked through a range of existing theories in order to see where some ideas would lead if applied. Through his reading of the work of Talcott Parsons and Alfred Schutz and thinking through the implications of their theories, he was able to explore in the true spirit of adventure the foundations and boundaries of social science.

What enabled Garfinkel to make a new contribution, even though the amount of work he produced is relatively small, was his ability to see possibilities in existing ideas. Making new insights is not merely about being able to synthesise difficult and large amounts of materials, it also involves knowing how to be creative and what it means to be original. This statement needs to be followed with an observation that cannot be sufficiently emphasised. To make a new contribution to knowledge does not mean one has to be a genius. The size of the contribution is not what matters – it is the quality of work that produces the insight. As will shortly be shown, creativity can be defined and is often systematic rather than ad hoc.

On the requirement to demonstrate scholarship

As a product, the thesis is something tangible. It is the only evidence of the work and effort that have gone into the research. For this reason, it needs to provide enough evidence, of the right type and in an appropriate form, to demonstrate that the desired level of scholarship has been achieved. A key part of the thesis that illustrates scholarship is the review of the literature. It is in this section that the balance and level of intellectual skills and abilities can be fully displayed for viewing and assessment.

The review chapter may comprise only 30 to 40 pages, as in a doctoral thesis, or 15 to 20 in a Master's thesis. The actual length often depends on the nature of the research. Theory-based work tends to require a longer review than empirical work. Either way this is a very short space to cover all that is required and expected. Typically, the review chapter is a grossly edited version of the massive amount of notes taken from extensive reading. What is being asked from the review is also very wide and demands concise, tightly structured expression. The material for a review is not all the literature one has searched, located, obtained and read. It is the literature that has been selected from what one has searched, located, obtained and read. This literature is much more than separate items or a bibliography. The reader of the thesis is being asked to see this literature as representing the relevant knowledge on your topic. It must also demonstrate the ability to think critically in terms of evaluating ideas, methodologies, techniques to collect data and reflect on implications and possibilities for certain ideas. Scholarship demands, therefore, a wide range of skills and intellectual capabilities.

If we take the methodological aspect of the thesis we can see that underpinning all research is the ability to demonstrate our utter familiarity with the respective strengths and weaknesses of a range of research methodologies and techniques for collecting data. It is, therefore, important to read widely around the literature on the major intellectual traditions such as *positivism* and *phenomenology*. This is because it is these traditions that support and have shaped the ways in which we tend to view the nature of the world and how it is possible to go about developing our knowledge and understanding of our world. Knowledge of historical ideas and theories, or philosophy and social theory, is essential. In a similar way to skills, knowledge of say Marx or the postmodernists may be seen as essential personal transferable knowledge.

As a scholar, you must also demonstrate the ability to assess methodologies used in the discipline or in the study of the topic in order to show your clear and critical understanding of the limitations of the approach. To do this is to show your ability to employ a range of theories and ideas common to the discipline and your ability to subject them to critical evaluation in order to advance understanding. This involves demonstrating the capacity to argue rationally and present that argument in a coherent structure. There is, therefore, the need to know how to analyse the arguments of others. This is because you can expect the reader of your thesis (an external examiner) to be familiar with some of the theories you have looked at in your review and argument. They will be looking, therefore, to see how you have analysed such theories and how you have developed independent conclusions from your reading. In particular, your reader will be interested to see how you have developed a case (argument) for the research you intend to undertake.

To demonstrate originality

The notion of originality is very closely related to the function of the search and analysis of the literature. We have already indicated that through a rigorous analysis of a research literature, one can give focus to a topic. It is through this focusing process that an original treatment of an old topic can be developed.

Core skill of creativity

Demonstrating originality, which lies at the heart of the literature search and review, rests on the core skill of creativity.

Placing aside until later chapters how this has and can be done we need to turn our attention to the concept of originality. In Figure 2.3 we show some of the associations that can be made from the different definitions of originality. Use these to get a grasp of the meaning of the term. This is important because

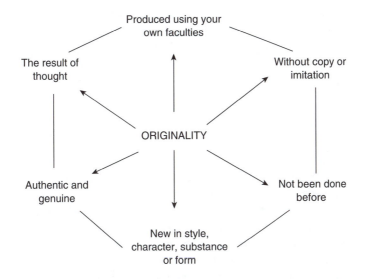

FIGURE 2.3 Map of associations in definitions of originality

in academic research the aim is not to replicate what has already been done but to add, albeit no matter how small, something that helps us to understand the world in which we live.

We can begin by noting that all research is, in its own way, unique. Even research that replicates work done by another is unique. But it is not original. To be original may be taken to mean to do something no one has done before or even thought about doing before. Sometimes this kind of approach to thinking about originality equates originality with special qualities assumed to be possessed by only a few individuals. The thing to remember is that we are all unique and there is nothing unusual about this. Therefore, we take the line that originality is not a mysterious quality; it is something all research scholars should be able to produce if they know how to think about, manage and play with ideas (Wallas, 1926).

A useful way of thinking about this is that of the *child in the adult*. Whereas the adult has learnt how to learn and has a broad range of skills, if they remember how to 'play' and 'imagine' they can use their adult skills and yet still enjoy play through the intellectual game (Walkup, 1967).

The research biography E = Mc²

All great discoveries have their own research biography. E = Mc² is no exception. David Bodanis (2000) uncovers the stories of love, tragedy and courage that made possible Einstein's historic formulations. Bodanis's book is an example of an historic chronological informative narrative review.

It is the playing with ideas, no matter how absurd they may at first seem or not knowing where they may lead to, that gives to research a sense of adventure. There is, therefore, an imaginary element to research: this is the ability to create and play with images in your mind or on paper. This amounts to thinking using visual pictures.

Extended example: Einstein

Theorists such as Einstein attribute their ideas to being able to play with *mental images* and to make up *imaginary experiments*. This technique is used to make connections among things that you would normally not see as connectable. Einstein, for example, described how he came to think about the relativity of time and space, in the way he did, by saying it all began with an imaginary journey. Einstein visualised himself as a passenger who rode on a beam of light. He held a mirror in front of himself. Since the light on which he was riding and the mirror were travelling at the same speed (velocity) in the same direction and because the mirror was a little ahead, the light could never catch up to the mirror and reflect his image back to him. Using the same notions about velocity, Einstein visualised himself in other situations to explore other dimensions of his idea. Einstein's imaginary situations are analogous to real events; they are a kind of episode, in which something fantastic can be visually synthesised to create a new or interesting view of reality. Einstein was able to follow his fantasy to produce his famous equation $E = Mc^2$.

The point to note is that Einstein's journey was a little *episode*; something most of us are capable of creating. Einstein's achievement was in *following through* his ideas to their theoretical conclusions. He stopped short his work when he realised that his ideas could have a dark side; that being the development of a nuclear weapon. It is reassuring to know that very few people will find themselves in the situation Einstein found himself. It is sufficient to say that such episodes are an essential part of the research imagination. You will often find yourself having what we have called 'little' episodes. This is a part of the process in thinking. You will often find yourself understanding things that just a few days or week previously seemed too difficult. This is because, as you apply more energy to your topic, you will increase your capacity for understanding. Therefore, notions and beliefs about having to be some kind of genius in order to be original can be placed to one side. Once this is done, we may be able to see and learn about how to be original in research.

These kinds of criteria can also be found in books such as that of Phillips and Pugh (1994). In their study of doctoral research, they identified nine definitions of what it means to be original. These are:

1. doing empirically based work that has not been done before
2. using already known ideas, practices or approaches but with a new interpretation
3. bringing new evidence to bear on an old issue or problem
4. creating a new synthesis that has not been done before

5.   applying something done in another country to one's own country
6.   applying a technique usually associated with one area to another
7.   being cross-disciplinary by using different methodologies
8.   looking at areas that people in the discipline have not looked at before
9.   adding to knowledge in a way that has not previously been done before.

Similarly, Francis (1976), working in the area of civil and mechanical engineering, observed seven ways to be original in research. These are:

1.   setting down a major piece of information for the first time in writing
2.   giving a good exposition of the ideas of another
3.   continuing a previously original piece of work
4.   carrying out original work designated by the supervisor
5.   providing a single original technique, observation or result in an otherwise original, but competent piece of research
6.   having followed instructions and understood the original concepts
7.   having an original idea, method and interpretation all performed by others under the direction of the postgraduate tutor showing originality in testing somebody else's idea.

We may agree with some of these and not others. For example, number 6 from Francis (1976) would not meet the criteria, at doctoral level, of originality expected in British universities. This list is more suited to undergraduate work. It seems to be oriented towards finding out for one's self how someone else did a piece of work by replicating it or explaining what it was about. These types of work can be extremely valuable for disciplinary socialisation and familiarisation with key concepts, ideas and approaches. One may argue that without this type of grounding good quality higher degree research is made much more difficult. The list presented by Phillips and Pugh (1994), on the other hand, is much closer to what may be expected from Master's and doctoral scholars. This is because it is oriented towards methodology and scholarship. It assumes the scholar already has an understanding of the subject knowledge. Much of what we have just discussed can be seen in the following example.

Extended example: Reviewing studies about communities

Before we can 'revisit' the community study, we have first to locate it, but unlike physical places, the community study is a social construction, which is highly adaptable, transportable and indeed, transient. It is one thing to know what and where it used to be: Frankenberg (1966), or Bell and Newby (1971), are useful as original Baedeckers in helping to map and access the early locations. It is another thing to position more recent studies and to understand the research imaginations that create them, and are created by them.

Sets out the purpose for the review by mentioning some of the problems of defining 'community'. Identifies some starting points and notes the C.S. have a history.

(Continued)

Once a sketch map has been drawn, 'the revisiting' can begin. In this brief re-exploration, we shall be less interested in the perennial questions of the definition of community, or the sociological purpose of studying 'communities', as with four questions of research methodology and imagination. Why is it that, from most sociological accounts, communities seem so full of such *nice* people? Why are small settlements apparently so receptive of middle class sociologists, and yet remain so hostile to other 'incomers'? How can sociologists know if their fieldwork is representative and comprehensive? And how can the sociologist evaluate whether a given finding is characteristic of 'communities', rather than of wider British Society?

A tourist map is the analogy for the review, showing different locations and interest points along the way.

A number of questions are asked as means for orienting the reader to the terrain.

Rediscovering the Community Study

Sub-section-title

After becoming a mainstream strength of British sociology in the 1950s and 1960s, community research rapidly became no more than a backwater interest by the 1970s. The familiar successes of Rees (1950), Williams (1956), Dennis et al. (1956), Young and Willmott (1957), Frankenberg (1957 and 1966), Stacey (1960), Littlejohn (1964), Rex and Moore (1969), etc. found little echo in the following decade. To some extent victims of their own success (what more was there to discover about the social life of small settlements?), criticised for spatial determinism and inadequate theorisation by Dennis (1958), Gans (1964), Pahl (1968), and Stacey (1969), they were swept aside by the tide of expansion and specialisation of the discipline that began in this country in the mid-1960s (Payne et al., 1981: 95–99).

Chronological arrangement is used, along with a contrast structure to show the popularity of C.S., their seeming decline and low impact on future work.

Indication of early criticisms of C.S., and part reason given as the specialisation of sociology.

It is important to recognise that community research did not completely cease during this shift in sociological fashion. It also evolved so that we had fewer studies of 'social places', and more accounts of problems studied in a location.

Seeming decline attributed to a change in focus of the C.S.

A decade after Newby's observation, Day and Murdock saw little sign of this gap having been filled:

Shows that little was done in over a decade to fill the knowledge gap.

> Bell and Newby's textbook account of this tradition (1971) turned out to be in effect its death knell. Rather than inspiring a new wave of case studies in community research, it seemed to provide ample justification for ignoring past work of the kind (1993: 83–4).

Beginning to see the use of testimony to shape the map.

They quote a voice from social geography in support: *relatively little of social scientific value could be said to have been bequeathed to later generations of researchers either by the concept of community or the methodology of community studies* (Cooke, 1988).

Use of sources from other disciplines.

An alternative interpretation can be found at the anthropological end of the discipline. By the mid-1980s, Cohen could reflect that whereas in the 1970s there had been a paucity of studies, things had since improved:

The 'however' movement is used to show that there was an alternative view of what had been happening in the area of C.S.

the problem we faced on the occasion of this present book was, therefore, quite different: we were confronted by an embarrassment of riches. Research seemed to be going on apace throughout the British Isles, in cities and countryside, on the remote periphery and in commuter villages (Cohen, 1986: viii).

Bulmer had also been cautiously optimistic the year before, perceiving: "*Some sign that the study of localities is being revived*" (1985: 433). While another study could see: "*a lively upsurge of locality and community studies in Britain*" (Warwick and Littlejohn, 1992: *xv*).

More testimony using a positive attitude in contrast to the negative attitude of the previous ones.

Are these assessments to be believed? On the whole, the answer should be yes. In the first place, several successful and very recognisable community studies had taken place, such as Brody's work on Inishkillane (1973), Stacey's revisit to Banbury (1975), Strathern's anthropology of Elmdon (1981), Giarchi's description of Troon (1984), or the fifteen of so studies reported by Cohen (1982, 1986). Other, less well-known work includes Stephenson (1984), Holme (1985), Fraser (1987), Morris (1987), Macleod (1990), Dean (1990), Goudy (1990), and Borland et al. (1992). These range over communal patterns of kinship, housing, migration, politics, drinking, religion, social control, localism, identity and cultural survival – for the most part the familiar themes of the earlier tradition of the 1950s and 1960s. In addition, there were several studies that were arguably not quite community studies, but which examined issues by looking at their manifestations in particular localities and which took these localities very seriously. Examples of this trend are Moore's 'The Social Impact of Oil' (1982), Davies' description of 'The Evangelistic Bureaucrat' (1972), Dennis' concern over 'People and Planning' (1970), Pryce's report on the 'Endless Pressure' of ghetto life (1979), MacKinnon's study of 'Language, Education and Social Processes in a Gaelic Community' (1977) or Wengler's account of 'The Supportive Network' in rural Wales (1984).

A question / answer is used to take the side of the positive view of C.S. More citations are given to provide evidence.

Links shown to previous studies; themes are said to be the same.

Citations to studies that have interesting titles; that are said to be about community but are classified not as C.S.

Next Door to the Community Study

On this brief and by no means exhaustive review, it seems reasonable to claim that the community study is tolerably alive and well, and living in British Sociology (albeit in a less fashionable or visible part of town). One reason for this survival has been that wider sociological concerns could be examined in specific sites (Moore, Davies, Dennis, Pryce, MacKinnon, Wengler). Another reason is that processes external to sociology put community back on the research agenda, as in the work of Martin Bulmer. On the one hand, his contributions can be seen as a development of his early career experience in the sociology department at Durham (Bulmer, 1978), a department which produced a series of local studies such as Moore (1974), Taylor (1979), Williamson (1982), and also Bulmer (1975). On the other hand, his work in the mid-1980s (e.g. Bulmer, 1986, 1987), was also related to the fresh stimulus of Peter Wilmott (1983, 1986), and Clare Wengler (1984),

The point of the previous section is emphasised: C.S. is still a major form of research. Note how studies classified on the fringe of the category are cited as the reason for the continuation of C.S. research.

We see an adaptation of the definition for C.S. to include studies of 'locality'. In the next

(Continued)

which marked the rediscovery of local systems as a potential basis for 'community care'. The setting of a new political agenda for social policy, in which a Government that did not believe in the existence of 'society', set about decanting the mentally ill and others into the care of 'the community', sharpened interest in kinship, networks and neighbouring.

paragraph note how the notion of locality study is consolidated as an important development of C.S.

A parallel political stimulus led to the rediscovery of the mining community, namely the Miners' strike in 1984–85. Drawing on the experiences of strikers and their wives, a number of sociological and polemical accounts appeared in the following years: Samuel et al., 1986; Gibbon and Steyne, 1986; Parker, 1986; Seddon, 1986; Allen, 1989; Winterton and Winterton, 1989; Gilbert, 1992 and Warwick and Littlejohn, 1992 (who also record the growth of something of a 'Featherstone history industry' – see Evans, 1984; Berry and Williams, 1986; Clayton et al., 1990). These are neither all 'conventional' community studies nor produced within normal canons of social scientific work, but draw on the idea of the community, communal sentiment, and in some cases specifically on contrasts and continuities with the classic study, *'Coal is Our Life.'*

The Miners' strike of the early 1980s is used to chronologically locate studies of locality. The gender dimension is mentioned. However, strong links are made with a classic community study, 'Coal is our life'.

These studies are said to have revived awareness of the concept of community

A third area of development was the shift away from the community per se towards the idea of *locality*. This has taken two forms. One is in the field of social geography, where there has been less antagonism towards space as a variable in social action. Although there have been debates about the status of space as a causal explanation of social relations, interest in where things happen has not weakened. Space and locality are seen as elements within broader and more general social theory, which call attention to the kinds of sub-cultural variation that Newby sought (above). The work of the Changing Urban and Regional Systems initiative (e.g. Cooke, 1989 and others like Soja, 1989), kept locality on the research agenda in social geography.

We are taken further into the notion of locality with a sub-division.

Other concepts are introduced such as 'space'. But emphasis is given to broader social theory that is used to explain geographical variation.

The second source of interest in locality within sociology was the study of the restructuring of industry and employment. This included work that connected directly with the social geographers (e.g. Gregory and Urry, 1985), as well as the explorations of economic life funded by the ESRC. For example, the study of economic change and labour market suggested how through the notion of 'occupational communities' (e.g. Salaman, 1974):

Variation in social relations between different localities is linked to economic change; which is one of the factors underpinning studies of mining areas.

Change in industrial structure affects the nature of community. Historically and in certain locations, such as mining and textile townships, the job recruitment process creates a strong link between work and residence and between work relationships and community relationships. An aim of research is thus to explore the nature of the link between work and community under contemporary conditions (Roberts et al., 1985: 7).

The idea of communities linked to occupation is followed.

The Social Change and Economic Life Initiative (SCELI) was also concerned with changes in production, work patterns, and household formation and strategies because SCELI concentrated on studies *in* localities, rather than *of* localities (Aberdeen, Kirkcaldy, Rochdale, Coventry, Swindon and Northampton), but these included 'Household and Community' surveys and some locally specific studies. It would be wrong to call these community studies: rather we see that in these and similar studies, the physical location of social relations is not irrelevant to those social relations, nor to the development of our ideas about the interconnection of work, the informal economy, households and networks (e.g. Bell and McKee, 1985; Beynon, 1992; Morris, 1988; Pahl, 1984; Stanley, 1992, etc.). Their emphasis however is on the interconnections with wider social forces, and to a large extent these researchers based in a locality represent the alternative and evolved perspective that has replaced the more traditional community study as a sociological fashion.

A distinction is made between studies in and studies of localities. The question is why is this distinction made?

The answer provided is that recent studies are in localities and form an alternative to and not a replacement for traditional C.S.

Relocating the Community Study

'Community' is more than just the inclusion of space in the analysis of social relations. One can think of the studies discussed above as ranged on a continuum from the single researcher doing an ethnography of an isolated (rural) settlement – such as the contributors to Cohen, 1982; Brody, 1974; Macleod, 1992 or Giarchi, 1984 – to the team using social surveys to explore the manifestation of economic restructuring in a given location or region (e.g. Gallie, 1988b or Roberts, 1985). In between are a variety of studies that to a greater or lesser extent are issue-based (e.g. Moore, 1984), localised (Stacey et al., 1975), ethnographic (Gibbon and Steyne, 1986), done by individuals or teams (Warwick and Littlejohn, 1992), and explicitly related to the origins of the idea of community (Strathern, 1981).

The map given of the terrain now allows for the major statement: the author wants to focus on what he has classified as 'pure' C.S.

At the same time he wants alternative studies to be recognised as important but different from his interests.

This sketch map suggests four characteristics, with which to locate studies about communities.

(a) Is the research carried out by a large team or one or two researchers?
(b) Is it predominantly qualitative or quantitative in style?
(c) Is the 'community' an identifiable settlement or simply an administrative creation?
(d) Is it concerned primarily with aspects of community per se, as against wider social processes, which just happen to be manifested locally?

A summative formulation is provided as a means for the reader to characterise the different types of research identified as C.S.

This acts to reinforce the author's classification and differentiation of what he has categorised as 'pure' C.S.

There is nothing absolute about these four questions. Their function is to provide a framework for thinking about a large number of differing studies. In the case of this paper, for instance, we wish to concentrate more on a 'purer' type of community study. In connecting Dennis et al. or Frankenberg to Cohen, one does not wish to exclude other studies but rather explain why one subset can, for particular purposes, be more relevant than another.

With the case made charity for the treatment of other studies is emphasised.

(Continued)

The inclusion of methodological style illustrates the flexibility of the framework. Key studies like Willmott and Young used a range of methods: indeed the first edition made great play of the latest technology of the IBM card counter/sorter (Platt, 1971; Payne et al., 1981). Brody's sensitive account of Inishkillane (*q.v.*) starts with a review based on historical and literary documents. Warwick and Littlejohn draw both on surveys and historical statistics, and pull together medical researchers, archivists, adult education classes and SCELI support (1992: xiv–xv). There is no reason to ignore their valuable contribution just for that, even if the main concern here lies in the research carried out by individuals using qualitative methods.

A short adjoiner: to emphasise the flexibility of the approaches to C.S. reinforces the author's argument about the value of C.S. research.

One purpose of this orienting framework is to explain how this paper concentrates on the more 'typical' community study, making links between some of the classics and some of the more recent studies. The observations that follow arise directly from doing that kind of single-handed ethnography, but to some extent they can be generalised to the other kinds of study. Two examples of such generalisation are the interconnected ideas of visual appearance, and the way the immediacy of 'issues' changes over time.

Conclusion of what the review has attempted to achieve.

Although the single researcher is mentioned the link is again made to the generalisability of single researcher work.

Source: Payne, 1993

The structure of this review displays an argumentative purpose. The author has the intent of persuading his reader that community studies are an important and productive avenue of research. This he does through a technique that we may call the *implied reader*. By this we mean that Payne seems to imply that some people have assumed that community studies are a thing of the past; and that they have no relevance for research today. Hence, he sets up an argument to correct this implied assumption by an implied reader. The review, therefore, uses the stance of 'contrary to popular belief'. The reader is taken through a range of material that cites many works. These works are classified to show continuity in the study of the community. The use of definition is a major resource in achieving the sense of continuity. The term 'locality' is used to argue that studies of locality are studies of communities.

Assessment criteria for the literature review

The outcome of all the work you do to produce your literature review will be subject to a formal assessment and peer evaluation. The formal assessment is what most students are concerned about. They want to know if their work measures up to the standards for their degree. Boote and Beile (2005) took the criteria from the first edition of this book (Hart, 1998), and with a review of the literature on dissertations and literature reviewing subjected the criteria to empirical testing.

Criteria and checklists

Criteria and checklists give us the basis for understanding what doctoral students need to become competent scholars. This topic will be explored further in Chapter 3.

The main assumption on which these original criteria were based (and are still based), as Boote and Beile (2005: 7) note, is that doctoral students need to become competent scholars before they are capable of being generative research-ers. The criteria were aimed at thinking about what it means to be a scholar. Table 2.4 shows the way, in which Boote and Beile (2005) devised a scoring rubric to rate literature reviews.

TABLE 2.4 Assessing the literature review in a thesis

Category	Criterion	1	2	3
1. Coverage	A. Justified criteria for inclusion and exclusion from review	Did not discuss the criteria for inclusion or exclusion	Discussed the literature included and excluded	Justified inclusion and exclusion of literature
2. Synthesis	B. Distinguished between what has been done in the field and what needs to be done	Did not distinguish between what has and has not been done before	Discussed what has and has not been done	Critically examined the state of the field
	C. Placed the topic or problem in the broader scholarly literature	Topic not placed in the broader scholarly literature	Some discussion of the broader scholarly literature	Topic clearly situated in the broader scholarly literature
	D. Placed the research in the historical context of the field	History of topic not discussed	Some mention of history of topic	Critically examined history of topic
	E. Acquired and enhanced the subject vocabulary	Key vocabulary not discussed	Key vocabulary defined	Discussed and resolved ambiguities in definitions

(Continued)

Category	Criterion	1	2	3
	F. Articulated important variables and phenomena relevant to the topic	Key variables and phenomena not discussed	Reviewed relationships among key variables and phenomena	Noted ambiguities in literature and proposed new relationships
	G. Synthesised and gained a new perspective on the literature	Accepted the literature at face value	Some critique of the literature	Offered new perspective
3. Methodology	H. Identified the main methodologies and research techniques that have been used in the field, and their advantages and disadvantages	Research methods not discussed	Some discussion of research methods used to produce claims	Critiqued research methods
	I. Related ideas and theories in the field to research methodologies	Research methods not discussed	Some discussion of appropriateness of research methods to warrant claims	Critiqued appropriateness of research methods to warrant claims
4. Significance	J. Rationalised the practical significance of the research problem	Practical significance of research not discussed	Practical significance discussed	Critiqued appropriateness of research methods to warrant claims
	K. Rationalised scholarly significance of the problem	Scholarly significance of research not discussed	Scholarly significance discussed	Critiqued scholarly significance of research
5. Rhetoric	L. Was written with a coherent, clear structure that supported the review	Poorly conceptualised, haphazard	Some coherent structure	Well developed, coherent

Source: Boote and Beile (2005); based on Hart (1998)

While Boote and Beile (2005: 9) only had a relatively small sample of dissertations to assess, they nevertheless were 'happy to report that the best literature reviews were thorough, critical examinations of the state of the field that set the stage for the authors' substantive research projects'. However, they did not have many of these. They reported:

> Our findings raise interesting questions about Doctoral candidates' ability to write a thorough and sophisticated literature review and what Doctoral dissertation committees will accept as adequate. Although our analysis of scores revealed differences in quality of dissertation literature reviews among the institutions, mean scores across all the institutions were surprisingly low. (2005: 9)

In the United Kingdom the major research councils, library organisations and Vitae have produced the Researcher Development Framework.

What is a Master's?

Many of the points in the discussion preceding this section are relevant to a Master's thesis and therefore need not be repeated. What we will focus on here is the skills element necessary for the Master's this. As the product of your time and research, the Master's theis (which some people call the *dissertation*) is a learning activity. The intent of this activity is that you acquire a range of skills at an appropriate level that are related to doing capable and competent research. The thesis then is the evidence that the research student has acquired the necessary skills and that they can, therefore, be accredited as a competent researcher. The kinds of skills listed here are those associated with research design; data collection; information management; analysis of data; synthesis of data with existing knowledge and evaluation of existing ideas along with a critical evaluation of your own work. Although these criteria are general they are important, and in a moment we will look at them in more detail. However, the thing to remember is that your thesis is the only opportunity you will have to demonstrate that you have the ability to apply these skills to a particular topic. This demonstration is the thesis. As such the thesis, as a product, should be coherent and logical, and not a series of separate and inadequately related elements. There should be clear links between the aims of your research and the literature review, the choice of research design and means used to collect data, your discussion of the issues, and your conclusions or recommendations. As a summary we can say that the research should:

- focus on a specific problem, issue or debate
- relate to that problem, issue or debate in terms that show a balance between the theoretical, methodological and practical aspects of the topic

- include a clearly stated research methodology based on the existing literature
- provide an analytical and critically evaluative stance to the existing literature on the topic.

A Master's thesis is, therefore, a demonstration in research thinking and doing. The thesis is, in the first instance, intended to show that the student has been capable of reasoning over which methodological approach to employ. Secondly, it is a demonstration on how to operationalise key concepts of methodology through the use of a range of data collection techniques. Clearly this is not all that a Master's thesis consists of. If one thinks of the Master's as *an exercise in research* then the whole process often becomes much more manageable both psychologically and in the actual doing of the work that produces the final product.

There is, then, a range of skills and capabilities that go into the Master's thesis. It is these skills and capabilities that often form the basis for the criteria on which a thesis is assessed. Table 2.5 provides an overview of the areas that are normally used as criteria for assessing the Master's worthiness of a dissertation. It also shows what is required of an excellent dissertation as well as what makes for a poor piece of work.

TABLE 2.5 Criteria for assessing a Master's dissertation

	Excellent and distinctive work	Competent work	Significantly deficient work
Aims, objectives and justification	Clear aims able to be operationalised. Explanation of the topic with succinct justification using the literature. Shows full awareness of the need to focus on what can be done.	Clear aims and objectives. Acceptable justification with identification of the topic.	Aims and objectives unclear due to no logical connections between them. Insufficient attempt to justify the topic. Actual topic not clear due to lack of focus.
Methodology and data collection	Choice of methodology explained in comparative terms showing considerable evidence of reading and understanding. Overall research design abundantly clear and logical for the student to apply. Strengths and weaknesses in previously used methodologies/data-collection techniques are recognised and dealt with.	Methodology described but not in comparative terms, so no explanation given for choices; nevertheless, an appropriate methodology employed. Research techniques clear and suitable for the topic. May have replicated weaknesses or bias inherent in previous work on the topic.	No explanation of the methodology, its choice or appropriateness for the research. No indication of reading on methodology or data-collection techniques, so no demonstration of ability to collect data in a systematic way. No overall research design.

	Excellent and distinctive work	**Competent work**	**Significantly deficient work**
Literature review and evaluation	Thorough review of the relevant literature; systematically analysed and all main variables and arguments identified. Critical evaluation firmly linked to justification and methodology.	Review of the main literature with main variables and arguments identified. Some links made to methodology and justification.	No review of the literature; annotations of some items but no attempt at a critical evaluation. Therefore no arguments or key variables identified relevant to the topic. No bibliography or too large a bibliography to have been used.
Style and presentation, including the use of graphic materials	Clear and cohesive structure. Very well presented, with accurate citations and bibliography. Impressive use of visual and graphic devices, and effective arrangement of materials. Accurate and proper use of the English Language, employing scholarly conventions.	Clear structure and arrangement of materials with accurate citations, appropriate use of visual and graphic devices.	Structured presentation but very thin on substantive content. Citations mostly correct but not consistent. Little evidence of thought about the use of visual or graphic devices. Sloppy use of language.
Overall coherence and academic rigour	Systematic and considered approach; critically reflexive; clarity and logic in the structuring of argument; proper use of language; assumptions stated; clarity of interpretation; identification of gaps and possibility for further research. Of a publishable standard.	Considered approach; clarity in the structure of presentation; satisfactory use of language; assumptions mostly stated though some implicit; conclusions and ideas for further research identified.	Not a considered approach, therefore, no planning evident. Poor use of technical terms and overuse of cliché. No argumentative structure evident. Some attempt at interpretation but not based on the data.

A Master's is, therefore, a limited piece of research. Taking approximately 10,000–15,000 words the dissertation is a relatively modest piece of writing; possibly equivalent to three or four decent-length essays. The key elements of the dissertation are the research; the design of the research; application of data collection techniques; management of the project and data; and the interpretation of the findings in the context of previous work. To do these things in a way that is scholarly demands management of the research.

Conclusions: Some common do's and don'ts in reviews

There is no such thing as the perfect review. All reviews, irrespective of the research question and audience, are written from a particular perspective or standpoint that belongs to the reviewer. This perspective often originates from the school of thought, vocation or ideological standpoint the reviewer has chosen. As a consequence, the particularity of the reviewer implies a particular reader. Reviewers usually write with a particular kind of reader in mind: a reader that they may want to influence. It is factors such as these that make all reviews partial in some way or other. This is not a reason or excuse for a poor review. At the same time, it can make a review interesting, challenging or provocative. Partiality in terms of value judgements, opinions, moralising and ideologues can often be found to have invaded or formed the starting point of a review. When reading a review written by someone else or undertaking a review you should be aware of your own value judgements in order that an attempt can be made to avoid a lack of scholarly respect for the ideas of others. Afolabi (1992) and Gall et al. (1996), offer some good advice about reviewing. Their observations and our own experience and research suggest that the following are some of the major rules for good literature reviewers.

Do ...	Don't ...
• identify and discuss the relevant key landmark studies on the topic	• omit classic works and landmarks or discuss core ideas with proper reference
• include as much up-to-date material as possible	• discuss out-dated or only old materials
• check the details such as how names are spelt	• misspell names or get the date of a publication wrong
• check spelling so as not to make silly mistakes, for example, orgasm in place of organic	• use concepts and jargon to impress or without definition
• try to be reflexive; examine your own bias and make this clear	• use jargon and discriminatory language to justify a parochial standpoint
• critically evaluate the material and look to show your analyses	• produce a list of items, even if annotated; a list is a bibliography not a review
• use extracts, illustrations and examples to justify your analyses and argument	• accept any position at face value or believe everything that is written
• be analytical, evaluative and critical and show this in your review	• only produce a description of the content of what you have read

• manage the information that your review produces: have a system for records management	• drown in information by not keeping control and an accurate record of materials
• make your review worth reading by making yourself clear, systematic and coherent, to explain why the topic is interesting	• be boring by using hackneyed jargon, pretentious language and only description
• specify your strategy for the review including inclusion and exclusion criteria	• omit the search vocabulary and parameters (criteria) for the search for relevant literature
• make clear the research question that the review is aiming to contribute to	• produce the review in isolation from the research question, broader aims and design

Source: Adapted from Afolabi, 1992 and Gall et al., 1996

These are most of the common do's and don'ts for literature reviews. Producing a good review, however, need not be too difficult. It can be far more rewarding than 'knocking something off' quickly and without too much intellectual effort. A large degree of satisfaction can be had from working at the review over a period of time. For a Master's or doctoral candidate this may be up to a year or more. A measure of that satisfaction comes from the awareness that you have developed skills and acquired intellectual abilities you did not have before you began your research.

In summary

- The literature review process is a research methodology in its own right. It should commence with a research question, followed by a research design, the presentation of results, and finally, a discussion of those results.
- The review can take a range of formats, but must include the core literature.
- The review has different uses in different parts of the research. There is the indicative review for the research proposal, the literature used in support of the rationale for the research question, the review itself, the review of methodology and data collection techniques and reference to the review, in the discussion of your own findings.
- A lot of information will be generated by the literature review so it is important to have a system of project and information management in place before you begin.

3

Classifying and Reading Research to Review

Key questions

- What types of research are there? How important are methodological traditions?
- How does one read analytically? What are the elements in research?
- What is the role of methodological assumptions in research?
- What kinds of criteria can be used to evaluate research? How can bad research be distinguished from good research?

Core skills

- Acquire knowledge and understanding of different research traditions and methods
- Critically analyse, synthesise, validate and evaluate new and complex information, data and arguments from a range of different sources
- Assess the credibility, quality, integrity and authenticity of primary and secondary information and data
- Incorporate new and older research into your own research and relevant literature
- Practise professional integrity and honesty with regard to information handling and apply appropriate standards when analysing the work of others.

Introduction

To be able to review research requires the prerequisite of understanding what research is about. In this chapter, we will give an overview of the different types of research. The aim is to show that different types of research are usually different because they have different research questions, are dealing with different kinds of phenomenon and are being undertaken within and from different research traditions (or paradigms). There are numerous textbooks on research and research design, so there is no intent to repeat what these have to say. We will, however, look at research from the standpoint of reading research for the purposes of producing a review.

The assessment of your review will be partially dependent on your demonstration of understanding different types of research. You need to show that you can go beyond mere description of methods, to show you understand how to analyse individual pieces of research, make informed, justifiable appraisals, critiques and offer new perspectives. Reviewing is not about expressing opinions. It is about evaluating the logical coherence of theories, methodologies and findings in a context of informed scholarship. A researcher must demonstrate understanding of the nature of research; of the ways in which it is presented and what it means to be scholarly. We begin this chapter, therefore, with an overview of research design before looking at the process of reading.

Typifying research

Research can generally be classified according to its design features and its intended outcomes. Reading a piece of research, therefore, involves making an effort to understand the reasons why the research was done, the way it was done, based on the research question and what was intended to be its outcome, i.e. intervention or knowledge.

Types of research

The bulk of research is aimed at explaining, exploring, describing or critiquing the occurrence (or non-occurrence) of some phenomenon. Although some studies combine, to varying degrees, there are distinctions between them. This is because the different purposes have different implications on the design of research, the ways in which it is presented (i.e. style), and the way it is intended to be understood and used. Only by understanding the reason for different styles will you be able to evaluate them on their own merits and in terms of what the researcher intended to produce. Table 3.1 shows some of the characteristics of different types of research.

TABLE 3.1 Types of research

Type of research	Purpose and features
Basic research	To contribute to theory or knowledge by formulating and testing hypothesis, applying a theory or method to a new area, and evaluating the generalisability of propositions across time and space. Research questions are often of a 'what' and 'why' form. In sociology, for example, the question may be, 'What is society?' and in management, 'What is quality?'
Applied research	To produce recommendations or solutions to some problem faced by a specific group of people in a situation. The aim is to take theoretical insights or work and apply these in real-world situations. Both qualitative and quantitative data are used. Questions tend to be of the form 'how' and 'when'. In anthropology, for example, the question may be, 'How can the structural functional approach explain witchcraft beliefs?' and in organisational studies, 'How can the low motivation of workers be increased through a specific organisational structure?'
Summative evaluation	To summarise and assess the main benefits of a policy, program or product, in order to judge its effectiveness or applicability to a specific situation or in a range of contexts. The aim is to assess the degrees of generalisability, therefore, abstraction and quantitative data are usually evident. Questions often follow on some initiative. In management the questions may be, 'How did changes to organisational structure change motivation levels?' and in social administration, 'What effect has community care had on voluntary agencies?'
Formative evaluation	To make improvements to a specific program, policy or set of activities at a specific time, place and with a specific group. The aim is to focus the research and often uses case study method and qualitative evidence. Questions are often focused and specific. In social policy the question may be, 'How can this agency be more effective in meeting the needs of its clients?' and in management, 'How can we maximise the benefits of this computer system for our research team?'
Action research	To help a group to help themselves through the research. The aim is to empower the respondents to 'research themselves and their situation' and on this basis, take responsibility for their own situation, make recommendations, possibly implement those recommendations and even evaluate the implementation. The focus is mainly on specific problems or issues and involves qualitative evidence. Questions are not usually set by the researcher but are issues subjects feel strongly about.
Illuminative evaluation	To make visible for contemplation key behaviours or attitudes in a given context. The aim is to enlighten policy makers or practitioners to the dynamics of behaviours in comparable situations, in order that those behaviours can be understood and attended to in a more appropriate way. A range of evidence, often qualitative, is employed.
Ethnomethodology	To describe the ways in which people make the sense they do, in and through the ways they communicate. The aim is to focus on the detail of the common-sense character of everyday life and the practices (methods) by which we make our actions understandable (sharable) to others. Close scrutiny of how people do what they do provides an explanation of what those people do and why they did it in the way they did.

Within any type of research there can be different types or combinations of the research act. For example, the aim of strategic research (sometimes called pure research) is to provide understanding. The emphasis is not necessarily on producing something pragmatic or even useful. A great deal of historically important research was research done *for its own sake*. Einstein's now famous views on time and space fall into this category. Einstein did not set out to 'invent' relativity or to make possible the building of atomic weapons; he used his imagination to reflect on what it would be like if he could travel at incredible speed. He undertook reflective research. This type of research act aims to examine or explore existing theories, practices or ideas and it does so in the spirit of creativity and imagination. There are therefore many aspects and dimensions to research. Within basic research for example, the research design may be shaped by the goal, which could be exploratory, descriptive or explanatory (see Table 3.2).

TABLE 3.2   The goals of different types of research

Type	Goal
Exploratory	(1) to satisfy curiosity, provide a better understanding or for general interest; (2) to examine the feasibility of further study by indicating what may be relevant to study in more depth and, (3) to provide 'illumination' on a process or problem. Questions focus on the 'how, what, when and where'. Studies tend to be small scale and often informal in structure, e.g. 'illuminative evaluation'.
Descriptive	(1) to understand common and uncommon social phenomena; (2) to observe the detail of the elements that make it the phenomenon; (3) to provide an empirical basis for valid argument. Questions focus on the 'how and what' – how may and how often does x occur or what do x's do, believe and understand? Studies tend to be small scale and qualitative.
Explanatory	(1) to explain the cause or non-occurrence of a phenomenon; (2) to show causal connections and relationships between variables of the types 'if A then B'; (3) to suggest reasons for events and make recommendations for change. Questions focus on the 'why and what' – what is the relationship between x and y and why does y happen? The aim is to uncover 'laws and regularities' of a universal nature. Studies are large and small scale and are often based on hypothetico-deductivism and associated quantitative data. Studies can be correlational and look for relationships between variables or causal and look to suggest cause and affect relationships. Both are associated with experimental research designs.
Critical	(1) to question and develop a sound critique of an argument, assumption or practice; (2) to identify the problems with and/or connections to the broader social/cultural factors and perceived social problems; (3) to suggest ways in which 'people' can be emancipated from the influences or a practice or assumption. Questions focus on the 'what' – what role does x have in the creation or maintenance of y? The aim is to uncover or make visible for analysis

(Continued)

Type	Goal
	influences from one practice or assumption to another phenomenon. Studies are often based on a realist position and are associated with qualitative data and/or rhetorical argument.
Historical	(1) to identify the conditions and events that may have led to a situation or discovery; (2) to attempt an explanation based on the broader social, economic, technological, religious or political conditions; (3) to place a situation or event into a timeline. Questions focus on the what – what preconditions were necessary for the occurrence of x? And how did the necessary conditions amalgamate to result in occurrence x? The aim is to make visible the diverse influences and variables that can explain the origins of a policy, practice, belief, event or discovery.

There are various ways in which these basic categories of research can be combined including, 'explanatory + descriptive', 'descriptive + explanatory + historical', 'explanatory + descriptive', 'exploratory + descriptive', 'explanatory + critical + emancipatory' and so on. In addition, there are also comparative (is y better than z?), prescriptive (y should be done), definitional (what is y?) and existential (does x exist?) aspects to some research.

Reading advice: Research designs

Research designs are varied and nuanced, depending on the goals of a particular piece of research. If you want to see a full discussion of the different types and designs of research, see Chapter 10 of my guide to postgraduate dissertations: Hart (2005) *Doing Your Masters Dissertation*.

The distinctions between the different types of research are not always clear or distinct. You will often find informal attitudes to research that grade it according to type. A common example is that of strategic research, which is often seen as superior to applied and other types of research. You need to avoid the fallacy of judging implicitly one type of research as better than another.

In terms of discovery very little research actually discovers anything new. Chance and the ability to make connections between seemingly unrelated factors are what often result in what we call discovery. The Hawthorne Effect (Mayo, 1933) is a common example of chance and observation of related factors. When studying working conditions in a factory it was noted that the act of carrying out the research influenced the behaviour of the workers. Physical conditions, it was observed, were not the only variable in productivity. The worker's perceptions of what they thought was happening (even when nothing was happening) were found to be a major influence on their attitude to work.

Relative standards and judgements

Nearly all subject areas have their own distinctive intellectual traditions, key authors, works and styles. In sociology, for example, Marx, Durkheim and Weber are some of the key theorists and some of their works are seen as classics of the discipline; psychology has Freud, Lacan and Pavlov. In part, it is the approach which the founders of a discipline took that gives the shape to the subject knowledge and practices of that discipline; it is the work and ideas of founding theorists that make different disciplines distinct from one another.

As a consequence, each subject area exhibits norms and conventions in research and writing that are particular to it. Different subject areas also have particular views on what is valid research and what the subject is about. This is not to say that all practitioners within a discipline agree about the nature of their subject or about any particular problem that concerns them. Differences exist within disciplines and between subject disciplines. Attitudes to subject areas with which you are familiar need to be put to one side when evaluating research from a discipline with which you are unfamiliar. It is the responsibility of the reviewer to recognise and acknowledge the nature of the discipline from which the work originates. For instance, sociology is essentially an argumentational rather than a knowledge discipline.

A considerable amount of empirical work is undertaken by sociologists although the main debates within sociology are about the subject itself. The argumentational nature of sociology manifests itself in its diversity of positions and approaches, for example, Marxism, functionalism, interactionism and ethnomethodology. An example of a knowledge subject may be physics, in which theories about matter progress as more hypotheses are tested and verified. This difference does not mean that physics is superior to a subject like sociology. Rather, the subjects are different and contribute in different ways to our understanding of the world. This pluralism found in and between the natures of different disciplines must be respected.

Implicit in choices about the kinds of issues we have just outlined is the question of comparative judgement. It is tempting for any reviewer to find advantages in one theory or type of research on the basis of their prior assumptions about what should constitute research. As a consequence, research that seems to confirm the reviewer's view of research may attract a favourable assessment. The problem with this is the generalising tendency (inherent in looking for research) that confirms prior assumptions; both morally and in terms of competent reviewing, the reviewer's credibility can be seriously compromised.

However, this tendency has another implication. In advocating the advantages of one theory or type of research over another, we implicitly make contrasts which can be misleading and which result in a gross oversimplification and severely restrain the innovative pluralism of literature reviewing. Take, for example, the differences between positivism and phenomenology. Where positivism is regarded as objective, phenomenology is, as a consequence, regarded as subjective. Similarly, Marxism is seen as theoretical in contrast to the empiricism of symbolic interactionism.

It is only through reading a piece of research that the developmental character of purpose and type can be teased out of the text. This act of reading is about understanding the researcher's project. We saw in Table 3.1 some of the major goals of research. In many cases it is a matter of 'horses for courses', but any project can – and many do – involve different kinds of study within the project. It is not uncommon for a study to report, for instance, on both applied and formative aspects of the project. Therefore, it is as important for the reader as for the writer of a piece of research to explicate the rationale of the research purpose and show understanding of the implications of choices made in its design. In the writing of a thesis it is usually the structure that allows the reader to follow the argument, but this is not simply a matter of structure and format. The writer must ensure that the substantive content of the report explicates the logic of the research – and not leave it to the imagination of the reader.

Design features

Very few accounts of a piece of research include the original design plan or proposal. Even master of philosophy (MPhil) and doctoral (PhD) theses omit the original proposal by which the research was designed. It is possible however to re-cover the design features and methodological choices made by a researcher. Pattern (1990) provides the following (shown in Table 3.3) summary of some of the main features of research design that the reviewer can look for and evaluate.

TABLE 3.3   Design issues and options in research

Issues	Options
What is the purpose of the study?	Basic research, applied research, summative evaluation, formative evaluation, action research.
What was the scope of the study?	What was included, excluded, why and to what effect?
What is the focus for the study?	People, policy, programmes. Breadth versus depth, case study, survey, chronological, comparative and so on.
What are the units of analysis?	Individuals, groups, programme components, whole programmes, organisations, critical incidents, time periods and so on.

Issues	Options
What is the sampling strategy?	Purposeful, probability, quota, random, size, representation, significance and level of generalisability.
What types of data were collected?	Qualitative, quantitative.
How were the data managed?	Organisation, classification, presentation, referenced and indexed and so on.
What analytical approaches were used?	Deductive, inductive.
How was validity addressed in the study?	Triangulation, multiple data sources, multiple studies
When did the study occur?	Currency of findings, long-term investigation, quick and cheerful, phased and piloted.
How was the study justified?	Literature review and analysis, problem definition, practical outcomes, intellectual endeavour and so on.
How were ethical issues handled?	Informed consent, confidentiality of information, reactivity, data protection and so on.
How were logistics handled?	Access to data and respondents, fieldwork, record keeping, data management and so on.

Source: Adapted from Pattern, 1990

The features outlined in Table 3.3 are not prescriptive for all research. They are indicative of the design features from which any piece of research can be constructed, and as such, some of them can be found in all written accounts of a piece of research. It takes a little practice in reading to identify the design features of someone else's research; effort is required to read research systematically and without prejudice. As some of these features have already been described, the remainder of this section will look at what is meant by focus and units of analysis.

By focus, we are referring to the specific dimensions and aspects of the topic that were studied. There are, in the main, three areas that a study can focus on: characteristics, orientations and actions. Characteristics are usually taken to be measurable or recordable attributes, such as age, sex, location and the like. In terms of social interactions these would be the where, how, when, between whom and in what context. Orientations refer to the characteristics of the people, group or organisation under study. The orientations of individuals may be their beliefs, attitudes, personality traits and so on. Actions are taken to be what people do. For example, a study that looks at consumer behaviour will be action-focused, while a study into new religious movements may look at either the demographic profile of members (and will therefore focus on characteristics) or the specific beliefs of the movement (in which case it will be looking at orientations). For the purpose of research design and the analysis of research reports, distinctions can be made between differences in focus. But be prepared for studies that mix and match in terms of what they have focused on at different times in the research.

By units of analysis, we mean the specific parameters of what was the subject for study. For example, if the topic is the UK Census, then the units of analysis are statistics based on responses by individuals; it is from decennial questionnaires filled in by the individual that demographic patterns can be measured. Units of analysis are therefore the units of observation: things we examine in order to study our chosen topic. In broad terms, there are four types of units: individuals, groups, organisations and social artifacts. As the unit of observation, individuals may be characterised by their membership of some group or organisation. However, if we were interested in the dynamics of the group as a whole, then the group is the unit of observation. This is because we may be aiming to generalise about the typical dynamics of group behaviour. Often in management research it is the organisation that is the unit of analysis. Comparisons made between different types of organisation in terms of structure, culture, size and the like are the characteristics observed in order to study the larger unit of analysis. Finally, social artefacts such as books, sculpture, pictures and buildings can be the unit of analysis. Also included in this category are other social artefacts such as jokes, songs, scientific experiments and rituals.

Methodological traditions

In many undergraduate courses and in textbooks on research, methods (techniques for collecting data) are regarded as separate from theory. This division may be practical, but it is artificial. In practice, it is your stance on key methodological questions that shapes the character of your research study. For example, if you believe that hard data, such as statistics, are to be preferred to soft data, such as ethnographic data, then a positivistic approach is being taken. If you prefer the rich detail of ethnographic data then you are taking an interpretivistic approach. The distinctions between these two are not always as clear-cut as this, so it is crucial that the origins and implications of both approaches are understood by the reviewer. Methodological issues are not something to be marginalised or ignored, because any serious attempt to understand an aspect of the world is almost inevitably based on some dimension of the intellectual tradition of Western knowledge. These traditions shape the different ways in which different subject disciplines frame their views of the world and how they go about investigating the world. Issues arising from differences between disciplines and methods can best be approached by understanding the connections between philosophical traditions and strategies for investigation. This is because if we aim to acquire knowledge of the world around us we need to appreciate the implications of what we take as the world, and acknowledge that our approach is not universally shared and that there are alternatives from which we can choose.

We may begin by noting that all research originates from some view of reality, which means that there are different ways of gaining an understanding of some aspect of the world and different ways of confirming our understanding (i.e. knowledge). If the two approaches, positivistic and interpretivistic, were applied to, say, atomic particles, then both may be seen to have a coherent logic. Empirically, we can't see atomic particles. We see such things through the intermediate use of instruments that measure them. Both accounts are consequently valid even though they are very different. In practice, we may be able to compare them, but we cannot judge them. This is because if we were to judge, we would be making a commitment to one or other methodological position, that is, an ontological and epistemological view of reality. In judging, we would make a value commitment to a position, which may compromise our attitude of open-mindedness.

In very general terms, we can say that it is important to grasp the philosophical meaning of ontology, epistemology and the methodological meanings of validity, reliability and data. This is because alternative views of reality lead to: different propositions about *what reality is* (ontology); different ways of establishing *what can be accepted as real* (epistemology); different strategies for *validating our claims* about reality; and different techniques for *collecting data* (questionnaires, observation, etc.). These dimensions for approaching the object of our research are present in all forms of knowledge whether that knowledge is scientific or common sense. While the kinds of issues and methodological implications of taking one position on the ontological status of reality and epistemological status of knowledge are outlined in the next section, you are advised to read further on this topic.

Reading advice: Methodological assumptions

Views of reality inform our methodological assumptions, which in turn shape the choices we make in our research design. For a more extended discussion of the consequences of methodological assumptions, see Chapters 7 and 8 in Hart (2005).

You need to be aware that there are no clear-cut prescriptions about how to translate theoretical ideas into research designs. Similarly, there are no rulebooks on how to do research. There are types of protocol that guide the researcher, and which assist those who would want to validate another's research. As a consequence, the reviewer is faced with the problem of acquiring sufficient understanding of the implications of methodology before beginning to review. Regrettably, there is no simple exposition of the implications of methodological doctrines on research. Added to this is the fact that the philosophical foundations of research are full of complexities and misunderstandings. We come back, therefore, to one of the main points: to assess the competency (rather than relevance) of a piece (or body) of research the reviewer needs to know what competent research looks like in the first place. The competent researcher needs to be able to demonstrate experience with research. Knowledge of research is therefore an essential prerequisite and is not something easily or quickly acquired.

In the research itself, the researcher may not show full awareness of the traditions from which their style or approach originates. It then falls to the reviewer to identify the methodological foundations of a study, particularly if the way in which a topic has been studied is to be mapped out. By mapping out the ways a topic has been investigated, the reviewer can see more clearly the general approaches, usual methods and what kinds of assumptions have tended to be made by an approach. Thus, the reviewer may be better able to identify opportunities for further research, using a methodological approach not yet tried with a particular topic. It is the very fact that the methodological or theoretical traditions underpinning all research can be teased out of an article or book that enables them to be challenged.

Researchers working within a Marxist framework, for example, can be expected to share, to a lesser or greater degree, a set of methodological assumptions. According to Cuff and Payne (1984: 78–9), Marx developed the following methodological assumptions.

- The social world like the natural world is always in a process of change.
- Like the natural world the social world is not chaotic, but ordered by patterns of relationships that can be observed.
- The structure of any society and forces on it for change can be found in economic relationships between social groups (e.g. classes).
- The structure of any society is made up of parts that are interrelated, e.g. family, education, religion, media and so on, all of which are shaped by the distribution of economic resources between social classes.
- Human beings are essentially rational and would use their social nature to live in co-operation; but human nature is subverted by the economic structure of society. The economic organisation of capitalism makes people selfish, greedy and individualistic, leading them to believe that such characteristics are natural.

Marx also believed that not all people are wholly caught up by the system, and that some, like himself, could transcend the system. Such individuals could rise above the deceptions of capitalism and study the workings of society and explain those workings to others.

Marx employed these methodological assumptions to explain rather than describe the mechanisms of change, social structures and social relationships. These assumptions were neither passive nor randomly chosen by Marx; he developed them through deliberate and systematic thought. His goal was not only to explain the hidden structures of capitalism but also to develop a set of ideas that would change society. Marx's assumptions were, therefore, motivated by a moral concern to bring about a different type of social order, which he thought would restore the nature of humankind.

Reading to review

Reading with the purpose of reviewing a piece of writing is very different from reading, say, for pleasure and leisure. Reading to review has the goal of producing a product: an *analytical evaluation* of the research on your topic. This means that you are expected to unravel the *reasoning* that informs the research and arguments that you find in the literature. Therefore, our first concern must be with the question of what it means to read analytically? Initially the process is one that progresses from the general to the particular.

Two types of review

Reading analytically can be accomplished with different approaches. In the next chapter we look at the two main types of review, the *traditional* and the *systematic* review, and how they are related to differing types of research.

Reading analytically is not something that can be done in one reading or in a short time period. It is often the case that three, six of even twelve months may be required for reading and reviewing a literature. It all depends on the level of your postgraduate work and how much time you have to do the work. In this time it is common for the reviewer to pass through several stages in their development as a research scholar. The initial difficulties of understanding or of attempting to do too much in too short a time are normally overcome through the experience of reviewing.

The processes of reading

Most people read a piece of writing in the same way. They tend to read from the general to the particular – from getting a gist of what the writing is about before looking for the details. Whatever it is that we normally read, we tend to first of all scan, then to pick out some details before reading more closely the other contents. When reading an article or monograph the scanning procedure is often the most effective.

Hierarchy of questions

Remember that in Chapter 1 we looked at the hierarchy of questions to be considered when reading to review. Different reading objectives can benefit from different procedures, but all generally follow the hierarchy from general to specific.

In your initial survey *scan* the title and the blurb on the cover before glancing at the structure of contents and the preface. A common mistake at this initial stage is to get stuck in and start reading every sentence. Remember that the detail can be looked at later, once one has become familiar with the general layout of the book. Look at the general structure of the text under consideration; making some tentative classifications as to what kind of research and theory the author may be using. Remember that this first classification is open to change once more detailed reading begins. Table 3.4 provides a snapshot view of the main purposes of reading to review. It lists the *information* components in a literature that you will be expected to be able to extract.

TABLE 3.4   The information components to extract when reading

justification	ways of thinking	perspective	theory
questions	hypothesis	politics	evidence
motives	interpretations	styles	arguments
definitions	problem	techniques	ethics
events	standpoint	concepts	conclusions

It may be useful to leave time between the initial scan and the detailed reading. Give your own intellect some space and time to digest what you have scanned. One often finds that leaving a day or so between the initial scan and the detailed reading enables one to read more effectively; that is, understand the item under consideration with greater ease. This is because you have allowed yourself time to become acquainted with the material in a way that is progressive rather than trying to do everything at once. An effective; basic format to follow then is the general to the particular by moving progressively through the item by re-reading it to extract different levels of detail and information. Here is a suggested scheme for reading monographs and articles.

Level one. Preliminary scan of the work (book, chapter, report or article) noting its structure, topic, style, general reasoning, data and bibliographical references.

Level two. Survey the parts of the book. If a book, this means scanning each chapter to get a general idea of the structure of the contents of the book as a whole and to identify the key chapters.

Level three. Scan and then read the preface and introduction. The purpose is to identify the idea, aims and logic for the work. These may be found in overviews of the book or an emphasis on stating a particular standpoint. The following extracts are from the preface of the book, *The Woman Reader, 1837–1914,* by Kate Flint (1993). She uses the preface to explain, briefly, the origins of her book:

> This book had its origins in a particular act of reading. In 1981, I was invited to write an introduction to Anthony Trollope's *Can You Forgive Her?* (1864–5). I pondered for some time on that title. Can *You* Forgive *Her?* That interrogative form involves the reader, and provokes a response. The pronoun with which the short query ends suggests, even before we open the novel, that we are to engage our moral judgement with the dubious behaviour, the peccadilloes of a specific female individual. Assessment of her conduct is necessarily related to her gender. Moreover, the novel proves to be concerned, throughout, with the specific conditions governing a woman's life in the mid-nineteenth century. Very soon, I came to see gender not just of the title's 'her', but also of the 'you', may matter. To what degree, I asked myself, could one postulate a difference in response between a woman and a man reading this story at the time of its original publication?

The topic for Flint's research, and subsequent book, came from thinking about the title of a book. She goes on to explain how she went about exploring the idea that men and women may have read differently a book such as Trollope's *Can You Forgive Her?* (1864–5):

> The more evidence of debates about reading that I amassed, the more instances that I gathered of individual reading practices, made me reformulate my initial questions. Asking 'how a woman may read' became increasingly problematical, indeed unanswerable, as I came to recognise the great heterogeneity among nineteenth and early twentieth-century women readers. Documentary material tends to suggest that the practice of reading provided a site for discussion, even resistance, rather than giving grounds for assuming conformity. Instead of my initial formulations about the possible relations of women and texts, I came to be fascinated by *why* the polemic should prove so pervasive and long lasting (for its roots lie way before the Victorian period). So rather than write a work of critical interpretation, I chose to examine the topic of the women reader, and its functioning in cultural debate between the accession of Queen Victoria and the First World War. (Flint, 1993: Preface)

These extracts from the Preface provide a quick overview of the *idea* of the book. To follow these up and add more detail one could look in the Introduction. It is here that we can see how the idea of the book is formulated into a set of aims. For example:

> One aim of the present book is to offer suggestions as to why 'the woman reader' was an issue addressed with such frequency throughout the period. (Flint, 1993: 10)

What this involves is then briefly discussed followed by a formulation of what the book can offer its reader. For example:

> This work offers a dual, though continually intersecting focus. Attempts to legislate about reading and its effects can be seen on the one hand as a means of gaining control over subjectivity, and, on the other, as a means of obtaining access to different types of knowledge, and through this, to different social expectations and standards ... It shows how notions about reading fed off attempts to define women's mental capacities and tendencies through their physical attributes, and, in turn, appeared to contribute to the validation of these very definitions. (Flint, 1993: 11)

Even with this amount of information a reader should be able to summarise the topic and aims of Flint's book. Using Table 3.4, we can see that a substantial amount of indicative information has been gathered about Flint's work. We know her research question, the challenge she wants to make to historical definitions, the subjects, the events and timeline and some of the concepts to be used and so on.

> *Level four.* Read the parts of those chapters that you have identified as being important to your needs. It is not necessary to read the whole book. Chapters to look out for are those that provide the rationale for the study; for example, chapters summarising theory and method. It is at this level that one needs to extract the main concepts and look to see how they have been defined and operationalised by the author.

Taking this procedure as our starting point, we can now look more closely at what one looks for when one is reading analytically. Overall, you should be looking to extract from an item or group of items the *project* of the author. What this means is that you will often find that a researcher had a particular *motive* for doing their research; and from this motive they constructed a project. We are using the term project in a very broad way – to include the motive, moral, political and methodological position that a researcher may start from and, therefore, use as the starting point for their research. It is your task to 'unpack' the project in order to identify the logic of what they produced by looking to see if you can identify how they produced their research. Figure 3.1

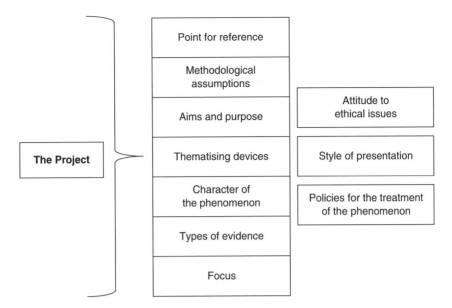

FIGURE 3.1   Elements for analysing the reasoning in research

shows some of the main types of component that make up a research project. You therefore need to put yourself in the role of the researcher and, importantly, stay close to the original materials. Resist attributing motives and methodological assumptions to a work or cohort of authors unless you have clear evidence.

The aim is to draw out of their work what it was they were attempting to achieve through their efforts. This means looking at their work or pieces of work to identify the *style and structure of their reasoning*. If it is a theoretical work this may mean looking for the structure of the argument employed for proposing a particular theory in favour of others. If it is an empirically oriented work it may mean looking at the methodological assumptions and research design that enabled the study to be undertaken. You should, therefore, be looking to see how, and importantly why, an author elected to employ a particular theory or tradition and why certain decisions were made concerning the design of their research. You are aiming to make explicit the nature of the connections between the methodological choices an author has made and the data they have collected through to the interpretations they have made of their data. The reviewer thus has to acquire the ability to assess *structures of reasoning* that different authors use in their work, and which identifiable cohorts of researchers have employed as a common starting point. This ability enables the reviewer to *critically evaluate* and *critically appraise* the degree of scholarship an author has managed to attain in their work.

Paradigms and methodological assumptions

In research there are at least three major paradigms: the interpretive (includes hermeneutics, phenomenology and symbolic interactionism), the empirico-analytical (positivism) and the critical (includes feminist, Marxist and psychoanalytical). Table 3.5 shows how seven basic questions can be used to guide one's reading, helping if needed, to make visible the particular researchers' methodological position.

TABLE 3.5   Comparison of three paradigms that influence research

Guiding questions	Paradigm		
	Empirico-analytical	Interpretive	Critical
What are the philosophical/ theoretical origins?	Positivism, natural sciences	Hermeneutics, phenomenology, symbolic interactionism	Marxist, feminist, psychoanalytics
Why conduct research?	To discover natural laws that enable prediction or control of events	To understand social life and describe how people construct social meaning	To uncover myths/ hidden truths that account for social relations, and empower people to change society radically
What is the nature of social reality?	Social reality contains stable pre-existing patterns or order that can be discovered	Fluid definitions of situations created by people through their social interactions with others	Social reality is multi-layered; events and relations based on hidden underlying social structures/forces that evolve in a historical context
What is the nature of human beings?	Self-interested and rational individuals shaped by external forces	Social beings who create meaning and constantly engage in making sense of their worlds	Creative, adaptive beings with unrealised potential, trapped by social forces that disempower/exploit
What constitutes an explanation/ theory of social reality?	A logical, deductive system of interconnected definitions, axioms and causal laws stated in probabilistic form	A description of how a group's meaning system is generated and sustained; contains detailed contextual information and limited abstraction	A critique that reveals the underlying social structure of conditions and helps people see the way to a better world

Guiding questions	Paradigm		
	Empirico-analytical	Interpretive	Critical
What does good evidence look like?	Based on precise observations that others can repeat	Embedded in the context of fluid social interactions, in which meanings are assigned	Informed by a theory of what the social world is like that unveils myths/hidden truths
Where do social/ political values enter into science?	Science is value-free; values have no place, except when choosing a topic	Values are an integral part of social life; no group's values are presumed superior to others	All science must begin with a value position; some positions are better than others

Source: Adapted from Fossey et al. (2002), Neuman (1994), and Guba and Lincoln (1994)

Although a simplification, the descriptions of the three paradigms in Table 3.5 show the differences between different approaches to research based on methodological assumptions about the nature of reality. All three paradigms are capable of being used to do either scholarly (traditional narrative) or interventionist (systematic) reviews of a literature (see the next chapter for more on these distinctions). It is not the case that an empirico-analytical set of assumptions is necessary for doing an interventionist review. Nor is it the case that elements from all three paradigms cannot be mixed to form a hybrid approach. The key question underpinning the questions in Table 3.5 is, 'what is the role of common sense in research and the evaluation of evidence?' The major problem with common sense is it cannot be taught – or can it?

Evaluating research

Once you have started to read and extract information and data from sources, you need to move on to appraise and evaluate the worth of those sources. This is a combination of reading the individual sources for yourself, looking at and thinking about what others have said about those sources and looking at how sets of sources have been knitted together to produce reviews of a literature for different purposes. Various schemes, composed of criteria, exist to evaluate different kinds of research. In this section, we will look at and discuss the idea of criteria-based evaluation of research but first what is the purpose of research? We need to know this, so we know what kinds of questions to ask.

What is the purpose of research?

The obvious answer is to find things out about things we do not know. In which case, given the number of academic journals, research reports and monographs published each year, we seem to be finding out a lot about a lot of things we knew little about. A more considered response is that much of what goes under the name research is something else. Some of this will be summative reviews of prior research, opinion pieces, discussions and contributions to debates over the meaning of some data or the applicability of a concept or method. Nevertheless, publications that are reports of primary research exist in plentiful numbers. Some are reports on research done by individuals as part of a qualification; others from research teams working on larger, often national and international, projects. Only some of these reports will have any applicability to practical problems. This is not an issue but means we need to understand that there are different types of research, done different ways, for different purposes. If some research we find has not been done the way we would have liked it to be done, it does not mean it is of a lesser quality or lesser relevance to others.

The point here is that there are lots of different kinds of research done for different reasons. If we are looking for research findings that may have a use for decision making, say about an intervention, then we may need to look at how a piece of research was done, to evaluate the *process*, before looking at the *outcomes*, appraising (judging) its relevance to our needs.

Evaluation and appraisal

The objectives of a piece of research will inform how it is organised and how the researcher approaches the literature. In Chapters 7 and 8, we will look more closely at some of the many different methods of organising, analysing and mapping the literature.

Therefore, evaluation may need to precede appraisal. One way of thinking about the differences here is to see evaluation as being about the uses to which the evidence (findings) can be put. Therefore, appraising can be about looking to see if findings from a study confirm or challenge other research. The focus is on the findings (the evidence). This aspect is looked at in the next chapter.

Evaluating different types of research

For the sake of explanation, we can say there are two approaches to research – the quantitative and qualitative. You will be familiar with both of these approaches. Most textbooks will tell you what these approaches are and what methods of data collection are usually involved (see Hart, 2005: 191–234). What follows are some simple but efficient and effective ways of identifying the strengths and weaknesses of both approaches. Each set of criteria assumes you have identified the core literature and are looking to assess the authority of these texts; the degree to which what they are saying and claiming is credible, and therefore, usable in your own research. Bearing in mind that nearly all reports of research undertaken are re-constructions written up for an audience we can, nevertheless, extract information that allows us to make an initial evaluation.

TABLE 3.6   Initial evaluations of qualitative studies

Key questions	Questions to delve deeper
How credible are the accounts? (Credibility)	Are there sufficient informant accounts to assess the interpretation given by the author? How much primary data are included? Is this enough? Is the interpretation plausible? Is it making an a priori argument?
Has the researcher been transparent? (Transparency)	Has the author discussed the methods used? Are the aims of the study stated? Are the methods suited to the aims and population and topic? Have contingencies when doing the research been mentioned?
Are claims substantiated with multiple sources of evidence? (Confirmability)	How many sources of data were used? How reliable is each? What alternative sources of data could the researcher have accessed? Are the data available for external scrutiny?

TABLE 3.7   Initial evaluation of quantitative studies

Key questions	Questions to delve deeper
Are all concepts and variables clearly defined and shown to be measurable? (Construct validity)	Have the dependent and independent variables been clearly isolated and defined? Is the aim to make predications (predictive validity) or confirm or falsify predictive validity (concurrent validity)?
Is the sample representative of the population? (Internal and external validity)	Has probability sampling been used (e.g. systematic random samples)? How has sample selection minimised bias and extraneous variables? What degree of significance does the sample give to the results? Are generalisations firmly based in the data from the samples?
How were threats to the accuracy of sample(s) and measuring instruments addressed? (Reliability)	Is the measuring instrument transparent, focused on the variables and suitable for the sample? How has the reliability of the measuring instrument been confirmed (inter-test, re-test or parallel forms of reliability)?

With these kinds of questions, you need to develop, through your own reading of methods, your own sets of criteria.

Whether qualitative or quantitative, research is done for one of three reasons, *theory* or *practice* or *policy* reasons. The purpose of doing the research will prioritise one of the three and be the emphasis in the research report. Any criteria applied to evaluating a research report will, therefore, need to be sensitive to the reasons for which the research was done. If improving practice is the reason, then criteria that are sensitive to application, best evidence and procedures alongside commensurability between studies may dominate. If theory is the concern then criteria sensitive to understanding, and possibly explaining, may dominate. And if informing policy is the reason for a piece of research then criteria sensitive to economic-political concerns and long-term goals may dominate.

Good and not so good research

Different priorities for a piece of research does not mean there is only good research, far from it. There is plenty of poor and sometimes bad research. Both good and bad have characteristics applicable (observable) in each type of research. Good research tends be reported in ways that encourage the reader to be able to see the context of what was done, why it was done and importantly, allow them to make their own interpretations or conclusions. Good research:

- has a clearly defined research question
- cites the funding source or reasons for doing the research
- provides an adequate description of the context, existing data or hypothesis about a problem
- summarises and discusses relevant standpoints and perspectives about the problem or existing data
- presents the findings and discussion in a language appropriate to the reader
- describes the methods used to identify and collect data in ways that can be understood and have the potential to be replicated
- discusses alternative interpretations and conclusions about what the data mean
- describes the limitations to the findings
- is polite and courteous when critiquing the work of others
- provides a complete and properly formatted set of references to all works that have influenced the work, not just those cited in the main body of the report.

The above is, in itself, a list of criteria. But it is not a long list and nor does it aim to be mandatory. Some research that is now regarded as classic and foundational for our understanding of the world would fail to meet most of these criteria. For example, Malinowski's *Argonauts of the Western Pacific* (1922), and his subsequent diary, *A Diary in the Strict Sense of the Term* (1989[1967]), may contain some terms and phrases that are not regarded as acceptable today. Words like 'primitive' and 'savages' were part of the language of early anthropology.

Malinowski, however, while using such words challenges many preconceptions about using the word 'primitive' as a derogatory classification. He makes a clear argument that the Trobrianders exhibited sophisticated social relations and structures, some (such as the high status and sexual freedom of women) far more advanced than to be found in his own Western society. Hence, while *Argonauts of the Western Pacific* (1922), would 'fail' on the basis of the criteria listed above our common sense should be applied to historical research; to dig out the project of the researcher in terms of the context of the assumptions in which they were working. In this case, Malinowski challenges many of the pre-conceived colonial assumptions of superiority taken for granted by his contemporaries.

Research techniques and understanding of methodological traditions have, to some extent, come a long way since Malinowski lived among and made notes about the Trobrianders. But while his descriptions may seem naive today and to not meet the strict criteria for qualitative research they are, nevertheless, an example of good research. His descriptions allow us, the reader, to understand what is going on, what people are doing and how they do things, what they believe and how they act on those beliefs, and most importantly, Malinowski leaves us room for our own interpretation of what is going on. His work does what research should do. It gives, in terms of outcomes, a theoretical lens, with which to understand (with which we can engage critically) the applicability of a method and approach and descriptions that resonate with what we already know. The product of understanding is not, by the standards of today, matched by the process of creating the materials for that understanding. These matters are not relevant for understanding *Argonauts of the Western Pacific*, because Malinowski's descriptions have believability (credible descriptions of experience) and authenticity (contextualised interpretations).

Not all research that fails to meet the standards defined by quality rubrics should be dismissed. There is, of course, research that is poor. Bad research tends to have one or more of the following features:

- a vague research question or no clear purpose/problem or the question is biased towards a particular answer
- ignores alternative perspectives and standpoints on the problem or dismisses them without serious consideration
- fails to give an adequate explanation for the context of the research
- claims to be research but is rhetorical and opinionated, bordering on and is bullshit (Frankfort, 2005)
- uses inappropriate methods to collect data that are not suited to addressing the data needs of the question
- patronises subjects
- citations are limited to those that confirm the views of the researcher
- the raw data are unavailable for reviewers to scrutinise.

Digging deeper: Criteria for appraising research

There are numerous sets of criteria and guides to evaluating the worth of research. For quantitative studies done to make recommendations for an intervention, organisations such as Cochrane have devised, implemented and published sets of criteria that come in the form of checklists. The aim of these checklists is to have a standardised method for evaluating individual studies and being able to find similarities and differences between studies. The overall goal is to build up bodies (a library) of evidence on the causes, spread and treatment of a range of particular health problems. The results are published as systematic reviews and sometimes as meta-analysis of data from many studies. With the application of common sense, some of the criteria from evidence-based schemes can be adapted for use in other research based on statistical methods.

The types of assessment done using schemes developed by Cochrane and other evidence-based organisations are largely mechanistic. They are about criteria that are decided upon and then applied to all the studies included in the set of research studies for review. The criteria identify data types and methods for producing the data.

Assessing the quality of research

The quality of research cannot be assessed merely by the application of a list of criteria. Criteria are useful for information extraction, providing a focus, but there is more to understanding research than just technical specification.

This enables a reviewer to combine findings from different studies of the same problem which have produced the same data type, using the same methods, and thereby corral bodies of evidence for recommending an intervention.

Statistically based reviews are able to have clear protocols because the research they are evaluating has been mostly done using a *closed-system approach*. This approach is informed by realism, experimentalism and predication. The realist assumption is that there is one real world independent of how people perceive it. Science and the scientific method of experimentalism attempt to uncover the mechanisms of the world in terms of cause and effect.

Reading advice: Criteria checklists

For some good examples of criteria checklists, I recommend *The Magenta Books*, guides from the National Centre for Social Research and the Rapid Evidence Assessment series.

Once the variables have been isolated and experiments made, then predictions on the behaviour of dependent variables can be made given a certain set of conditions.

Qualitative research can also be used to make predictions and inform practice and policy. It can also be done from a *realist* ontology. However, there are several seemingly contradictory sets of criteria that have been proposed for the assessment of studies labelled qualitative. In addition, some of the concepts found in the schemes are difficult to use. For example, fidelity, believability, representation and authenticity can be difficult to apply. Even more problematic are criteria such as resonance, coherence and verisimilitude. Therefore, when looking for schemes of criteria for evaluating qualitative research, you will find a lot of debate, discussion and some philosophical bartering. There is a good reason for this. Qualitative research can, like quantitative research, be done for a number of reasons. Unlike some experimental quantitative studies, qualitative studies tend to be characterised by an open-approach as opposed to a closed-systems approach. This does not mean they are less worthy as research; far from it. It means we may have to invest more intellectual effort, and a broader knowledge base, than we would with statistical-experimental studies. To apply any set of criteria to a qualitative piece of research may mean we need to know about different philosophical traditions, debates within these traditions, about ways of doing empirical studies based on methodological traditions and how to understand complex arguments. The following list, adapted from Spencer et al. (2003: 11–15), shows an example of a checklist approach to appraising qualitative research.

Research question Is this a question that can be addressed through research?

What kind of research question has been stated? Is its justification reasonable? What kind of research does the question imply be used to address it? Is there a discussion and evidence of the main assumptions/hypotheses/theoretical ideas on which the research question is based and how these affected the research design? (*The assumption here is that no research is undertaken without some underlying assumptions or theoretical ideas.*)

Design How defensible is the research design?

How does the design of the research strategy address the research question and aims of study? Is there a clear rationale for the study design? Is there a convincing justification for different features of the research design (e.g. reasons given for different components or stages of research; purpose of particular methods or data sources, multiple methods, time frames, etc.)? Is there a description of background or historical developments and social/organisational characteristics of study sites or settings? Are the aims and design of study set in the context of existing knowledge/understanding; identify new areas for investigation (*for example, in relation to policy/practice/ substantive theory*)?

Sampling How well defended is the sample design/target selection of cases/documents?

Is there full explanation and description of the sample composition or case? Is the selection of the study locations/areas explained adequately? Does the sample allow for comparisons to be made? Is missing coverage in the samples/cases and implications justified? How have access and methods of approach affected participation and/or coverage and/or data collection?

Data collection How well was the data collection carried out?

Who conducted data collection? What procedures and/or documents were used for collection/recording, checks on the origin/status/authorship of the documents? How were primary data recorded? Where are the raw data? If audio or video recording of interviews/discussions/conversations was not done, then why not? Is there a balanced discussion of how fieldwork methods or settings may have influenced the data collected? Have sufficient data been collected to meet the specifications of the sampling design?

Analysis How well has the approach to, and formulation of, the analysis been conveyed?

Is there a clear rationale for choice of data management method/tool/package? What evidence is there of how descriptive analytic categories, classes, labels, etc. have been generated and used (i.e. either through explicit discussion or portrayal in the commentary)? Is there a discussion, with examples, of how any constructed analytic concepts/typologies, etc. have been devised and applied? What evidence is there of attention to negative cases or exceptions, and of opposing or differing positions? This includes discussion of explicit and implicit explanations and the detection of underlying factors/influences. Have patterns of association/conceptual linkages within data been identified and discussed? Is there a discussion of how error or bias may have arisen in design/data collection/analysis and how this was addressed, if at all?

Findings How credible are the findings?

Are the findings/conclusions supported by data/evidence (i.e. the reader can see how the researcher arrived at his/her conclusions; the 'building blocks' of analysis and interpretation are evident)? Do the findings/conclusions 'make sense'/have a coherent logic? How has knowledge/understanding been extended by the research, e.g. in revisiting the literature review (where appropriate) in the conclusions, summarising knowledge to date, key issues raised by previous research and what this research contributed? Is there a sensible discussion of what can be generalised to the wider population from which a sample is drawn/case selection has been made?

Reporting How clear and coherent is the reporting of the research?

Does the report state the research question and demonstrate clear links between it and the research design? Is the report constructed so as to provide a narrative/story or clearly constructed thematic account of the research, thereby having a structure and signposting that usefully guide the reader through the commentary? Is the information for intended target audience(s) understandable and written at an appropriate level? Are the key messages highlighted or summarised? How clear are the assumptions/theoretical perspectives/values that have shaped the form and output of the research/evaluation? Is there a credible/clear discussion of how findings have contributed to knowledge and understanding (*e.g. of the policy, programme or theory being reviewed*) and may be applied to new policy developments, practice or theory?

Ethics What evidence is there of attention to ethical issues?

How much evidence is there of thoughtfulness/sensitivity about research contexts and participants with documentation of consent procedures? Are the consent procedures and information provided to participants documented? Where appropriate is potential harm or difficulty through participation discussed?

Auditability How adequately has the research process been documented?

Are all citations detailed and correct? Are the databases searched for information all listed? Is there a clear discussion of the strengths and weaknesses of data sources and methods? Is there access, if required, to the raw data? Have the changes made to the design been justified with the implications for study coverage highlighted?

Have all relevant documents been made available (e.g. letters of approach, topic guides, observation templates, data management frameworks, etc.)?

There are a lot of listings of criteria available from various sources. You will need to look for these and how they have developed from those ones that are suited to the research you are doing and looking at. Chapter 4 discusses which types of research are more suited to evaluation using formal criteria.

Criteriology and common sense

By looking at sets of criteria for the assessment of research we are engaging in a debate that has many standpoints, positions and beliefs. Criteria are useful but must be treated with caution. One way to do this is to ask, 'Says who and why?' Who says these are the criteria to be used? Why these and not others? What are these criteria for? What are the consequences for research that fail these criteria? Seale (1994: 171) argues that:

> In qualitative research the project of criteriology experiences particular contradictions because of the difficulty in regulating and constraining an endeavor whose guiding philosophy often stresses creativity, exploration, conceptual exploration and a freedom of spirit.

Malinowski is an interesting example. Our discussion of Malinowski suggests that research from more than a few decades ago is historic and has little to contribute to our current concerns. Many of the sets of criteria currently advocated relate to recent research and may, therefore, not capture the essential aspects of historic research. Strict adherence to criteria can limit our understanding and box us into narrow discourses, thereby stifling our creative perspectives. Whatever criteria are used these need to be transparent but also need to be used intelligently. The aim is to make visible for discussion the purposes of a research project, the processes by which the research was done and the arguments that were made. From the standpoint of the reviewer, the aim is to be able to talk intelligently about the position of a researcher, the logic of their research, the concepts they employed, the theories they accepted and rejected, and the influence they had on subsequent research. The project to construct definitive criteria is one that in itself can be subject to critical evaluation.

Conclusion

There are different types of research done for many different reasons using different methodological assumptions and methods of data collection. There is no easy way to understand these except through concerted reading of books on research methodology, some of which will have their origins in philosophy and history.

What is often written in research articles is a reconstituted version of what was done. It is your job to read analytically, in order to identify the design issues and options of the research so that the motives of the researcher can be made visible.

It is important to get to grips with the different methodological positions from which research is conducted. Some of these you may not like, nevertheless it is your professional responsibility to understand the logic of those positions. Otherwise, you cannot legitimately critique them or propose another in their place.

There are generic and specific criteria for evaluating research and these can be very useful for extracting information or to make comparisons and for aggregating findings. However, all schemes of criteria have been devised from a particular standpoint that their authors regard as useful for identifying 'proper' research (valid and reliable). There are research traditions such as some ethnographic studies or historic studies that require the application of common sense when it comes to making judgements on their worth – a charity of interpretation. This same common sense also needs to be applied to research that exhibits the formal properties associated with statistical-based research grounded in 'scientific realism'.

Reading research analytically also means reading with a sceptical mind. Take nothing for granted or at face value. It may be the case that a particular author has been venerated and often cited. This does not mean you must do likewise. Challenge all research with an equal scepticism.

In summary

- It is crucial that you teach yourself how to read research critically and analytically.
- Knowing about the elements that make up choices in research is an important prerequisite to being able to understand an author's argument and research project. This awareness can be practised through reading research and undertaking analysis of that research.
- Develop, through research and reading different sources, knowledge about the different methodological traditions that researchers use, but do not always discuss, as the epistemological basis of their research.
- Practise analysing and evaluating research. Look for the reasoning an author has employed for their research, and ways it has been used to make claims.

4

Different Types of Literature Review

Key questions

- What are the different types of literature review?
- Which type of literature review do you need to do?
- What are the consequences of doing a radical critique of the literature?
- What methodological and epistemological issues need to be taken into account?
- What qualities do the reviewer and review need to exhibit?

Core skills

- Understand different research traditions and methods
- Analyse research from a generic and subject specific standpoint
- Demonstrate theoretical and practical knowledge
- Evaluate the quality and usefulness of research
- Apply bibliometric analysis to publications when managing complex information
- Apply problem solving techniques.

Introduction

The kind of literature review you need to do will be dependent on the purpose of your research. There are two general types of review, the scholastic (traditional) review and interventionist (systematic) review. The traditional review has been used in dissertation research for many decades. The typical scholastic review tends to be theory and methodologically focused and is based on analysis and discussion with, normally, no implication for intervening in the lives of people. The interventionist review is more recent. It was developed to help provide the best available evidence for an intervention, providing empirical guidance for medical treatments and policy changes. Which type of review you will need is dependent on your research question, the purpose of your research and your ability to do the review.

This chapter is, therefore, about making decisions about what your research needs, and how a review of the literature can help you with those decisions. It is not about claiming one type of review or source of knowledge is better than another. All reviews, if done with a transparent methodology, can have equal status in current research.

Different types of literature review

As there are different types of research that use different methods to collect data and are based on different research traditions, there are different types of literature review. Table 4.1 summarises the two main types of review. Take note that this is a summary that needs a lot of details to be assumed.

TABLE 4.1   The two main types of literature review and their audiences

Interventionist	Scholastic
The general purpose is to use all available, valid and reliable evidence to make decisions in reaction to a condition (medical, social, economic, etc.) or proactively to lessen some occurrence.	The general purpose is to use dialectical reasoning to examine arguments, look for and resolve contradictions, challenge propositions and make inferences through rigorous conceptual analysis.
The types of audience are those needing to make decisions about practical matters and include medical, educational, criminal justice, transport, housing and environmental practitioners and policy makers.	The types of audience are those, such as dissertation supervisors, needing to be assured the writer of the review has reached a level of cognitive ability to apply logical techniques and has the capacity to use high level conceptual thinking.

The purpose and the audience are two of the determining factors for which type of review one looks for or aims to produce. Having looked at some scholastic reviews in Chapter 2 the following extract shows the range of practice-based audiences for an interventionist review. The following extract, from Stein et al. (2009), is about safeguarding children. Its intended audience are practitioners, policy makers and researchers.

They state that the aims of the review are:

1. To provide an accessible summary of relevant literature on adolescent neglect and to draw out the implications for further developments on this topic.
2. To inform the preparation of guides for multi-disciplinary teams and for young people.

The authors then state what the implications are for a group of stakeholders:

Implications for practice, policy and research for young people

The review suggests the need to raise awareness amongst young people about the meaning of neglect and the potential consequences, so that young people who may be experiencing neglect feel able to seek appropriate support. The guide for young people being produced as part of this project will be one means of pursuing this objective.

Practitioners and practice managers

Similarly, there is a need to raise professional awareness of definitional issues, and of the scale and outcomes of adolescent neglect, in order to promote more effective responses to the needs of this group of young people. The guide for professionals will contribute to this objective.

Senior managers and policy makers

At a management and policy level, the review suggests a need for additional documentation to support age-specific assessments in cases of potential neglect; potential improvements to official definitions and measurement of maltreatment; and the need for more dedicated funding to undertake further research and to pilot new interventions in this area.

Researchers

Finally the review presents a major challenge to the research community to pay more attention to neglect and to issues affecting adolescents within the field of maltreatment research. The lack of previous work presents an opportunity to develop a consistent set of definitions and measurements, which can support a coherent strand of UK research on this topic.

The potential consequences of adolescent neglect

Much more is known about the potential consequences of child neglect and specifically of neglect during adolescence. There are some limitations to this body of evidence however, most notably that it generally indicates correlations rather than causality.

Stein et al.'s (2009) review is typical of the recent attempts to corral national and international research into one place for the use by a range of service users.

The main point to note about this dichotomy (see Table 4.1) is that it is not definitive. It is not a matter of either this one or the other one. Both types rely on the people producing them to have the same kinds of skills in searching, handling information and data, and being able to think through what the data and concepts mean. The skills set required is outlined in Chapter 1 where we discussed the Researcher Development Framework. However, using this useful dichotomy, we now turn to say more about the features of these types of review.

Scholastic (traditional) review

The typical scholastic review is about reading research to acquire greater levels and degrees of understanding. That understanding can be about almost anything but would usually involve understanding the origins and history of an idea, the arguments about a theory, the development and application of a methodology and so on. It is not about reading the literature as a pastime. Scholastic research is a serious activity and can be a challenge to do. There are some very dense ideas and complex arguments out there. Unlike the interventionist review the scholar-researcher is not necessarily looking for guidance on how to do something better. They do not have prior research condensed into packets that can be easily disseminated and digested. The scholastic reviewer has the aim to understand the different contributions that have been made to a problem and then to make interpretations about what each one means. This same aim is extended into reviews that are produced for practice and policy based audiences. This is because there is a substantial pool of information and understandings about all kinds of topics, issues and problems in social science and humanities research that can provide necessary contexts for interpreting the meaning of a recommendation.

Definitions of the scholastic review

The scholastic review is not always separate from an interventionist review. The general purpose of the scholastic review is to identify sources relevant to the objective of the review. The sources can be primary research, existing theories, models and arguments (including interpretations). The review can be focused on one or more objectives such as:

- integrating existing knowledge and argument on a topic or problem, to find the boundaries and assumptions that have been deemed necessary for research in a particular field
- examining and evaluating theoretical positions to see how well they describe or explain a phenomenon or inform research, to see if existing theory can be applied to new problems or if a new theory is needed
- an analysis of particular themes within research from different perspectives, to make comparisons between approaches

- evaluating the usefulness of different methodological approaches and data collection techniques
- looking at the historical development of a topic or problem
- looking for state-of-the-art research to identify emerging themes, points of criticism that may be integrated into suggestions for research.

In terms of a working definition we can say that a

> scholastic review can examine the findings, development or argument about a topic or the methodological literature in ways in which a topic or problem has been researched. The resulting review(s) will exhibit tightly reasoned critical evaluation on the findings and interpretations of a justified selection of sources and will throughout focus on a clearly stated research question.

The knowledge contained in the scholastic review is, therefore, an essential prerequisite to any type of review. It is a necessary step in the production of insight that can lead to more sophisticated and progressive research.

Variations on the scholastic review

The idea of the literature review is nothing new or strange to research. Social science and humanities researchers are used to and expected to be familiar with a wide-ranging set of sources across several fields of study. The postgraduate student in sociology would be expected to have a sound working knowledge not only of their area of research but with the general founders of the discipline, key theoretical and methodological studies and with contemporaneous arguments within their area. The scope of the scholastic review tends to be much wider than that of interventionist reviews. The scholastic review encompasses reviews for dissertation research, conceptual discussion and clarification, argumentation, historical description and cross-disciplinary learning.

Examples of the scholastic review

There are many examples of scholastic reviews. Depending on your needs, look for reviews that address the kind of question you have, and if possible, the topic area in which you are working. The suggestion is not to copy what others have done but use previous work as a learning resource. The example that follows illustrates this.

Epistemological assumptions

Types of review are informed by the epistemological assumptions of the researcher. Here is a snapshot guide to the definitions:

Subjective idealism: there is no shared reality independent of multiple alternative human constructions

Objective idealism: there is a world of collectively shared understandings

Critical realism: knowledge of reality is mediated by our perceptions and beliefs

Scientific realism: it is possible for knowledge to approximate closely an external reality

Naïve realism: reality exists independently of human constructions and can be known directly. (Spencer et al., 2003: 45–6, quoted in Barnett-Page and Thomas, 2009: 11)

There are different types of scholastic review. The differences between the types are mostly dependent on the epistemological preferences of the researcher; this is often assumed by their adherence to a specific paradigmatic worldview. Barnett-Page and Thomas (2009) undertook a comprehensive review of the literature on methods used to synthesise qualitative studies and data. From their hand-eye based reading of the literature they were able to make some very useful categorisations of the methods currently being used. They found nine distinct methods being used to synthesise studies and were able to further say what made each type different.

Barnett-Page and Thomas (2009) describe each method in turn, citing the studies placed into the categories. The following extract is their description of grounded theory and who has used it to synthesise qualitative research.

Kearney (2001), Eaves (2001) and Finfgeld (1999), have all adapted grounded theory to formulate a method of synthesis. Key methods and assumptions of grounded theory, as originally formulated and subsequently refined by Glaser and Strauss (1967) and Strauss and Corbin (1990, 1998), include: simultaneous phases of data collection and analysis; an inductive rather than hypethetico-deductive approach to analysis, allowing the theory to emerge from the data; the use of the constant comparison method; the use of theoretical sampling to reach theoretical saturation; and the generation of new theory. Eaves cited grounded theorists Charmaz (1983) and Chesler (1987), as well as Strauss and Corbin (1990), as informing her approach to synthesis. (Barnett-Page and Thomas, 2009: 6)

Barnett-Page and Thomas (2009) is an example of a detailed analytical review. It exemplifies both the review *of* the literature and the review *for* research. The first part of their analysis enabled them to categorise the research studies into nine types based on the methods each type had in common as the means to synthesise qualitative research. These nine categories tell the reader about the kinds of methods currently being used. This work was an essential prerequisite to showing the epistemological origins and other features of the nine methods. From their discussion of epistemological differences that distinguish the nine types from each other, the reader is able to make an informed decision on which method is most suited to their kind of research question, and which fits with their paradigm. The reader is thereby able to make a recommendation on which method they regard is needed *for* their research.

The following table (Table 4.2) is from Barnett-Page and Thomas (2009: 23–5). They show the ways in which they have attributed a range of dimensions to the nine methods. Table 4.2 shows two of the dimensions; the continuum from idealist to realist and the tendency for groups of methods to be either heterogeneous or homogeneous in their selection of studies to be included in an analysis.

TABLE 4.2 Dimensions of difference

Idealist--Realist

Subjective idealism			Objective idealism		Critical realism			Scientific realism
Meta-narrative	CIS	Meta-study	Meta-ethnography	Grounded theory	Thematic synthesis	Textual narrative synthesis	Framework synthesis	Ecological triangulation
Heterogeneous			Homogeneous		Heterogeneous			Not clear

Source: Barnett-Page and Thomas, 2009

The strength of this kind of review is that it shows the choices available to the researcher when designing their own research. The initial categorisations are not of a lesser value than the later identification of epistemological assumptions. The initial nine categories are essential to bringing clarity and order to what can seem a very confusing literature. From this, the researcher is able to make an informed decision on which studies to read. This decision is based on their intentions. Barnett-Page and Thomas (2009) state that some methods are more suited to describing the data and others to making fresh interpretations of the data.

> the methods reviewed here vary in the extent to which they attempt to 'go beyond' the primary studies and transform the data. Some methods – textual narrative synthesis, ecological triangulation and framework synthesis – focus on describing and summarising their primary data (often in a highly structured and detailed way) and translating the studies into one another. Others – meta-ethnography, grounded theory, thematic synthesis, meta-study, meta-narrative and critical interpretive synthesis – seek to push beyond the original data to a fresh interpretation of the phenomena under review. (Barnett-Page and Thomas, 2009: 15)

Therefore, if you are doing an undergraduate dissertation then methods that can be used to describe multiple studies may be suited to your needs. If you are doing a doctorate then methods that can be used to make fresh interpretations of data on a phenomenon may be suited to your needs.

The key features and requirements of the scholastic (traditional) review include:

- focusing on increasing knowledge of a particular topic, problem or methodology used within a field of interest
- the need to read very widely across subject disciplines including history and philosophy in order to understand complex assumptions and arguments
- being capable of analysing arguments, comparing positions and making visible methodological assumptions and their logical consequences
- the need for a sound and extensive working knowledge of the resources and sources available (e.g. databases and archives), how they are organised and how research is reported
- the need to understand the research process, including the strengths and weaknesses of methods (often alongside statistical techniques)
- the ability and mental capacity to organise information and see relationships between ideas, theories and arguments
- identifying new possibilities for research and not merely mirror what has already been done and said.

Interventionist (systematic) review

The interventionist review is essentially about trying to minimise doubt by finding out, as far as possible, about what works. It is about using evidence obtained from primary research or evaluation to guide decision making. This type of review is not restricted to medical practice but is often used by different government departments to inform social and economic policy. In the UK a range of organisations have been given responsibility to set standards for the collection and dissemination of evidence such as the Economic and Social Research Council. In 2000 the UK government called on the social sciences to develop methods and processes to provide evidence about what policies work, and which ones are more likely to be effective.

> Social science research evidence is central to development and evaluation of policy ... We need to be able to rely on social science and social scientists to tell us what works and why and what types of policy initiatives are likely to be most effective. (Blunkett, 2000: 24)

Definitions of the interventionist review
The phrases 'systematic review' (SR) and evidence-based practice' (EBP) are more commonly used than interventionist review. The word 'interventionist' is used in this book to make a distinction about the *purpose* of a review and to

challenge claims about the worth of different types of review. This is because in many definitions of the different types of review, the word 'systematic' implies that any other type of review is not systematic. For example, Sweet and Moynihan (2007: 1) claim that

> systematic reviews provide a systematic, transparent means for gathering, synthesising and appraising the findings of studies on a particular topic or question. The aim is to minimise the bias associated with single studies and non-systematic reviews.

It is not true to claim non-interventionist, so called traditional, reviews are unsystematic or that they do not appraise evidence. There now exists a rigorous protocol for the production and evaluation of scholastic reviews.

Reading advice: Guides to meta-analysis

The ESRC National Centre for Research Methods, based in the UK, has a number of excellent guides, available online, on the meta-analysis and synthesis of research findings. I highly recommend them even if you are not based in the UK, and they are easily located on the ESRC website (www.evidencenetwork.org).

An interventionist review is usually a research report (or article) specifically undertaken to provide the best available evidence in support of a decision to make something better, do something more efficiently, do the right thing and ultimately do the right thing in the right way. An interventionist review does not tell one what should be done or how to do something; it cannot provide definitive answers or solutions. It informs decision making when a decision maker, individual or organisation has finite resources, lacks knowledge of current research, and is working within a value system. The review, therefore, gives supporting evidence for translating research into practice, to address a particular need, and in so doing aims to do more good than harm, at a cost acceptable to the organisation and society.

Variations on the interventionist review

All types of review are the actualisation of putting into practice a range of skills and processes supported by common sense and interpretation. Interventionist reviews, while usually following a set protocol, have differences based on the needs of the reviewer. There are two main types of review commonly associated with interventionist – the systematic review and the meta-analysis. But note that both of these reviews can be done by researchers for reasons not directed towards intervention and can also be undertaken by scholastic researchers looking to understand the contexts of a problem. Victor (2008) summarises (see Table 4.3) the three main types of scholastic review aimed at advising policy makers and practitioners in decision making.

TABLE 4.3   Different types of review for social science policy research

	Traditional	Extended	Integrative
Summary of approach	Originated in clinical medicine where it was designed to reach rigorous conclusions about the effects of medical interventions.	Covers a range of approaches, involving extension and/or adaptation of the traditional approach to widen its use and applicability within the social sciences.	An emerging set of approaches based upon the view that knowledge should be cumulated in an integrative rather than an additive way.
Key methodological features	A highly prescribed, staged methodology. Prioritises the inclusion of randomised controlled trials whose data are extracted via a standardised template, pooled and analysed through statistical meta-analysis.	Varying extensions and/or adaptations of the traditional staged methodology. Potentially includes a wide range of types of research and accordingly various approaches to quality appraisal. A narrative form of synthesis is often used.	Centred upon theory development. A less prescribed more iterative process that proceeds according to the researcher's expertise and judgment. Purposive sampling and appraisal of the evidence.
Research questions best addressed by this approach	Questions measuring the effect of an intervention. For example, what reduction in the level of homelessness does a new government programme cause?	Intervention effect questions where little RCT evidence is available. Also questions about intervention processes and actors' views of interventions. For example, what are homeless people's views of a new government programme?	Any question about the social world concerned with building theory. For example, what theoretical model best explains how a new government programme designed to tackle homelessness works?

Source: Victor, 2008: 2

Examples of the interventionist review

There is a substantive and detailed literature and resources on systematic reviews. For example, there is the Campbell Collaboration, the ESRC UK

Centre for Evidence Based Policy and Practice, the Evidence for Policy and Practice Information and Co-ordination Centre (EPPI-Centre) and the Cochrane Collaboration. These organisations and others provide a substantial set of resources including guides to conducting a systematic and related review, such as meta-reviews and analysis. Table 4.4 shows some of the systematic reviews available from EPPI.

TABLE 4.4   Example systematic reviews available from EPPI

Date	Title
2012	A systematic rapid evidence assessment of late diagnosis
2012	A systematic review of selected interventions to reduce juvenile re-offending
2012	Commissioning in health, education and social care: Models, research bibliography and in-depth review of joint commissioning between health and social care agencies
2012	Communities that cook: A systematic review of the effectiveness and appropriateness of interventions to introduce adults to home cooking
2012	Do micro-credit, micro-savings and micro-leasing serve as effective financial inclusion interventions enabling poor people, and especially women, to engage in meaningful economic opportunities in low- and middle-income countries? A systematic review of the evidence
2012	Evidence on the relationship between education, skills and economic growth in low-income countries: A systematic review
2012	Impact of national health insurance for the poor and the informal sector in low- and middle-income countries: A systematic review
2012	Plain tobacco packaging: A systematic review
2012	Providing access to economic assets for girls and young women in low-and-lower middle-income countries: A systematic review of the evidence
2012	The impact of economic resource transfers to women versus men: A systematic review

The systematic reviews listed in Table 4.4 tend to use a common template and approach. Moodie et al.'s (2012) study looked at plain tobacco packaging and is a typical example. This is shown in Figure 4.1. Once the definitions and criteria for selection had been determined (an important research stage in itself), a range of databases was identified and searched along with other web resources such as archives. Full details of the search strategy and quality assessment criteria are given in the report. Some 4518 records were found, from which 3232 were excluded because they failed to meet the criteria. The result of scanning the abstracts and reading the texts, as well as removing duplicate records, was

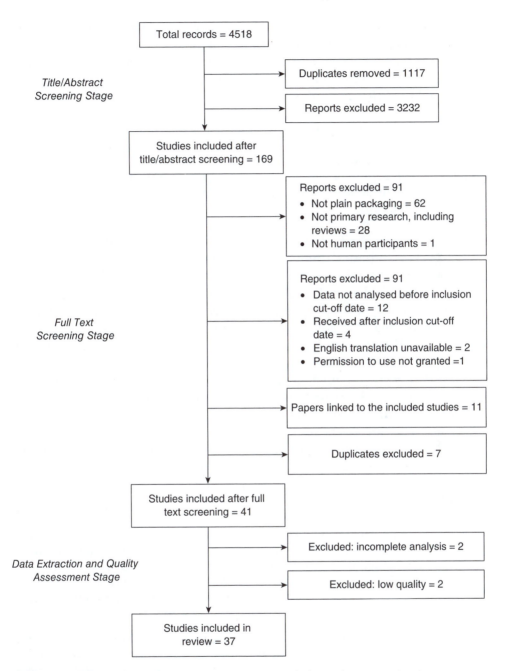

FIGURE 4.1 Flow of studies for a systematic review of plain tobacco packaging

Source: Moodie et al., 2012: 109

37 studies retrieved for analysis. Although some archive materials were looked at, the bulk of the work in the review consisted of searching databases using the search terms the team had decided would retrieve the most records – to provide

all of the best available evidence. The records retrieved were a combination of studies using qualitative and quantitative methods.

The other type of review associated with interventionist researchers is the meta-analysis. For organisations such as the Cochrane Collaboration (Higgins and Green, 2011: 15) meta-analysis is:

> the use of statistical methods to combine results of individual studies. This allows us to make the best use of all the information we have gathered in our systematic review by increasing the power of the analysis. By statistically combining the results of similar studies we can improve the precision of our estimates of treatment effect, and assess whether treatment effects are similar in similar situations.

Meta-analysis is a specific kind of systematic review. In medicine, it is almost wholly based on statistical analysis (not aggregation or adding up the numbers) of results from randomised control trials that have researched the same question. To do meta-analysis takes time and you will need to be knowledgeable and competent with the necessary statistical techniques. This is because there are alternative methods for doing a meta-analysis. The Cochrane Collaboration discuss three (Higgins and Green, 2011): the Mantel-Haenszel method (which is more specific to dichotomous data and weights studies in a slightly different way), the Peto method (which is useful for rare events) and the Random effect inverse-variance model (which assumes that all studies are estimating their own true effect, and these effects are normally distributed).

Meta-analysis can also be used with non-statistical studies and to synthesise qualitative and quantitative research studies. The Cochrane Collaboration have recognised the value of non-statistical research. Noyes et al. (2013: 3), writing for readers of the *Cochrane Handbook for Systematic Reviews of Interventions,* say:

> it is increasingly being recognised that evidence from qualitative studies that explore the experience of those involved in providing and receiving interventions, and studies evaluating factors that shape the implementation of interventions, have an important role in ensuring that systematic reviews are of maximum value to policy, practice and consumer decision-making (Arai 2005, Mays 2005, Popay 2005) ...

> A synthesis of evidence from qualitative research can explore questions such as how do people experience illness, why does an intervention work (or not), for whom and in what circumstances? In some reviews, particularly those addressing healthcare delivery, it may be desirable to draw on qualitative evidence to address questions such as what are the barriers and facilitators to accessing health care, or what impact do specific barriers and facilitators have on people, their experiences and behaviours? These may be generated, for example, through ethnographies and interview studies of help-seeking behaviour. Evidence from qualitative research can help with interpretation of systematic review results

by aiding understanding of the way in which an intervention is experienced by all of those involved in developing, delivering or receiving it; what aspects of the intervention they value, or not; and why this is so. These types of qualitative evidence can provide insight into factors that are external to an intervention including, for example, the impact of other policy developments, factors which facilitate or hinder successful implementation of a programme, service or treatment and how a particular intervention may need to be adapted for large-scale roll-out (Roen, 2006).

Meta-analysis does not have to be statistical. Some meta-analytical studies are focused on a range of issues that have multiple methodological approaches. For example, the European Union funded a number of meta-analytical studies into gender and science (www.genderandscience.org). They analysed research done on a broad range of topics, questions and issues related to the gender gap in science research. Topics covered included wage gaps, stereotypes and identity, labour activities, policies and integration. They also produced a synthesis report from the meta-analysis of the separate reports. What is interesting about some of the meta-analyses is that they are of ethnographic studies. They show how qualitative research can be subject to systematic and meta-analyses in ways that are rigorous and valid in findings.

Key features and requirements of the interventionist review include:

- the focus is on answering a particular question where an intervention is required to address a condition or situation
- the use of explicit and clearly stated search terms so as to produce a re-producible audit trail of actions and decisions over what was included and what was excluded
- allocation of sufficient time and resources to what can be a time consuming, multi-person and costly project
- the need for a sound and extensive working knowledge of the resources and sources available (e.g. databases), how they are organised and how research is reported in statistical terms
- the need to understand the research process, including the strengths and weaknesses of methods alongside statistical techniques
- the need to be as comprehensive as possible (that may mean inclusion of contrary evidence), knowing how to apply a recognised and accepted method called a protocol to the design of the search, its implementation and reporting of findings
- a broad knowledge of the contexts in which, and reasons why, research has been done in the first place, including the pressure to publish and the possibility of misreporting findings.

Which type of literature review do you need to do?

Which type of literature review you should do depends on the reasons you have for doing your research. To a large degree your research question and the intent it has will direct you to the kind of materials you need to inform your research.

The interventionist goal will lead you to primary research directed to policy and practice, while the scholastic goal will lead you to arguments over concepts and theories and the relative merits of different methodological and political stand-points. As you are a critical researcher, you should expect that matters are not so clear-cut. There are other issues to take into account. The main one is your metaphor for the review – are you adding to the existing building and doing verificationist work or are you looking to make a building of your own and doing generative research?

Adding to or making a new building: Generative and verificationist review

When thinking and planning your research, especially the review, you have choices. One of these choices is to work within an existing body of research and add to what, from that approach, is already known. The second choice is to examine the existing literature on a problem and aim to establish an alternative or different way of understanding the problem. A couple of analogies may help here.

The first is the analogy of 'the pond'. When searching the literature on a substantive problem and methodology, you will find authors whose work has had a measurable impact on the problem. Let us call these the rock throwers. Other authors who have done similar work to the rock throwers, we can call the pebble rollers. The pebble rollers have formulated their research problems from reading the existing literature and have done research that aims to add greater degrees of verification to an existing position. They have, in short, tried to verify the propositions of the rock throwers. All subject areas have their own ponds populated by a small number of rock throwers and many pebble rollers. The pebble rollers do not disturb the pond because they take care in adhering to the theoretical, methodological and political conventions of the rock throwers by carefully rolling their research into the larger pond. The rock throwers have become what they are because they established the problem, applied a research technique not used before or developed the theoretical metaphor to talking about the problem.

The second and related analogy is the building. Most research activity can be seen as a series of elements that form an interlinked construction, like a building. The building has structure, form and shape. Through a search and analysis of the literature on a topic, we can construct diagrammatic representations of different disciplinary problems.

Critique of existing works

Remember in Chapter 1 we discussed core works and critiquing an existing body of literature.

These diagrams can show the foundations, the methodological assumptions, on which the building rests, along with the main sections, the ways in which different researchers have built on the same foundations. With recourse to the methodological foundations and other researchers within the building a researcher can explain, justify and communicate their research. This means that some researchers form communities of interest and share common views on what a problem is, how it should be investigated and what stance should be taken towards it. They share, in other words, a distinct set of cognitive premises.

Reading advice: Dogma in research

A literature review and critical analysis of core works can reveal the edifice behind some methodological assumptions. For a more elaborate discussion of the consequences of dogmatic imperialism in research and the abuse of authority, read Chapter 8 in Hart (2005).

These premises, what we may call beliefs or assumptions, are not always made clear in individual publications. They are often only made visible through critical analysis of the core works of a literature on a problem. All literature reviews should aim to make clear the methodological assumptions used by core texts in their field of study. Whether one decides to accept those assumptions (theoretical, methodological or political) or not, is the matter.

Pond or building, these are only analogies. But how you act on them can have real consequences. The point is you have a choice here. If you throw a rock into the pond there will be repercussions. Alternatively, you can add to the existing building, even be a little radical by adding a small extension. You could even begin a new modest building of your own. Therefore, how we use the literature can be either to add more evidence for a position or we can critique the rock throwers and aim to throw in a rock of our own or even go to another pond. Mixed analogies apart, there are inherent dangers in challenging established researchers. For professional standing and career progression making a challenge to the orthodoxy can mean a lonely existence in the research world. For new researchers and especially established researchers here is some advice from David Grahame-Smith (1998: 7–8):

- never feel absolutely certain of anything
- never discourage thinking, for one will always succeed
- have little respect for the authority of others, for there are always contrary authorities to be found
- do not fear to be eccentric of opinion, for every opinion was once eccentric
- find pleasure in intelligent dissent, rather than in passive agreement, for the former implies a deeper agreement than the latter
- do not feel envious of the happiness and contentment of those who live in a false paradise for only a fool will think it is paradise.

Mix the metaphors

Paradigm boundaries, once delineated, can be used as a resource, extended and challenged. One way to do this is to think about mixing the metaphors from different disciplines and research traditions. For example, the work of Howard S. Becker can be seen as the mixing of a number of approaches and traditions within the social sciences. From the social psychology of George Herbert Mead, the European philosophy of Georg Simmel and to the pragmatism of Everett Hughes, Becker takes a number of ideas, concepts and theories, as well as ways to approach research and data. This continuing synthesis can be seen in his varied works and topics of study, as well as in his use of metaphors. Becker says this about metaphors:

> A metaphor that works is still alive. Reading it shows you a new aspect of what you are reading about, how that aspect appears in something superficially quite different. Using a metaphor is a serious theoretical exercise in which you assert that two different empirical phenomena belong to the same general class. But metaphors work that way only if they are fresh enough to attract attention. If they have been used repeatedly enough to be clichés, you don't see anything new. In fact, you think that they actually mean, literally, what they allude to metaphorically. (Becker, 1986: 113)

Synthesising ideas, metaphors and research designs was very productive for Becker. It enabled him to look at a range of social processes including the production of art, making jazz music, drug use, deviance, writing, photography, medical education, methodology and evidence – among other topics.

Becker and other researchers whose works span many topics and problems are not working outside of normal science or practice. They do not take the stance that different research traditions and theories are incommensurable. Their approach is one of what Thomas Kuhn (1970) called problem solving. This is about understand the language used by others in their research and methodological tradition to understanding what it is they are doing and for what reasons. The principle of charity is, therefore, about understanding the conversations others have to see if there is any purchase from joining in for one's own research. In Kuhn's words this is about

> ... what the participants in a communication breakdown can do is recognise each other as members of different language communities and then become translators. Taking the differences between their own intra and inter-group discourse as itself a subject for study, they can first attempt to discover the terms and locutions that, used un-problematically within each community, are nevertheless foci of trouble for inter-group discussions. (Locutions that present no such difficulties may be homophonically translated.) Having isolated such areas of difficulty in scientific communication, they can next resort to their shared everyday vocabularies in an effort to further elucidate their troubles.

Each may, that is, try to discover what the other would see and say when presented with a stimulus to which his ... verbal response would be different. If they sufficiently refrain from explaining anomalous behavior as the consequence of mere error or madness, they may in time become very good predictors of each other's behavior. Each will have learned to translate the other's theory and its consequences into his own language and simultaneously to describe in his language the world to which that theory applies. That is what the historian of science regularly does (or should) when dealing with out-of-date theories. (Kuhn, 1970: 202)

This does not entail a conversion to a different way of seeing and doing things. It is about understanding as many views on reality as one can, to explore if other metaphors and concepts can 'suggest new questions requiring new methods, and mixing methods can generate new questions leading to new metaphors' (Brewer and Hunter, 2005: 58). One way of approaching this is to think through just what it is you need to know from the literature before you start searching and reading.

Questions for the review

Different research purposes require different kinds of questions. It is because there is a wide range of questions, topics and problems that have been investigated by social scientists, humanities and arts researchers that there are a variety of methods used to collect data. The different ways of approaching research mean that there is a diverse range of research designs. This is a strength and weakness. The strength lies in the rich diversity of research studies. The weakness is the problem of making meaningful comparisons between diverse studies. One approach to this initial problem is to be sure that your research question is a researchable question.

Do you have a research question that is capable of being answered? This depends on the data. Is it available in sufficient quality and quantity? Can you get access to the data? Do you know how to analyse the data? Do you have the time to do the research? These are basic but essential questions. In part, your answer to them is dependent on your knowledge of what different types of research, and particularly reviews of the literature, involve. It is common sense to find out at an early stage whether or not research has already been done that answered the same kind of question you have.

Stages for a literature review

There are a number of ways in which the basic steps to doing a search and review of the literature can be listed. Broadly following Cooper and Hedges (1993), the basic steps for doing any review are as follows:

1. formulate a focused researchable question
2. develop a strategy with a search vocabulary for locating potentially relevant evidence – include explicit criteria for the inclusion and exclusion of studies
3. develop methods for abstracting, summarising and synthesising the evidence
4. locate the relevant studies and assess their methodological validity or quality – include explicit criteria for the selection of content and assessment of quality
5. abstract and synthesise the relevant information, concepts and/or argument – this may be done qualitatively or quantitatively or as a synthesis of both
6. map out the main themes, questions, methods and methodological assumptions in the literature
7. draw conclusions about methodological assumptions, practice, policy or future research, which are backed by evidence, taking into account quantity, quality and consistency.

Cooper (1984) provides a scheme of stages (see Table 4.5) for the literature review in terms of the stages involved in a typical research project.

Table 4.5 is useful as it helps us see the whole process and what may be involved. The literature review, combined with the research problem, should lead to the formulation of empirical research questions.

Reading advice: Planning your search

For a guide to getting started in the whole process, see Hart (2001) for more guidance on planning your search.

Although Cooper does not include the planning stage in his (1988) 'Taxonomy of literature reviews', it is an essential part of research. At this point, the dissertation author explains, using evidence from the review, how the dissertation makes a meaningful contribution to knowledge in the field. It is about placing your work within the existing body of literature or showing how it differs from the literature. Translating these general schemes into a clear plan of action is a necessary part of reviewing. Table 4.6 gives an idea of what two types of scholastic review may involve.

For systematic and policy reviews the research questions should shape and drive the process and stages. The question should:

1. be clear and as precise as possible
2. indicate the scope of what is to be included and what excluded
3. be capable, if the data are available, of being answerable
4. be worth the effort of the research (and costs) necessary to search and review the relevant literature.

TABLE 4.5 The research stages in conducting a literature review

Research stages

Stage characteristics	1 Problem formation	2 Data collection from the literature	3 Evaluation of data for quality	4 Analysis and interpretation of data	5 Public presentation
Research questions asked	What evidence should be included in the review?	What procedures should be used to find relevant evidence?	What retrieved evidence should be included in the review?	What procedures should be used to make inferences about the literature as a whole?	What information should be included in the review report?
Primary function in review	Constructing definitions that distinguish relevant from irrelevant studies.	Determining which sources of potentially relevant sources to examine.	Applying criteria to separate 'valid' from 'invalid' studies.	Synthesising valid retrieved studies.	Applying editorial criteria to separate important from unimportant information.
Procedural differences that create variation in review conclusion	1. Differences in included operational definitions. 2. Differences in operational detail.	Differences in the research contained in sources of information.	1. Differences in quality criteria. 2. Differences in the influence of non-quality criteria.	Differences in the rules of inference.	Differences in guidelines for editorial judgment.
Sources of potential invalidity in review conclusions	1. Narrow concepts may make review conclusions less definitive and robust. 2. Superficial operational detail may obscure interacting variables.	1. Accessed studies may be qualitatively different from the target population of studies. 2. People sampled in accessible studies may be different from the target population of people.	1. Non-equality factors may cause improper weighting of study formation. 2. Omissions in study reports may make conclusions unreliable.	1. Rules for distinguishing patterns from noise may be inappropriate. 2. Review-based evidence may be used to infer causality.	1. Omission of review procedures may make conclusions irreproducible. 2. Omission of review findings and study procedures may make conclusions obsolete.

TABLE 4.6 Stages and processes for two types of qualitative literature review

Qualitative literature reviews

Conducting a literature review with qualitative studies	The phenomenological method for conducting a qualitative literature review
Gall et al. (1996) have broken down Ogawa and Malen's (1991) method into the eight steps.	The goal of phenomenological research is to arrive at the essence of the lived experience of a phenomenon (Moustakas, 1994). Applied as a review technique, the goal is to arrive at the essence of researchers' empirical experiences with a phenomenon.
Step 1: Create an audit trail. In this step, the reviewer carefully documents all of the steps that are taken. The audit trail serves as documentation to make clear the evidence that supports each finding, where that evidence can be found, and how that evidence was interpreted.	*Step 1: Create an audit trail.* In this step, the reviewer carefully documents all of the steps that are taken. The audit trail serves as documentation to make clear the evidence that supports each finding, where that evidence can be found, and how that evidence was interpreted.
Step 2. Define the focus of the review. The problem formation stage mentioned earlier is similar to this step. In this stage, the constructs of the review are defined and, thereby, it is determined what to include in the review and what to leave out.	*Step 2: Bracketing.* In phenomenological research, the first step is to identify the phenomenon to be investigated. The researcher then 'brackets' his or her experience with the phenomenon by explaining his or her own experiences with and positions on the phenomenon.
Step 3: Search for relevant literature. This step is similar to the data collection stage mentioned earlier. According to Ogawa and Malen (1991), in addition to qualitative research reports, non-research reports such as memos, newspaper articles or meeting minutes should also be included in the review and not necessarily regarded as having less value than qualitative research reports.	*Step 3: Collecting data.* The next step is to collect data about the phenomenon. In primary phenomenological research, the researcher would interview a set of people who had experienced the phenomenon. In using the phenomenological method as a review tool, the reviewer would read the reports of scientists who have done research on the phenomenon. As in quantitative reviews, the reviewer still must decide on criteria for inclusion and define the research strategy.
Step 4: Classify the documents. In this step, the reviewer classifies the documents according to the types of data they represent. For example, some documents may be first-hand reports of qualitative research, others may be policy statements about the issue in question, and still other types of data may describe projects surrounding the issue.	*Step 4: Classify the documents.* In this step, the reviewer classifies the documents according to the types of data they represent. For example, some documents may be first-hand reports of qualitative research, others may be policy statements about the issue in question, and still other types of data may describe projects surrounding the issue.

Qualitative literature reviews

Conducting a literature review with qualitative studies	The phenomenological method for conducting a qualitative literature review
Step 5: Create summary databases. This step is similar to the data evaluation stage. In this stage, the reviewer develops coding schemes and attempts to reduce the information in the relevant documents.	*Step 5: Create summary databases.* This step is similar to the data evaluation stage. In this stage, the reviewer develops coding schemes and attempts to reduce the information in the relevant documents.
Step 6: Identify constructs and hypothesised causal linkages. After summary databases have been created, the task is to identify the essential themes of the documents and create hypotheses about the relationships between the themes. The goal here, unlike meta-analysis, is to increase the understanding of the phenomena being investigated, not to integrate outcomes.	*Step 6: Identifying meaningful statements.* The purpose is to identify meaningful statements. The researcher may do this by highlighting empirical claims made about the phenomenon of interest and collecting those claims, word-for-word, in some kind of spreadsheet or qualitative software to make the data manageable.
Step 7: Search for contrary findings and rival interpretations. In the tradition of primary qualitative research, it is necessary to actively search for contrary findings and rival interpretations. One may, for example, re-read the documents at this point to search for contrary evidence.	*Step 7. Giving meaning.* After identifying meaningful statements, the next step is to give meanings to those statements. That is, the reviewer may put the meaningful statements into categories and then interpret and paraphrase them as groups.
Step 8: Use colleagues or informants to corroborate findings. The last step in Ogawa and Malen's (1991) method – corroborating findings – also parallels primary qualitative research. In this step, one shares a draft of the report with colleagues and informants, such as the authors of the documents included in the review, requesting that they critically analyse the review. In this way, based on the extent of agreement among the informants, the reviewer can confirm the degree to which the review's conclusions are sound.	*Step 8. Thick, rich description.* The final step is to create a thick, rich description of the essence of primary researchers' experiences with the phenomenon. The goal is to describe the essence of the phenomenon as seen through the eyes of the researchers who investigated that phenomenon.

Interventionist reviews often use a rubric called PICO to formulate a researchable question. PICO stands for Patient, Population, or Problem (P), Intervention, Prognostic Factor, or Exposure (I), Context or setting (C) and Outcome (O) or other evaluative measures you would like to measure or achieve. Here is an example from McLellan (2010) using PICO:

Title: A systematic review of the corticosteroid regime for pediatric patients with steroid-responsive nephrotic syndrome

Population: pediatric population with steroid-responsive nephrotic syndrome

Intervention: corticosteroids

Comparison: Randomised Controlled Trials (RCT)

Outcome: optimal responsiveness, decreased hospital readmission.

Not an either/or choice

It is the case that one chooses either a scholastic or an interventionist review. Both types have their place and usefulness and can often inform one another. Hammersley (2002: 4–5) comments, 'To say that traditional reviews are unfocused because they don't concentrate on a specific question is like complaining that a map is of no use because it covers a wider area than the one we are currently interested in'. Hammersley makes the point well – that criticism would be better reserved for the quality of the actual research subject to a review, rather than different reasons for doing a review. Nonetheless, when deciding which review to do, there are some other factors worthy of consideration. Within the broader debate of the relative value of different types of review, it is the purpose of the review that drives the choice of the kind of evidence that is needed. From the kind of evidence needed to meet the need at hand, we can select the most appropriate strategy for seeking it out. Boaz et al. (2002) summarise (see Table 4.7) the nature of the evidence currently available for five different interventionist needs.

TABLE 4.7   Evidence and review type in different policy areas

Evidence in different policy areas

Policy areas	Methodological preferences and debates	Nature of the evidence base
Healthcare (especially NHS clinical services)	Gold standard of RCT with additional methodological safeguards. Growing interest in qualitative methods to give complimentary view.	Expensive and accessible via national initiatives such as the Cochrane Collaboration and local clinical effectiveness strategies.
School education	Much research is considered less than robust. Paradigm wars. Eclectic methods competing rather than complementing. Large datasets are analysed but there is relatively little true experimentation.	Fragmented research community. No accessible database of research evidence (but fresh initiatives underway). Few systematic reviews.

Evidence in different policy areas

Policy areas	Methodological preferences and debates	Nature of the evidence base
Criminal justice	General acceptance of experimental methods in determining what works. Preference for theory driven rather than method driven approach to evaluation.	Large, but still limited research base. No online, up-to-date database of research in the UK, but Home Office research reports are available online.
Social care	Preference for qualitative methodologies. Quantification and experimentation often viewed with suspicion and even hostility.	The *Care Database* of research findings is available via the Social Care Institute for Excellence website. Concept of evidence is still hotly contested.
Welfare policy (focus on social security benefits)	Eclectic use of methods to provide complimentary insights. Some longitudinal study but almost no experimentation (because of legal impediments due to the statutory duty to provide equitable benefits).	Evidence created in response to perceived policy problem. Little apparent collation into a stable evidence resource.

Source: Boaz et al., 2002: 7. Originally in Davies and Nutley, 2000

The interventionist review (systematic and meta-analysis) is, therefore, a series of technical tasks aimed at retrieving and synthesising findings from a range of studies that have usually been done in the last couple of decades. The main source of information and data is research articles published in peer reviewed journals and reports. The scholastic review also includes technical tasks not dissimilar to the interventionist review but has the added weight of going beyond findings and journal articles. Books, monographs, biographic materials and gray literature, and more, all come within the scope of the scholastic review. Where the interventionist reviewer is looking for the best available evidence on which they can make a recommendation, the scholastic reviewer is looking at philosophical, methodological and political argument that may have influenced theories, concepts and perspectives on problems. The ability to do competent statistical analysis in the interventionist review does not mean the scholastic review is the easier option. Far from it. The amount and scope of reading they are expected to do can often be far greater than that expected from the interventionist reviewer. This is indicated by Barnett-Page and Thomas (2009), who produced Table 4.8. It shows which kinds of methodological approach and type of research are most likely to be able to be assessed using standard criteria and those that are not. The non-criteria approaches tend to be theory-based and, therefore, have a heavier load of literature than the criteria-based approaches.

TABLE 4.8   Criteria and non-criteria research methods

Non-criteria-based--- Criteria-based

Critical Interpretive Synthesis	Grounded theory	Meta-ethnography	Meta-study	Meta-narrative	Textual narrative synthesis	Framework synthesis	Thematic synthesis	Ecological triangulation

Source: Barnett-Page and Thomas, 2009: 23–25

Conclusions

Whatever type of review you determine is necessary for your purpose, it needs to meet the criteria expected by your readers – it needs to do the job it was designed for. Some of the schemes of assessment in Chapter 2 may help you. There are, of course, two main standpoints here. One is yours, from which you want to produce a valid set of findings and interpretations from your review.

The other standpoint is being able to assess the quality of a review that has already been done. This could be your own review being assessed by others or a review you have found and need to assess. In this section, we will look at some general features to be aware of before specifying a scheme for systematically assessing a review.

Regardless of the type of review you do, there are some common features shared by all good reviews. These include being rigorous, transparent and honest, as well as showing the implications for research methodology, policy and practice. To this end there is a growing, though small, literature, directed to specifying what is to be looked at in a written dissertation. Fitt et al. summarise the literature on literature reviewing in the following way:

> The Doctoral dissertation is a singular opportunity for a PhD candidate to demonstrate they have the capabilities and necessary preparation for independent scholarly work (Isaac, Quinlan, & Walker, 1992; see also Association of American Universities, 1998 and Council of Graduate Schools, 1997, 2004). As part of the only tangible evidence of a candidate's research (Bruce, 1994; Hart, 1999), the literature review allows them to showcase their ability to critically analyse what work has already been done in the field and how it was conducted, what lines of inquiry have yet to be investigated, their ability to synthesise research from their specific field as well as others, and their ability to resolve ambiguities in the vocabulary and literature (Creswell, 2008; Fraenkel & Wallen, 2006; Gall, Gall, & Borg, 2007; Gay, Mills, Airasian, 2006; Johnson & Christensen, 2004; McMillan,2008; Schumacher & McMillan, 2006). As such, the Doctoral dissertation literature review can be viewed as one barometer of the overall health of Doctoral research training. (Fitt et al., 2009: 4)

It may be useful, at this stage, to summarise the general skills and capabilities that this chapter has indicated will be required to do a literature review. There are four that are very important, and which require special attention by the research student and practitioner alike.

1. Prior understanding: you will be expected to demonstrate a sufficient level of prior under-standing of the topic and methodology. The focus for this is normally in the literature review and chapter on methodology. The latter, is, of course, often heavily dependent on the use of the literature dealing with methodology. Therefore, if your main methodology were survey-based you would be expected to show familiarity with the literature on surveys. This may involve a critical appraisal of key works that advocate a positivistic approach to research, identifying core authors and relevant studies as exemplars of the approach. This is required because you need to justify your choice of approach; this involves the construc-tion of an argument. The literature will help you provide evidence and substance for a justification for your choice of approach. At the same time, you will become familiar with the literature on the methodology and be able to show this in your thesis.

2. Persistence and diligence: you will not normally find all the information you require in a few weeks. You will therefore need to be persistent in your work. This is especially the case with the search of the literature. Initial search strategies may not reveal what you may have wanted; you therefore need to be flexible and search more widely or use more complex combinations of words and phrases. Persistence also means being thorough in your search; by making detailed records of how you managed the administrative function. This is because a comprehensive search for the literature on a topic is very much a matter of managing the administration of search sheets, records, databases, references located, items obtained and those ordered from the library and so on. The use of all relevant sources and resources is therefore required to be shown in your thesis. This can be written up in the methodology chapter or the review of the literature.

3. Justification: a major requirement is that you provide sufficient argument to justify the topic for your research. This means showing that what you propose to research is worthy to be researched. This normally involves the use of existing literature to focus on a particular context. This context may be *methodological*, that you propose to employ a methodology on a topic in one area that has not previously been used in this area. This may involve constructing an argument to show how this methodology relates to the topic and thereby suggest what its potential may be, if tried. Alternatively, you may provide a summative or *integrative* review. This would involve summarising past research and making recommen-dations on how your research will be an addition to the existing stock of evidence. In this case, you would be proposing to apply a tried approach to your topic. Whatever you use as the focus for your justification, one thing must always be seen; that is, evidence from the literature. You are therefore expected to avoid using personal opinions and views; and never submit a statement without sufficient backing.

4. Scholarly conventions: something of this expectation has already been covered in a previ-ous section but there are a few points to add. You are required to use the literature in a way that is proper. At the most basic level this means citing references in a standard for-mat recognised by the academic community. It also means using the literature in a way that is considered and considerate. You may not be able to cite all the references that you

locate in your search. You will therefore need to exercise judgement as to which references are the most important, which means the most relevant to your purpose. An attitude of critical appraisal will be necessary to avoid a simplistic summative description of the contents of articles and books. This involves being charitable to the ideas of others while at the same time evaluating the usefulness of those ideas to your own work.

In summary

- There are different kinds of review: the two main ones are the scholastic and the interventionist. Neither is better than or superior to the other.
- It is the case, though, that the scholastic review needs to precede an Interventionist review. Both types of review need the researcher to be able to understand different epistemological positions and their relative strengths, weaknesses, arguments and reasons for existing. This includes understanding the consequences of each epistemological position for research, practice and ethical issues.
- Different types of review and their associated methodologies can be synthesised. The choice of which type of review to do is largely a matter decided by your research question or hypothesis. It is not the case that either type of review is politically neutral.
- You may aim to verify existing research on a topic or problem, or to generate a new position or understanding of an event or behaviour. Either way this decision is a political one.
- Finally, the wider your knowledge of philosophical debates, the more you will be able to extract from the literature and the more likely it is you will develop a deeper, more innovative interpretation of your field of study.

5

Argumentation Analysis

Key questions

- What is an argument?
- Why is understanding argument necessary?
- How can we understand the structure of an argument?
- How can arguments be analysed and evaluated?
- How do arguments relate to the nature of debate in research?

Core skills

- Evaluate arguments in ways that are clear and systematic
- Use analytical techniques that make visible methodological assumptions used in a research study
- Identify the consequences of methodological assumptions when used for policy and in practice
- Critically analyse, synthesise, validate and evaluate complex arguments from different sources
- Assess the credibility, quality and integrity of different standpoints and perspectives in a piece of research.

Introduction

Argument is in the spirit of many disciplines. A researcher seeing fault, error or other possibilities in the work of another and making and suggestions for improvement or change is what makes for what we call progress in the ideas and practices of human studies. Being able to recognise the structure and substance of an argument is a necessary ability in everyday life but especially so for the successful academic researcher. If you cannot see the logic of even the simplest argument, then you cannot legitimately develop the work of another, and suggest alternative courses of actions, or other ways of interpreting a phenomenon.

This chapter is about how to analyse an argument, in particular, those types most commonly found in the social sciences and humanities. As can be demonstrated by a visit to the library, almost any article in a social science journal is based on argument and most research is based on the one or other position that the researcher has chosen to use as a starting point. Such positions are usually based on what the researcher believes is the best method for acquiring knowledge about, and a standpoint on, a range of debates. There are, for example, a number of questions that social scientists face when undertaking research. Should the researcher inform subjects that they are being studied? Should the researcher remain impartial when the research has a moral element? Should the views of subjects be taken into account? There are many more questions like these that the researcher has to deal with in their work. The main consideration in this chapter is with methods for analysing and understanding an argument.

What is an argument?

An argument involves putting forward reasons to influence someone's belief that what you are proposing is the case (Hinderer, 1992). Whichever way someone makes an argument they are attempting to convince others of the validity (or logic) of how they see the world and convince us that we should see it the way they do. An argument therefore has at least two components, a *point* and a *reason*:

> making a point (or statement) by providing sufficient reason (or evidence) for the point to be accepted by others.

These two elements are related and the movement can go either way to form the argument, a movement from either a point to reason, or from evidence to conclusion (the point). The movement from one to the other can be supported by other components called inferential devices. These are rules or principles that permit the making of a claim on the basis of some evidence (or warrants). We will be looking more closely at these later.

In our definitions of the types of argument given below, we exclude arguments based purely on what is called formal logic. Our concern is with those types of arguments most commonly found in the social sciences, based on supposition, inference and assertion (see Table 5.1). These are much less structured and often more difficult to analyse than arguments based on formal logic. Fisher, whose work we will be looking at shortly, illustrates this point. He defines argument as consisting of 'giving reasons for some conclusion: the reasons are put forward in order to establish, support, justify, prove or demonstrate the conclusion' (1993: 140). He also shows that there are elements in formal logic that are useful when analysing assertion and supposition. He states that:

> Every argument contains its reasons and its conclusions: the reasons presented for a conclusion are usually called premises of the argument. The question the logician is interested in is whether they are good reasons for the conclusion; if they the premisses are said to entail or imply the conclusion, and the conclusion is said to follow from the premisses or to be implied or entailed by them. (Fisher, 1993: 140)

TABLE 5.1 Definitions: Inference, assertion and supposition

Inference	an assertion made on the basis of something else observed or taken as knowledge; used in deductive and inductive arguments.
Assertion	to make a declaration on the existence or cause of something with or without the use of evidence.
Supposition	making an assumption about what is, or is not, a case or state of affairs.

Regardless of how many components an argument has or how complex it may be, all arguments are open to question and can be challenged.

The importance of argument in the social sciences

Words such as *logic, valid, premise, reliable, reason* and *conclusion* make up the vocabulary of argument. A whole discipline has developed, dedicated to logic and the search for undeniable propositions. It is not necessary to be an expert in formal logic or philosophy to construct and analyse arguments. But why should social scientists take an interest in logic and argument? There are so many reasons for understanding argument that we could write another book. However, the main reasons are outlined in the following three points.

1. A great deal of research is done by researchers who may, for the sake of illustration, be classified as interactionist, linguist, feminist, Marxist, ethnomethodologist, post-structuralist, behaviourist and so on. Researchers working within these and other approaches tend to hold different or differing opinions on the nature of reality (ontology) and how knowledge can be acquired of that reality (epistemology), and therefore what counts as valid knowledge. Hence, we have the basis for debate and argument between researchers.

2. Many researchers are particularly knowledgeable about the complexities and implications of holding one view rather than another about what counts as research and argument. Hence, they are able to understand the different types of argument and the implications of different standpoints. This enables them to be active participants in the debates that are known in their fields of study.

3. For many people the debates that go on between researchers seem esoteric and this often leads to bewilderment and confusion. Researchers do not always make clear the origins of their ideas or explain the rationale for them. Students are left wondering what a debate is *really* about and why people invest so much time and effort in them. However, if we work from the premise that differences of opinion over matters such as the interpretation of data, the meaning of concepts, the validity of knowledge, and the topic for inquiry, are the basis of scientific progress, then there is a need to be able to understand and analyse argument.

Classical tradition

An understanding of the origins of logic can be a useful knowledge base from which to start argumentation analysis and understand the importance of debate to research. In this section, we look at the classical traditions of argument and at some of the forms that debate has taken in the social sciences and humanities.

What does deductive mean?

It is commonly a statement or theory whose truth or falsity is known in advance of experience or observation (a priori: prior to experience) – referring to instances of reasoning, in which the conclusion follows from the premises. Deduction (or inference) can proceed from the general to the particular, general to general and particular to particular.

The Greek thinkers, such as Socrates (circa. 469–399 BC), Aristotle (384–322 BC) and Plato (circa. 427–347 BC), are most commonly associated with laying the foundations for our concern with logical thinking. Being able to understand

and challenge an argument was a valuable skill in ancient Greece. This is because in legal cases you had to defend yourself. Some people earned their living from teaching others how to present an argument and defend themselves from accusations. The Sophists, as they were called, taught others not only argumentation analysis but also how to convince others of something when that thing was wrong. Today the term 'sophistry' is used as a derogatory name for when a person employs false reason to deceive others. It was Socrates, however, who began the development of argumentation analysis. His method, called *Socratic dialogue* (or the Socratic Method), consists of a question and answer technique. Opponents are asked different types of question in ways that dissect their argument into its basic elements including the unsubstantiated assumptions on which it is based.

What does inductive mean?

This is commonly a statement whose truth or falsity is made more probable by the accumulation of confirming evidence (a posteriori: based on experience) – referring to instances of reasoning, in which statements are made about a phenomenon based on observations of instances of that phenomenon. It consists in arguing that because all instances of *a* so far observed have the property *b*, all further observations of *a* will also have the property *b*.

Questions are asked that entice opponents to contradict themselves or reveal the assumptions on which they base their position, or admit extreme consequences that may emanate from their stance. The elements of the argument are then repackaged or reassembled to present the opponent with the flaws in their reasoning. Socratic dialogue, although it often appears to be a conversational art form, is based on logical thinking and can be learnt by most competent people. Socrates was so good at the technique, he annoyed too many people who regarded themselves as 'wise'; he was put on trial for heresy and sentenced to death. Part of the reason for other people being frustrated with Socrates was his ability to produce humorous arguments.

For the Greeks logic was not a theoretical or abstract pastime. For Aristotle, logic was a poietic science, or what is known as an organon (an instrument) of science. Aristotelian logic aimed to set criteria for proper scientific thinking. His approach was essentially deductive (as opposed to inductive).

The deductive approach dominated until the sixteenth century when challenges were made to it, and other forms of systematic thinking began to develop. One of the more pervasive forms was positivism. This led to a more abstract approach to logic, based on mathematical concepts. Twentieth-century philosophers such as Bertrand Russell and Alfred Whitehead aimed to construct universal systems of logic. Positivism, however, failed to provide the basis for a universal scheme of fundamental descriptive laws from which predictions could be made.

Positivism

The idea that logic could be used as the basis of a method for investigating the nature of the world took hold during the Enlightenment in the eighteenth century. From the aim to uncover the laws that governed the workings of the universe, to a view of what constituted reality (ontology) and of knowing about that reality (epistemology), developed a standpoint that we commonly call the attitude of scientific inquiry. In part, this involved a particular doctrine applied to the method of science, which consisted of a set of principles about how scientific (i.e. valid and reliable) knowledge could be acquired. Table 5.2 shows the main principles and what they mean.

TABLE 5.2   The principles of the scientific method

Principles	What they mean
Observation	Only that which can be observed can be measured. All basic concepts must be clearly defined, for example, what is meant by length and what is to be measured, before they can be used (operationalised). Systematic observation is therefore necessary for science.
Hypothesis	On the basis of systematic observation, the scientist formulates a hypothesis (a formulation proposition) that explains what has been observed.
Experimentation	The hypothesis is tested to ascertain its validity. This involves attempting to verify the hypothesis by trying to show the hypothesis is wrong (i.e. falsifiability). Hence if the hypothesis cannot be shown to be wrong, it must be true.
Scientific laws	From the results of experimentation, general explanations (or laws) can be developed that wholly or partly explain particular phenomena, for example, the law of gravity.
Theory formulation	The discovery of particular laws can lead to the development of more general theories (or models) that enable more things to be explained using a unified approach.
Flexibility	If new evidence is found that falsifies or changes an explanation the scientist should acknowledge this and change the law and theory.
Replicability	The procedures used, including definitions of main concepts along with data, should be open for other scientists to scrutinise, thereby enabling others to replicate the work.
Objectivity	Scientists should be neutral observers of the world and not concern themselves with morality or ethics, nor should they be motivated by anything other than the pursuit of knowledge.

It was the logical positivists (e.g. Carnap et al., 1973[1929]; Ayer, 1946[1936]; Hempel, 1965; Schlick, 1974[1918]), associated with the Vienna Circle of the 1920s, who were mostly responsible for the debate on and about positivism, along with Wittgenstein (1972[1921]) and Popper (1959[1934]). For the logical positivists, science was concerned with the problem of verifying, using reliable methods, the meaning or existence of something.

Reading advice: Positivists vs realists

If you're interested in a full account of how positivists and realists differ in their assumptions and what this means for research, see Hart (2005).

They tried to limit inquiry and belief to those things that could be firmly established. Hence, ideas about aesthetics, morality, ethics, judgement and religion were assigned to metaphysics – as being outside the interest of, what they took to be, proper logical empirical science (see Hospers, 1988; Trigg, 1993).

Debate among researchers

The standpoint that positivism (especially logical positivism) demanded from science was questioned by scientists wanting to investigate the social world. Many social scientists were particularly keen to rid themselves of the stricter forms of positivism. Social order, patterns of social relationships and modes of thinking did not fit with the belief that there was only 'one absolute logic' and one form of approach to rational understanding (i.e. truth). The connection between human reasoning and the procedures of positivistic science therefore came to be a subject for debate. In opposition to absolutism, it was proposed that there were many logics. This counter-position, known as relativism, found expression in such areas as linguistic semantics and psychology. For example, Piaget and Inhelder (1955) argued that the variety and complexity of natural language and behaviour implied that there was no single logic, but that there may be a range of acquired rules, encoded in the brain, that people follow. Hence, what could be considered rational, logical and even the truth was a matter for debate.

Logic became seen as normative; that standards of behaviour follow cultural conventions rather than ideal standards of rationality established by formal logic (Turner, 1984). In economics, for example, models and theories were developed to describe real life decision making (Simon, 1957). Examples and illustrations were devised and case studies undertaken to show how real decision making deviated from rational models – what actually happened was compared with what ought to have happened in an ideal situation. The aim was to improve decision making by identifying the key variables that all effective decisions needed. In this way, some theorists, such as Cohen (1986), maintain the usefulness of normative logic because it provides what they consider to be an ideal standard for comparison.

Extended example: The Azande people and the logic of believing in witchcraft

Not all social scientists, however, aimed to produce comparisons of everyday logic with that of science. The anthropologist Edward Evans-Pritchard (1902–73), for example, undertook a study of the Azande people from southern Sudan (1937). His interest was with the mental life of what were then commonly called 'primitives'. Contemporary views held the position that tribal peoples tended to have a primitive mentality: they were intellectual inferiors to Europeans. Comparing Western scientific logic with the superstitions and myths of tribal people was the norm for research. Evans-Pritchard's fieldwork refuted this comparison and belief; it demolished the divide between 'us' and 'them'.

Evans-Pritchard did this by focusing on the mythical beliefs and practices of the Azande. The defining feature for Azande life was the pervasive belief in witchcraft and sorcery. For example, no Azande would venture out on a journey or similar undertaking without first consulting an oracle. The purpose was to see if any misfortune would be likely to befall them on a journey, or to see if anyone had bewitched them. To European science, this kind of belief was not a religion or the basis of logical thought; it was a measure of the primitiveness of tribal societies. Evans-Pritchard opposed this view. He showed that the metaphysical ideas of any society could be treated with the same seriousness as those of any of the great world religions. Added to this, he showed that the logic of such beliefs was *situational*, being dependent upon the cultural conventions or ways of viewing the world of particular groups.

Hence Western science, according to Evans-Pritchard, is just one way of understanding the world, and although successful in terms of technology, it is not the only or dominant form of understanding to be found in human cultures. If we want to understand such beliefs as Azande magic, we need to understand the use and nature of them as experienced by the Azande in their everyday lives. Trying to compare and measure notions about intellectual superiority was, according to Evans-Pritchard, inappropriate due to the fact that Western science and Azande witchcraft were incomparable; they were two different ways of thinking about the world and organising daily activities.

Therefore, in terms of our debate, we can identify two key points. The first is that Evans-Pritchard argued that non-literate peoples' apparent irrational (illogical) beliefs formed a coherent and logical system of ideas. The second point is the approach Evans-Pritchard took to understanding the logic of Azande belief and practices. His approach was informed by science. It was based on close observation, questioning and inquiry into what was going on in Azande culture, leading him, and us, to a more balanced, unprejudiced and even objective view of such beliefs. Hence, the procedures of science can help us understand science itself, as well as non-scientific based phenomena, and what could be considered logical.

Through this potted and condensed history of logic, we can see how some social scientists have been classified into different camps depending on their degree of allegiance to particular (and somewhat idealised) methodological traditions. Another point to note is that when we talk about different positions, we are entering the grey area at the boundary of social science and philosophy: the place where understanding not only becomes difficult, but also reveals the reasons for many of the fundamental differences within the social sciences. That locale (place) is the realm of philosophy where questions about the nature of reality and how we can acquire knowledge are the subject matter.

Many researchers, however, still hold to a notion of the possibility of positivism. Even those theorists who want to counter the extremes of positivism still have to enter into the debate over positivism. Positivism therefore still exerts a strong influence on the aims and structure of social science thinking and the nature of argument. We can reiterate our point about the nature of debate in the social sciences by saying that differences are based on different approaches and answers to questions and issues related to methodological policies, perspectives and standpoints to do with research. Table 5.3 summarises some of the issues for the design of research.

TABLE 5.3   Issues for research design

What is reality?	*Ontological issues* are concerned with what we believe to exist and able to be investigated. For example, what is the subject matter for psychology? Is reality singular and objective, existing apart from me and my perceptions and cultural biases? Or, is reality shaped by my prior understanding and assumptions?
What procedures can be used to establish what can be accepted as real?	*Epistemological issues* are concerned with how we can know anything. For example, is my knowledge wholly 'gained through senses' and is, therefore, objectively real or is my knowledge a matter of how I perceive the world? Can I include intuition, personal experience or only the data to make claims?
What is the process of research that can ensure valid knowledge?	*Methodological issues* are concerned with how we can validate what we claim to be knowledge. For example, how can we have a logic of inquiry that gives us assurance in our knowledge? Should we use a deductive or inductive process, and aim for generalisation and explanation or context-based description aimed at an emerging design, categories and theories? Are we interested in prediction, explanation or understanding?
What is the role of values and ethics?	*Axiological issues* are concerned with the personal values, morality and ethics of the researcher. For example, whose side should a researcher be on, if any – the underdog or the elite? Should I aim to ignore the moral issues of the subject matter and my own feeling or use these as part of my research?

(Continued)

What are reliable techniques for collecting data about claims?	*Data-collection issues* are concerned with which techniques are the most reliable, and which kinds of data the more accurate. For example, is the survey questionnaire better than the observational case study? Shall I use quantitative data rather than qualitative because people regard these as more objective? Or is qualitative evidence better because it will show that all data are dependent on interpretation for their meaning?
What is the language of research?	*Rhetorical issues* are concerned with how to talk about and write up research. For example, is writing in the third person more objective than doing so in the first person? Should I be formal, precise with definitions and aim to quantify or use informal language that is easier to understand and show how understanding evolved?

A continuing debate exists, therefore, between many different camps about what we should use as the standpoint for thinking about and investigating the social world. We can clarify this debate without over-simplifying it by saying that there are two main protagonists – realists and anti-realists. Realists take the positivist line that there is a world to be investigated which exists independent of human belief, perception, culture and language: reality and truth are therefore to be uncovered or discovered. Anti-realists take a different view. They believe that the world exists, but its character and the ways we understand it are constructed and shaped by the language we use to describe it. What we understand as reality is, according to anti-realists, not something that is universal but plural: there are many or multiple realities, each separate and based on different assumptions for understanding.

Logic, in the broad sense of the term, refers to various forms of reasoning over why one position rather than another should be the one used to study a particular subject matter. There is no single absolute logic from which universal truths can be determined. In social science, logical reasoning takes a range of forms and is presented in many different styles. The logic of a piece of research or school of researchers is not always clear as it can be based on unstated methodological assumptions. These assumptions shape the ways in which such researchers approach the social world and how they investigate it and eventually report on their investigations.

Methodological assumptions, like those we attributed to Marx in Chapter 3, are important to understand. This is because they orient a researcher towards certain ways of thinking about the subject matter in which they are interested and help them to make decisions on how to undertake research. These assumptions frame the view a researcher will have of the meaning and operationalisation of concept and influence what they regard as the goals of social science. In this case, the dominant goal for Marxist researchers is structural analysis of covert forces and relationships that give rise to manifest inequalities and forms of oppression; theoretical explanatory analysis therefore dominates many Marxist-inspired studies. By understanding the methodological assumptions from which a researcher starts, you can analyse the use of these in any particular study that claims to have used them. You could compare, for instance, how different Marxist studies have used the concept of alienation. The comparison may seek to analyse the different arguments put forward for why the concept has been used differently from other studies. In this way, all approaches, whether they have an explicit argument or not, are open to analysis.

Analysing and evaluating arguments

If our objective is to analyse and then evaluate an argument, we need some methods for doing so. Whatever method we use, it needs to be clear, consistent and systematic. It is these qualities that give coherence and intelligibility to analysis and evaluation. They can also help with the main difficulty of producing an explicit evaluation; laying out the steps and reasons for what has been undertaken. We need these kinds of ground rules because of the divergent nature and styles of argument in the social sciences. We will shortly be looking at two methods on how to deal intelligently and fairly with whatever argument we come across. They have been chosen because of the flexibility they offer and because they can provide a systematic approach to analysis and evaluation. The first method, Argumentation Analysis, was developed by Stephen Toulmin (1958) during the 1950s. Toulmin developed an approach to argumentation analysis that was rooted in the practice rather than the theory of logic. Toulmin provides a flexible approach to the examination of actual procedures used in practical argument. Complementing Toulmin's philosophical approach, Fisher (1993) provides a method for a systematic reading of texts. This initial reading technique enables the reader to systematically extract the main elements of any argument for the purposes of evaluation. These flexible but explicit approaches to argumentation analysis are especially useful to the social scientist in that they allow both analysis and evaluation of arguments based on assertion and methodological commitment.

Toulmin's method of argumentation analysis

In his book, *The Uses of Argument* (1958), Stephen Toulmin sets out a model of argumentation and provides a method for its analysis. The basis of Toulmin's approach is relatively simple. He proposes that an argument can be broken up into a number of basic elements. Figure 5.1 shows these elements and the relationships that exist between them.

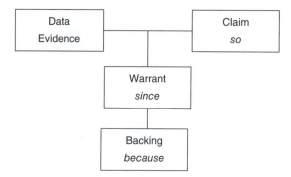

FIGURE 5.1   Toulmin's structure of an argument

For example, if we were to say, 'performance at university depends on age and gender', we would be making a claim. It is a contentious claim that is open to challenge. It is claiming that a relationship exists between academic performance, age and gender: hence we have three variables. What evidence (data) would allow us to accept such a claim? We may expect such a claim to be based on empirical research by reliable researchers using reliable methods. If this were so, the claim would be based on evidence. The evidence would be made available in the research report. The pedigree of the reports may be shown in who produced them, that is, who undertook the research. If those who had undertaken the research were respected academics, then backing will have been provided for the initial claim.

A challenge can be made to any or all elements. Is the claim justified? Are the evidence, warrant and backing justified? Added to these, we can ask whether the claim stands up to major challenges. Is it sufficiently robust or does it need to be reworded? For example, a challenge to the warrant may be made on any or all of these grounds: the research was out of date; the conclusions in the reports did not logically follow from the data collected; the evidence was inappropriate; or the data collection techniques were unreliable.

Therefore, we have claims, evidence, warrants, and backing:

Claim – an arguable statement.

Evidence – data used to support the claim.

Warrant (or *permit*) – an expectation that provides the link between the evidence and claim.

Backing – context and assumptions used to support the validity of the warrant and evidence.

Figure 5.2 is an example from everyday life. In dry summers, consumers are asked and expected to save water through careful and limited use. This is normally taken to mean water should only be used for essential things – watering lawns,

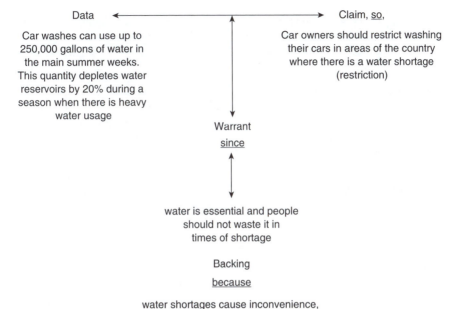

FIGURE 5.2 An argument for saving water

filling swimming pools and washing cars are prohibited. The argument for this could have the structure shown above.

There are a number of ways in which these main elements can be assembled to produce an argument. There are also variations on the use of each element. Claims, for example, come in five main types: *claims of fact, claims of value, claims of policy, claims of concept* and *claims of interpretation*. These are explained in Table 5.4.

TABLE 5.4 Different types of claim

Claims of fact are statements that can be proven to be true or false. For example, statements such as London is the capital of England, or there are three universities in Manchester, are either true or false: they can be verified or refuted using evidence such as an authoritative reference (e.g. encyclopaedia). The difference between a claim based on facts and other forms of claim is that others require additional warrants and backing for their acceptance.

Claims of value cannot be proven true or false: they are judgements about the worth of something. For example, someone may make the statement that watching *Coronation Street* is a waste of time: this is a judgemental statement. To back it up they may add a qualifying standard, such as watching soap operas does nothing to improve the mind or enhance our understanding of the world around us. One may agree with the value claim or make a challenge through the counter-claim that modern living is stressful, that people need relaxation, and that watching *Coronation Street* is a form of relaxation and therefore good for people.

(Continued)

Claims of policy are normative statements about what ought to be done rather than what is done. For example, someone may claim that public libraries are an essential part of the culture of a civilised country and should therefore be protected from budget cuts. In this case, we see a claim of policy combined with a claim of value.

Claims of concept are about definitions and the recognition of the language used. For example, when comparing views on abortion or euthanasia, the way the claim was worded would be important. Some organisations, such as Life, would claim abortion was the murder of an unborn child. The claim employs particular definitions that are not only restrictive but also emotive. The use of words is not therefore as given in dictionary definitions, but is a matter of interpretative use.

Claims of interpretation are about proposals on how some data or evidence is to be understood. Facts mean nothing without interpretation and interpretations can and often do differ.

The range in the types of claims from which an argument can be constructed shows that almost everything is arguable. Facts can be verified, but their interpretation can be a matter of dispute. Opinions over an interpretation also require substantive support in much the same way as any structured argument. Facts alone are not always sufficient or available. Intellectual debate also employs scenarios, illustrations, analogies and models to provide substance and backing to an interpretation.

Other difficulties arise in distinguishing opinions from personal preferences, judgements and inferences. There may be little dispute about the ingredients for a pint of Guinness, but a great deal of dispute can arise over, say, whether it tastes sweet or bitter, or whether it is acceptable to consume alcohol and so on. There is no methodical or prescriptive way of resolving such disagreements.

Inference and personal preference can, however, be identified and analysed. An inference is an interpretation we make on the basis of observing something else. For example, we may see a student standing on a chair in the library shouting 'Fire!' and infer that there was a fire in the library. This is because people *do not usually* stand on chairs shouting 'Fire!'

Like claims, there are also different types of warrant (or permits). The two main types of warrant are stated warrants and unstated warrants. The function of all warrants is to link or provide a bridge between a claim and what is presented as support (backing) for that claim. Warrants are therefore about the basic assumptions underlying claims; they are basic beliefs or fundamental premises about something, from which a person makes a statement. For example, in the American Declaration of Independence, Thomas Jefferson made it clear what his assumptions were by stating that, 'all men are created equal, that they are endowed by their creator with certain unalienable Rights, that among these are Life, Liberty and the pursuit of happiness'. He prefaces this declaration (claim) with the warrant, 'We hold these truths to be self-evident ...'

In the social sciences. most approaches have sets of methodological assumptions about social order. We can take an example from sociology to illustrate what we mean here. Sociologists working from within a structuralist approach tend to regard social order as an outcome of relationships between institutions and dominant values. How they perceive these relationships makes for a significant difference between them. Structural functionalists perceive a relationship as based on consensus while conflict structuralists perceive a relationship as based on domination. While each of these approaches has a long and complex philosophical backdrop, it is the basic assumptions that theorists in each approach use that shape the nature of the warrants they use for their claims about the world.

A more commonplace example of an argument can be seen in the attitude many British people have towards their elected representatives in Parliament. The broad assumption among the electorate and press is that elected members of Parliament should be accountable, honest and exhibit high standards of ethical behaviour, but in practice this is not always the case. In Toulmin's terms, the situation would look like this. Some members of Parliament have behaved in ways not becoming to their position by taking money to ask questions in Parliament: these are the data, for which concrete examples could be given. The claim could be: members should not be permitted to take money or other incentives to ask questions in Parliament (a value claim). This is based on the warrant: members should be honest and act in the best interests of the general public and not a minority of vested interests.

The excerpt from the Declaration of Independence is an example of a stated warrant. But not all assumptions are stated in an argument. There may be a number of reasons for this, including that the author assumes the reader is familiar with the assumptions of the argument or that the author wishes to disguise the assumptions used.

Extended example: Unstated assumptions in an argument

The following extract shows an argument from an unstated assumption. It is by Vickie Shields (1990) who is writing for the converted.

> Any critical study of visual communication must necessarily address the question of how meaning is communicated through visual images. Meaning is not found intricately woven into the fabric of the text to be unearthed by a trained scholar, nor is the meaning of a text to be defined solely in individual psyches. The ability of a visual text to communicate meaning involves an intricate interplay between the codes and messages encoded into the text at the time of its

(Continued)

production and the cultural experience of subjectivity the spectator brings to the viewing of that image. The production of visual texts takes place within dominant ideological structures. Texts therefore, have the ability to reflect or reproduce dominant cultural discourses about such things as gender, race, ethnicity, class, age, education and sexual preference.

This extract is from the introduction of an article. What we have is, in the first instance, a text aimed at a friendly audience of like-minded people. The language and concepts used are vague and without reference. To the converted these concepts and words will be familiar. The author also expects her main statements, for example, 'meaning is not found intricately woven into the fabric of the text to be unearthed by a trained scholar, nor *is* the meaning of a text to be defined solely in individual psyches', to be meaningful and expects the reader to know to whose work she is referring.

This may be taken to be Judith Williamson's *Decoding Advertisements* (1979), which is a major milestone in the feminist analysis of advertising. Similarly, the statement, 'The ability of a visual text to communicate meaning involves an intricate interplay between the codes and messages encoded into the text at the time of its production', has a literature behind it. This may be the semiological approach of Ferdinand de Saussure (1966), and Barthes (1967); and the ways in which it has been employed by academics such as Nichols in *Ideology and the Image* (1981), and Sut Jhally in *The Codes of Advertising* (1987). Hence, our investigations would take us into some interesting areas of cultural studies, providing us with the opportunity to read and understand some of the major developments, arguments and applications of methodologies and techniques used over the past decade and more.

Some other points to note about this short extract are its general methodological approach and polemical character. References to broad social concepts such as class, race, age, education, ethnicity and gender tend to show a bias towards a structuralist approach within cultural studies. You could therefore expect many of the methodological assumptions of structuralism to be part of Shields's general argument, and if we wanted to inquire further into her argument, we would need to become familiar with those assumptions and styles of discourse used by structuralist theorists. We would need to learn about the conventions of the approach – the styles of presenting argument and analysis about the broad, as well as subtle differences between sub-schools within the approach. More particularly, it can be seen that these assumptions are motivated by a standpoint or perspective originating in the works of Marx. This can be seen in the vocabulary of 'dominant ideological structures' and reference to the notion of 'reproduction of cultural discourses'. Therefore, from this basic starting point, the reader could begin to describe the assumptions of this argument as motivated by a moral standpoint. These are not stated, but are apparent in the language of this extract.

Critical evaluation

Remember in Chapter 1 we explored another aspect of this debate, with a critical evaluation of the literature on advertising.

Whether it is easier or harder to write for a readership that has predigested your position and found it agreeable is open to debate. There is no reason why you should not agree with the moral, political, religious, or methodological attitude of an author. But it is your responsibility to analyse first, to think about the argument you read and then evaluate it. The act and process of argumentation analysis involves a reflective attitude; you must put to one side (i.e. bracket) preconceived allegiances and preferences, as well as prejudice and political opposition to approaches.

Some prejudicial forms of assumptions can originate from ethnocentrism – the belief that one's own culture is more important and better than any other. Many of the founding theorists in social science, such as Durkheim, Tönnies and Simmel, made ethnocentric assumptions. They assumed that modern industrial urban society was superior to rural non-industrial society; that is, people in industrial society were mentally and socially more advanced than so-called tribal peoples with their primitive mentality. This kind of armchair ethnocentrism was challenged by anthropologists such as Bronislow Malinowski and Evans-Pritchard, who actually lived among other cultures. Nevertheless, the notion of cultural development in terms of a hierarchical contrast remains a major tradition in Western social thought.

Along with the task of identifying warrants, the reader must also look for qualifiers and restrictions. Some arguments use words such as *probably, some, many* and *generally,* which often indicate a qualifier. The function of a qualifier is to limit the scope of a claim in order to make it more acceptable and to place limits on its application. For example, in Britain there is an ongoing debate about arming the police force. Some people have made the claim that the majority of police officers should be armed. The word *majority* is a qualifier: it limits the scope of an armed police force by allowing for exceptions. The claim is stating that not all, only the majority, of police officers should be armed. The claim has allowed for a possible restriction. This may be that only police officers trained and psychologically able to use firearms should be allowed to carry them.

The other major element of an argument is backing. Backing can take the form of additional information, perhaps an account of personal experience or a hypothetical scenario. In the example of the British police force, the backing may include recounting incidents in which unarmed officers were faced with armed criminals. Concrete illustrations are usually much more convincing than hypothetical or generalised scenarios. However, the main and most common form of backing is the legitimacy conferred on an argument through the use of academic style.

Fisher's method of critical reading

Fisher (1993) provides us with a systematic technique for reading analytically. His technique enables the evaluation of any argument to be done by analysis of its formal structure. Words that are used to structure an argument are the focus for the analysis. Words such as *thus* and *therefore* are highlighted, because they are used to link evidence with claims and suggest inference, reasons and conclusions. From this, the structure of the argument can be seen or even rewritten as an argument diagram. Like Toulmin's approach, Fisher's technique can be very effective because it allows you to think through the argument you are analysing. Fisher's approach differs from Toulmin's in that he provides us with a systematic set of procedures for the analysis and subsequent evaluation of an argument. We will look first at his method for systematically extracting an argument.

The purpose of the following procedure, adapted from Fisher (1993), is to extract the conclusions (C) and reasons (R) of an argument.

1. First look quickly through the text in order to get an initial sense of the author's project and purpose.
2. Read the text again circling any inference indicators (thus, therefore, etc.) as you read.
3. Look for conclusions and any stated reasons for these. Underline the conclusions and place in brackets < > any reasons.
4. Attempt at this stage to summarise the author's argument. If there is no clear argument, ask what point(s) the author is trying to make and why.
5. Identify what you take to be conclusions by marking them up with a C – remember that there may be interim conclusions as well as the main one. Typical indications of a conclusion are the use of the following words: therefore, thus, hence, consequently, and so on. Be careful not to assume that a summary or formulation provided by the author of their argument, so far, must be the conclusion.
6. Taking the main conclusion, ask yourself what reasons are presented in the text for believing this conclusion or why you are being asked to accept this conclusion. Typical indications of reasons are words and phrases such as 'because', 'since', 'it follows', and 'so on'.
7. The reasons provided for the argument can be ranked into a structure. Go through each reason (R) asking whether it is essential or secondary backing for the argument. From this, you will be left with the core reasons for the argument. You will then be able to construct an argument diagram with the following structures:

    R1 + R2 = (therefore) C [for joint reasons]

    R1 or R2 = (therefore) C [for independent reasons]

Variations on these structures are common. For example, a main conclusion may be supported by an interim conclusion and several basic reasons. So, taking the first equation above:

R1 + R2 = (therefore) C1 (interim conclusion)

C1 + R3 = (therefore) C2 (main conclusion)

This is a relatively simple method to use and depends only on close reading. We are not yet asking whether the reasons identified make good (i.e. sound) reasons;

this stage is about analysis, not evaluation. It is not a prescriptive method that will instantly reveal an argument. This is especially the case in the social sciences, where many arguments are based on assertion and hypothetical statements and it is important to become skilled in recognising such arguments in order to avoid committing the fallacy of taking for real a hypothetical scenario. Typical indicators of hypothetical and assertive arguments are: if, suppose, provided that, and so on. Finally, the extent to which you can adequately analyse and evaluate an argument, depends on your grasp of the subject-specific language and its problem definitions. Bearing these points in mind we can now look at the evaluation of an argument.

Practice with Fisher's notational technique should enable most competent research scholars to extract the details of any argument. It is essential to have the structure of the argument laid out before you can evaluate it. When evaluating an argument, you are attempting to assess not only the logical but also the contextual structure of the argument as a whole and of its parts. Fisher's method for argument evaluation can be applied to most forms of analysis. His method is based on what he calls the assertability question. This is a method involving questioning both the premise and conclusions of an argument. The main assertability question is: what argument (what *you* would need to believe) or evidence (what *you* would need to know) would justify the acceptance of the conclusion?

Note that this question is not attempting to establish truth. It is about establishing justified reasons for accepting an assertion. The question is not therefore delving into the realm of philosophical scepticism, where truth, reality and meaning are all open to abstract debate and doubt. Fisher's method is about using normal everyday standards of evaluation and judgement. For this reason, his method should be usable by any competent person. In practice, therefore, the assertability question assumes that most people can apply an appropriate standard and that such a standard will need justification and will be open to critical scrutiny. Hence, Fisher personalises the evaluation of an argument thereby avoiding a prescriptive dogma, because a prescriptive method would stifle imagination and lateral thinking. Returning to the assertability question, we can now treat it as a practical approach to evaluation in that real arguments are evaluated by questioning the relationship between the premise and conclusion.

For most arguments, you should ask whether the conclusion follows from the premise. For a conclusion to be acceptable, the following conditions must be satisfactorily established by the analyst:

Its conclusion must follow from its premises.

Its premises must either be true or, if suppositions, justifiable.

Even if the premise of an argument could be true or justifiable, the conclusion could be false or doubtful. Similarly, the conclusion could be acceptable, but one or all of the premises doubtful. In a more complex analysis, you may find the premise to be justifiable, but the conclusion able to be inverted; that is, the consequences of the premise seen in two ways. Putting this into practice, Fisher claims that clarity can be achieved through addressing the following kind of question to an argument: could the premise be true and the conclusion false, judging by appropriate standards of evidence or appropriate standards of what is possible?

Therefore, you need to ask what argument or evidence would justify your acceptance of the conclusion. It is because standards are not universal, but historically, culturally and subject specific that care is needed here (see Turnbull, 1971, for an interesting example of a description of a culture that through a change in the physical environment changed radically). Different cultures, like different disciplines, differ in what they accept as standards of proof. When dealing with subject specific disciplines ask what should be taken as proof and why. However, avoid taking for granted what the discipline accepts as justification for asserting a conclusion or what its adherents assume to be knowledge. You should, in other words, think about and think through for yourself the arguments and assumptions you are dealing with. In this way, you will understand more because you will have applied a healthy natural scepticism. Turning this into practice is not too difficult.

Many standpoints and perspectives in the social sciences have their origins in moral, political and ethical positions. For example, very early on in his life, Karl Marx was politically committed to the idea that capitalism was morally perverse and should be replaced. He spent the rest of his life developing a methodological approach to show how and why this should happen. All of his work was therefore an immense effort to elaborate the basis of his original position. By asserting a conclusion, someone puts forward a proposition they take to be true. The basis therefore of some arguments is assertion. This does not mean such arguments are wrong. Rather they need to be constructed very carefully; paying attention to their reasoning, using evidence systematically and coherently, and relating ideas in as rigorous a way as possible. You can, therefore, develop an argument from assertion and analyse one by the same approach. Example A at the end of this chapter shows how an argument based on assertion can be analysed for evaluation. In the following example based on Marx, the notational system developed by Fisher's procedure (looked at above) is demonstrated. Inference indicators are marked to make the structure of the author's argument clear.

Extended example: Karl Marx – logic of argument

The following extract is from Marx's 'Value, prices and profit' (1950[1898]). It is an argument well known to scholars of Marx. It has been used extensively to demonstrate the impeccable logic of his argumentation analysis, especially the kind of analysis he uses in much longer and sophisticated texts like *Capital*. The target for Marx's analysis is the assertion that working people act irrationally when they combine (i.e. unionise) in the pursuit of higher wages. Marx attributes this assertion to 'Citizen Weston'. Marx skillfully dissects Weston's argument. He shows how Weston's premises do not follow from each other and how his conclusion does not follow from the premises. Added to this, Marx takes Weston's own premises and recasts them into a logical argument to show the rationality of unionisation for higher wages. A possible way to approach this extract is to read it through first. Afterwards read the notes, adapted from Fisher (1993), which accompany it. Note that Marx's analysis is not linear but combinational – Marx expects his reader to re-read the argument, moving back and forth through its different sections.

TABLE 5.5   Analysing Marx: Worked example

Quotes from Marx	Argumentation analysis
Citizen Weston's argument rested, in fact, upon two premises: firstly, the *amount 'of national production'* is a *fixed thing*, a *constant* quantity of magnitude, as the mathematicians would say. Secondly, the *amount of real wages*, that is to say, of wages as measured by the quantity of the commodities they can buy, is a *fixed* amount, a *constant* magnitude.	In this first paragraph Marx sets out the premises of Weston's argument as: (1) **production is a <u>fixed thing</u>** *therefore* (2) **wages are fixed** (as measured by what they can buy) *therefore* given (1) + (2) the conclusion is: the working class cannot gain higher wages through combined struggle (e.g. unionisation). In the next two paragraphs Marx sets out to show that (1) and (2) are false, that (2) does not follow from (1), and even if the conclusion was true, it is not true because of (1) and (2). Marx's analytical reasoning looks like this:
Now, his first assertion is evidently erroneous. <Year after year you will find that the value and mass of production increase, that the productive powers of the national labour increase, and that the amount of money necessary to circulate this increasing production continuously changes. > < What is true at the end of the year, and for different years compared with each other, is true for every average day of the year. > <u>The amount or magnitude of national production changes continuously. It is not a constant but a *variable* magnitude</u>, and apart from changes in population it must be so, because of <the continuous change in *the accumulation of capital* and the *productive powers of labour*.> It is perfectly true that if a *rise in the general*	The value of production and the productive power of labour increases every year, and the amount of money in circulation is variable (changes) because increased production requires changes in money circulation. Therefore, national production and circulation of money are variables and not constants. Presumably, national production can decrease as well as increase. Therefore, Marx is claiming that Weston's assertion is false. To show the validity of his point Marx would need to produce sufficient historical evidence that shows variability of national production, labour output and amount of money in circulation.

(Continued)

Quotes from Marx	Argumentation analysis
rate of wages should take place today, that rise, whatever its ulterior effects may be, would, by *itself*, not *immediately* change the amount of production. It would, in the first instance, proceed from the existing state of things. But if *before* the rise of wages the national production was *variable*, and not *fixed*, it will continue to be variable and not fixed *after* the rise of wages.	
But suppose <the amount of national production to be constant instead of variable.> Even then, what our friend Weston considers a logical conclusion would still remain a gratuitous assertion. <If I have a given number, say eight, the absolute limits of this number do not prevent its parts from changing their relative limits.> Therefore, <if profits were six and wages two, wages may increase to six and profits decrease to two, and still the total amount remain eight.> Thus the fixed amount of production would by no means prove the fixed amount of wages. How then does our friend Weston prove this fixity? By asserting it.	Marx points out through an illustration that Weston's position is an assertion and not a logical argument. He points out that even if it was true there is no reason to accept the conclusion. Marx uses the illustration to show that the total amount of the whole may be constant but the elements making it up, i.e. national production, wages, labour output and money in circulation, are variable in quantity. The elements can change relative to each other without affecting the whole. Therefore, Weston's conclusion is, as Marx points out, an assertion. Marx has therefore dealt systematically with Weston's reasoning and shown it to be flawed. But Marx does not stop here; he continues his analysis before making his claim, which is based on Weston's own rationale. This is the clever bit.
But even conceding him his assertion, it could cut both ways, while he presses it only in one direction. If suppose <the amount of wage is a constant magnitude> it can neither be increased nor diminished. If then, in enforcing a temporary rise of wages, the working men, act foolishly, the capitalists in enforcing a temporary fall in wages would act not less foolishly. Our friend Weston does not deny that, under certain circumstances, the working men can enforce a rise in wages, but their amount being naturally fixed, there must follow a reaction. On the other hand, he knows also that the capitalists can enforce	In this paragraph Marx asks the 'what if ...' question. He asks what if one accepts Weston's assertion that wages are a constant? In asking this, Marx's motive is to show the dual nature of the assertion. If working people act irrationally in pursuing wage increases, then, capitalists in pressing for lower wages act equally irrationally. This is Marx's first step. His second leads him to his main conclusion. Marx points out that if capitalists force a reduction in wages, working people will be acting rationally in resisting such pressure. This is because the working people would be abiding by Weston's assertion in trying to maintain wages as a constant.

Quotes from Marx	Argumentation analysis
a fall of wages, and, indeed, continuously try to enforce it. According to the principle of the constancy of wages, <u>a reaction ought to follow in this case</u> > not less than in the former. <The <u>working men,</u> therefore, <u>reacting against the attempt at, or the act of, lowering wages, would act rightly.</u>> <u>They would,</u> therefore, <u>act rightly in enforcing a rise of wages,</u> because <every reaction against the lowering of wages is an action for raising wages.> <u>According to citizen Weston's own principle of the constancy of wages, the working man ought,</u> therefore, <u>under certain circumstances, to combine and struggle for a rise of wages.</u>	Marx makes his main conclusion but it emphasises a restriction under certain circumstances.
If he denies this conclusion, he must give up the premise from which it flows. He must not say that the amount of wages is a constant quantity, but that, although it cannot and must not rise, it can and must fall, whenever capital pleases to lower it.	In typical Socratic style, Marx presents his opponent with the reality of his own reasoning. Weston would presumably have little choice in accepting Marx's argument because Marx has left him with no logical basis for argument.

As you can see, Marx's main conclusion is, 'the working man ... ought ... under certain circumstances ... to combine and struggle for a rise in wages.' The clever thing about this is that Marx bases this conclusion on Weston's own premise of the constancy of wages. Following through the reasoning of the extract one can see not only the systematic logic but also the impeccable style of Marx's argumentation.

Although the exposition of this extract (in the right-hand column) has worked in a linear direction, one could have started from the conclusion and worked in multiple directions. From that conclusion, 'working men ... would act rightly in enforcing a rise in wages', working backwards will reveal how Marx came to this conclusion. To do this read deductively, looking for a structure of reasoning that supports this main statement or conclusion. However, whichever way you read Marx's argument it reaches the opposite conclusion to that of Weston.

There is another point also to note in this short example – the ways in which Marx's methodological assumptions underpin his analysis of Weston's argument. In Chapter 3, we outlined what are generally taken to be the methodological assumptions Marx developed. We can use these to show once again (Table 5.6) the importance of methodological assumptions and how they are used as the starting point for a challenge.

(Continued)

TABLE 5.6　Marx's methodological assumptions and Weston's assertions compared

Marx's methodological assumptions	Weston's methodological assertions
Everything is in a process of change, therefore, change is rational.	Structures in the world are fixed and therefore change is irrational.
Singular events only appear chaotic because we do not look for the structure of relationships that connect events into a whole, therefore look for what connects events and situations.	Challenges to the status quo must be challenged and prevented to avoid chaos.
The force for change resides in the economic relationships between social classes, therefore look at the relationships between the classes for an explanation for change.	Social classes are related but ought not to be in conflict as conflict is irrational because it will not change anything for the better.
People are encouraged to see their situation in isolation rather than in terms of broader structures of social inequality, therefore they may act in ways contradictory to the good of society.	People should accept the status quo because it cannot be changed for the better. Change would lead to chaos.
People are essentially rational but the individualising force of capitalism makes them selfish. Therefore, certain forms of community (society) are better than others because they encourage the essential rationality of human nature.	People are essentially irrational and therefore need to be controlled by people that know better. Selfishness and individualism encourage self-help, innovation and enterprise, which are good for society as a whole.

Fallacies in arguments

The term fallacy comes from the Latin *fallere*, which means to deceive. It was Aristotle (384–322 BC) who first identified the nature of fallacious reasoning. In a moment, we will look at some common fallacies. But first, it is important to note that it is not normal for academic authors to deceive their readers. Although there have been some notable exceptions to this norm (e.g. the Cyril Burt scandal – see Beloff, 1980). Therefore, the first working assumption is that the author is genuine and has not gone out to hide information, distort facts or slander opponents, in order to make a more convincing case for their argument. Rather it is sometimes the case that the writer has misled him- or herself; he/she has made a mistaken assumption, not examined the assumptions that have been made or has not noticed the faults in his/her reasoning.

There are two ways of looking at fallacies: fallacies other people make in their arguments and fallacies you can make when evaluating other people's arguments. What we will do here is to look at some of the most common errors people make when constructing arguments. We begin with some simple fallacies before describing an example.

A number of authors have highlighted the main fallacies common in arguments. Hinderer (1992), for example, discusses some of the main fallacies that are a result of confusion, while Thouless and Thouless (1990) provide a long list of tricks often used to bolster argument. Out of the 37 tricks identified by Thouless and Thouless the ones most likely to be encountered when reviewing a research literature are shown in Table 5.7.

TABLE 5.7   Fallacies common in arguments

Fallacy	What it is and how to avoid it
1. of implied definition	Referring to something without clearly defining it. Always define what you refer to, especially concepts
2. of illegitimate definition	Closing down alternatives by giving a restrictive definition. Acknowledge alternatives to show you know about them
3. of changing meanings	Defining something as A, then using A in a different way B
4. of emotional language	Using value or ethically loaded terms
5. use of all rather than some	Using bland generalisation to incorporate all variables and thereby minimise contradictory examples
6. ignoring alternatives	Giving one interpretation or example as if all others could be treated or categorised in the same way
7. of selected instances	Picking out unusual or unrepresentative examples
8. of forced analogy	Using an analogy without recognising the applicability of other contradictory analogies
9. of similarity	Claiming there is no real difference between two things even when there is
10. of mere analogy	Use of analogy with no recourse to real world examples
11. of false credentials	Exaggerating one's credentials or experience to convince others of your authority
12. of technical language	Deliberate use of jargon intended to impress the reader and/or hide the lack of a foundation to an argument
13. of special pleading	Claiming a special case to raise one's argument above other similar positions. This is often associated with the use of emotive language

(Continued)

Fallacy	What it is and how to avoid it
14. of playing on the reader	Telling readers what they want to hear rather than challenging their thinking and assumptions
15. of claiming prejudice	Attributing prejudice to an opponent in order to discredit them
16. of appealing to others for authority	Claiming some other in authority has made the same argument as oneself in order to strengthen one's position
17. of false context	Giving examples out of context or using nothing but hypothetical scenarios
18. of extremities	Ignoring centre ground positions by focusing only on the extreme ends of a spectrum of alternatives
19. of tautology	Use of language structures to get acceptance of one's argument from others. This is often in the form of 'too much of X is bad' therefore X itself is good

Source: Based on Thouless and Thouless, 1990: 139–44

Examples of bad and good research and argumentation analysis

There are many examples of good and bad research. In Chapter 3, the features of both were listed. In this section, we will look at research that appears plausible but is not. We will then look at a longer example, to show how a series of focused questions can make visible fallacies in complex arguments.

Extended examples: False logic and food panics

This example is about bread. Here are 12 points about bread.

1. More than 98% of convicted felons are bread eaters.
2. Half of all children who grow up in bread-consuming households score below average on standardised tests.
3. In the eighteenth century, when virtually all bread was baked in the home, the average life expectancy was less than 50 years; infant mortality rates were unacceptably high; many women died in childbirth; and diseases such as typhoid, yellow fever and influenza ravaged whole nations.
4. More than 90% of violent crimes are committed within 24 hours of eating bread.
5. Bread is made from a substance called 'dough'. It has been proven that as little as one pound of dough can suffocate a mouse. The average American eats more bread than that in one month!

6. Tribal societies that have no bread exhibit a low occurrence of cancer, Alzheimer's, Parkinson's disease and osteoporosis.
7. Bread has been proven to be addictive. Subjects deprived of bread and given only water begged for bread after only two days.
8. Bread is often a 'gateway' food item, leading the user to 'harder' items such as butter, jelly, peanut butter and even cold cuts.
9. Bread has been proven to absorb water. Since the human body is more than 90% water, consuming bread may lead to dangerous dehydration.
10. Newborn babies can choke on bread.
11. Bread is baked at temperatures as high as 400 degrees Fahrenheit! That kind of heat can kill an adult in less than one minute.
12. Bread baking produces dangerous air pollution, including particulates (flour dust) and volatile organic compounds. (www.geoffmetcalf.com/bread.html)

Given such a number and range of apparent facts about bread, is it legitimate to assume there is an association between bread making and consumption and social and physical problems? Further, is it legitimate to claim bread is a causal variable leading to such things as crime? On the basis of these points and statistics a number of claims and recommendations could be made. If we take them at face value, then bread is clearly dangerous. Therefore, we could recommend that something should be done to minimise or prevent these dangers. The evidence points to the need for action, for if the state of affairs is allowed to continue, we could claim the problems will persist and could get worst. Therefore, what is to be done? A public awareness campaign to warn of the dangers of bread? A ban on advertising for bread and bread-based foods? Moving bread production to depopulated areas? We could go on but the points are:

• legitimate sounding statistics can be applied with false logic to support absurd arguments
• association does not prove or automatically lead to causation
• application of Toulmin's or Fisher's schemes of argumentation analysis and common sense can reveal such nonsense in seemingly academic arguments.

This next example is about Dihydrogen Monoxide. Here is an extract from an official looking web page called the United States Environmental Association Centre (www.dhmo. org/facts.html).

Dihydrogen Monoxide (DHMO) is a colourless and odourless chemical compound, also referred to by some as Dihydrogen Oxide, Hydrogen Hydroxide, Hydronium Hydroxide, or simply Hydrochloric acid. Its basis is the highly reactive hydroxyl radical, a species shown to mutate DNA, denature proteins, disrupt cell membranes, and chemically alter critical neurotransmitters. The atomic components of DHMO are found in a number of caustic, explosive and poisonous compounds such as Sulphuric Acid, Nitroglycerine and Ethyl Alcohol.
    For more detailed information, including precautions, disposal procedures and storage requirements, refer to one of the Material Safety Data Sheets (MSDS) available for DHMO:

(Continued)

- Kemp Compliance & Safety MSDS for DHMO
- Chem-Safe, Inc. MSDS for Dihydrogen Monoxide
- Applied Petrochemical Research MSDS for Hydric Acid
- Original DHMO.org Material Safety Data Sheet (MSDS) for Dihydrogen Monoxide (html).

A list of dangers from DHMO are listed below and include,

- death due to accidental inhalation of DHMO, even in small quantities
- prolonged exposure to solid DHMO causes severe tissue damage
- excessive ingestion produces a number of unpleasant though not typically life-threatening side effects
- DHMO is a major component of acid rain
- gaseous DHMO can cause severe burns
- contributes to soil erosion
- leads to corrosion and oxidation of many metals
- contamination of electrical systems often causes short-circuits
- exposure decreases effectiveness of automobile brakes
- found in biopsies of pre-cancerous tumors and lesions
- given to vicious dogs involved in recent deadly attacks
- often associated with killer cyclones in the US Midwest and elsewhere, and in hurricanes including deadly storms in Florida, New Orleans and other areas of the southeastern US.
- thermal variations in DHMO are a suspected contributor to the El Nino weather effect.

Making sense of information in an argument is important. The bread example above shows this. In this case DHMO sounds like it is even more harmful than bread. This example illustrates the need to evaluate by being sceptical about information from all sources, especially the Internet. In the example below from Francis we see questions being asked. In this case we need to ask only two questions:

1. What is Dihydrogen Monoxide (DHMO)?
2. Who is the United States Environmental Association Centre?

Analysing the much-cited source

All disciplines have their 'must cite' sources. These can be primary and secondary publications that are regarded as core texts. In critical theory of consumerism, Judith Williamson's *Decoding Advertisements* (1979) is such a source. The following is an example of how to apply critical thinking to make visible methodological assumptions that become taken-for-granted givens for subsequent researchers.

Extended example: Debate over methodological fallacies

In his analysis and subsequent critique of Judith Williamson's *Decoding Advertisements* (1979), Francis (1986) provides a good example of the kind of debate over fallacies and understanding that arises in the social sciences. His analysis also shows an example of the use of the phenomenological reading technique. Before we look at the debate, we need to understand two things: why Francis chose to look at *Decoding Advertisements* and what we mean by phenomenological reading.

Francis chose to look at Williamson's book because in the early 1980s it was a major development in feminist analysis of advertising; it showed the kinds of work that could be produced using a feminist standpoint within the methodological assumptions of structuralism and psychoanalytical analysis. Choice of which works to critique is therefore important, especially if you are making a critique of a major argument. Francis chose a landmark study for his critique. So, whatever else he aimed to do in his analysis, he needed to be very careful as to how he analysed the argument in *Decoding Advertisements* and how he argued that it is based on a number of methodological assumptions that are fallacies.

Phenomenological reading technique

In his analysis Francis used what may be called the phenomenological reading technique. The basis of this technique has its origins in the work of the philosopher most commonly associated with phenomenology, Edmund Husserl (1859–1938). Although his work is complex, we can get an understanding of it through some simple illustrations. Take, for example, the interest that experimental psychology may have in the relationship between hunger and the image of food. Husserl would not be interested in the relationship between the image of food and hunger but with a more fundamental (or a priori) question. He would ask: What exactly is it that is to count as an image of food? Husserl is interested in a pure description of the phenomenon (noumena) that humans experience. He is not interested, therefore, in the causation of such experiences or the history of the phenomenon. Husserl is recommending that if we want to know what a thing is like, what its essential features must be in order that it can be recognised as an example of that thing, then we must place brackets around the assumptions and understanding that we take for granted. Issues about the ethics, morals, politics, consequences and especially reality (ontology) of a thing should not, Husserl recommends, be of primary concern.

When used by sociologists like Francis, Husserl's phenomenology places a priority upon describing the different ways in which the intention people have influences the ways they understand everyday life. For example, the drawer in a jeweller's shop may be full of rings, some of which are classified as wedding rings. Once purchased, these wedding rings may come to have an emotional meaning for the wearer, symbolising love and commitment. To the jeweller they mean something different: they are a commodity for sale. Hence, the same object can be constituted in different ways depending on the intentionality of different people. The main point to note here is that both realities are equally valid.

(Continued)

Applying this attitude to science, the mathematical approach of, say, physics, and the analytical approach of, say, semiotics, are only two from many ways in which the world can be understood. This leads to a second point that is important for Francis. The scientific approach, whether in the natural or social sciences, takes for granted that there is a world having prior existence to the world of causality and relationships between things that scientists aim to describe. The mundane world in which we all exist (*Lebenswelt*) is the one from which the scientific approach is derived.

Hence, following Husserl's ideas, Francis takes the position that the kinds of analysis produced by scientists are abstractions and idealisations about the world in which we live, and have little to do with the properties of the things that we experience in everyday life. What we see in accounts about the world is the operation of procedures for analysis, based on assumptions subscribed to by the analyst about the intent of the phenomenon studied. Hence, those things that are classified as belonging to this or that class of things (phenomena) are not a matter for study as things in themselves. Added to this is the point many phenomenological social scientists make – the 'correctness' of any scientific analysis of a phenomenon is not validated by comparing it with how it is usually experienced in everyday life. Rather, the issue of validity is looked at from within science by ensuring that the procedures used were correct and rational. Ironically, when the world of everyday life is used, it is used with the intent to provide a correction to what is assumed to be our partial view of reality. Hence, one of Husserl's followers, Alfred Schutz (1967), argued that the procedures and intent of science are incomparable with the procedures and intent used by people in everyday life.

Although there are many ideas here, we should be able to see that Francis is working within an approach that is different to that from Williamson. Francis is interested in two main things. The first is the assumptions Williamson accepts about advertising and how she employs a set of procedures to arrive at her analysis of advertising. The second is what it may take to describe the essential features of an advertisement. This approach can be seen in the following list of questions that Francis asks about *Decoding Advertisements*.

1. What assumptions have been made that enabled the account to be made?
2. What are the consequences of these assumptions for understanding the thing (i.e. phenomenon) itself?
3. What happens if we suspend these assumptions?
4. What assumptions would we need to make in order to analyse the phenomenon as a thing in itself rather than as an instance of something else?
5. What consequences may these have for our understanding of that phenomenon?

Francis subjected *Decoding Advertisements* to a critical reading. He claims to have identified a number of major fallacies in the assumptions made about advertising, products and viewers, which impact on the status of several methodological assumptions within structuralism and its use to analyse advertising. Francis argues that there are three main fallacies on which *Decoding Advertisements* is based. He calls these the description fallacy, the technical reading fallacy and the formal knowledge fallacy.

The description fallacy, according to Francis, is assuming that the function of an advertisement is to describe the details of the product. Williamson, claims Francis, criticises advertisements for not describing products: this criticism is based on her assumption that the function of an advertisement is to describe a product and advertisements that do not do this are deceptive. As a case in point, she cites a perfume advertisement for Chanel No. 5, in which Catherine Deneuve (a French model and actress) is pictured with a bottle of Chanel. Williamson claims that advertisements like those for perfume are 'hollow referent' images – they are used because no real information can be given. Francis observes, however, that 'if we cease to conceive of descriptions as essential to the nature of advertising, the basis of Williamson's charge of deception disappears' (1986: 209). He follows this up with: 'I assume Williamson is not suggesting … that we cannot describe smells. In everyday life we routinely do so' (1986: 209). What Francis has done here is to show the fallacy of making an assumption about the function of something, in this case, an advertisement. He has also shown that if one changes or drops (suspends) that particular assumption, the substance of much criticism about advertisements disappears.

A second fallacy, the technical reading fallacy, made by Williamson is that of assuming viewers of advertisements have insufficient mental ability to see the structures by which she believes an advertisement works. She assumes that advertisements have hidden structures that cannot readily be perceived by looking at the manifest image. On the basis of this, she criticises advertising agencies for hiding the technical work that went into the production of an advertisement. Williamson has, Francis observes, conflated 'two different perspectives on advertisements. She has conflated the everyday and routine viewing of advertisements with a technical interest in adverts. It is because of this that Williamson is able to claim that, '"we" the general viewer do not "see" the "real" structure and purpose of advertisements' (1986: 210). Williamson fails to realise, Francis argues, that the whole objective of the technical construction of an advertisement is aimed at the production of an 'object that can be understood ... by anyone' (1986: 221).

The third fallacy Francis finds in *Decoding Advertisements* is the 'formal knowledge fallacy'. On the basis of assuming advertisements convey messages, Williamson proposes that these are structured and work at a level where most people are unaware of them. Viewers of advertisements do not know they are receiving a powerful advertising sales pitch. Referring to the work of Toulmin, Francis points out the formal tautology in this. In attributing objective existence to unconscious and covert structures of ideas, Williamson is attributing concrete reality (misplaced concreteness) to an ideational notion. But for the notion to hold she must continue to assume that viewers cannot see how advertisements are structured. She therefore claims that the only way to get at these structures is through analysis and uses elements from psychoanalytical theory to do this. But as Francis makes clear, 'unless we clearly distinguish between the phenomena and the representations we use to picture them, our theories will remain self-sustaining tautologies' (1986: 213). In short, what *Decoding Advertisements* does is to claim the existence of formal structures and then

(Continued)

apply formal analysis to demonstrate the adequacy of the approach: it does not describe advertisements or products, it describes the procedures of its own theory.

We can see that Francis intends to approach advertising not as a phenomenon, but to examine properties as the phenomena. It is this difference of project that sets the two apart. There is no reason why we should see Francis's critique as negating the work of Williamson. We may even want to look at what criticisms could be made of Francis's reading of *Decoding Advertisements*. Assessing the original argument and the critique is a common theme in the social sciences. In terms of Francis's critique, we may see a counter-argument develop on the lines of a clarification of what Williamson intended, thereby attempting to correct the reading Francis gives us. For example, it may be claimed that Williamson did not criticise advertisements for not describing products. If this is the case – and we can only see if it is by reading *Decoding Advertisements* for ourselves – then Francis's claim about Williamson regarding advertising as deception may be thrown into doubt. But let us assume Williamson did argue that advertisements contain no real information, we have the issue of what we mean by information. This takes us back to Husserl's phenomenology: we need to inquire into what makes information what it is in order to be able to recognise it as such. Williamson may, therefore, have an idea about what information 'is' and it is this that Francis is criticising. It is these kinds of problems that can often lead to new topics for research. Again, following this through, we may then show in defence of Williamson that she thought some products, such as perfume, were difficult to describe. Hence, what she is critical about is the association of perfume with certain images. It is this association, not the product or even advertising as an institution, that she is interested in. Williamson is therefore concerned with the issue of persuasion. If this is the case her analysis is of the strategies used by advertising to persuade. But does this clarification distract from the original critique made by Francis? From a phenomenological approach, there are strong grounds for claiming that Williamson is more concerned with procedures of analysis than with the thing in itself, whether an advertisement or information.

But why should Williamson be interested in a phenomenological approach? As with most research, the answer is that it is up to the researcher to make choices about what their topic is to be and how they are to study it. However, Francis may observe that a researcher also has the responsibility to understand the consequences of the choices they make. In this case, he may claim that the choices Williamson made had more to do with demonstrating preconceived views about advertising than with describing the properties of advertisements. Here, then, Francis would be looking to show the motivation for Williamson's interest in advertising. Again, a correction of this maybe attempted by saying that Francis has misunderstood the methodological tradition in which Williamson is working. As a consequence, he misunderstands her arguments about how smell is packaged as a perfume and how this has meaning for consumers. This line may, therefore, take us towards another aspect of the debate – that of understanding the traditions in which different researchers work.

The importance of this cannot be overestimated. We have already shown something of this in our explication of the origins of the phenomenological reading technique. The same, therefore, could be done for the tradition in which Williamson worked. Again, it is such inquiries that can form the basis of further research. It is finding these unexplained areas in arguments or assumptions that have not been defined that can often be the starting point for a new piece of research. For example, we have just seen that Williamson may, it could be claimed, be interested in the symbolic and cultural meaning and signification of perfume. If this is the case, then Francis's criticism could be the starting point for research into perfume, such as the question of what makes a particular smell classifiable as perfume.

Asking relevant questions as a core skill

In terms of the core skills as outlined by the RDF Framework, Francis is showing Creativity: an inquiring mind, intellectual insight and making connections to make visible methodological assumptions and their consequences. This is done, initially, by asking relevant questions.

This takes us back to the debate. Francis may be criticised for not defining what he takes an advertisement to be or what he takes to be the essential properties of perfume. He may therefore have made a number of fallacies, principally of referring to something without clearly defining it. But is this serious criticism of the critique Francis has put together? There is no definitive answer to this question. It depends on how you, the reader, want to understand the argument; and this itself may be based on your prior interests, concerns and ideas about the role of social science. It is in many ways the different idea that Williamson and Francis each have about social science that makes their positions incompatible. Williamson works within a tradition that seeks to apply semiological theory, a tradition that aims among other things to show the ways in which messages are structured to convey certain meanings. Her book, *Decoding Advertisements*, was a major step in synthesising work in structuralism and psychoanalysis from a feminist perspective. Francis, however, works from within a different tradition. As we have seen, his interests are with foundational issues that centre on the general question of *just what*, rather than how and why. He wants to redirect our attention to the question of just what is an advertisement: to think first about what it is that we are going to research.

Critical appraisal and evaluation

Throughout this chapter, we have looked at three main standpoints to an argument. One you take when critically evaluating the arguments made by others. Then the standpoint taken by those authors you are evaluating. Finally, the standpoint taken when you develop your own argument.

The proposer of an argument needs to marshal sufficient and relevant evidence to support their argument. The method by which this is accomplished is producing valid, sound and coherent arguments, devoid of fallacies, and not easily undone. The evaluator of an argument needs to identify the structure of the reasoning used; looking carefully at the premise and conclusion; seeking to show why the proposed conclusion is not the only one to be derived from the reasons provided. Alec Fisher (1988: 129) gives some sound advice:

> Starting with the main conclusion C, ask,
>
> What immediate reasons are presented in the text for accepting C?
>
> or
>
> Why (in the text) am I asked to believe C?

Using methods to evaluate argument, evidence and practices involves thinking critically. There is a lot of advice given on what it means and how to do critical thinking. Some of this is overtly complicated. For practical purposes, critical thinking can be characterised as follows.

> Critical thinking involves developing the ability and capacity to be sceptical, to a degree appropriate to the needs of the project.

Fisher's (1988: 128–39) method is a sceptical one. It is about asking questions about an argument in a systematic way, based on consistent application of the *assertibility question*. A common problem is that many authors have a poor understanding of informal, let alone formal logic and hence know little about how to structure a clear, accurate, precise, thorough and fair argument.

Steps in critical evaluation

Critical evaluation involves the following basic steps. Once you have identified the main publications, group them roughly into sets based on similarity of argument.

- For each set itemise the reasons given for the conclusions made. Pay particular attention to inference indicators. Group reasons together along with any evidence offered. Group conclusions together. Pick out quotes for each author that illustrate clearly and fairly their argument.
- Think about the reasons and conclusions. Ask what assumptions have been made, what are the origins (heritage) of these assumptions, were these assumptions necessary, what other assumptions could have been used? At this level of study, you should be familiar with methodological assumptions and traditions.
- Think about the logical consequences of the conclusions made based on the assumptions underpinning them. What would the likely outcomes be if the assumptions were taken to their logical conclusions? Look for distinctive chains of reasoning and new ideas.
- Assign weights – high weight to strong chains of reasons with thought out conclusions and low weight to weaker chains of reasoning.
- Use mind maps (Buzan, 1995) and relevance trees as tools to organise and evaluate the relative usefulness (strengths) of the different camps and individual studies.

Methods to avoid bias

Reflect on and consider your evaluation. Look to see if you have introduced explicit or implicit bias into your evaluations. There are various methods you could use here. The Socratic Method and De Bono's Six Thinking Hats could be useful.

The Socratic Method is based on systematic questioning of others and your own opinions and beliefs. For example, ask of your evaluations, what do I mean by? How did I come to that conclusion? Why do I believe that I am right? What is the source of my information? What assumption led to this conclusion? What happens if I am wrong? What sources disagree with me, and why? Why is this significant? What is an alternate explanation for this phenomenon?

Edward De Bono claims that there are several types, orientations and approaches to thinking and that most people only use one or two. People, he claims, use what they have become used to (habitual). He advocates that we learn to use several approaches; in this way, we could become much more effective thinkers. He asks us to think about problems using a range of 'hats' (different approaches). These hats are:

White hat	(Blank sheet)	Information and reports (*objective*)
Red hat	(Fire)	Intuition, opinion and emotion (*subjective*)
Yellow hat	(Sun)	Praise, positive aspects (*objective*)
Black hat	(Judge's robe)	Criticism, negative aspects (*objective*)
Green hat	(Plant)	Alternatives, new approaches and 'anything goes' (*speculative*)
Blue hat	(Sky)	'Big Picture', 'Conductor hat', overall process, 'Meta hat', 'thinking about (*overview*) thinking'

Conclusion: Fair play

Argumentation analysis and evaluation aims to de-construct and then re-construct differently the ideas of other people. Inevitably some things will be lost or cannot be included, while other things may suffer in translation. What I am saying here is that any analysis and evaluation of a body of literature will incur some costs: certain things will have to be sacrificed in order to obtain other things. Clarity, consistency and coherence are not easily achieved; and to make an analysis intelligible not all the detail and contexts analysed can be included in the final synthesis. It is not necessary to short-circuit this problem by presenting things as if simple choices could be made; that different ideas were competing rivals. To do this would most certainly commit one to the error of over-simplification and gross comparison.

At the heart of this problem is the fact that not everything you find interesting will be relevant to your topic or method. For example, if one were looking at the topic of 'economic determinism' this would entail reading both Marx and Weber. This would amount to tens of thousands of pages of difficult and sophisticated argument and analysis. There would also be a very wide secondary literature to read. If one were interested in the history of social thought on economic determinism this task may not be a problem. But if the interest is in looking at the applications of ideas about economic determinism this task would be too large; it would prevent one getting on with the job of doing empirical work. Therefore, a certain amount of ignorance is also inevitable. Practical considerations mean some texts cannot be closely read, while others can only be read selectively and casually. Some texts may not get read at all. It is for these reasons that Anderson et al. (1985) make a number of recommendations. One is the need for the scholar to be charitable in their interpretation and approach to the work of others. It is an attitude that allows us to recognise our own limitations and to show some of the characteristics of scholarship: modesty and understanding.

Charity of interpretation means 'playing fair' when assessing the strengths and weaknesses of other people's ideas. Although this may sound like an old notion, fair play is an important part of scholarly activity. Having an inquisitive attitude to different ideas, other ways of looking at the world and approaches to researching the world one is exercising an intellectual attitude; the kind of attitude from which differing ideas can be synthesised into new and exciting ideas. The value of this attitude repays several-fold the effort needed to exercise it. One major benefit is that it can save us from making victims and fools of ourselves. Social science is replete with articles exposing discovery: that a new idea has been developed or a new breakthrough made and that we should dump existing ideas and follow this new one. All too often one finds that the breakthrough is another case of what Anderson et al. (1985) call the Christopher Columbus Complex – this is like going to Disneyland and believing one has 'discovered' America. The main causes of this complex are ego and laziness. This can come about because the researcher can easily fall victim to their ego: believing that they, as part of the contemporary world, have a greater degree of insight on and intellectual understanding of society. As a consequence, the works of dead social theorists, like Sorokin, go unread or are only understood through derivative sources. Ideas by predecessors are, therefore, glibly criticised for what is perceived to be their weak purchase on current issues or problems of the discipline. As Anderson et al. (1985: 70) point out:

> victims of such a complex tend to overestimate our contemporary achievements because they underestimate those of our predecessors, the tasks they faced and, perhaps failed at, largely because victims of the complex have not tackled those tasks themselves.

Charity of interpretation and fair play are, therefore, practical considerations and not merely scholarly altruisms. Together they can make argumentation analysis not only rewarding but also an intellectually stimulating activity; resulting in genuine developments that the research scholar can be justifiably proud of.

In summary

- It is necessary to become knowledgeable, proficient and practised in analysing and making an argument.
- There are some useful, easy to apply methods for reading an argument, for extracting the essential methodological assumptions in an argument and on how to challenge claims made by others. It is important you can use these methods.
- The Socratic Method has been recommended as the main approach, or attitude, to take when reading and thinking about an argument. With practice and patience this method and attitude can become almost natural and an essential intellectual skill.
- Throughout research you find arguments for the use of methodology, data collection techniques and the interpretation of data. All research is, therefore, open to challenge.

6

Evidence, Evaluation and Critical Realism

- Develop an enquiring and sceptical attitude in order to recognise new trends, develop insight and go beyond the obvious
- Confidently enquire, challenge and question the taken-for-granted.

Introduction

Evidence is a core requirement for argument, interpretation and recommendations. Evidence is what your discipline and common sense say it is – subject to the rules of proof, authentication and production. That is, statements made about some phenomenon must (now or hypothetically in the future) have a corresponding proof. It must be authentic; not false, not incomplete or a surrogate. It must be able to be produced, in full, and if possible in its original state. In research it must, if produced from a research method, be replicable; other researchers should (actually or in principle) be able to produce the same results using the same methods. Figure 6.1 summarises the relationship between research and professional practice, argumentation and critical thinking; placing evidence at the centre of these activities.

What evidence actually 'is', is not always clear. Nor are the methods used to produce evidence commonly agreed on. Both are subject to critique and evaluation, and the data produced are subject to contested interpretation. How evidence was produced is subject to questions about the reliability and validity of the method(s), process and application of the method(s). Once produced, evidence is subject to evaluation in terms of its merit, completeness and utility for recommendations and making changes. Critical evaluation of evidence is essential for reviewing a literature, claiming changes should be made to a practice or procedure (as in medical treatment) or offering an explanation for the occurrence of a phenomenon. Evidence is published in documents. If your interest is in claims for intervention or explanation then the literature with the evidence, rather than rhetoric, should be your focus.

This chapter begins with the most complex question and that is, what is meant by evidence and proof? We will look at the kinds of evidence used in three kinds of literature review – the interventionist, scholastic and realist review. In all three it is important to understand what each kind of review takes as evidence. This is because we need to know what it means to evaluate

FIGURE 6.1   Evidence, argumentation, practice and critical thinking

and critically assess what is being claimed, on what basis, by studies using the same assumptions about the nature of evidence required to establish acceptance of that claim. Along the way, we look at a cautionary tale about not getting caught up in believing something is important simply because it is hard to understand or because everyone else has cited the source.

What do we mean by evidence?

Evidence can come in all manner of forms. It can be eyewitness testimony, a photograph, a letter, a DNA test, some indices, an anecdote, your own experience and so on. As technology develops new ways of obtaining evidence, the number of forms and sources of evidence increases. For example, in recent years virtual ethnography has become a new field in itself, the Internet becoming the source of data on patterns of behaviour (see Dicks et al., 2005; Coleman, 2010). Virtual ethnography illustrates the issues we have with evidence. When reading a study based on observations of Internet behaviours then we can ask, as we can of any report of findings:

What is the source?

When were the data collected?

How were the data captured?

What were the units of measurement?

How were the phenomena defined and operationalised?

What techniques were used to analyse the data?

Can I see all of the evidence?

Can I collect the same kind of evidence?

Evidence for one discipline is not, however, necessarily the same as for another discipline. While there can be cross-disciplinary agreements of what is, and is not, acceptable as evidence, this does not entail all evidence has equal standing for all subjects. It is far from it. Since the mid-1970s aspects of the humanities and social sciences have developed the view that evidence and our belief in an external reality is socially constructed through language. Hence, proponents of this standpoint believe there can be no unbiased and culturally neutral observations. As a consequence, the work and findings of scientists are characterised as embedded within, and biased by, economic and cultural circumstances. A number of authors, for example, Snow (1963[1960]), Kimball (2008), Brockman (2013) and Gould (2003), and others, have made comment either for or against this opposition between science and non-science. What this illustrates is the continuing debate, going back to F.R. Leavis, Matthew Arnold and T.H. Huxley, over the differences between the humanities and the physical sciences. Within all of this, is the standing of evidence and what it means to be able to supply sufficient and necessary proof for a claim.

As an aside look at the brief list of citations given above. Here, we see a literature on a topic, that topic being the debate over differences between attempts to systematically understand our world. Be that world social or physical. One could do a review of the literature on such a topic.

Different kinds of evidence

As there are different kinds of research, there are different kinds of methods producing different kinds of evidence. The purpose of a research project often determines the kind of evidence required to validate or falsify a thesis statement (theoretical knowledge) or provide answers to a question (empirical knowledge). Evidence is not fixed but part of a process of how we come to know something (research knowledge), and then questioning what we take as being known. While this seems complex, it is all about epistemology; this is the limit to human knowledge. In everyday life, we rarely have problems using our knowledge and cognate abilities to find out what is going on, identifying what a situation is. In research 'things' are different. When we make a claim, we need to have sufficient and necessary evidence to give 'it' backing. This becomes more important when we make a recommendation for an intervention; when 'real' people will be affected by the implementation of that decision. Therefore, when we think in research terms (taking a research attitude), we need to reflect much more carefully and systematically on the quality and quantity of evidence being produced and invoked as proof for something. When in the research attitude (you may think of this as the scientific approach), we need to be more cautious of what we take as proof; questioning what we take for granted.

Hierarchy of evidence

Both qualitative and quantitative research studies produce evidence that can, based on the methods of its production and quantity, be ranked. Stratifying evidence and the methods by which it was produced can be done in a number of ways. For example, careful questioning of many people provides stronger evidence than eliciting the opinion of a few people. The basic assumption underlying ranking such schemes is that some methods provide evidence that has more certitude than others. This is not universal but conditional; any degree of certitude and resulting hierarchy of evidence is based on the kind of question that has been asked, the methods used to obtain data and the needs of the user. Depending on the needs of the user, different kinds of evidence can be assigned numerical weights. Table 6.1 shows this practice for evidence-based decision making, for health and medical practitioners, in terms of methods and outcomes. The greater the weight, the greater the degree of certitude in the methods and results.

These kinds of matrix are largely based on the medical hierarchy of evidence. This hierarchy is shown in Table 6.1. This kind of hierarchy reflects the general needs of practitioners working in and researching biomedical and non-biomedical

TABLE 6.1   Methods and their applicability to provide an increasing degree of certitude

| Intervention | Type of research | | | | |
	Qualitative research	Case control	Cohort	RCT	Systematic review
Diagnosis			✓	✓ ✓	✓✓✓
Treatment			✓	✓ ✓	✓✓✓
Screening				✓ ✓	✓✓✓
Managerial innovation	✓	✓	✓	✓ ✓	✓✓✓

Source: Gray, 2001: 118

health conditions. While there is some debate as to the degree to which randomised control trials (RCT) can be used for all questions, it is generally agreed that RCTs combined into systematic reviews and meta-analysis have greater authority than other types of method.

Medical and other decision-based schemes for weighting evidence normally exclude such sources as intuition, anecdotal and personal experience. These three sources along with the testimonial and professional opinion of scientists are, however, the main sources used in a court of law. Evidence that is presented in a court illustrates the contested nature of all evidence. With the inclusion of objects, legal representatives seek to produce a greater probability of belief in their evidence than that of their opposition. Regardless of the often personalised nature of legal evidence, any evidence presented by the prosecution services is subject to rules of reasonable proof. Whether it is legal evidence or evidence for an intervention, or evidence for a policy, or evidence for a claim in an argument, there are similarities between all of them. These are not in the use or application of a universal hierarchy but in the need to be able to show:

1.   use of an appropriate method or methods to collect the evidence (validity and reliability)
2.   the confirmability of the evidence (transparency and credibility)
3.   justifiable inferences (theory/explanations) can be made having been tested by the evidence.

Whatever we take evidence to be in terms of its source, quantity and quality, there are no clear-cut automatic, universal criteria that can easily be applied. We can see this in a discussion of evidence and explanations and the place of evidence in claiming causality and correlations.

Evidence and explanations

The discipline we work in, do research in and read in, tends to shape the way we do research, what we take as evidence and how we make interpretations. A commonality, however, between researchers in different disciplines, is that most know, research takes time. Think how long it takes to complete a doctorate. Sometimes, however, evidence-based research is needed to inform a decision and there is little time, in the normal sense of research, to do the research.

Rapid Evidence Assessment

Rapid Evidence Assessment (REA) is reviews of research aimed at policy makers. These can be a sound resource for obtaining an indicative review of a topic or methodology.

Evidence-based research is often required by government, charities and commercial organisations. Governments need to make informed choices from alternative policies. Charities need evidence of their value to the public to secure funds. Commercial organisations need information on their competitors, the market and for the development of products. There are many sources on how to do research for different organisational sectors.There are several organisations and sources that produce rapid evidence assessments. These include:

- The Centre for Evidence Based Intervention (CEBI) (www.cebi.ox.ac.uk/home.html)

The CEBI tell us, 'we investigate what works, with whom, and in which contexts, particularly through high-quality randomised trials, systematic reviews and other evaluation designs. We also carry out basic research into the causes of social problems, to understand better how and why interventions are effective. Our ultimate aim is to help develop successful interventions that translate into effective social policies and programmes.'

- The online journal *Systematic Reviews* (www.systematicreviewsjournal.com/#)

The journal tells us, '*Systematic Reviews* encompasses all aspects of the design, conduct and reporting of systematic reviews. The journal aims to publish high quality systematic review products including systematic review protocols, systematic reviews related to a very broad definition of health, rapid reviews, updates of already completed systematic reviews, and methods research related to the science of systematic reviews, such as decision modelling. The journal also aims to ensure that the results of all well-conducted systematic reviews are published, regardless of their outcome.'

- Alliance for Useful Evidence (www.alliance4usefulevidence.org)

This is an open-access, free to join network that gives access to resources from many organisations interested in evidence-based practice and policy.

- The British HM Treasury under the title *Magenta Book* (www.hm-treasury.gov.uk/magentabook)

The purpose of the *Magenta Book* (2003) is to help us to understand or use evidence, particularly for the purposes of improving current policies and using that learning for future policy development. It is aimed at anyone commissioning, managing, working, or advising on an evaluation of a policy, project, programme or delivery of a service. Work such as the *Magenta Book* makes a common assumption about evidence. That is, some kinds of evidence are better than others. Evidence from randomly controlled trials (RCTs) is believed to be better than evidence from case studies and other non-experimental research. This belief has two aspects. One is adherence either tacitly or overtly to there being a hierarchy of evidence. The other is about research strategies for producing explanations.

- Researchfish (www.researchfish.com)

From 2014 research councils in the UK (the AHRC, BBSRC, EPSRC, ESRC and NERC) began to collect research they had funded in order that they could track the impacts of the grants they had awarded. The resource is currently used by over 100 funders to gather information about the outcomes of their research.

Causality and correlation

There are different assumptions about the meaning of causation and how it can be established. Nonetheless, it is necessary to provide an outline, for the sake of coherence, of what we are talking about and how it fits into the literature review. We can begin by saying that when we talk about explanations we are using notions about the cause of something. Throughout research, in all disciplines, is the notion of causality – that one thing was the cause of another thing. Around and based on this notion there has developed the systematisation and institutionalisation of methods and procedures to investigate the relationships between an event and its cause(s). This endeavour has been spectacularly successful, in all fields of study, in confirming inferences of correlations and causal relationships. There is an extensive literature on many aspects of the history of discovery, and on the methods for doing research. A feature of this literature is that it is not uniform in holding a consensus about how to establish inferences or about what counts as reliable evidence for claiming an inference. For so many reasons this lack of agreement is a positive and not a negative feature of research. It allows for argument about and critical appraisal of inferences and continuous institutional vigilance of research methods and policies. It does not, however, negate the assumptions from some disciplines about the value of different kinds of procedures for doing research nor the stratification of evidence. These differences can be seen in Table 6.2 that shows the different kinds of review we have so far looked at in this book, namely the interventionist and scholastic reviews.

TABLE 6.2 Ontology, causation, evidence and the literature review

	Positivist/sucessionist	Realist/generative	Constructivist/ configurational
Ontological assumptions	An external world exists regardless of the researcher's beliefs or perspective. Through objective methods the real, universal reality can be uncovered.	Material and social realities exist which interact through a combination of the senses, language and culture making for differences in understanding and interpretation.	Reality, as we know it, exists as an outcome – for an individual – based on how they use their knowledge and language to categorise, frame and construct understanding and meaning.
Notion on causation	Through experimentation and control, causal variables are distinguished from other variables, and a linear relationship is established, from which conjectures are made.	Relationships are not seen as linear but multifaceted. As behaviours (regularities) occur in open systems, variations can exist in mechanisms and contexts.	Cases of observable phenomenon are compared for similarities and differences. Attributes (like variables) that have the power to influence a situation (event, behaviour, belief) with larger social systems are identified.
Evidence types	Evidence is in the form of data sets from experiments and surveys that have measured relationships between dependent and independent variables. Explanatory variables (x) are shown by recourse to the data, to bring about a change in the dependent variable (y).	Evidence is sourced from primary research and secondary sources on the problem, with no strict protocol regarding exclusion. Evidence is used to develop theories that explain the pattern of CMOC*, and can include common sense.	Evidence can be a combination of quantitative and qualitative data. It is obtained by the identification and description of a series of attributes, which through comparison with other combinations of attributes lead to the explanation of an event in terms of such a configuration of attributes, that at a specific time and place is the reason for the event happening.
Uses in the literature review	Data from RCT are included and data from non-RCTs usually excluded. The use of the same or similar criteria for inclusion and exclusion across different studies on a	Theories and hypothesis developed for studies can be examined in the light of changing contexts and patterns of behaviours (outcomes). The generative process allows for subsequent	Studies include numerical and non-numerical data and sources that can be contemporaneous and/or historical and cross-cultural. Studies are gathered on the basis of similar conditions to

(Continued)

	Positivist/sucessionist	Realist/generative	Constructivist/ configurational
	particular problem allows for meta-analysis that provides answers to what is likely or not likely to work.	researchers to build on and produce cumulative explanations, some of which will have the potential to be used to investigate different regularities in other kinds of behaviours (transferability).	analyse changes in attributes through comparative analysis. Studies are usually included to show useful frames of reference for interpretation or show inadequacies in data or to justify the method itself.
Examples including protocols	Masters et. al. (2006); Ciapponi (2011); Dowden and Andrews (1999); Hanson and Jones (2015); Jacobs et al. (1999); Richardson et al. (2015).	Lodenstein et al. (2013); Gaventa and Barrett (2010); Jackson et al. (2009); Mills et al. (2015); Otte-Trojel et al. (2014).	Cakir (2008); Jacobs et al. (1999); Kantar (2014); Mills et al. (2006); Trowler (2010).

*CMOC = context, mechanism, outcome-configuration.

The sucessionist position is mostly associated with the traditional intervention-ist, as of the kind found in the Cochrane Review Library. The configurationalist position is often mostly associated with the scholastic review, as of the kind found in reviews based on argumentation. The position in the middle, the generative approach, is most often associated with the realist review (and evaluation). This matching is, of course, a little crude but it allows us to think about the role of evidence in different approaches to research and to the status given to evidence types by different disciplines. Something new has, of course, been introduced in this typology. While the traditional interventionist and scholastic reviews have been discussed elsewhere in this book, the *realist review* has not. The reason for this is the standpoint some realists take regarding evidence and theory. In order to understand the realist review, it would be useful to know more about the sucessionist position. This we can do by looking at an example.

Extended example: Intercessory prayer

Regardless of the differences in assumptions both ontological and epistemological, many primary studies and literature reviews have been done to look into the relationship between praying and its effects on a sick person. Masters et al. (2006) asked if intercessory prayer 'works'. The following extract is from a typical meta-analysis of some such studies. In this example, we can see how evidence is sourced in terms of the selection of studies to be included and excluded, how the evidence is presented and how certain interpretations are made on its significance for answering the common question.

Extract	Observations
Both lay and professional interest in non-medical treatments for illness has grown exponentially in recent years. Perhaps the greatest evidence of this trend is the establishment of the National Center for Complementary and Alternative Medicine (NCCAM) within the US National Institutes of Health. In 2002, 62% of Americans reported using some kind of alternative medicine.	*The context for the meta-analysis (MA) is set with reference to an official body having been established for complementary treatments.* *The word 'medicine'. What is medicine? How does it differ from 'treatment' and 'therapy'? Are there differences and what significance do they have?*
Of the 10 most often utilised alternative medicine procedures in the United States, prayer for self (43%) and prayer for others (24.4%) are the two most commonly named therapies, and being in a prayer group (9.6%) ranks 5th. Prayer is a quintessential example of a health practice that is rooted in one's beliefs and philosophical orientation toward life and the cosmos. Nevertheless, it is important to note that prayer in and of itself may not qualify as a treatment that lacks a plausible biomedical explanation.	*Prayer is categorised as an alternative medicine and not complementary therapy. It is further defined as a health practice. What this means is some types of prayer are being categorised as aimed at biological intervention. The caveat is added that prayer may not count as treatment because it has no biomedical properties. If this is so, then why classify it as a treatment in the first place? This is when we need to look at the methodological paradigm that the authors are using as their reference point for their MA, namely materialism (also called physicalism).*
Simply defined, IP is prayer said on behalf of someone else, but the person doing the praying (i.e., the intercessor) is not present with the recipient of the prayer, thus making the prayer distant. Prayer occurs when intercessors pray for individuals who are not present with them and may, in fact, not even know that others are praying for them. Many believe that prayer is effective in and of itself, and it does not require that the recipient of the prayer be an active participant in either the prayer or the knowledge that someone is praying for him or her. Studies to be examined in this meta-analysis are that the participants (mostly patients) did not know if they were receiving prayer, that is, they were blind as to whether they were in the prayer or control group. By implementing these rigorous methodological procedures, the authors of these studies removed known psychological processes or placebo effects from the set of possible explanatory mechanisms that could account for significant findings.	*Regardless of the known status of prayer as an open system, metaphysical belief, the authors proceed to further their definition of it as interventionist – as if it were causal.* *Methodologically the authors move quickly to matters of control and variables. The point is made that some recipients of prayer did not know they were recipients and therefore could be regarded as part of a control group. This feature of the research to be included in the MA then reinforced the materialist assumptions of the authors. They are treating prayer as if it were a material force that could have causal power.* *Therefore, the assumption is the test of the power of prayer will be determined by selecting studies that have a control group.*

(Continued)

Extract	Observations
This meta-analysis is the most comprehensive and up-to-date quantitative review of the literature and includes the first published multi centre IP intervention study, a study not available to previous reviewers. It is also notable that prior authors reached highly discrepant conclusions regarding the proper future course for this research.	*The claim is made for this MA being the most comprehensive, but is it? This needs to be shown in the number of studies included alongside a transparent explanation of the inclusion and exclusion criteria. That other reviews have not reached a definite conclusion on the effect of prayer or future research into prayer seems to be a problem for the authors – why is this? Is it because they hold the belief there is a single, universal answer to the research question?*
One study with a large effect size supporting the efficacy of IP turned out to be unusual in a number of ways. When originally published, the study had three authors. However, one author removed his name from the study, stating that he only provided editorial input for the investigation, which did not merit inclusion as an author. Another author, Wirth, was recently convicted of fraud-related charges unrelated to the study and a newspaper report casts considerable doubt on whether the prayer groups in the study were actually conducted. We thought that the strange circumstances surrounding this article warranted examination of the overall results both including this study and excluding it from consideration.	*This is an interesting paragraph. It explains why one study was excluded. The authors show they have a sceptical stance towards the research they have collected for possible inclusion. Newspaper reports may raise suspicions but they should not be the sole reason for omitting a study unless clear evidence is obtained. This is good practice and something all researchers should adhere to. Did the authors, however, subject the other studies identified for inclusion to the same scrutiny?*
A comparison of the effect of IP on participants randomly assigned to conditions versus participants non-randomly assigned revealed no significant difference ($Q = .038$, $p = .85$). In addition, the mean effect size of studies that utilised daily prayer showed no significant difference compared to studies that utilised less frequent prayer ($Q = .33$, $p = .57$). A WLS regression analysis revealed no relationship between mean effect size and duration of prayer intervention ($\beta = -.02$, $p = .94$). The fore-mentioned analyses indicate that study design characteristics did not serve as moderator variables in this analysis. A test of homogeneity yielded non-significant results ($Q = 15.07$, $p = .30$), indicating that the studies were likely clustered around a common mean that is reasonably representative of each study in the set.	*This set of analytical statistics is offered as the main evidence for conclusions made about the answer to the research question. Statistics can be powerful methods for describing behaviours and for inferring relationships between variables (or not in this case).*

Extract	Observations
All of these studies suffer from a major and unsolvable methodological flaw, that is, receipt of prayer cannot be controlled and therefore it is impossible to know to what degree individuals in the control groups were actually the recipients of the 'intervention' (IP). There is no scientifically discernable effect that differentiates the status of individuals who are the recipients of IP initiated by a research team from those who do not receive research team initiated IP.	*The earlier claim for the methodological advantages of the research design is not seen as a problem. This problem is directed towards the studies included rather than this MA itself. Nonetheless, the claim is made that there was no significant effect for either the control or non-control group. As this is seen as a methodological flaw, it means the results of the MA must incorporate this flaw in its own analysis. The question is, why was it used in the first place? What status does this confer on any conclusions this MA makes?*
In the absence of supportive empirical data, the role of a defensible theoretical rationale gains greater prominence if this line of research is to continue. However, the development of such a rationale may, in and of itself, prove challenging. Chibnall, Jeral, and Cerullo offered a brilliant criticism of the theoretical and methodological underpinnings of this research and pointed out many significant and seemingly insurmountable logical difficulties with IP studies. A couple of final caveats are in order for a proper perspective. First, we did not study prayer for one's self or prayer said in the presence of the prayer recipient. This research has nothing to say about these practices. We are also not trying to persuade believers to stop their practice of IP as it is carried out within their faith traditions. We see no health risk to patients or others from IP, and, in fact, believe that there may be as yet unspecified and unstudied benefits for the intercessors themselves. We encourage those interested in how spiritual variables may impact health to investigate areas of research that are grounded in theoretically defensible constructs and related models. Nevertheless, given that the IP literature lacks a theoretical or theological base and has failed to produce significant findings in controlled trials, we recommend that further resources not be allocated to this line of research.	*The primary studies are seen as providing no empirical data. No clear set of reasons with evidence is given for this claim. The citation for Chibnall, Jeral, and Cerullo (2001), is given but not the substance of their criticisms. This citation is meant to give evidence for the claim about the lack of empirical data. But it is left 'hanging', that is, no description of Chibnall et al.'s (2001) criticisms are provided. Is there a 'proper perspective'? Does this mean other perspectives are not proper, or as good? The language used here indicates the authors have a particular view on the status of prayer and how others should regard it in health settings and it is this they are trying to justify.* *Moderation is introduced with the claim the authors are not talking to people with religious faith. For some reason that is not made clear, for there may be – the authors acknowledge – benefits of prayer but to understand these 'defensible theoretical constructs and models' will, the authors state, be needed. Will these be from the Galtonian materialist paradigm or from other methodological positions? This is not made clear.*

(Continued)

Extract	Observations
	Finally, a recommendation is made that no further resources be allocated to the study of intercessory prayer because the controlled trials they have analysed have not produced results that are statistically significant or have a justifiable theoretical base – what kind of base this would be is not indicated.

Masters et al. (2006) undertook a meta-analysis of primary studies on intercessory prayer using the protocols common to traditional interventionist literature reviews. The critical comments made of Masters et al. are intended to show the importance of applying a critical standpoint not only to evidence but also the methodological framework, in which evidence is offered as the basis of a claim or recommendation. The statistical calculations are some of the evidence offered by Masters et al. (2006), but they also have three tables and these are worth looking into. Table 6.3 (Table 2 in Masters et al., 2006) summarises the statistical calculations.

TABLE 6.3   Effects of intercessory prayer summarised across studies

Condition	Number of comparisons	g^a	Z	P
Overall	14	.100	1.35	.18
Patient	11	.169	1.93	.05
Healthy	3	−.061	.58	.57
Patient (without Cha and Wirth, 2001)	10	.066	.72	.47
Overall (without Cha and Wirth, 2001)	13	.012	.17	.87

a Positive value for g favours effect for intercessory prayer

Source: Masters et al., 2006: 24

The second table Masters et al. (2006: 24) present shows lists of the studies included in their review. While Cha and Wirth (2001) were excluded, it is not clear if this is the list of actual studies included. This is because in the references another list is indicated by the use of asterisks.

Masters et al. (2006: 24) also include a forest plot (see Figure 6.2) as evidence for their conclusions. A forest plot is a graphical representation used in meta-analysis. Each line shows the direction of association found in individual studies. Lines on the right-hand side of the plot indicate a positive association (it is said to favour experimental). This indicates that participants

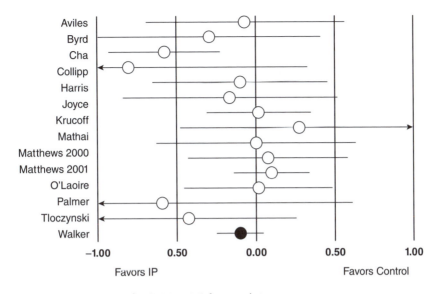

FIGURE 6.2 Masters et al.'s (2006: 24) forest plot

who received the intervention showed or reported more changes than those who received the control (another intervention or no intervention). The black dot at the bottom shows the mean effect size of the studies. The clear dots shows the standard mean difference for each study (the difference between the mean score for the intervention group and the control group). The black dot (in Figure 6.2) is slightly to the left of centre and, therefore, favours some intercessory prayer. This is not a significant degree of favour but it does show a positive outcome.

These positive findings (though very small) should not be taken at face value. They need, as evidence, to be interpreted within a context. That context is the assumptions about the homogeneity and heterogeneity between the studies included in the meta-analysis. If similar studies are asking similar research questions and investigate similar interventions then a higher level of consistency across the studies could reasonably be assumed. If this is the case, then why do these 13 studies (excluding Cha and Wirth, 2001) not arrive at the same or very similar results? Masters et al.'s (2006) forest plot seems to show a high level of heterogeneity. To compensate for this Masters et al. (2006) applied a test for heterogeneity. Tests for heterogeneity/homogeneity work like this. If the calculation results in a percentage higher than 50% then the heterogeneity between studies is said to be high. If the calculation results in a percentage lower than 50% then the heterogeneity between studies is said to be low. Therefore, calculations for hetero-geneity aim to look at the presence and effect of variability between studies and make 'a moderation', where necessary, for apparent variance. Tests for heterogeneity include the Q Test and I^2 index (see Huedo-Medina et al., 2006, for a discussion of these tech-niques). Masters et al. (2006: 24) have a figure of >30, indicating, they claim, 'the studies were likely clustered around a common mean that is reasonably representative of each study in the set'.

(Continued)

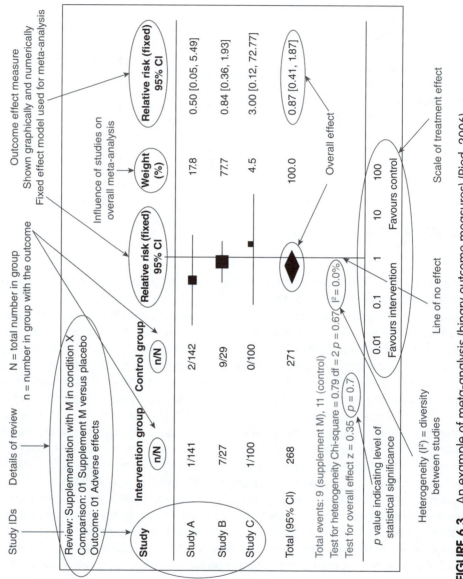

FIGURE 6.3 An example of meta-analysis (binary outcome measures) (Ried, 2006)

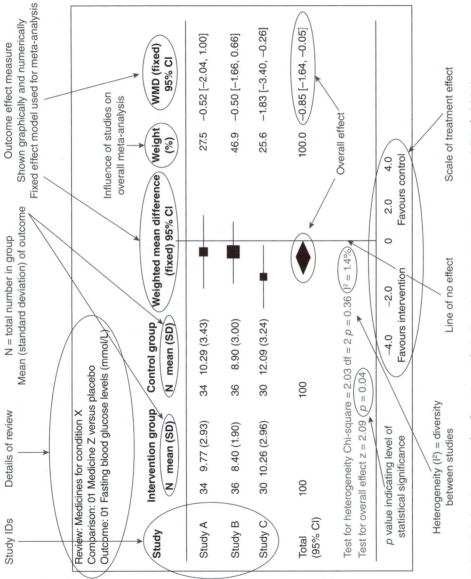

FIGURE 6.4 An example of meta-analysis (continuous outcome measures) (Ried, 2006)

(Continued)

Even with a calculation of >30, Masters et al. (2006) have a number of problems and most of these are about the details they have given about their meta-analysis. The tables presented in their article lack the necessary details for a full scrutiny. A typical meta-analysis will have at least one table with all the details. Table 6.4 and 6.5 are examples of what we should expect in any meta-analysis. In these two tables Ried (2006) shows how to read meta-analysis data.

The differences between Figures 6.3 and 6.4 come down to the variables being looked at in a meta-analysis. Figure 6.3 combines data from randomly controlled trials. It shows comparisons between an intervention group and a control group. Binary variables result in yes/no results. That is, did the intervention work or not. The outcome measure is normally ratios. Figure 6.4 shows the use of continuous variables such as height. The outcome measure is normally stated as weighted mean difference (WMD). Therefore, a basic understanding of statistics and different kinds of variables shows that Masters et al. (2006) used continuous outcome measures. The 0 is the line of no effect and is used when using WMD. Having looked at Figure 6.4 the details in Masters et al. (2006) are somewhat sparse.

In the example of intercessory prayer, the name Galton was mentioned. This is relevant because when we attribute a position to a piece of research, such as this meta-analysis, we are implying it will hold, to a lesser or greater degree, a set of assumptions. These assumptions will be about the nature of reality and knowledge. Masters et al. (2006), in their meta-analysis of intercessory prayer, hold a worldview that can be traced, in Western culture, to Francis Galton (1822–1911) and his popularisation of materialism (Levine, 2010).

Causality and the materialist worldview

The search for causal variables may be as old as Homo sapiens. It is an intellectual and practical activity that has been remarkably successful for human kind. However, it is a radical step to claim that all that exists is matter (whatever matter is). The belief being that if it extends into space then it is material and hence nothing non-spacial can exist. This proposition is deceptively attractive and simple. This is because in our everyday lives 'things' seem to happen for a reason. We may not know the details of how something works, like a toaster, but take it for granted that once the handle is pressed the toaster will heat up and toast a slice of bread.

Originating (most likely) in third century Indian thought, it gained popularity in European thought in the nineteenth century. It was Francis Galton who in 1872 made the first statistical analysis of intercessory prayer. His strict materialist position led him to propose, in statistical terms, the hypothesis that if prayer worked then members of the British Royal family would live forever.

His hypothesis is based on the practice then found in many Anglican services of praying for the monarch and her/his family. Galton devised a simple test of this belief in intercessory prayer. Prayers were given over a selection of plants to see if they would grow any faster than plants not subject to prayer. Galton found no correlation between the control group and the non-control group. In the studies looked at in Masters et al.'s (2006) meta-analysis of intercessory prayer, we see the continuing influence of the materialist worldview on the search for causal variables and exclusion of other worldviews.

There is nothing inherently wrong with the materialist position regarding the workings of the world (and universe). A problem does arise, however, when materialism is presented as the only true position to take regarding understanding the world.

There is more than materialism

While the materialist worldview is not to be denied it is not to be accepted at face value. Take Karl Marx's famous inversion of Hegal's idealism. What came first, Marx's *idea* of revolution or his *materialist* conception of history that justified the idea? If we take away historical materialism is the power of the idea of revolution/change also taken away?

While there are different standpoints within the materialist position, textbook portrayals tend to be of the more dogmatic variety. They tend to negate the possibility of other worldviews. For all practical purposes, there is no need to develop a systematic challenge to materialism in the ways in which adherents of materialism have thought it necessary to challenge other worldviews. This asymmetry is often maintained in studies, such as that done by Masters et al. (2006). These reviews and the research on which they are based are reliant on the assumptions we can trace back to Galton – the sucessionist epistemology and measurement of variables. There is, it should be stressed, nothing wrong in this. But (there should always be room for a but question) there are some basic questions about materialism, as there are for all worldviews that are part of what makes us conscious sentient beings. As such, we are able to question and reflect on our experiences and feelings, to experiment and study, to systematically categorise and record, and importantly to think creatively about what something could be, is and means. These abilities are part of the scientific as well as everyday attitude. The point being made here is this. Dogma in any worldview is to be challenged. In some fields of physics, this has been happening for over 100 years.

Over the past 100 or so years physicists have developed the theory (or more accurately, theories about the minimum amount of physical stuff needed to do things) of quantum mechanics. Like many investigative and theoretical endeavours quantum mechanics is a story containing ideas and challenges to those ideas. In his telling of the story of quantum mechanics, Manjit Kumar (2014) calls his book *Quantum: Einstein, Bohr and the Great Debate about the Nature of Reality*. Kumar (2014) not only tells the story of quantum mechanics, he also shows how ideas have a history, create divisions and are often described using non-physical terminology. In the preface he writes,

> Paul Ehrenfest was in tears. He had made his decision. Soon he would attend the 'week-long' meeting where many of those responsible for the quantum revolution would try to understand the meaning of what they had thought. There he would have to tell his old friend Albert Einstein that he had chosen to side with Niels Bohr ...
>
> In a note to Einstein, as they sat around the conference table, Ehrenfest scribbled: 'don't laugh! There is a special section in purgatory for professors of quantum theory, where they will be obliged to listen to lectures on classical physics ten hours every day.' 'I laugh only at their naiveté;' Einstein replied. 'Who knows who would have the (last) laugh in a few years?' For him it was no laughing matter, for at stake were the very nature of reality and the soul of physics.

Kumar (2014) also shows the politics of ideas, personalities and assumptions inherent in research and philosophy. The particulars of quantum mechanics do not need to be understood. What we have here are two positions regarding quantum mechanics, Einstein's and Bohr's. Other scientists had to make choices over which of the two to ally themselves with. There were no objective criteria for making such a choice. In a similar way, Kumar's book is not an objective account (or telling) of the story – an historian could question the sources he uses, while a philosopher the meanings he gives to them. Like all narratives, Kumar's gives emphasis to some people and events over others. The benefit, however, of trying to read works like *Quantum* (Kumar, 2014), is what such accounts reveal about the ways ontological and epistemological positions, including assumptions about causality, are portrayed in textbooks. In the main, most portrayals are (including the ones in this book) far too simplistic and naive.

Contextualising research findings

The traditional interventionist review, as seen in the library of Cochrane, are powerful tools for decision making. However, those reviews aimed at policy improvement have a major problem. That problem is they ask, 'what works?', when they should be asking 'what works for whom, in what circumstances and in what respects, and how?' Pawson and Tilley (1997; 2004) use this difference in question to summarise their recommendations and research programme based on the assumptions of *realist evaluation*.

To understand the relevance of Pawson and Tilley (1997) and how their approach has been used, we must first place their argument within the context of literature reviewing. Figure 6.5 shows a typical selection process for a typical interventionist review.

TABLE 6.4   Sucessionist and generative inclusion and exclusion criteria protocols compared

Sucessionist inclusion and exclusion criteria (from Jadad et al., 1996: 7 and Treadwell, 2011)	Generative inclusion and exclusion criteria (from Lodenstein et al., 2013: 9)
Was the study described as randomised? • Number of studies that were RCTs • Existence of important unmeasured confounders • Degree of relevance to Key Questions in studies that did this • Whether the outcome is harmful • Is randomisation ethical (e.g., is there equipoise between interventions)? Was the study described as double blind? • Number of studies that did this • How difficult it is to blind study participants or maintain blinding • Whether study participant knowledge of intervention group can influence outcomes • Degree of relevance in studies that did this • Whether the outcome is a harm • Is blinding ethical (e.g., would it require an unethical comparison group)? Was there a description of withdrawals and dropouts? Were the objectives of the study defined? Were the outcome measures defined clearly? Was there a clear description of the inclusion and exclusion criteria?	Relevance The document addresses interventions or reforms that aim *explicitly* (in their objectives) to strengthen citizen engagement or social accountability in the health sector (health service delivery and/or health policy making processes) or the document describes opinions on, and experiences with, citizen engagement or social accountability in the health sector (case study, descriptive study). The document addresses interventions that more *implicitly* (in the process or outcomes) relate to citizen engagement and social accountability in the health sector. In these cases, the studies will only be included if they report on voice and/or responsiveness or relational issues. Setting The document deals with at least one country with medium to low levels of governance capacity and quality. The list of countries is derived from the Worldwide Governance Indicators (WGI) database from the World Bank. The document deals with interventions at local (community, district) or national level. Type and characteristics of studies The document is based on primary research (additional code 'P'). Documents will have been developed/published between 2003 and 2013.

(Continued)

Was the sample size justified (e.g., power calculation)?

Was there a clear description of the interventions?

Was there at least one control (comparison) group?

- Number of studies that did this
- Whether disease course allows intervention effects to be predicted accurately without an independent comparison group
- If there would be substantial carry over effect if study participants received both interventions sequentially
- Whether the outcome is a harm

Were the methods used to assess adverse effects described?

Were the methods of statistical analysis described?

English, French and Spanish language.

For grey literature the credibility and quality will be assessed using these criteria:

- a recognisable research process, not just anecdotal reporting
- the independence of the author (if from the organisation, a level of external peer review should have taken place)
- the contact details of the organisation or authors are provided.

Exclusion criteria

- the document is not about the health sector
- the intervention has a global character (e.g. global mobilization campaigns, etc.)
- the document is based on secondary research (additional code 'S') or is a conceptual paper.

The conventional interventionist review is based on excluding research through the application of selection criteria. These criteria are well known and are commonly applied standards used to evaluate reviews. In the case of Carr et al. (2011), they started out with 269 possible studies.

Criteria-based protocols

Examples of criteria-based protocols for the selection and rejection of studies are included in the following manuals and guides:

- Systematic Reviews CRD
- EPPI Centre
- PRISMA Statement (2009)
- AHRQ
- NICE

Once the criteria had been applied 243 were excluded. Of the remaining 26 studies, 23 of these were RCTs. The three non-RCTs included one ethnographic study. It is not, however, the criteria that should have given relevance weightings to study selection or rejection but the aims of the review. Carr et al.'s (2011) aims were:

To identify, describe, classify and analyse the range of models developed to date for delivering health-related lifestyle advice (HRLA), or training, for effectiveness, mechanism of effect, cost-effectiveness, equity and acceptability in improving the health and wellbeing of individuals and communities, with particular reference to the reduction of inequalities in the UK. (Carr et al., 2011: ix)

After the review was completed Carr et al. conclude:

Overall, the evidence was not sufficient to support or refute the use of LAs [lifestyle advisor] to promote health and improve quality of life (QoL). Although there is likely to be considerable uncertainty about statements of interventions' cost-effectiveness because of the sparse evidence base for effectiveness, lessons can be drawn from the realist analysis of the included studies. (Carr et al., 2011: x)

Carr et al. (2011) produced a 284-page report. We can take it for granted that this required a substantial amount of work. Given their overall conclusion they do, however, have some positive recommendations to make based on their review, but these are about specific lifestyle behaviours. There is nothing inherently wrong with Carr et al.'s (2011) work. What we can note is that the criteria for inclusion may have been too restrictive. This is because the use of hierarchies of evidence, largely based on methodological assumptions about the level of rigour used in a study, excluded studies that may have provided contextual and historical information, and importantly understanding relevant to the problem. Carr et al. (2011) had many exclusion criteria:

This review will exclude interventions delivered without the explicit aim of health improvement. For example, community-based secondary prevention for chronic disease will be included, but lifestyle advice or training delivered as part of treatment or care for acute illness will be excluded. Other exclusion criteria will include: interventions focusing solely on the delivery of training or advice to children or adolescents as intervention methods and factors determining effectiveness are likely to be very different from those in adults; and studies or reports detailing descriptive accounts of programmes, without any evaluation. (Carr et al., 2011: 190)

Taking Carr et al. (2011) as an example of a sound conventional and non-realist synthesis review, we can compare it to reviews that take into account context. By context Pawson and Tilley (1997; 2004) mean the interactions between the participant, setting and programme mechanisms. This includes such features as the history of the organisation, the people working in it, the biography of participants, beliefs, staffing, region, ethnicity, age, gender, sexuality, geography, and anything else that can be identified as part of the situation. Importantly context is also about the different understandings and interpretations participants have of a situation and programme.

Realist analysis: Theory-driven reviews

Realist analysis and evaluation are the starting points for the realist literature review. To understand the realist review, we must first grasp the standpoint and approach to research held by key proponents in the realist evaluation movement. The realist review developed out of realist evaluation (Pawson and Tilley, 2004). Both are theory-based approaches (theory driven) to gathering and synthesising evidence. The main focus is theory and not programmes. Programmes are conventionally regarded as an intervention to bring about change. Conventional interventionist reviews normally focus on programmes as the main units of analysis. They assume the analysis and synthesis of data (especially from RCT) from different studies can provide a weight of evidence for making a recommendation for, or against, an intervention. Pawson and Tilley (2004) argue that the focus should be on theories about how programmes operate. This shift in focus from programmes to theories is not minor. It represents a significant intellectual shift in how to do evaluation and a literature review aimed at intervention. It also changes the ways in which we view the hierarchy of evidence. So, why theorise? Pawson and Tilley (2004: 3) explain why:

> Programmes are theories incarnate. They begin in the heads of policy architects, pass into the hands of practitioners and, sometimes, into the hearts and minds of programme subjects. These conjectures originate with an understanding of what gives rise to inappropriate behaviour, or to discriminatory events, or to inequalities of social condition and then move to speculate on how changes may be made to these patterns. Interventions are always inserted into existing social systems that are thought to underpin and account for present problems. Changes in patterns of behaviour, events or conditions are then generated, by bringing fresh inputs to that system.

The realist review like the realist evaluation, therefore, begins with a theory about a programme and once evidence has been collected, the theory is tested. The review ends, as does the evaluation, with a refined theory about a programme. On the way to the refined theory several initial or rough theories may be examined.

Realist analysis resources

If you want to read more on realist analysis and evaluation, I recommend the following resources which are easily located online:

- BetterEvaluation
- Realist synthesis: The website
- The RAMESES Project

These do not have to be 'realist' but must be useful in addressing the questions 'what is supposed to happen?' and 'why is it assumed to work?' In a review, different 'programme theories' can be compared using a much broader range of evidence than would normally be found in conventional interventionist meta-analysis. Hence in the realist review, evidence for programmes and programmes themselves are seen as 'open systems' rather than as 'closed systems'. Analysis at the level of theory results in abstraction. This means the abstracted comparison of theories allows for the review to make explicit assumptions and ideas embedded within a programme. This shift from closed to open systems can be seen in the extension of the interventionist question. Where conventional interventionist reviewers ask 'what works', the realist reviewer asks 'what works for whom, in what contexts, in what respects and how?' Hence, every intervention (programme) is testing an implicit or explicit theory about what may cause change. The realist reviewer, therefore, aims to make visible for analysis the theories on which a programme is based. This is done by developing hypotheses about how programmes work for whom, when and in what contexts. The hypotheses are tested against evidence from studies that have used a range of approaches and methods, not just RCT.

In the realist literature review, Wong et al. (2013: 10) list the main reasons for starting with theory:

1. there are always more questions that you could ask in a review than you will have the capacity to answer – using theory helps to focus the review, and to decide which questions to ask
2. there is always more literature that you could examine than you will have the resources for – theory helps to determine which literature is most relevant
3. the information gathered in a review always has to be interpreted and theory provides a guide for interpretation
4. the information gathered in a review is usually complex and messy – theory provides a basis for abstraction and for understanding 'the patterns in the data'
5. given that evaluations of the 'same' programme (or kinds of programmes) almost always show different results in different situations (or for different groups), theory provides a basis for explanation of the patterning of outcomes
6. attributing outcomes to programmes is complex – in primary evaluation, theory provides a basis for causal attribution; in reviews, theory provides a framework with which to assess the plausibility of attributions made by original authors.

Realist reviews: Key concepts – context, mechanism and outcome-pattern

There are four interrelated concepts common to explanations in realist evaluation and reviews of programmes. They are, 'context', 'mechanism', 'outcome' and 'configuration' (CMOC). All programmes have a context. This means any situation has a history, location, stakeholders, politics, interpretations and so on. Contextual thinking is used to address the question, 'for whom's and in 'what circumstances' did the programme work – or not as the case may be? The realist evaluation like the realist review has the difficult task of identifying, with confidence, conditions which are relevant to a programme. A mechanism is something that generates an outcome. This may be positive or negative, intended or unintended. Mechanisms include people, beliefs, interpretations, processes and structures. All mechanisms operate within particular historical contexts and social structures. Realists generally assume mechanisms are hidden and are not, therefore, always obvious; they are, nonetheless, causal. These can be structural and include social class, gender and economic relationships and/or a process, and also include sequences of events with later ones dependent on earlier events.

An important point for realists is that mechanisms are not linear, simple or inevitable and are not, therefore, always measurable via the control of variables. This is because at the programme level, it is the interpretations people make that are often key mechanisms. It is not inevitable that subjects will make predicted interpretations and change behaviours. Rather, subjects will bring their interpretations to a context. Therefore, the studies included in realist reviews may have employed a wide range of methods and kinds of sources. This is seen as the strength of the realist review. It is a feature of the realist review but necessitates the review to explicate the logic of interventions they include.

Outcomes are referred to as outcome-patterns or outcome configurations. This phrase points to the assumptions that mechanisms can and often do result in more than one outcome, but in some cases the outcomes have patterns. This allows for theories to be developed and tested regarding what brought about the patterns, and importantly allows for comparisons to be made between outcome-patterns between different realist evaluations. Hence, it is not a simple case of saying (making the claim) an intervention 'worked' and will 'work' for similar situations. It is a matter of identifying the outcome-patterns, to list which outcomes did seem to work and which did not in a given context.

Extended example: The protocol of a realist review of citizen engagement in health service delivery

In a review titled 'A realist synthesis of the effect of social accountability interventions on health service providers' and policymakers' responsiveness', Lodenstein et al. (2013: 4) asked 'when and how do social accountability interventions influence providers' and policymakers' responsiveness in health service delivery in countries with medium to low levels of governance capacity and quality?' Their paper is not a review but an explication of the protocol they used for their review. The key to understanding what they are aiming to find out is given in their specific research questions (Lodenstein et al., 2013: 4):

What is the expected chain of results of the social accountability intervention (programme theory)?

What are the reported (favourable and unfavourable) outcomes of the interventions?

At what levels – individual, organisational, societal and so on? In particular, what are the reported responsiveness outcomes?

Who is reported to be both positively and negatively affected by the intervention and its outcomes?

What mechanisms and contextual elements help to explain the outcomes of the intervention?

These questions are driven by testing a hypothesis that Lodenstein et al. (2013: 4) have. They state, 'By answering these questions through a realist synthesis, the reviewers expect to be able to refine the hypothesised program theory ...' The review was initiated by, according to Lodenstein et al. (2013: 1), the following situation:

> One of the effective strategies for building equitable health systems and providing quality health services is the strengthening of citizen-driven or social accountability processes. The monitoring of actions and decisions of policy makers and providers by citizens is regarded as a right in itself but also as an alternative to weak administrative accountability mechanisms, in particular in settings with poor governance. The effects of social accountability interventions are often based on assumptions and are difficult to evaluate because of their complex nature and context sensitivity.

Lodenstein et al. (2013: 1), therefore, state the overall aim of their review:

> This study aims to review and assess the available evidence for the effect of social accountability interventions on policy makers' and providers' responsiveness in countries with medium to low levels of governance capacity and quality. For policy-makers and practitioners engaged in health system strengthening, social accountability initiatives and rights-based approaches to health, the findings of this review may help when reflecting on the assumptions and theories of change behind their policies and interventions.

An interesting feature of Lodenstein et al.'s (2013: 5) paper is the inclusion of definitions, based in the wider realist literature, of context, mechanism, outcome and C-M-O configurations. Each definition is used to give examples relevant to their core research question. For example, context is defined as, 'Actors or factors that are external to the intervention, occurring independently of the outcome or influencing the outcome ... context can also be understood as anything that can trigger and/or modify the behaviour of a mechanism'. These definitions are exemplified by:

(Continued)

The issue/problem: The issues citizens are confronted with, or about which they express demands, claims, suggestions, opinions, preferences and so on. For example, they may be about the quality, acceptability, accessibility or availability of health services and policies, equality (gender, class or ethnicity) or particular medical aspects of the citizen–provider interaction (disease recognition, treatment and so on). The issues at stake may also be about equity, discrimination, exclusion and demands for changes in the underlying power relations.

Political/institutional factors: The nature and strength of civil society; models of deliberation, information, capacities and awareness of citizens; the strength of the health system; the capacities, power and incentives of providers and policy makers; the nature and scope of existing social accountability relations; the legal context of citizen engagement; media and press; the historical context; pre-intervention activism; political economy factors; formal and informal political processes; general views on participation; cultural norms and the history of the community where the intervention is implemented.

Other interventions: Other participatory interventions, government-led accountability initiatives, initiatives to strengthen citizen participation in general or for health.

Mechanism is defined as the 'interplay between structure and agency, how the social structure interacts with individual or group agency. Mechanisms can be found at individual, group, organisational or societal levels. They are psychological or social explanations of behaviour. They may be the cognitive or emotional responses of people who want to participate (or not) in an intervention'. These definitions are exemplified by the following:

In documents they may be referred to as barriers or facilitators and/or successful or unsuccessful elements of the intervention and its outcomes. They are most likely presented in the discussion or lessons learned section. Mechanisms may be expressed through interpretations, considerations, decisions or behaviours of humans, including the authors of a document. Within the factors being discussed, the behavioural elements will need to be distilled. In the context of citizen engagement and social accountability, mechanisms may refer to triggers that make a citizen or a provider decide or act in favour or not in favour of the intervention. His/her considerations may be a simple cost–benefit analysis, the expected success for the individual or the collective, the mandate of the activity, the trust in, and behaviour of the facilitators, and so on.

Outcome is defined as the 'intended or unexpected outcome of an intervention. It can be defined as intermediate or final ... it can be reported at the individual, organisational, institutional, policy or legislative level. It can be both positive and negative'. These definitions are exemplified by the following:

The reviewers distinguish between process outcomes and health, rights and development outcomes (called impact). Process outcomes can be found on the citizens' side and on the providers' side. For citizens, outcomes can be levels of empowerment, voice, agency, awareness, knowledge, satisfaction and trust. Change in providers' and policy makers' responsiveness can be levels of accountability: receptivity, responsibility, recognition of issues and concerns, inclusion, acceptance, discrimination, coherence, cohesion, confrontation, conflict, trust, quality and performance (e.g. related to accessibility, acceptability) reflected in changed behaviour, policies and practices. Impact refers to health outcomes such as increased utilisation of or attendance at health services, prevalence and treatment rates.

In addition to definitions and examples, Lodenstein et al. (2013) also provide an indicative review of realist evaluation sources, a framework for the extraction of data from sources, inclusion and exclusion criteria, discussion of quality assurance, a list of previous reviews on the situation/debate and a discussion of internal and external validity. What this protocol illustrates is the prior thinking and preparation that need to go into any review and particular realist reviews.

Realist reviews: Theory

In realist evaluation four levels of theory can be distinguished: philosophical theory, evaluation theory, programme theory and substantive theory. Realism is a philosophical theory about reality (ontology). Realist evaluation is part of the realist tradition and is grounded in complex systems theory. Realist evaluation uses in its programme theory the CMO configuration. Finally, realist reviews look for the use of substantive theory to explain a programme. All disciplines have their distinctive substantive theories. These are normally concerned in explaining substantive social concerns such as crime, divorce and prejudice.

Substantive theories are considered to be transferable rather than the basis for generalisation. Realist evaluation means transferring learning from one context to a similar context. For example, Lodenstein et al. (2013: 7), in outlining their protocol for a realist review, tell their readers:

The preliminary program theory presented in this protocol is based on a review of literature and preparatory sessions with the authors and external experts. It is formulated in a broad way with a limited number of predefined assumptions to allow a better understanding of the variety of ways of working of social accountability interventions and responsiveness dynamics. An inductive approach to data collection and analysis will help the reviewers to enrich the preliminary program theory gradually and make the underlying assumptions more explicit ... Later in the synthesis process, the results of previous systematic reviews and literature reviews will, where relevant, be used to contextualise or strengthen the findings and support the review of the hypothesised program theory.

In a realist review (or synthesis) the reviewer (or review team) will usually start with a rough, preliminary theory. Through testing the rough theory can be refined until a middle range theory or programme theory is developed. The programme theory is, at that time and context, put forward as the best possible explanation for the C-M-O pattern. It is, of course, important to understand what is meant by and how to use middle range theories.

Briefly, middle range theory is the suggestion made by Robert K. Merton (1967) that the findings from empirical research need to be subject to a level of practical abstraction, so that they could be used to form generalisations. This could be done, he argued and demonstrated, by developing theories from which hypotheses could be derived and empirically investigated and tested:

> Theories that lie between the minor but necessary working hypotheses that evolve in abundance during day-to-day research and the all-inclusive systematic efforts to develop a unified theory that will explain all the observed uniformities of social behaviour, social organisation and social change. (Merton, 1967: 39)

Substantive situations or social phenomenon (such as deviancy) would generate their own middle range theory and hypotheses, from which, in turn, more general conceptual schemes could be developed to explain empirical regularities (patterns of behaviour). Merton (1967) was mostly concerned to develop middle range theorising for the social sciences, especially sociology. His work, however, has been adapted and applied across many disciplines in both the social and natural sciences. The basic scheme of middle range theory is shown in Figure 6.5.

There are many middle range theories to be found across different disciplines. In sociology, we have had the theory of anomie (Durkheim, 1952/1970[1897]),

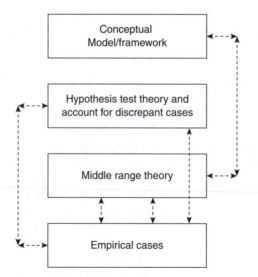

FIGURE 6.5   The place of middle range theory in research

role set theory (Merton, 1957), dissonance theory (Cooper, 2007), and many more. Most middle range theories have their origins in a conceptual model.

A conceptual model is normally a set of general concepts that have been proposed to define a situation or behaviour that is of interest to a discipline.

Reading advice: Frames of reference

There is a lot written on conceptual models. To help you understand frames of reference in more depth, I recommend Hart (2005), Anderson et al. (1985) or Putman (1981).

For example, in nursing there are various conceptual models such as Johnson's (1980) Behavioral system model, Levine's (1991) Conservation model and Roy's (1976; 1988) Adaptation model. Conceptual models can be derived from several middle range theories or from grand, more abstract theories (a kind of top-down approach). The function of these models, so to speak, is to provide a frame of reference for the researcher. This frame of reference guides the researcher on such matters as how to define certain concepts, what kind of vocabulary is to be used in descriptions and explanations and how to produce interpretations. Frames of reference are usually discipline specific.

It is sometimes the case that from one conceptual model, the range of situations or behaviours observed needs more than one middle range theory. Hence, some conceptual models generate several middle range theories. Take, for

TABLE 6.5 Uses of Roy's (1976; 1988) Adaptation model to develop middle range theories in nursing

Roy's (1976; 1988) Adaptation model

Middle range theories developed from Roy (1976; 1988)	Use of Roy (1976; 1988) to develop conceptual-theoretical structures
Theory of psychosocial adaptation to termination of pregnancy for foetal anomaly (Kruszewski, 1999)	Cross-cultural responses to pain (Calvillo and Flaskerud, 1993)
Theory of adapting to diabetes (Whittemore and Roy, 2002)	Adaptation to chronic illness (Pollock, 1993)
Theory of adaptation during childbearing (Tulman and Fawcett, 2003)	Preparation for caesarean childbirth (Fawcett, 1990)
Theory of caregiver stress (Tsai, 2003)	Preparation for caesarean childbirth (Fawcett, 1990)

example, Roy's (1976) Adaptation model. This was initially developed in the 1970s to frame, describe, define and explain the relationship of the patient and their particular adaptation to their condition in terms of their place within a system composed of their biological, social and psychological environment over time. From this initial model, several middle range theories were developed (mainly in the 1990s) with other associated conceptual structures to guide empirical research. Some of these can be seen in Table 6.5. This shows that a conceptual model, if it has sufficient explanatory power, tends to be applied to various behaviours within a discipline.

Middle range theories are not always explanatory. They can be descriptive or predictive. Whereas explanatory theory aims to show the relationship between one concept and another, descriptive theory classifies (using typologies and taxonomies) the commonalities observed in a phenomenon. Predictive middle range theory aims to assert more precise relationships between concepts, so that claims can be made about outcomes to a situation given specific changes to one or more of the main concepts.

Doing a realist review

The realist review shares many of the approaches found in the scholastic review. Both try to be as inclusive, rather than exclusive, as possible. The mind-set they share is about looking for studies and conceptual works that can provide useful insight relevant to the main review question. A part of this mind-set is ensuring relevant theory and concepts to drive the search and analysis of studies. A key element here is the generative and iterative nature of the realist review. Through theory driven searching and analysis the overall goal is to generate explanations that account for what outcomes (O) were generated by what mechanisms (M) in what contexts (C). This often means alternating between searching and analysing, following new leads, incorporating these into the analysis and so on. It is not a linear process of the structure found in conventional interventionist reviews. The realist reviewer is, to use an analogy, a detective.

The evidence for the realist reviewer can seem boundless. Given the assumptions of realist analysis any programme is multifaceted, complex and operates in an environment that is changeable. The same programme can be expected to operate differently given different contexts. Hence, efforts need to be focused. If they are not, the process will become amorphous, lacking focus and purpose. The task will be akin to nailing jelly to a wall. Guidance to the realist reviewer is at hand. There are some basic stages, shown in Table 6.6, that can help.

TABLE 6.6   Stages in the realist review of a programme literature

	Stages	Brief explanation
Gain knowledge and understanding	**Stage one:** Search for and read the key works on realist evaluation	Ensure you are familiar and conversant with the main methodological assumptions of realist evaluation and analysis. It is essential to have read Pawson and Tilley (1997; 2004), Pawson (2006; 2013), Bhaskar (1978) and Archer (1995).
	Stage two: Search for and read realist reviews	Realist reviews are a learning resource. Look for the ways in, which of the assumptions, philosophy and logic of realist analysis have been used. Examples include Daykin et al. (2007), McMahon and Ward (2012), Connelly et al. (2007) and Jackson et al. (2009).
Define the boundaries	**Stage three:** Focus your review question	State the review question in such a way that it is focused on specifics rather than generalities. Take into account how much time you have to do the review. Remember that the question can be subject to revision as different studies are located and analysed. This is part of the iterative process.
Understand causes	**Stage four:** Identify the main theory underlying the programme under consideration	Realist analysis assumes all programmes are based on a theory. This needs to be identified and described. This theory is a candidate to guide the search for studies. Again, the process is iterative: information obtained from studies may necessitate that the theory and its description be changed. The aim is to make visible for analysis the relationship between the programme theory and relevant substantive theory. This means producing initial explanations for the pattern of contexts, mechanisms and outcomes (CMOs).
Identify the evidence for testing	**Stage five:** Identify data that enable the testing and refining of the theory and concepts	Initial explanations need to be tested against the data available. There should be no strict criteria for the inclusion of study. This stage is about searching for relevant studies from different disciplines, using different methodological approaches. No preference should be given to hierarchies of evidence.
Test, evaluate and synthesise	**Stage six:** Select relevant studies that allow sense to be made of the topic, theories to be tested and refined and initial inferences to be made about mechanisms	Studies identified in the search need to be sorted for relevance. Selection should be based on what a study can bring in terms of data, understanding, interpretation or specificity. Studies claiming findings need to be evaluated for the plausibility, rigour and coherence of the methods used. The aim is to obtain as much understanding as possible, in the time available, that

(Continued)

Stages	Brief explanation
	allows for a justifiable interpretation of the relationship between CMOs. This may mean further refinement and theory testing as needed. The refined theory needs to be consistent with the evidence provided.
Report and support / **Use of the findings** — **Stage seven:** Write the review showing understanding of the topic and identifying the mechanisms that work in what contexts	The methods, processes and decisions made in the review need to be explained. The philosophy, logic and analytical approach of realist analysis need to be demonstrated. The pattern of CMOs needs to be explained in ways that allow for current and future applications of a programme to understand the complexities and role of contexts, and thereby be able to make local adaptations to suit local situations.

Source: Adapted from Rainbow Framework, 2014: 1–10

Extended example: Realist review

Ziebland and Wyke (2012) asked, 'What is written in peer-reviewed journals and scholarly books about the health effects of access to and use of online patients' experiences?' Using a template similar to the one above in Table 6.6 and based on Pawson et al. (2005), the authors summarise the steps they took:

Step 1: Clarification of scope

- We settled on the review question: 'What is written in peer-reviewed journals and scholarly books about the health effects of access to and use of online patients' experiences?'
- We refined the purpose of our review: to provide 'a conceptual map' of what is known about the health effects of access to and use of online patients' experiences about health and illness.
- We articulated the key ideas to be explored in a multidisciplinary project meeting, in which we developed our initial matrix.

Step 2: Search for evidence

- Exploratory background reading gave us 'a feel' for the literature based on our own and colleagues' bibliographic databases.
- A wide-ranging search (with assistance from a librarian at the Oxford Knowledge Centre) sought to identify any studies that had tested the effects of exposure to online patients' experiences or that described theories or ideas about the potential effects of exposure to online patients' experiences.
- Both of us scanned all resulting titles and abstracts and after discussion chose potentially promising papers that could inform our thinking.
- We sought more papers and books by 'snowballing' from reference lists as promising ideas emerged.

- Our final search for additional studies came when we had nearly completed our review or when we came across them in the course of our professional lives, for example, through discussions and seminars.

Step 3: Appraise studies and extract data

- At least one of us read full papers. Although we used no formal quality appraisal tools, we considered papers in relation to their relevance.
- Relevance: Does the research address the topic and enable us to add to, adapt, or amend the initial matrix developed in Step 1?
- Rigour: Does the research support the conclusions drawn from it by the researchers or the reviewers?

Both of us identified papers containing important ideas, explained them, and discussed their relevance during a period of intensive working together.

We added categories and specific instances to the initial matrix, which became our main data extraction framework.

Step 4: Synthesise evidence

- We developed our initial 'map' or overview in a tabular form, identifying potential effects of access to and use of personal experiences of health and illness on the Internet, the potential negatives relating to that, and potential mechanisms through which each effect may work.
- A constant comparison between reading and the working table identified the point at which no new ideas were emerging and we were confident that we had achieved 'saturation'.
- We drew up a glossary of terms defining, recording and explaining key concepts; our understanding of them; and their application in this overview.

Step 5: Disseminate and evaluate

- We presented and discussed the table and glossary at a full team meeting and made some modifications and clarifications regarding how the table should be presented.
- We discussed the table in a workshop with 30 members of a health service user panel, who suggested the emphasis and importance of topics.
- A final search and discussions at a conference identified the importance of visual as well as written and read presentations of experiences.
- We identified and described seven domains – finding information, feeling supported, maintaining relationships with others, affecting behaviour, and experiencing health services, learning to tell the story and visualising disease.

[A point to note about this account is how understandable it is and how it reflects the Research Development Framework, especially Domain A. According to the authors, 'the objective was to review the literature to identify theories, mechanisms of action and potential impact of patient experiences'. The review underpinned all of the later work in the programme.]

(Continued)

- We clarified which aspects of health are liable to be affected by exposure to online patient experiences
- We identified different types of patient experience and theories relevant to the underlying mechanisms of action through which online patient experience might operate
- We identified the different types of outcomes that might be relevant to online patient experience and the outcome measures that are now used in the research literature on health information, support and decision making
- We contributed to the assessment tool development.

Cautionary tale: Language, evidence and credibility

There is a problem with the application of the evidence-based scheme. The problem is the best evidence does not mean that there is ample evidence covering every problem. It is not the case, for example, that the literature in health care is equally interested in all illnesses. Frankel and West (1993: 11 cited in Gray, 2001: 120) showed through an analysis of published papers in health care that researchers were more interested in, and published mostly on, diseases that were relatively uncommon. Whereas there were 40 discharges or deaths from slow virus diseases, there were 2000 papers on the illness compared to 7.7 papers on cerebrovascular disease that had 111,250 discharges or deaths. There is, therefore, a relevance gap in medical knowledge. Since Frankel and West's (1993) publication, a number of initiatives have addressed this issue including, in the UK, the NHS R&D Programme and Cochrane Collaboration. The main issues to be taken into account when using the hierarchy of evidence include that electronic databases have limitations, indexing methods vary between sources, abstracts can be misleading and bias exists in published papers.

From resources such as *Retraction Watch* (an online surveillance of journals that retract articles for a range of reasons including fraudulent data, unsubstantiated conclusions, image manipulation, plagiarism, and all other misbehaviours) we should not assume all published research is genuine or reliable. A number of studies, organisations and websites show that there is continuing dishonesty and even fraud in research. The deviant and criminal behaviours include using false or misleading data to make a claim, altering data to obtain the desired result, omitting data that could have unwanted impacts on conclusions and fabricating data without having done any research.

Fashionable nonsense in writing

Sometimes something can read very well. It reads as if it is an authentic piece of research. As a consequence there is no evidence to show that it is not what it purports to be, and that it is not a genuine contribution to a debate. This is normally because if you read an article in a reputable journal you know to have published articles that have been influential in the past, then you have no reason to suspect matters are not what they seem. All subject disciplines have journals that are normally taken to be reputable, publishing articles that have been peer reviewed. Such journals are seen as upholding standards of quality when it comes to the validity of the articles they publish. But this is not always the case. In 1996 the respected journal *Social Text* published an article by Alan Sokal.

The title of Sokal's article is 'Transgressing the boundaries: Towards a transformative hermeneutics of quantum gravity'. I do not know much about quantum gravity. I know something about hermeneutics. This is the kind of article that looks, from its title, to be about the relationship between the social and physical sciences. If I read it I may get the gist of it and trust in the editorial procedures of the journal that its author has something to say that has relevance. In addition, the biographical information supplied with the article tells us Alan Sokal is,

> a Professor of Physics at New York University. He has lectured widely in Europe and Latin America, including at the Università di Roma 'La Sapienza' and, during the Sandinista government, at the Universidad Nacional Autónoma de Nicaragua. He is co-author with Roberto Fernández and Jürg Fröhlich of *Random Walks, Critical Phenomena, and Triviality in Quantum Field Theory*.

The reputation of the journal plus the credentials of Sokal imply that there is nothing amiss with the article. In the summer of 1996 Sokal published an article in *Lingua Franca,* in which he revealed that the article in *Social Text* was a parody. Sokal admitted that the article was 'chock-full of nonsensical, but unfortunately authentic, quotes about physics and mathematics by prominent French and American intellectuals' (Sokal, 1997: 17) – and in a subsequent book authored with Jean Bricmont, Sokal expands on the main purpose of the article. He says,

> We show that famous intellectuals such as Jacques Lacan, Julia Kristeva, Luce Irigaray, Jean Baudrillard and Gilles Deleuze have repeatedly abused scientific concepts and terminology: either using scientific ideas totally out of context, without giving the slightest empirical or conceptual justification – note that we are not against extrapolating concepts from one field to another, but only against extrapolations made without argument – or throwing around scientific jargon to their non-scientist readers without any regard for its relevance or even its meaning. We make no claim that this invalidates the rest of their work, on which we are explicitly agnostic. (Sokal, 1997: 17)

Sokal told the truth. He did so because he wanted to make a point. Sokal and Bricmont (1997: xi) made several points that are worth noting about what to look for, and avoid, in an article. They advise to look out for:

- the use of scientific or pseudoscientific terminology without bothering much about what these words mean
- concepts that have been imported from the natural sciences into the humanities without the slightest justification, and without providing any rationale for their use
- displays of superficial erudition by shamelessly throwing around technical terms where they are irrelevant, presumably to impress and intimidate the non-specialist reader
- the manipulation of words and phrases that are, in fact, meaningless
- self-assurance on topics far beyond the competence of the author and exploiting the prestige of science to give discourses a veneer of rigour.

But how did Sokal do what he did? He explains how:

> my article is a mélange of truths, half-truths, quarter-truths, falsehoods, non sequiturs, and syntactically correct sentences that have no meaning whatsoever. (Sadly, there are only a handful of the latter: I tried hard to produce them, but I found that, save for rare bursts of inspiration, I just didn't have the knack.) I also employed some other strategies that are well-established (albeit sometimes inadvertently) in the genre: appeals to authority in lieu of logic; speculative theories passed off as established science; strained and even absurd analogies; rhetoric that sounds good but whose meaning is ambiguous; and confusion between the technical and everyday senses of English words. (Sokal, 1997: 17)

As evidence, just what is the Sokal article evidence of? It may be that we, as readers of journal articles, place too much faith in the journal itself – that we trust journal editors and reviewers to know what a 'fake' looks like. Or it may be evidence of a claim made by several social theorists including Edward Sapir (1985: 162):

> Language is a guide to social reality. Though language is not ordinarily thought of as of essential interest to the students of social science, it powerfully conditions all our thinking about social problems and processes. Human beings do not live in the objective world alone, nor alone in the world of social activity as ordinarily understood, but are very much at the mercy of the particular language, which has become the medium of expression for their society.

In place of the word 'society' in the quote above, we could use discipline, standpoint, perspective or approach. Different traditions in theory such as interpretivism, postmodernism, realism and so on have a particular language that is used by its adherents (members) to converse in ways that reflect their assumptions about the status of evidence.

Wrongdoing in research

There are institutions and groups that carefully monitor and report on wrongdoing in research. To find out more, the following have ongoing investigations that they make available online:

- *Retraction Watch*
- US Food & Drugs Administration (FDA)
- Lock and Wells (1997)

Sapir expressed this position in the early twentieth century. It is a position based on empirical field research among several different cultures. Sapir's argument has, unlike that of Sokal's parody, empirical data. Possession of data is not, however, a criterion for soundness in interpretation, theory or argument. Sapir's arguments were during his lifetime and afterwards subject to criticism and even dismissal.

What we can make of the Sokal affair and of work by any social theorist such as Sapir, is that we can expect a literature based on confirming and refuting their work to have developed. No matter what the evidence in amount or quality the meaning of that evidence (data) will always be subject to re-interpretation, critique and defense. In addition, we can also note that no one theory or theorist has yet produced a definitive account of how research should be done, what counts as unequivocal evidence or how evidence should be interpreted.

To understand the role and place of evidence in research, therefore, requires more than a sceptical attitude. It requires reading beyond your subject area and certainly beyond your research topic. Try to understand some of the big ideas that have and are being proposed in disciplines alien to you, such as theoretical physics, astronomy, history, mathematics, economics and so on. C.P. Snow captured this when he said,

> A good many times I have been present at gatherings of people who, by the standards of the traditional culture, are thought highly educated and who have with considerable gusto been expressing their incredulity at the illiteracy of scientists. Once or twice I have been provoked and have asked the company how many of them could describe the Second Law of Thermodynamics. The response was cold: it was also negative. Yet I was asking something which is about the scientific equivalent of: *Have you read a work of Shakespeare's?*

> I now believe that if I had asked an even simpler question – such as, What do you mean by mass, or acceleration, which is the scientific equivalent of saying, *Can you read?* – not more than one in ten of the highly educated would have felt that I was speaking the same language. So the great edifice of modern physics goes up, and the majority of the cleverest people in the western world have about as much insight into it as their neolithic ancestors would have had. (Snow, 1963[1960]: 20–1, quoted in Sokal, 1997: 17)

Conclusions

Evidence has a major, embedded function in all reviews. In Chapter 1, the main reasons for doing a review were discussed. All of these reasons are about making a sound case (argument) for framing a research problem in a particular way and making the further case for how it is to be investigated. The review is the evidence, presented in a structured way, for the recommendations made in a research proposal. In the thesis itself, the review is both a description of current research on a problem and an argument. As an argument, it makes recourse to evidence to justify what has been done. This is done by placing the research and findings within a suitable disciplinary context. The review makes visible the context in which the research student wants the reader (research committee) to understand the case for researching a particular problem.

In summary

- The literature review is a process of evaluation and adjudication between definitions, assumptions, approaches, research methods, analytical techniques and interpretations found across the literature. Therefore, take your time to make sense of alternative positions, approaches and interpretations in the literature.
- Evaluate and assess rival positions in your research field and adjudicate between what supports the position you are recommending and what does not. Making a recommendation for one approach over another is a political action.
- What is taken as sufficient and necessary evidence in a literature review can, therefore, be different between different subject disciplines. Medicine, for example, will take evidence produced by randomly controlled trials, archaeology may take crop marks shown on an aerial photograph, while advertising may look at drawings consumers have made as a result of projective techniques.
- The realist approach to the review is worth noting. This is because the realist review is, like other reviews, never definitive or comprehensive because the emphasis is on adjudication between alternative theories about how and under what conditions a programme works.
- Evidence in the literature review is, therefore, a pragmatic matter. Definitions of concepts, specification of methods for data collection, use of stated or unstated methodological assumptions, ideological influences and interpretations can, amongst other matters, be classed as evidence for the review of any literature from any discipline.
- Pragmatically there can never be a definitive review or a review that is a source for claiming certainty.

7

Understanding and Analysing the Ways Ideas are Organised

Key questions

- What is meant by analysis and synthesis?
- How are analogy, metaphor and homology used to present ideas and theories?
- Why is definition important in research and argument?
- How can definition be used to determine the topic for analysis?
- How can we compare and contrast the ideas of different theorists?

Core skills

- Critically analyse and synthesise ideas from different sources and disciplines
- Appreciate how research topics were established and developed
- Understand the role and purpose of philosophy to research
- Compare research traditions in order to provide opportunities for generating novel ideas, new research questions, and imaginative and new interpretations of existing phenomena.

Introduction

Once you have undertaken a comprehensive literature search you will need an array of tools for a comprehensive analysis of its content. Obtaining numerous items relevant to your topic should not be too difficult. What tends to be difficult is subjecting the literature to a thorough analysis. There are some very basic tools which enable analysis and that are essential for the application of more sophisticated methods. Without an understanding of these tools and the techniques for using them, a great deal of time and effort can easily be wasted. The previous chapter examined how arguments may be analysed. In this chapter and the next chapter, we go on to look at some of the techniques of analysis, which many authors use to arrange and structure their arguments and can be used to map ideas in a body of literature. An understanding of the ways in which ideas are structured is an essential prerequisite for a systematic analysis and critical evaluation of ideas and arguments. At the same lime, as analyst-cum-evaluator, you will be seeing how others have managed information and ideas in order to construct what they take to be a plausible argument.

The aim is to show you ways in which you can undertake a competent analysis, evaluation and assessment of the literature in order to be able to: map out the main issues on a subject; examine the use of concepts and the ways in which comparisons have and can be made; see how complex ideas can be described; and to understand the role that methodological assumptions have in shaping the ways in which ideas and arguments are presented. At the same time, the objective of analysis is not only to understand, but also to see if you can make connections between ideas, and find a gap in the literature that can become your own topic or even produce a new synthesis. What follows is an overview of what we mean by analysis and synthesis, in the context of what knowledge is and what it means to comprehend the literature.

Analysis and synthesis

Analysis is the job of systematically breaking down something into its constituent parts and describing how they relate to each other – it is not random dissection but a methodological examination. There is a degree of exploration in analysis. You can play around with the parts, rearranging them in various configurations to explore possible leads. You should not be afraid to try things out purely to see how they fit together. Nevertheless, when it comes to analysing several items, such as a batch of articles, you should attempt to be systematic, rigorous and consistent. If a range of arguments is being analysed, you will need to explicate the claim, data and warrant for each argument. In this way, the identification of the individual and similar elements in a range of items can be compared and contrasted.

In any literature review the data for analysis are information; that is, the interpretations, understandings and arguments that others have proposed that they want you to accept as a plausible story.

Analysis vs synthesis

Analysis = taking an idea, argument or piece of research apart to see how it was constructed. Doing the same with multiple ideas, arguments and pieces of research.

Synthesis = re-assembling the pieces of an idea(s), argument(s) or piece(s) of research in a different way to support new claims, interpretations and proposals for research.

These can come in a variety of structures and formats, styles and mediums. Although text is currently the most prevalent form, statistics, film, images and diagrams, both in print and on computer, are now being used more frequently as ways to present an interpretation or as the materials for research. The point to note here is that the information we are dealing with is not data collected via a research instrument, such as a questionnaire, but published materials relevant to your topic.

The kinds of analysis relevant to literature reviewing are those that systematically extract key ideas, theories, concepts and methodological assumptions from the literature. For this reason, techniques such as discourse analysis, conversation analysis, content analysis, semiological analysis and the like are beyond the scope of our interests.

Synthesis, therefore, is the act of making connections between the parts identified in analysis. It is not simply a matter of reassembling the parts back into the original order, but looking for a new order. It is about recasting the information into a new or different arrangement. That arrangement should show connections and patterns that have not been produced previously. Table 7.1 outlines some of the connections between analysis and synthesis and gives indications of what we mean by knowledge and comprehension.

Synthesis requires you to have a comprehensive knowledge of the subject and a capacity to think in broad terms, because a range of viewpoints, methodologies and stances often requires connecting. This means that as an analyst you will usually find yourself battling to keep control of a large amount of information. Also, you should not refrain from considering ludicrous suggestions and generalisations, or dealing with eccentric ideas in the literature. In some cases, it is the seemingly novel position that is the most interesting and with greater potential than the conventional and familiar one. New, interesting and potentially useful ways of looking at some aspect of the world can be generated at all levels and in all subject fields. The subsequent synthesis does not have to be

TABLE 7.1   Analysis, synthesis, knowledge and comprehension

Analysis	Select, differentiate, dissect, break up	Unpacking a thing into its constituent parts in order to infer or determine the relationship and/or organising principles between them; thereby isolating the main variables.
Synthesis	Integrate, combine, recast, formulate, reorganise	Rearranging the elements derived from analysis to identify relationships or show main organising principles or show how these principles can be used to make a different phenomenon.
Comprehension	Understand, be able to explain, distinguish, interpret	Interpreting and distinguishing between different types of data, theory and argument; thereby being able to describe, discuss and explain in various ways the substance of an idea or working of a phenomenon.
Knowledge	Define, classify, describe, name, use, recognise, become aware of, understand, problem solve.	Perceiving the principles, use and function of rules, methods and events in different situations; classify, characterise, generalise, analyse the structure of and learn from experimentation on the meaning of concepts and their application.

outstanding or in a class in which we may place the ideas of Copernicus, Newton and Einstein. It does, however, need to be coherent and explicit. This means providing a clear exposition on the origins of the elements in the synthesis and showing how the connections were made. The latter is about describing and showing how a bunch of ideas compare and differ, and how they can be related to a problem.

Apart from looking for a topic, a researcher undertakes to analyse and synthesise ideas in the literature for a number of other reasons, one of which is to practise and develop competence in the skills of analysis. Through practice you will develop a style of your own and begin to enjoy the confidence it will give you in your own competence. A second reason is the need to gain knowledge of the subject area. The foundation for analysis is thinking in various ways about what you are reading. This process will enable you to dig beneath the surface of an argument and see the origins of a piece of research or theory. In this way, you will make direct mental connections between what would appear at face value to be separate arguments or articles. In other words, you will come to know the typology of origins and assumptions, which most authors on a subject employ, but rarely state, in their work. With practice you can become an expert and be able to assess critically a piece of work in a broader context rather than merely regurgitating it as a single item in a list. As a researcher at postgraduate level, you will be expected to demonstrate these capabilities; this requirement is often stated in criteria as 'a critical exposition of previous work' and 'an ordered presentation of knowledge of the subject'. Adequate demonstration of an appropriate level of analytical thinking is therefore very important.

Analogy and homology

In the eighteenth century, there was a relatively manageable stock of theories about the world and many academics had an understanding of ideas in both the natural and social sciences because disciplinary divisions had not yet fully emerged and the academic community was still relatively small in number. However, with succeeding generations the academic disciplines have proliferated and diversified – manifested in the range and scope of the many ideas, concepts and theories in the social sciences.

What is analogy?

Analogy is often used as part of an argument. The intent is to show how one thing is like another.

If this is accepted then the thing being described or explained by analogy can be said to share similar properties of that analogy.

Many of the approaches to understanding society have developed into very complex disciplines in their own right and to become competent in at least one major approach, say feminism, can take several years of hard work.

Two techniques which social scientists use to overcome some of the initial difficulties that they think others may have in understanding their theories, are analogy and homology. Analogy compares one thing with another. For example, you could describe the workings of the human brain as similar to that of a computer. This analogy, originally developed to explain the working of a computer, is now used interchangeably to describe the brain and computer. Analogies, therefore, help us to understand what is being talked about. They can give us a starting point: a reference to something with which we are familiar in order to help us grasp the complex and unfamiliar. Homology is used to look at one phenomenon in terms of the structure of another, very different, phenomenon. The particular structure of social class relations at a given period in history may, for example, be used to explain the structure of messages found in the writing of an author. Those messages may be said to have a structure that is related to the structure of the social class relationships of the society in which the author lives. A homologous relationship will have been proposed to exist between two separate things. Homology, therefore, takes as a starting point the assumption that the ideas of an individual can be explained by reference to social structures and social relations.

Arguing from analogy

One of the major reasons for the use of analogies is that the social sciences have very particular vocabularies. A feature of all academic disciplines is the unusual and often abstract vocabulary needed to converse in that discipline. For example, a student of information studies may use the term *dialog*. The student is not referring to the common use of the term *dialogue* in the sense of people conversing or exchanging views, but to an organisation (Dialog) that provides access to online databases. You should not be put off by the difficulties in understanding the language of a subject. Nor should you be over critical of a discipline that seems heavy with jargon. Most discipline-specific terms have been developed for good intellectual reasons – they help us to describe concisely very complex ideas and theories about society. It is your responsibility as a research student to work at understanding the language of a subject – if you cannot understand the vocabulary of a subject then you cannot analyse and evaluate the relevance of that research to your work.

Those unfamiliar with sociology often find difficulty with the lack of agreed definitions of key concepts. The specific meaning of a concept is usually dependent upon which particular strand of the discipline you are studying and, without a standard definition, comparisons in the use of any concept can be difficult. Added to this is another problem: just as you think you have grasped a concept and have pinned it down by a definition, it soon begins to elude you again. Unlike facts, ideas and concepts are not static; they shift and re-form their meanings in whatever way a theorist determines. Defining most concepts is therefore like trying to nail custard to a wall. This is why analogies are common in the social sciences – they help us to describe the intangible in ways that make them more concrete. If you are to analyse the use of any concept, theory or idea you must be able to evaluate the use of analogies. Some common analogies used in the different disciplines in the social sciences include:

Discipline	Analogy
Sociology	the 'living body' of society
Management	the 'pyramid' of organisation
Economics	the 'flow' of currency
Librarianship	the 'web' of information

One of the oldest and most pervasive analogies in the social sciences is the organic analogy. Although it originated in the sociological work of Herbert Spencer (1820–1903), it has been used across many disciplines. Spencer's basic concept was that evolution was a unifying principle. He contended that society, like nature, undergoes evolutionary processes of transformation into higher and more advanced forms. The general principle behind this is the development of complexity from simplicity and differentiation from homogeneity. Whatever exists, according to Spencer's concept, is in constant struggle – a struggle between the forces of change and forces attempting to maintain equilibrium. Spencer therefore viewed society in the way he viewed nature. He described this conceptualisation through analogy, claiming that society could be viewed as a living organism.

Extended example: The organic analogy

The following two examples are based on Herbert Spencer (1969[1884]) and Radcliffe-Brown (1952), both of whom used analogies related to a living organism to describe and explain the properties of societies.

Spencer's organic analogy	Observations
Societies agree with individual organisms in four conspicuous peculiarities:	
1. That commencing as small aggregations, they insensibly augment in mass: some of them eventually reaching ten thousand times what they originally were.	*The idea of simple to complex through expansion: the continuum of development. The implicit notion of progress.*
2. That while the first are so simple in structure as to be considered structureless, they assume, in the course of their growth, a continually increasing complexity of structure.	*Increasing size leads to the development of structures. The implicit notion that some societies are 'simple' and others 'advanced'.*
3. That though in their early, undeveloped states, there exists in them scarcely any mutual dependence of parts, their parts gradually acquire a mutual dependence; which becomes at last so great that the activity and life of each part is made possible only by the life and activity of the rest.	*Gradual rather than sudden change from 'sameness' and independence to 'difference' and dependence. The implicit notion of labour division and individuality.*
4. That the life of a society is independent of, and far more prolonged than, the lives of any of its component units; who are severally born, grow, work, reproduce, and die, while the body-politic composed of them survives generation after generation, increasing in mass, in completeness of structure, and in functional activity.	*The whole and the parts: the whole is greater than the parts. The implicit notion that society has a life independent of its parts but influences those parts.*
(Spencer, 1969[1884])	

(Continued)

In analysing this analogy, we can see that Spencer preferred and advocated a systems model of society. He argued that society was made up of parts that were interdependent; the relationship between the parts was structured into determinate patterns and each part had a function in the maintenance of the whole. We also see the idea of the whole (society) being larger or greater than the parts from which it was composed.

Spencer's organic analogy is interesting in itself as a piece of sociological reasoning. It is also interesting for the influence it had on empirical work in the discipline. Thinking about society as a body made up of organs led others, such as the anthropologist Radcliffe-Brown (1881–1935), to look at the functioning of the parts of society in relation to each other and the whole. Like Spencer, Radcliffe-Brown (1952) analytically divided a society into parts such as the kinship system, political system and belief system. In the following extract from his work we see how he uses the organic analogy to develop a metaphor for thinking about the function of the parts of a social structure. This functionalist theory enabled him to go beyond a description of activities observed to explain how these activities functioned to maintain society. This you can see in the following extract.

Radcliffe-Brown's development of the organic analogy	Observations
As the word function is here being used the life of an organism is conceived as the functioning of its structure. It is through and by the continuity of the functioning that the continuity of the structure is preserved. If we consider any recurrent part of the life-process, such as respiration, digestion, etc., its function is the part it plays in, the contribution it makes to, the life of the organism as a whole. As the terms are here being used a cell or an organ has an activity and that activity has a function. It is true that we commonly speak of the secretion of gastric fluid as a 'function' of the stomach. As the words are here used we should say that this is an 'activity' of the stomach, the 'function' of which is to change the proteins of food into a form, in which these are absorbed and distributed by the blood to the tissues. We may note that the function of a recurrent physiological process is thus a correspondence between it and the needs (i.e. necessary conditions of existence) of the organism.	Here we see some of the essential features of organic life described. The focus is on continuity of the organism.

An example is given that is intended to apply to all processes and organs in a body. Radcliffe-Brown is arguing that every activity found in the body has a function in contributing to the maintenance of the body, as a whole, itself.

Repeated definition of activity is used to emphasise the point that to uncover the reason for an activity look for its function in terms of the larger structural whole.

The idea of 'needs' is introduced; that the body has functional needs that are required to be fulfilled in order for its survival. |
| To turn from organic life to social life, if we examine such a community as an African or Australian tribe we can recognise the existence | Having described an organism Radcliffe-Brown turns to a comparative description of society. |

Radcliffe-Brown's development of the organic analogy	Observations
of social structure. Individual human beings, the essential units in this instance, are connected by a definite set of social relations into an integrated whole. The continuity of the social structure, like that of an organic structure, is not destroyed by changes in the units. Individuals may leave society, by death or otherwise; others may enter it. The continuity of structure is maintained by the process of social life, which consists of the activities and interactions of the individual human beings and of the organised groups, into which they are united. The social life of the community is here defined as the functioning of the social structure. The function of any recurrent activity, such as the punishment of a crime, or a funeral ceremony, is the part it plays in the social life as a whole and therefore the contribution it makes to the maintenance of the structural continuity. (Radcliffe-Brown, 1952: 178–80)	*The idea of the whole being greater than the sum of its parts is maintained. 'The parts are thought to be organised' into patterns of social relationships that are a part of general structures.* *The idea of continuity is followed through to emphasise the role of social structures.* *All activities are seen as a part of the structure of social relationships. From weddings to court cases, to telling jokes, are to be seen as recurrent activities and as such to be treated as having some function in the maintenance of the structures making up the whole.*

The functionalist view of society was developed by Parsons (1951), Merton (1938), Erikson (1966) and others. By the time Parsons was developing his systems approach, the organic analogy was no longer in popular use. Nevertheless, it allowed social researchers to analyse any society in terms of the functional needs of all societies. Each part was looked at, as if belonging to one of three groups: a group which fulfilled regulatory functions (e.g., political-power arrangements), a group which fulfilled sustaining functions (e.g. agriculture) and a group that fulfilled distribution functions (e.g. money). The parts of society included language, religion, morals, beliefs, stratification and agencies of education and socialisation. Any regular and routine phenomenon was treated as an institution for analysis in terms of the function it fulfilled for the maintenance of the whole.

The organic analogy is, therefore, a way of expressing a number of assumptions about the nature of any society. These assumptions can be and have been operationalised in a range of empirical studies, for example, Erikson's (1966) famous functionalist study of the Salem witchcraft craze. Whether you are dealing with an empirical study or theoretical development within the functionalist approach, the assumptions being used can be extracted from both for evaluation. The assumptions in the organic analogy are now well known and include the following: all societies grow and their growth is inevitable and cannot be prevented; social change in the arrangement of the parts is therefore ever present, hence, growth is associated with increasing specialisation of parts (i.e. an increased division of labour) and this entails increased interdependence – each part needs the others even though there may be no direct link between them.

In the research literature analogies are found in various forms and guises, organic and non-organic. Some theorists use extensive analogy to communicate the principles of their theory; others use relatively simple phrases, for example, 'the white heat of technology' and 'the cutting edge of research', which are metaphors. Metaphors are usually used for the purpose of quick illustration and most are part of some analogous conception of the world and therefore shape a theory's standpoint and perspective. For example, 'the white heat of technology' implies that lack of technology is cold, and possibly backward looking. A writer using such a phrase is expressing an argument about how we should see the use of technology: bright, dynamic and extremely 'hot'. They are also setting up an implicit structure for a contrast in which the use of technology is seen to be preferred and lack of technology is seen as a poorer alternative. Of course, context (including the purpose of the writer) influences the impact of the metaphor and will need to be taken into account.

Analogies are used to communicate to others certain views of the world. As such they are either a standpoint or perspective on the world, which makes them open to question; an analogy, the assumptions upon it is based and the consequences it may have, are all open to question, analysis and evaluation by the researcher. There are certain ways in which analogies can be analysed. The starting point is to understand the principles of good and bad analogies. The basic principle of analogy is comparison of one thing with another, which means that when someone uses an analogy they are arguing that what is true of one thing, will also be true of another. In the organic analogy 'growth' is regarded as applicable to both living things and societies. Analogies have the following structure: x is like y; y has many features common to x; therefore, what is true of x will also be true of y; y can be described like x. This logic can be analysed through an interrogation technique similar to the one developed by Fisher (1993). The following are questions you can address to assess the usefulness of an analogy:

- Is this analogy apt; is it valid?
- Are the claims made, in the reasons for the analogy, plausible?
- If so, where are they comparable and to what degree?
- Is the analogy similar in more features or principles than not?
- If so, are these key features or not? What are the consequences of the analogy?
- To what kind of research and theorising does this commit its use to?
- Is this kind of research acceptable?

If we look more closely at the organic analogy, we can see that there are some serious reasons for the careful use of analogy. The first point to note is the tendency of the organic analogy to encourage the assumption that what exists in a society must have a function. Even though something may seem to have no function or be dysfunctional (i.e. disruptive) for the whole, it is nevertheless regarded as being functional. The analogy encourages the analyst to look for or uncover the hidden rationality, and thereby a function for everything. Analytical attention is tied to the positive functions rather than negative functions of institutions and behaviours. In the human body, however, some organs appear to have no positive function or even no function at all; the appendix, for example. This kind of counter-evidence from the analogy could pose a challenge to the conventional bias inherent in the assumptions of the organic analogy.

A second point to note is the assumption of societal needs. A society or social system is assumed to have needs, and if these needs cannot be fulfilled then the social system will, it is assumed, 'die'. There is a certain attraction in assuming that all societies have certain prerequisites, but it can lead to some unusual and doubtful conclusions. For example, religious belief is often assumed to be a prerequisite of all societies. In societies rooted in religious beliefs, it is assumed that religion provides the moral basis for behaviour and therefore holds the society together. But what of those societies where there appears to be no formal religion, as in the former USSR? This assumption (or proposition) can only be maintained if a surrogate for religion is found – an assumption that could result in non-religious cultural movements being identified as fulfilling the function of formal religion. In the case of the former USSR the claim could have been made that communism was a form of religion. Similarly, one may claim that television and pop culture are forms of religion – these are things that people follow and engage with. However, claims that religion helps to maintain social order are propositional. They are claims made on the basis of a particular theoretical standpoint, and so are open to debate and challenge – as are alternative interpretations about the phenomenon of religion itself.

These points about the organic analogy are also applicable to other analogies, including any that you, as the researcher, deem appropriate to devise for your own ideas. Analogies are, nevertheless, very useful and can save a great deal of time and effort when describing the principles of a theory or process. As in the case of the organic analogy, however, no conclusions or claim can be accepted on the basis of, or with reference to, an analogy, regardless of how good the analogy is. This is because analogies are not evidence or data; they are devices used to make complex ideas and theories more understandable. Therefore, no analogy is proof of anything claimed or evidence for any proposition; if it were proffered as such then that claim would be invalid.

In your research you need to look for the ways in which analogies are misused by authors, either deliberately or mistakenly. In particular, look for analogies used to induce belief or mitigate critical evaluation or negate alternative possibilities. Picturesque metaphors (ways of thinking about society) and similes are what induce belief in or acquiescence with a claim and the reader is more likely to accept them without critical questioning. Try to question all metaphorical turns of phrase used by an author. Ask what alternative metaphor could have been used; then ask what difference these other forms or analogies would make to the picture being proposed. Always bear in mind that an analogy or metaphor is an abstraction and that care needs to be taken in order to avoid mistaking it for reality. Through the use of this technique you can build up a critical attitude and a bank of typical metaphors and analogies with corresponding recipes for their analysis and evaluation.

The metaphor in research

The use of metaphors is evident across all subject disciplines. How and why metaphor is used has a literature in itself (see Prewitt et al., 2012 for example). Metaphor use is the subject of contested debate and controversy (Gentner, 1982; McGlone, 2007). One subject field that is generally comfortable with the use of metaphor is education and pedagogy.

What is metaphor?

Metaphors are usually figures of speech but in research and theory they are sometimes used to represent a conceptualisation of abstract concepts, ideas and notions. They provide ways of thinking about processes that lead to phenomenon. For example, in media studies and social policy the 'hypodermic needle' metaphor is commonly used.

Common metaphors in education and pedagogy include 'education as production', 'education as cure', 'teacher as supportive parent', 'the mentor teacher', 'the hero student', 'a symphony conductor', 'a gardener', and so on (Hyman, 1973; Oxford et al., 1998; De Guerrero and Villamil, 2001; Chen, 2003).

Metaphors are not usually selected at random. Most have a connection to the methodological and pedagogical framework preferred by the researcher using them. For example, adherents of the Social Order, Cultural Transmission, Learner-Centered Growth, and Social Reform standpoints have their preferred metaphors (Oxford et al., 1998: 8). Table 7.2 summarises some of the different metaphors and shows how particular metaphors are associated with particular perspectives on the nature of education.

If metaphor is important then how can we analyse them? Quite often the metaphor a theorist or researcher is using is stated in their work. Practice looking for metaphors can lead to the kind of analysis done by Cornelissen et al. (2008). The literature using metaphor in the field of organisational research can, according to Cornelissen et al. (2008), be mapped onto one of four dimensions. Figure 7.1 shows the analysis done by Cornelissen et al. (2008).

What Figure 7.1 shows is a selection of authors whose metaphors for behaviour in organisations have been isolated and mapped onto four dimensions.

TABLE 7.2   Educational perspectives and associated metaphors

Perspectives on education	Metaphors
Social Order perspective	The individual is reduced 'to some malleable medium, which can be shaped into a socially useful product'. The teacher is involved in the process of social engineering and becomes a 'manufacturer', 'doctor', or 'mind-and behaviour controller'.
Cultural Transmission perspective	Stress is placed on initiating the learner into 'the correct cannon of a certain culture'. The teacher becomes a 'gatekeeper' who controls the learner's entry into 'the inner sanctum' of the elite.
Learner-centered Growth perspective	The focus is on the development of the learner's full potential. The teacher's responsibility is to create 'the optimal environment, in which the inner nature of the mind could grow and flourish'. Metaphors for the teacher are 'nurturer', 'scaffolder', 'delegator', etc.
Social Reform perspective	Adopts elements from each of the other three views on schooling and aims to fuse and harmonise the needs of society with the needs of the individual learner. The whole process of education is 'reconceptualised around the interactive character of life'. The teacher and students must become 'miniature democratic communities' where the role of the teacher is to promote the development of a democratic, scientifically and culturally advanced society.

Source: Nikitina and Furuoka, 2008: 164–7 and Oxford et al., 1998: 8–41

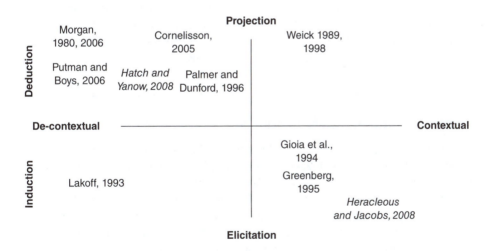

FIGURE 7.1   Example literature on metaphor mapped

The majority are, according to Cornelissen et al. (2008) deductive in their use of metaphor. That is, authors such as Morgan (1980; 2006) impose their metaphor onto organisational reality. Morgan uses these kinds of metaphors: *machines, organisms, brains, cultures, political systems, psychic prisons* and *domination.* Alternatively, authors such as Greenberg (1995) look for metaphors that emerge or surface from organisational contexts, in which focus groups were asked to construct drawings that represent feelings about organisational change.

Reading for metaphors is not always an easy task. But when a literature exhibits a tendency to use metaphors, as does educational and organisational research, then analytical mapping of metaphors can reveal methodological preferences and differences in the literature. This in turn can provide the basis for comparisons and assessment of the descriptive and explanatory power of the metaphor.

The argument from homology

Homology is a word not often used in the social sciences even though, as a methodological principle, it is the basis of some notable studies. Much of the work done by the structural anthropologist Claude Levi-Strauss (1963; 1964–72), the studies of classic literature by Lucian Goldman (1964), and studies of scientific knowledge by Shapin and Schaffer (1985) employs the notion of homology. Homology may be seen as having a tenuous relationship with analogy and metaphor, each being distinct positions on a continuum. At one end, analysis using analogy looks for similarities between different phenomena, and the use of metaphor takes the line 'think about one thing as if it were the same as another thing' (Law and Lodge, 1984: 104–20). Homology takes a position at the other extreme, that there are direct and corresponding relationships between structures existing in the natural world and structures existing in culture and the human mind. A short example may help here.

Extended example: History of science

Investigations (Russell, 1983; Shapin and Schaffer, 1985) into the work and thought of the famous scientist Robert Boyle (1627–91) claim that he looked on the laws of society in much the same way as those of nature. He believed that matter was innate and irrational, by which he meant that matter could not organise itself because it had no free will. Using this as a starting point, Boyle, it is argued, looked for the determining factors that shaped matter, such as air pressure, heat and weight leading to the corpuscular theory of matter. This was radical thinking in the seventeenth century. Previously even Boyle himself had subscribed to an animist theory of matter, which involves the personification of the natural world. In attempting to account for Boyle's transformation from an animist position to a corpuscular position, Shapin and Schaffer (1985) argue that a structural homology existed between the political context, religious belief and ideas in science in the seventeenth century. Politically, the period was one of radicalism that questioned traditional social and religious hierarchies. Radicals such as Gerard Winstanley, leader of the Diggers, believed that people and not the Church were responsible for the organisation of society.

Alarmed at the growth of such radical religious-cum-political movements, a counter-position developed, called Latitudinism. The Royal Society, of which Boyle was a key figure, advocated Latitudinism. This was the belief that knowledge was not God-given, but had to be acquired and accumulated through hard work. Added to this was the assumption that the pursuit of knowledge was to be guided by men of learning such as ministers and gentlemen. Therefore, what we have here is a homology. On the one hand were the radical movements, and on the other the Royal Society and the Church. The radical movements advocated self-activity by the masses to organise themselves. Followed through, this may mean revolutionary change in the structure of society. Boyle reversed this view. He insisted and demonstrated through experimentation on gases that matter was inert and he then applied this to social structure. In homologous terms Boyle claimed that differences in nature were equivalent to differences in society. Nature could not organise itself, therefore society could not change itself. For inert matter read people, for active principle read Church, and for natural hierarchies read social hierarchies. In short, Boyle is said to have thought about the science of chemistry in the same way as he thought about the politics of society, applying the same structures of thinking to both. This is characteristic of the use of homology in the social sciences.

Assessment of argument based on homology (or its variant, correspondence theory) is not an easy task, because arguments based on the notion of homology or correspondence are usually very complex. There are, however, a number of levels, on which any argument based on homology can be assessed. The goal of many theorists who use homology in their arguments is to give what they believe to be a scientific explanation of the social world, so we can use this as our starting point. The focus of any assessment would be the theory of the relationship said to exist between phenomena in the natural world and phenomena in the social or mental world. In short, examine first the plausibility of the theory itself in the light of the evidence and then see if there is sufficient evidence for the argument and what kind of evidence it is. If there is both necessary and sufficient evidence, then an argument based on homology may be a powerful validation of the methodological assumptions used. Conversely, if the evidence is thin or counter-examples have been ignored or dismissed as not relevant or not as good, then the plausibility of the theory can be doubted.

In a similar way, the significance attributed to individual thinkers can also be questioned. Was Boyle, for example, as influential on the thinking about social organisation as it is claimed; or does the claim rely on extrapolation from the evidence? Finally, you could look into the role of analysts, asking how have they been able to see this connection when others have not. In most cases analysts take on a position of special status; one in which they claim their analytical framework has enabled them to show us the real picture. When this kind of self-attributed status is used in conjunction with a political starting point, the result is often like the work of the evangelist: converting us by encouraging us to see the world as they do. Therefore their work is motivated by the urge to change some state of affairs that they regard as wrong. Given these pointers you should be able to explore the plausibility of arguments based on homology and reflect on your own preconceptions about the use of analysis and what kinds of goals motivate your own research.

Definition: Constructing meanings

In order to be able to think and express your ideas clearly and systematically it is important that you use words and concepts in appropriate ways. Conversely you will also need to know how to analyse the ways in which others have used words and concepts; especially in defining the subject matter. Therefore to think clearly and to make sound arguments, you will need to understand how to deconstruct the ways in which a word or concept has been used in an argument, and also how to follow the development of an argument based on definition. The aim of this section is to raise awareness of the use of words in order to avoid sloppy and avoidable misuse, equivocal meaning and misinterpretation.

Defining is about placing boundaries around the meaning of a term; it comes from the Latin *definire* – to put boundaries around. The boundaries relate to the way in which a term or word is used in a given context. There are different types of definition, such as formal definitions and stipulate definitions, which we look at later. One of the main things to notice at this stage is the way in which a definition can have different focal nodes. In her work on academic writing and reading Giltrow (1995: 187–96) maps out the nodes of three main focal groups to show how a definition can be developed though different phases (see Table 7.3).

TABLE 7.3   Focal nodes of a definition

Focus	Nodes
Focus on the phenomenon itself, isolated for scrutiny	Formal definition Reflection on the world itself Comparison Division
Focus on the 'career' of the phenomenon	Examples Account of variation Associations
Focus on the phenomenon's situation in a larger context	Role in system Cause and effect Frequency

When the definition focuses on the phenomenon, 'the thing' itself is made different from other things. The phenomenon is isolated from similar phenomena and potentially grey areas are clarified. This may be done by making it clear what is and is not included in the definition, a procedure that limits the phenomenon and therefore helps to focus attention on the topic of analysis. The same procedure can be used to extend what is to be included in the definition (i.e. classification) and, thereby, what is to be the scope of the topic.

For example, if our topic was broadcasting we may want to look at a specific kind of media or all types of broadcast media. Either way a formal definition could be used to limit or expand the class of media for our study. We may, for instance, want to differentiate terrestrial from satellite broadcasting; then a formal definition of terrestrial broadcast media would differentiate it from satellite broadcast media. Conversely, we may want to look at the effects of broadcast media; in this case our definition may place media into a larger class, say agencies of control, along with other agencies, such as education, the courts and psychiatry. Formal definition, therefore, is based on differentiation and classification. Although many are offered as authoritative, you need to remember that all formal definitions are offered as plausible proposals and are, as a consequence, open to critical analysis.

Another technique associated with a focus on the phenomenon is reflecting on the word itself. Focusing in on a word draws attention to that word. This means that a concept or word can be analysed into its constituent parts and those parts defined as the features of the phenomenon. For example, broadcasting may be defined in terms of different technology, the production process, message encoding and decoding and message consumption. Similarly, focusing attention onto the word itself means that you can differentiate it from other words in the same class. For example, television broadcast media may be differentiated from radio broadcasts by reference to the visual aspect of television.

When we focus on the career of a phenomenon, we are defining the context and history of 'a thing' in order to give it a location as a topic for research or theorising. This can be done by tracing the history of the phenomenon by looking at the preconditions that indicate its development. Key landmarks and examples are often a feature of the career definition. Examples and instances can also be used to show variation from a theme or core; to show the ways in which a phenomenon splits into various strands of sub-development, each with its own career and special features. The idea of the career itself is largely a process of selection and therefore abstraction; it is the analyst who proposes what is to be seen as the key features and developments of the phenomenon. As such, key features are selected for their associative and contrasting relevance between other elements that may also be associated, and which may be used to construct a different career definition. Therefore, career definitions are propositional and are also open to critical analysis.

In contextual terms, a phenomenon and its parts may be defined in relation to the function or role each plays in a larger system. For example, the notion of the 'professional' can be applied in numerous situations. If a common definition is given to the concept of professionalism then its use across different contexts can be proposed. If defined as the power of the expert, professionalism can be placed into the class of phenomena associated with power and control; its frequency and different forms of manifestation can therefore be measured. You may often find, as many student researchers do, that it is economical to use pre-existing definitions and views of a phenomenon. If, however, the point of the research imagination is to be analytically creative, you should resist passive acceptance of traditional and habitual ways of defining phenomena.

There are a variety of methods you can use (individually or in combination) to construct and analyse definitions or the use of words including the following:

- *Synonyms* – tracing the development of a word
- *Etymologies* – stating the dictionary meaning of a word
- *Writing formal definition* – showing the meaning of a word through the use of examples
- *Definition by example and counter example* – listing the things to be associated with a word
- *Listing attributes* – explaining the everyday use of a word
- *Lexical or reportive definition* – stating how you intend a word to be understood
- *Stipulative definition* – eliminating a particular meaning of a word or showing inaccurate uses of a word in order to emphasise a more precise or different use
- *Defining by negation* – using words to give an emotive slant, either a positive or negative meaning to something.

The most obvious thing at this stage is the use of dictionaries and encyclopedia.

Extended example: Etymological analysis of the concept 'community'

Some concepts in the social sciences have relatively long and complex histories. Tracing the ways in which a concept has been defined and operationalised is called etymological analysis. In Table 7.4 different uses of the concept community are mapped and chronologically arranged.

The first thing that strikes you is the widespread use of the concept throughout the history of the social sciences. But also note the way in which the origins of the concept lie in the late 1880s, in the works of the classic studies produced by Marx, Tonnies (1957[1887]), Weber (1965a[1930]) and Durkheim (1984[1893]). The etymological map proposes that the concept of community, although widely used in many different ways, has a common frame of reference (or paradigm). That frame is made up of the assumption that a major transition from a rural way of life to an urban one occurred in the mid-nineteenth century.

Hence, running through these studies is the methodological assumption of contrast. This is the belief that industrial society can be compared and contrasted with pre-industrial society in respect of the kinds of community that characterised each mode of living. Rural, pre-industrial society 'is thought' to have been characterised by a qualitatively different kind of community from industrial society – one in which social relationships were much closer and family bonds much stronger. The works of Tonnies (1855–1936), Weber (1864–1920) and Durkheim (1858–1917), along with that of Marx (1818–83), have all shaped the development of social theory in the twentieth century and will probably continue to be an influence on the social sciences in the next millennium.

TABLE 7.4 An etymological summary of the concept 'community' 1880–1990

Author	Period	Key Points	Framework	Seminal Works	Argument
Durkheim, Marx, Tonnies, Weber	1880s	Rural–Urban Continuum. The Great Transition. Positivism.	Theoretical Positivist	*Gemeinschaft and Gesellschaft* (Tonnies, 1957[1887]); *Division of Labour* (Durkheim, 1888)	Social change affecting traditional social bonds and community life. Community based on the notion of will. Great Transition establishing a new basis for the division of labour. Social intervention to rebuild community will eventually be necessary.
Burgess, Lloyd Warner, Lynd, Park	1920s	Empirical research. Chicago School of Sociology. Outsider community studies.	Ethnographic Naturalistic Inductive	*Middletown* (Lynd, 1922); *Local Community Fact Book of Chicago* (1923)	Importance of fieldwork as a method to examine social structure. Importance of social statistics in community studies. City life has an ecological structure/base.
Harrison, Shaw, Wirth, Young	1930s 1940s	Mass observation of British society. Community within an urban setting. Participant observation. Research method description.	Ethnographic Descriptive Inductive Deductive	*The Jackroller* (Shaw, 1930); *Yankee City Series* (Lloyd Warner, 1937); *Urbanism as a Way of Life* (Wirth, 1938); *Street Corner Society* (Whyte, 1943); *Scientific Social Surveys & Research* (Young, 1944)	Urban life weakening traditional social bonds, subsequent decline in family life. Chicago School has had a positive impact on community study methodology. It is possible to map out concrete community study methodology.

(Continued)

Author	Period	Key Points	Framework	Seminal Works	Argument
Arensberg, Dennis, Hillery, Janowitz, Nisbet, Reiss, Stein, Wirth	1950s	Problem of community definition. Questioning community theory. Consideration of alternative concepts e.g. neighbourhood.	Empirical Spatial Evaluative	*Community Press in an Urban Setting* (Janowitz, 1952); *The Quest for Community* (Nisbet, 1953); *Towards a Description of Community Areas of Agreement* (Hillery, 1955)	Need to rethink approach to community and community studies. 94 separate definitions, only commonality is the inherent idea of people. Searching for community based on Tonnies' concepts will prove fruitless.
Arensberg, Frankenberg, Nisbet, Stacey, Vidich, Warren, Wilmot and Young	1960s	British community studies. Myth of community. Questioning methodology. Insider community studies.	Empirical Analytic	*The Sociological Tradition* (Nisbet, 1967); *Community and Conflict* (Arensberg, 1968); *Communities in Britain* (Frankenberg, 1969); *The Myth of Community Studies* (Stacey, 1969)	Community based on shared traditions, most fundamental of sociology's unit ideas. Continuity of community life. Sociologists are not studying community – they are studying area and locality.
Bell and Newby, Benson, Bernard, Elias, Filkin, Gusfield, Macfarlane, Plant, Scherer	1970s	Rethinking the concept of community. Comparative community studies. Community in social policy.	Theoretical Normative Summative	*Contemporary Community: Sociological Illusion or Reality* (Scherer, 1972); *The Sociology of Community* (Bernard, 1973); *The Concept of Community* (Gusfield, 1974); *The Origins of English Individualism* (Macfarlane, 1978)	Need to redefine community. Anomalies in models for understanding community life today. Paradigm in crisis. Community has taken on so many meanings as to be meaningless.

Source: Adapted from Jones, 1997

Why do etymologies matter?

The meaning of a word is not given in that word itself. A word has no formal properties. The meaning a word has is given in the context (the situation and how it was used) of its use as informed by the culture in which it is used.

The meaning of a word can be changed over time. For example, the word gay once meant to be happy and carefree and can often be heard in cinema films made between the 1930s and 50s. Now it refers to same sex preferences.

They all used a framework that assumed the break-up of community. Tönnies refers to *Gemeinschaft* and *Gesellschaft* (community and society), while Durkheim termed non-industrial society, mechanical solidarity, industrial society and organic solidarity.

What community has been taken to mean may therefore differ between the different studies but, as the etymological map shows, a set of methodological assumptions is common to all uses of the concept. The map shows the approach to community; the ways in which a key conceptual construct, although subject to much debate, has distinct methodological boundaries.

Hence, if you were undertaking a study of community, Table 7.4 shows the relevant literature you would look at. As a consequence, you would be working within and with a long-standing framework of methodological assumptions. Breaking free from these assumptions would be a difficult task because the framework is historically established and has enjoyed widespread use throughout the social sciences.

What is a paradigm?

In social science, the concept of paradigm derives from the work of Thomas Kuhn, in particular *The Structure of Scientific Revolutions* (1970). It is used to describe how scientists work within accepted (usually unquestioned) ways of defining, assigning categories, theorising and procedures within disciplines and during particular historical periods. Different eras of science are characterised by particular worldviews (paradigms) that are taken as knowledge, and are used as standard forms of solutions to problems, of explaining events and of undertaking research. Paradigm shifts occur when the dominant paradigm is successfully challenged by another paradigm able to incorporate the existing paradigm and also offer wider explanatory power and understanding.

Working within the framework has advantages; you would be relatively safe because you would not be attracting attention by doing something different. Paradigm shifts do sometimes occur, for example, the Ptolemanic paradigm was incorporated into the Copernican paradigm. Those who do step outside established and cherished paradigms, however, often have their work marginalised. For example, the historian Alan McFarlane in his work, *The Origins of Modern English Individualism* (1979), cast doubt on the methodological assumptions about the idea of the transition from rural community to urban individualism. Even though his argument is systematic, it has not been incorporated into the popular expositions that disseminate the stock of knowledge underpinning the social sciences.

Challenging an established position – a position many other theorists take for granted – is not something to be done lightly. It requires a thorough knowledge of the consequences of using different assumptions and the ability to construct a carefully reasoned argument. But having produced this kind of map, you will be able to see more clearly, in global terms, the concepts you are using. Hence, you will give yourself a choice over which definitions you may find useful, because you will have analysed how others have defined and operationalised the concept in their studies.

However, even within the tradition itself we see a great deal of healthy debate. As a key concept within the social sciences, community has attracted considerable attention. The concept of community, its meaning and ways in which it can be operationalised, is a major source of debate, criticism and research. As such, its literature is massive, running into hundreds of items, and has considerable potential for analysis. However, a major problem with such a concept is that most researchers who have sought to give a definition of community have done so by adding more examples or seeking more information about the concept. This has led to more confusion than illumination of just what is meant by such a nebulous concept. Table 7.4 attempts to summarise the main developments in its use by showing the historical continuity of interest in the topic. It also shows the ways in which different theorists at different times have re-evaluated the use of the concept and at the same time argued against previous definitions and ways of operationalising it.

The next example looks at a very familiar work to see the re-evaluation of another topic. In his classic work, *Suicide: A Study in Sociology* (1952/1970[1897]), Emile Durkheim demonstrates how to construct a rigorous argument through the use of definitions. Durkheim's aim was to demonstrate the scientific status of sociology.

Extended example: Defining the topic for analysis

In the three books (all in one volume) that make up *Suicide,* Émile Durkheim demonstrates through definitional analysis the existence of a social reality as a phenomenon for serious scientific study. In order to show conclusively the importance and distinctiveness of social, as opposed to psychological and biological, explanations of behaviour, Durkheim chose suicide as his topic. We can see why Durkheim chose suicide in the statement that is his hypothesis: 'Suicide, perhaps the most intimately personal action that an individual can take, is a phenomenon, which is nevertheless, not to be understood in terms of individual psychology, biology or physiology, but in terms of social forces wholly external to the individual' (1952/1970[1897]: 46).

In this hypothesis, we see Durkheim defining the subject, as he saw it, for sociology. In identifying the pattern of suicide rates among peoples of different European countries Durkheim is insisting that he is not concerned with suicide as an individual action. He wanted to show that the rate of suicide was a social phenomenon (a social fact) and that it could be explained in terms of the social relations to be found in different societies and cultures. The evidence he uses for this initial statement is the invariability of the suicide rate for a number of nationalities. Using statistics showing the number of suicides in European countries, Durkheim makes a number of interesting observations.

> The statistics for one and the same society are almost invariable. This is because the environmental circumstances attending the life of peoples remain relatively unchanged from year to year. To be sure, more considerable variations occasionally occur; but they are quite exceptional. They are also clearly always contemporaneous with some passing crisis affecting the social state. (1952/1970[1897]: 46)

Durkheim's argument is that social rather than other factors are largely responsible for the invariance in the rate of suicide; the suicide rate of a society or community 'is not simply a sum of independent units, a collective total, but is itself a new fact *sui generis,* with its own unity' (1952/1970[1897]: 46). Durkheim's topic was, therefore, the distribution of suicide. It was this topic that he had distinguished from the circumstances of particular individuals who commit suicide.

To do this, in Book One of *Suicide* (Extra-social Factors), Durkheim attempts to show that explanations relying on factors other than social ones are inadequate. He does this through a systematic elimination by definition, that is, he eliminates other possible explanations of suicide. In this book Durkheim eliminates the following: insanity, gender, geographical location, alcoholism, race and heredity, cosmic factors, and imitation. He begins this by building up his own definition of suicide and he starts by showing the need for a definition:

> Since the word 'suicide' recurs constantly in the course of conversation, it may be thought that its sense is universally known and that definition is superfluous. Actually, the words of everyday language, like the concepts they express, are always susceptible of more than one meaning, and the scholar employing them in their accepted use without further definition would risk serious misunderstanding. (1952/1970[1897]: 41)

Durkheim is therefore claiming that everyday language is too imprecise for serious scientific argument. This is because, he argues, words as used in everyday conversation are indefinite and are likely to vary in meaning from one situation to the next. Therefore, Durkheim is arguing for a precise definition of suicide before any serious study of the topic can be made. He approaches this task by proposing a series of formulations of suicide. His first formulation is, 'the term suicide is applied to death, which is the direct or indirect result of a positive or negative act accomplished by the victim' (1952/1970[1897]: 42).

(Continued)

He then amends this definition because he shows that it is incomplete and could be ambiguous. The same definition of suicide could, argues Durkheim, be given to individuals suffering from hallucination who throw themselves out of a building, as to those who do so knowingly. Similarly, he argues that a person's motive cannot simply be inferred, because motive cannot be observed. Moving through such examples, Durkheim turns to the problem of how to classify the deaths of people who sacrifice themselves for others. In the following extract we can see what he means by this problem.

> In general an act cannot be defined by the end sought by the actor, for an identical system of behaviour may be adjustable to too many different ends without altering its nature. Indeed, if the intention of self-destruction alone constituted suicide, then the name suicide could not be given to facts, which despite apparent differences, are fundamentally identical with those always called suicide, and which could not be otherwise described without discarding them. The soldier facing certain death to save his regiment does not wish to die, and yet is he not as much the author of his own death as the manufacturer who kills himself to avoid bankruptcy? (1952/1970[1897]: 43)

Durkheim continues with such examples in order to show that there is a need to study suicide as a social fact rather than as a psychologically or personally motivated action; although people commit self-destruction for a variety of reasons, whatever the reason 'scientifically this is suicide' (1952/1970[1897]: 44). It is through this kind of reasoning that Durkheim is able to reach his conclusive definition of suicide: 'the term *suicide is applied to all cases of death resulting directly or indirectly from a positive or negative act of the victim himself, which he knows will produce this result*' (1952/1970[1897]: 44).

Note that this definition already excludes certain types of suicide, for example, the suicide of animals, victims of hallucination, alcoholics who drink themselves to death, dare devils who accidentally kill themselves and scholars who work themselves to death.

Having constructed and explained his definition of suicide, Durkheim goes on to show, through careful analysis, that existing explanations of suicide are inadequate. He proceeds by a process of elimination by argument, through the use of a range of quantitative data such as statistics and maps to substantiate his arguments. He rules out factors such as insanity, gender, alcoholism and race. He eliminates alcoholism by comparing a map of prosecutions for alcoholism with one of the suicide rates in areas of France and Germany (1952/1970[1897]: 77–81). He found that there was no significant connection between them. He therefore concludes that a 'society does not depend for its number of suicides, on having more, or fewer alcoholics' (1952/1970[1897]: 81). In a similar way, Durkheim eliminates insanity as a cause for the invariance of the suicide rate. By definition, if all those who commit suicide are classified as insane, then there would be little case for a social (structural) explanation. But, as Durkheim points out, there is an enormous difference between certifiable madness and the depression of an otherwise 'normal' balanced person. Yet both may commit suicide. From available statistics, Durkheim shows that more women than men were to be found among the populations of asylums for the insane (in the late nineteenth century), but in society at large, more men commit suicide (1952/1970[1897]: 71). He also shows that insanity rates peak at about the age of 35 years of age remaining constant until about 60 years of age. However, Durkheim shows that suicidal tendency increases regularly from childhood to the most advanced old age (1952/1970[1897]: 73), suggesting again that insanity is an unlikely cause of suicide. As a consequence of using the available data Durkheim is able to conclude that:

> As insanity is agreed to have increased regularly for a century and suicide likewise, one may be tempted to see proof of their interconnection in this fact. But what deprives it of any conclusive value is that in lower societies where insanity is rare, suicide on the contrary is sometimes very frequent. (1952/1970[1897]: 76)

Suicide shows how definitions used as the basis of an explanation, once scrutinised, can be shown to be ambiguous; if they are treated in strict stipulative terms the evidence that could be used to support them often shows an inverse relationship exists. For example, when examining the claim that insanity was the cause of suicide, Durkheim takes the rates of insanity not generally but for three different religious groups: the Protestant faith, Catholic faith and Jewish faith. He shows, contrary to the opinion of his day, that in this case 'suicide varies in inverse proportion to psychopathic states, rather than being consistent with them' (1952/1970[1897]: 73).

There have been, over the course of the twentieth century, many critical evaluations of Durkheim's famous study. Nevertheless, most are agreed that Durkheim's style of argument is a classic illustration of how definitional analysis combined with comparative data can be used effectively to eliminate explanations. Systematically questioning the evidence of any explanation or argument can, therefore, be an effective method of analysis. It helps to clarify your understanding of those arguments and also to show (or not, as the case may be) the strength of the arguments you are proposing.

Comparing and contrasting

A common practice in the social sciences is to make comparisons between the works and ideas of different authors. This usually involves finding common points of interest between, say, definitions of main concepts, kinds of data collected and the interpretation of findings. The practice can be useful in identifying common areas of interest and differing positions on similar topic areas. Figure 7.2 shows that comparing and contrasting can be done at several levels. The point to note is that comparing theorists has inherent difficulties, mainly to do with the selection of criteria or points of reference, which are valid and comparable.

Not all things can be compared with all other things. Any number of phenomena belonging to the same family of things (e.g., methodological assumptions) can usually be analysed in a comparative framework, but rarely can all the elements in one phenomenon be compared to those of another with equivalent degrees of similarity and difference. There will be certain elements in one phenomenon not present in others and vice versa (see Figure 7.2). Selectivity, therefore, is essential to any successful comparative analysis.

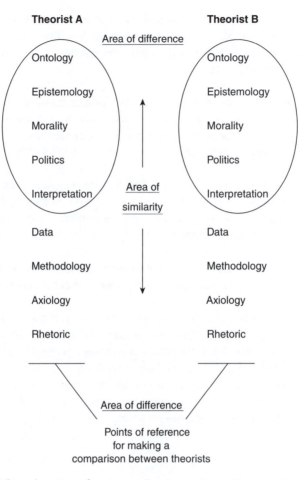

FIGURE 7.2   Identifying locations for comparison

One of the requirements of selection is that the choices made need to be clear, explicit and justified, because the choice of which elements to compare may affect the degree to which the reader agrees with the analysis. The detail required for a justification (i.e. argument) depends on the audience and the degree of novelty of the comparison. Taking account of, and writing for, a particular hypothetical readership is important. When setting out on the analysis, you need to have in mind just what type of person will read the research report. Try to think about the level of knowledge you can reasonably expect from your potential readers. Similarly, the more novel or even radical the comparison, the greater the need for detailed explication. Conversely, the more familiar the comparison, the less will be the need for explication.

In their small but very enlightening book called *The Sociology Game,* Anderson et al. (1985: 60–9) make a comparison between the ideas of Karl Marx and Max Weber. Their short explication demonstrates the kind of attitude that we have been looking at throughout this book. The first is the need for an interpretation that is open-minded, clear and based on demonstrating understanding. They show how the relative ideas of Marx and Weber (1965a[1930]; 1965b) share certain assumptions, but differ in others; but the differences are not necessarily a reason for championing one of them to the detriment of the others – a preference for one does not invalidate the ideas of the others and cannot be used to this end. The second approach the authors show is the need to understand the consequences of the differences and similarities in the ideas of Marx and Weber. They do this by discussing some of the more moderate and non-controversial interpretations of Marx and Weber and contrasting these with more extreme and controversial interpretations. Through this method they show that a reader can make choices about how to interpret a theorist, but in doing so, the reader needs to be aware of the logical consequences of choices. The following example illustrates these and other relevant points for making comparisons.

Extended example: Comparing Marx and Weber

We begin this example by looking at how Anderson et al. set out what it is they are attempting to achieve. They start with the ideas of Marx: 'any theorist can be interpreted in many different ways … if the recent … treatments of Marx have done much to improve our understanding of his work, it has done nothing to make him any more conclusively interpreted' (1985: 60).

In order to focus on the main themes in the work of Marx and Weber, Anderson et al. examine a number of places in which Marx and Weber are commonly assumed to be different, such as the questions over economic determinism and idealism.

Economic determinism

Both Marx and Weber had proposed arguments based on the role of economic relations and modes of production. Anderson et al. begin by outlining what they see as the main points in Marx's thesis:

> Marx gives economic relations an important position in the understanding of society and its working. Irrespective of how this is eventually worked out, there is no question that for Marx understanding the structure of economic relations is fundamental to understanding the nature of society, and it is at this point that the fullest range of interpretations have centred. The range stretches from the readily acceptable claim that economic relations limit the possibilities of social life to the stronger claim that there is a specific causal connection between economic structures and other elements of social structure. (1985: 60)

(Continued)

That Marx emphasised the importance of economic relations in the formation and shape of society is not in doubt. However, as Anderson et al. also point out, at the time Marx was writing, people may have found it difficult to make the connection between economic forces and art, culture, religion and activities like literature. The fact that theorists have made connections between the economic conditions of a society and cultural activities shows that Marx's initial thesis has been developed in ways not developed by Marx himself. This development is therefore an area open to debate. For instance, have Marx's ideas been developed in ways consistent with what Marx himself would have recognised and agreed with? Or have Marx's ideas been used in ways not consistent with his original aims? Either way, the ideas of Marx, and how they may have been used, are open to comparative analysis. However, Anderson et al. make another important point about the methodological strategy Marx suggested, 'We can read Marx as making what is now an inoffensive "heuristic" suggestion about a strategy social inquiry may adopt for understanding a wide range of social phenomena, including many which may seem far removed from economic spheres of life' (1985: 61).

It may, therefore, be the different methodological strategies that different theorists suggest which can be a point for comparative analysis. In the case of Marx, Anderson et al. suggest that the role of economics may therefore be seen as the base of society. Such things as religion, art, education and the family can therefore be treated as the superstructure. In terms of methodology, the superstructure can be described as determined by the base. This thesis, as Anderson et al. point out, is a much more contentious thesis than merely suggesting that the economic base has an important role for society. Although a contentious claim, it is also a claim that is bold and original but less plausible than saying that the economy is a precondition for the cultural aspects of social life. As Anderson et al. mention it is 'not uncommon a situation in sociology where often the interest in a claim is inversely related to its plausibility' (1985: 61). This difference between the bold and less bold thesis is, according to Anderson et al., the basis of a difference between Marx and Weber:

> If we take Marx as advancing the less bold thesis, the more plausible one, that economic relations are important in social life, then there is little difference between them. Weber is no less convinced than Marx that economic relations are important for our understanding of society and its workings. He also emphasises that there cannot be a simple and one-sided connection between economic and other social phenomena. But if we use the Marx of the bolder thesis, namely, as advancing the position of 'economic determinism', then there is a wide gulf between him and Weber. Weber does deny that economic relations are the only determinate and influential forces in history, though this denial is not one intended to minimise their contribution, but to deny that they have exclusive sway. (1985: 62)

There is no need to cast Marx's ideas in terms of an either/or, as if we had a choice between extremes. Anderson et al. emphasise that the analyst has other choices and can impose limitations on an interpretation:

Marx could be interpreted as concentrating on those aspects of social life in which economic relations are influential, so imposing self-constraints on his theorising; that is, being interested in phenomena only in so far as they can be seen as influenced by economic relations. Restricting theorising in this way to certain kinds of influences does not have to deny other kinds of influences. (1985: 62)

Idealism

A second area in which Marx and Weber are often contrasted, is the question of idealism. Where Marx is often said to have been a materialist, Weber is said to have been an idealist. In contemporary social theory, materialism is a label that denotes superiority over other positions, especially the idealist position. This simple and hierarchical contrast is a case of naive labelling. Marx and Weber were, of course, far too sophisticated in their thinking to have opted for a simplistic position. So any comparison needs a much more sensitive and informed treatment. To understand fully the nature of thinking in a materialist or idealist conception, a degree of knowledge about the history of ideas is required. One way to do this is to refer back to the work of the German idealist philosopher Hegel (1770–1831). Anderson et al. provides a succinct summary of the relationship between the thought of Marx and that of his tutor Hegel:

> Hegelian Idealism postulated history as the development of thought, which meant, in practice, the development of art, religious thinking, and, especially, philosophy. Thought developed, or so Hegel could be uncharitably understood to be saying, as if it were something which existed independently of human beings in some ethereal world of its own. Marx, however, was sceptical of Hegel's Idealism or, more accurately, the idealism ascribed to Hegel, for two reasons: first, history is the history of real, actual human beings, not abstractions; second, although Hegel thought developments in art, philosophy, and so on had brought people freedom, as far as Marx could see it left them as impoverished and as enslaved as before. Marx could not accept that a philosophical theory, on its own, could so change the world as to set genuine people free. (1985: 63)

Anderson et al. make their readers aware that any position attributed to either Marx or Hegel cannot be simple – that various interpretations can always be made. They show that ideas can neither be presented as if they develop in a straightforward way, nor can the theories of any theorist be classified without challenge to that classification. Classifying one theorist in a single word can lead to the subsequent oversimplification by other theorists following the same classification. The case made for Weber being an idealist originates in his interest in the role of ideas, especially in his study, *The Protestant Ethic and the Spirit of Capitalism* (1965b):

> Weber did not dismiss the importance of ideas in shaping the course of history. *The Protestant Ethic and the Spirit of Capitalism*, argues not against Marx but against a certain kind of materialism, which denied that ideas have any independent role what so ever ... . (1985: 63)

(Continued)

The fact that Weber did not dismiss ideas and their social role does not make him an idealist. In looking at the role of ideas, Weber is also looking at the kinds of relationships people engage in together when they have some ideas in common. This is entirely consistent with Marx's view that history is created by real people and not metaphysical forces. Weber's argument is not that religion or other ideas are a cause of material conditions as in this case, the development of capitalism. *The Protestant Ethic and the Spirit of Capitalism* is not a challenge to Marx's materialist view of history, nor is it a challenge to Marx's distinction between the base (material conditions) and superstructure (ideas and mental life). This is because neither Marx nor Weber suggest that there was a strict one-way causal relationship between the base and superstructure. Marx's contention that the most important influence on the institutions of society was the economic one does not mean that it is the only one. Hence, although Hegel thought that consciousness (ideas and thought) determined material being and Marx did not, Marx reformulated the argument to put the emphasis on the material rather than on consciousness. From this example, we can see that the development of any social theory is not a matter of constructing a diametrically opposed position; in this instance, materialism is not the only alternative to idealism or idealism the only alternative to materialism. Anderson et al. reinforce this point when they say:

> So far *as* the development of religion is concerned, Weber attempts to give a thoroughly materialist account of how it is interwoven with political and economic interests, the structures of power and inequality in society, the development of states and so on, as well as depending on the interests and problems that arise from within religion itself. (1985: 64)

If Weber's account is a materialist account of the relationship between religion and material changes then how is it that he has been labelled idealist? The main reason for casting Weber in the role of an idealist is simply that he examined religion, and religion is seen as belonging to the realm of ideas. This shows the kinds of mistakes that can be made by making quick assumptions that lack a sufficient knowledge base about the history of ideas. The second reason often comes from not appreciating the purpose a theorist has when presenting an account. If Weber's thesis is seen as idealist, then his purpose may be read as that ideas alone can have the power to transform the world. However, if we follow Marx's argument that ideas can only have any effect if they are acted on by groups following their own interests, then Weber may be seen as being in general agreement with Marx. Hence, Weber's thesis was that ideas, if taken up by a certain historically significant group, could have a decisive influence on historical events. This is very different from saying that ideas determine history, which would mean arguing for an idealist conception of history.

In their analysis of Marx and Weber, Anderson et al. demonstrate a number of important issues about making comparisons. The main point is that many of the differences between Marx and Weber, 'are not located … in places where they are usually sought. The critical difference is not that one is a materialist, or economic determinist, and the other an idealist, for, in most respects, neither is more nor less materialist than the other' (1985: 68). Another point that Anderson et al. bring to the fore is the need to dig beneath common understandings about a theorist. That is, do not take secondary expositions at face value – they need critical evaluation in relation to the original work.

Now that you have read the example above, the message you should bring away with you is this: if someone has offered an interpretation of a theorist based on some form of comparison, that account is open to examination. You can do this by identifying the main places at which comparisons are normally thought to be located. These can then be examined in detail to see why such places have been located and what has been made of them by others and for what reasons. As Anderson et al. show, if this procedure is followed, you will usually find that things are not always what they seem.

Lessons from philosophy

In this chapter we have examined ways in which ideas, interpretations and methodological assumptions can be presented to advocate acceptance of an argument; and conversely, how we can analyse such techniques and practices. Underpinning this chapter has been an implicit prompt to employ philosophical scrutiny when reviewing a literature. We need to think about and question the plausibility of what is being proposed as an interpretation of a state of affairs. What we are doing when we analyse the works of others is to dissect and reorganise all ideas and arguments, many of which are very complex and difficult to grasp.

It is often the case that what makes an argument difficult to understand is the way in which it has been constructed. The author of an argument may have committed, quite unknowingly, a number of methodological fallacies and mistakes in the use of language, and these create a confusing and misplaced position on a matter or question. Through philosophical scrutiny we can usually make visible these kinds of errors in logic and fallacies. There are two philosophers whose work is particularly relevant here: one is Gilbert Ryle (1900–76), and the other is Ludwig Wittgenstein (1889–1951).

Both Ryle and Wittgenstein had, amongst other concerns, reservations about the ways in which language and concepts were used to construct explanations and arguments about the nature of reality. In their separate ways, each came to the conclusion that many problems in science were the result of a widespread and inappropriate use of concepts; and it was this that usually led to confusion. Ryle focused his attention upon the use of misleading expressions and mistakes made with inappropriate use of categories, while Wittgenstein had serious reservations about the attitude of science, and in particular, the attitude towards generality and truth.

If we look first at Ryle, we can see something of the nature of philosophical scrutiny. Ryle (1949) was interested in the details of how a conclusion was made. He was, therefore, interested in the routes by which an argument was put together. Through analysis he showed that the ways in which we tend to think about the world are based on long-standing mistakes. The first set of mistakes Ryle identified was what he called systematically misleading expressions. Here is an example: a robin is a bird; Stephen Hawking is a man. What is it,

Ryle would ask, about these statements that makes them factual and able to be understood (i.e. meaningful)? Ryle was not interested in the particular facts in such statements; his interest was in what scientists and philosophers take to be the formal properties of such statements. That is, factual statements have syntactical similarities that can lead to confusions. One 'confusion' is to treat facts as if alike: a bird is a thing, just as a man is a thing, therefore both are objects. If this is the case then both can be studied in the same way.

This kind of logic may lead down a number of routes, all of which compound and continue the confusion. Firstly, it may be assumed that birds and humankind are the same (a reductionist argument) which would be incorrect, if not meaningless. A similar assumption can be applied to some analogies. Defining society by comparing it to an organism may give it a quasi-ontological character leading us to believe that society is a real object rather than an abstract term, or, to take another analogy, defining the mind as if it were a computer may lead us to believe that the mind is a physical (i.e. material) object.

A similar misplacement can be seen in the use of words like beauty, justice, equality, intelligence, creativity, knowledge, wisdom and the like. The expression 'one is born beautiful' is a generalisation; it assumes some universal understanding about the concept of beauty, as well as implicitly assuming some causal link based on the inheritance of physical features. It fails to ask a number of relevant questions, such as the following. What is meant by beauty? Who defined beauty? When was the definition given? What comparisons were made or what comparisons could we make to establish criteria? Beauty therefore is a concept not a fact: it is not an object in the world, and is not therefore something we could collect information on and thereby eventually arrive at some stipulate definition. Like the concepts of justice and equality, beauty is a characterisation of actions and conventions in social relations that are relative and context dependent. As such, movement from the universal to the particular can, at best, be misleading and, at worst, meaningless.

Secondly, treating facts or interpretations as if alike may lead us to be confused about the alternative ways of thinking about the world. Take, for example, the statement that I may make: the chair I am sitting on is solid. My colleagues in the Department of Physics, however, tell me that my chair is nothing more than particles held together by forces I cannot see. How can my chair be two things at the same time? I cannot choose between the two seemingly alternative views on reality. This is because what seem to be contradictory positions are different positions; they cannot therefore be subjected to a comparative evaluation to assess relative accuracy and so determine which position is the more truthful or better.

What we have here, according to Ryle, is a muddling of the technical with the non-technical (i.e. common sense) attitude. The muddle has its origins in trying to say that one kind of reality is superior to another, rather than saying it is different. The point here is that great care needs to be taken when attempting to compare things; judgements of relative worth cannot always be settled through a comparative exercise. The usefulness of one social theory cannot easily be compared with that of another, or one society shown to be superior to another, by subjecting each to a comparative evaluation. When such exercises are attempted they often have to leave out residual elements or make claims of a moral superiority in order to argue for one position over another. Recourse to morality or politics is, then, due to mistakenly attempting to compare things which are different, and which cannot be judged in terms of universal logic.

We may go on to apply research methodologies and techniques that are incongruent with the phenomena we are studying. A classic example here comes from the body/mind debate. It is commonly assumed that the mind is different from the physical body, that it is resident somewhere in the brain of the body, and that it is the mind of a person that causes the person to act rather than merely respond. It is therefore assumed that the presence of a mind is what distinguishes humans from other forms of life. In particular, scientists have wanted to treat mental phenomena, such as attitudes, emotions and intellect, as if they were physical things. The motivation for this is the belief that events in the world can be explained in terms of causal relationships. Categorising the mind as separate from the body is, according to Ryle, a major category mistake.

The nature of this category mistake resides in treating the mind as if it were a physical object rather than a process. For example, events in the physical world tend to be episodic – one thing happens and then another thing; such happenings occur in space and time. Mental events, however, do not have the same kind of episodic character as objects as they do not exist in a space or as a distinct entity. Ryle suggests that in making assumptions about a mind/body dualism we can commit a number of misplaced descriptions due to the inappropriate use of the categories we use. He gives numerous examples of the category mistake, such as assuming that a university is something distinct from the buildings that we can see around it, or that team spirit is something that can be observed along with the activity of the sporting event itself.

Ryle is therefore drawing attention to the variety of ways in which categories (i.e. concepts we associate with the mind) are used to relate different things and thereby produce descriptions of those things. He is suggesting that we need to reflect on the categories we use, especially when using the appropriate 'mental' verbs to describe dispositions; that is, tendencies to act in certain ways. This is because many actions are not easily described using dispositional verbs. For example, we can describe the physical activity of someone mowing the lawn but find it more difficult to describe the process involved when someone is doing mental arithmetic. We cannot, according to Ryle, reduce the latter kind of activity to the former, because they are different. Added to this, Ryle observes, we do not need to reflect on the intricate rules or propositions of arithmetic in order to do arithmetic. The ways in which people do arithmetic can be very different; they may use a pen and paper, or employ objects to count with or do it in silent contemplation. Ryle therefore warns against assuming that such activities as arithmetic are somehow mysterious, as hidden away somewhere in an entity called the mind. What Ryle recommends is the use of thick description. He believed that it is only through a detailed, thick description that we can show the variety of processes people use to do what they do. This leads us to the work of Wittgenstein.

In his later work Wittgenstein (1953) had a great deal to say about the nature of making comparisons through the use of language and the benefits to be had from a thick description of phenomena. Although he did not deal with these as separate issues, for the sake of clarity we will consider them separately. The first point that needs to be made when looking at the work of Wittgenstein is that one of his main interests was with the attitude of science. Wittgenstein was not interested in saying anything about the findings of science but, like Ryle, was interested in, and had some serious reservations about, the ways in which scientific argument was constructed. Also like Ryle, Wittgenstein's ideas are difficult to translate into the social sciences, but we can get an idea of their usefulness with a simple example. When looking at something like witchcraft we may say that its outcomes are false. We may add, through a comparative assumption, that the deductions of science are true. But to some people the outcomes of witchcraft are true.

Therefore, as social researchers, we have a difficulty concerning the status of truth and falsity. Wittgenstein's interest was in such difficulties. He was not interested in establishing criteria for determining what is and what is not true. His interest was in what makes something either true or false and what kinds of statements are inappropriate for even trying to determine their truth or falsity.

Wittgenstein was therefore not assuming that everything that has syntactical similarities based on logical form is capable of being empirically proven to be true or false. His interest was in investigating the boundaries of factual discourse. The problem is, of course, that factual statements can look very similar to non-factual statements. It is easy to mistake a statement for a statement of truth. It is because people tend to think within certain institutional frameworks, i.e. that some things are accepted as true, and other things outside that way of thinking are regarded as false. Science, which dominates Westernised culture, and the witchcraft beliefs, which dominate life in Azande culture, are both institutionalised. Therefore, according to Wittgenstein, it only makes sense to talk about the truth of science within the theoretical basis of the institution of science, just as it only makes sense to talk about the use of witchcraft within the everyday life of Azande people.

Therefore, Wittgenstein had reservations about the goal of generality in science. He was not critical of science or of the emphasis it placed on general explanatory frameworks. He was, however, concerned with the degree of emphasis placed on generality to the exclusion of other ways of understanding the world around us. His basic contention was that not all puzzles and problems require generality in order to be explainable. This, he thought, was especially the case with conceptual puzzles often associated with debates over methodology and theory; such things as clarification, analysis and even an understanding of how a phenomenon happens, cannot wholly be had from a generalising approach. This is because, according to Wittgenstein, the ways in which a problem is stated, can often lead to an inappropriate strategy for its investigation.

Conclusion

We stay with Wittgenstein to conclude this chapter. Wittgenstein makes a simple but useful distinction between puzzles that require information (i.e. more facts) and those that require clarification (i.e. sorting out). Many of the things we have said throughout this chapter are to do with clarification, about sorting out confusing and diverse ideas in order to recast them to make them clearer. Once we have collected sufficient literature, we can begin to tackle our problem of understanding. But in collating the literature we are tackling the problem of information. Wittgenstein's distinction therefore informs much of what we have been advocating. He maintained that there are two main kinds of problem: problems of ignorance (there are things existing that we do not know enough about and therefore we require more information), and problems of confusion (we have the information but we do not understand what it amounts to). We therefore need to seek clarity in the information we have, rather than acquire more. The consequences of this distinction are many, but for us there is one that we specifically need to acknowledge. If we emphasise description, use core texts and subject them to careful analysis, we can be more assured that we will clarify our understanding and be saved from endlessly searching for more information and thereby compounding our confusion.

In summary

- The analysis, evaluation and assessment of a literature require the application of a diverse range of tools and cognitive abilities. It takes time and practice to acquire research skills and abilities and is something that will, once learnt, last a lifetime.
- The importance of doing analysis and evaluation is it allows for higher-level sustained engagement with the ideas, arguments and theories in the literature – at the centre of analysis is extracting the meaning an author has tried to present for understanding a particular phenomenon.
- Take metaphors and analogies for what they are – ways of describing something but not the 'thing itself'. Treat all metaphors and analogies with caution.
- All problems are based on a definition that provides the basis for claiming that there is a problem. Always critically interrogate definitions for alternative ones.
- Proposing meanings and interpretations is central to all disciplines, and as they are expressed in language then they take us into the realm of the philosophy of research.

8

Mapping and Analysing Ideas

Key questions

- What do we mean by mapping ideas?
- What techniques can we use to map ideas on a topic or methodology?
- How can analysis be used to map the use of tropes?
- How can analysis help to construct the historic influences on a topic or development?
- How can we use analysis of citations to re-construct the history of a topic?

Core skills

- Select and apply tools for undertaking detailed bibliometric and citation analysis of research
- Identify methodological connections between complex ideas from different disciplines
- Apply techniques of analysis that make visible questionable claims in research
- Understand how research is communicated in text, graphs and diagrams.

Introduction

The information contained in the literature is often made up of specific theories based on certain choices people have made about the methodological assumptions they wish to employ in their work. The aim of a review is to extract, to a degree appropriate to the level (Master's, Doctorate), the methodological assumptions in a literature (from several authors) on a specific problem. This means eliciting such things as the key concepts, analogies and arguments from the literature; and to make visible the assumptions underpinning work in given approaches to particular phenomena. This is done by eliciting from the literature the ways in which core ideas, concepts and methodologies have been employed in an argument and how they have been operationalised for empirical work. Eliciting this kind of information forms part of the *analysis element* of the review.

> ## Reading advice: The bedrock of research
>
> Methodological assumptions are the bedrock of research. They are often not stated in a study but need to be made visible for analysis, evaluation and possible adaptation for you to use, or not, as the case may be. See Chapter 7 of Hart (2005) for more on methodological assumptions.

This analysis is essential if core ideas and concepts are to be properly identified from individual items and, thereby, used to produce a *map of the knowledge* on a phenomenon, topic or problem.

This chapter looks at some of the ways in which the literature of any topic can be mapped out. The main use of mapping a topic is to acquire sufficient knowledge of the subject to develop necessary understanding of methodology and research techniques; to comprehend the history and diffusion of interest in the topic; and to undertake an analytical evaluation of the main arguments, concepts and theories relevant to the topic in order to synthesise from the analysis an approach or thesis that is unique, i.e. your work. Mapping the literature enables analysis and synthesis to be undertaken. This is because, in mapping 'out' work on a topic, you undertake the task of construction; putting together the different strands and elements of work that make up the corpus of knowledge on a topic. Different researchers coming from different subject backgrounds often map out a topic in different ways. This means that your map will never be definitive; it will always have the potential to be developed either by yourself or by another scholar at a later stage.

The point to note here is that the reviews produced by other researchers are essentially maps of a topic. It is these maps that you are expected to analyse in a way that is evaluative and critical. The first thing we will look at, therefore, is some relatively simple techniques based on a diagrammatic representation for producing a range of different maps on a topic.

Mapping ideas and research

Given the amount of information usually found in a search of the relevant literature (the topic literature and literature on methods) some form of organisation of that information is essential. Organising the content based on key themes can help you make connections between different publications.

Your summary sheet for analysis

In Table 8.2 I've included a basic classification grid (or matrix) for organising content on key themes. You should use this as a summary sheet to record your analysis.

Classification is a necessary part of the analytical stage of a review. There are two reasons for this. The first is that the analysis provides a *descriptive* foundation (i.e. map) for a future evaluation and assessment of ideas on the topic. Without the use of classification, large amounts of information could not be processed in a way that is both systematic and progressive. Secondly, mapping ideas from a literature can be done in different ways to produce different maps. Try to be methodical in spelling 'out' how the map or maps were produced. This means being explicit on why you chose to represent connections between authors that another scholar may not have made.

Classification

In everyday life, we tend to classify 'things' as we encounter them and this we do quite routinely without giving the process of how we typify things much thought. There is nothing that we, as humans, do not typify and place into some category of things. For example, we classify objects into types, such as cars, houses, offices, and 'the like'. People do not give, unless requested, the descriptive details of the object or process. We have, therefore, different levels of classification based on the needs of the situation and our particular purposes.

We can often give a simple *gloss* (overview) of an attitude or behaviour; and normally this will be adequate. However, we are sometimes required to give more detail in terms of a description that has increasing depth and/or breadth. This basic principle of a sliding scale of descriptive detail is also the basis of classifying and mapping ideas from the literature. However, when organising ideas from the literature, we are classifying for a purpose that is different from everyday classification. Rather than taking a routine attitude to classification, we are adopting a *technical attitude*. Here is an example from Anderson et al. (1985: 36):

> Consider the task of describing a wood yard and its contents. We can talk of pieces of wood, perhaps, but of what kind? There is teak, mahogany, oak, plywood, hardwood, pine, etc. and, if the person making the description knows their woods, then it is likely that such descriptions will be right. But there is another way we could proceed. We could describe the wood yard as consisting of tongue and groove boards, window frames, doors, wall panelling, and so on. This description, too, can be perfectly sound and correct.

Whatever we are describing and classifying there can be different levels of detail and specificity. In the example from Anderson et al. (1985), 'wood' is a general categorisation while 'teak' and 'mahogany' are classes within the category.

This involves taking a *reflexive* approach to how we are classifying. This means looking to critically evaluate the ways in which ideas on the topic have been conventionally organised. This is because classification, at its most basic, involves sorting and organising things, such as ideas, into categories and labelling those categories. The process of assigning ideas into categories is based on making decisions about how an idea is to be classified. Classifying is about creating and attaching labels to things. It is also about convincing others that the labels used to classify particulars are plausible. There is, therefore, an argumentational element to all classification schemes. In the following example from Savage et al. (2013), we can see how the concepts, measures and resulting classification scheme can be challenged.

Extended example: Social class

Savage et al. (2013) argued that there was a need to take another look at the way in which social class was measured and classified. In association with the BBC (British Broadcasting Corporation) the researchers used data from an online survey augmented with data from a market research company. Savage et al. (2013: 2) devised what they claimed was an 'up-to-date multi-dimensional model of social class.' The seven part hierarchical classification scheme for social class in the UK they proposed is as follows: elites (this group has the highest levels of all three capitals), established middle class (scoring second highest for cultural capital), technical middle class (distinguished by its social isolation and cultural apathy), new affluent workers (young class group which is socially and culturally active), traditional working

(Continued)

class (scores low on all forms of capital), emergent service workers (young, urban group which is relatively poor but has high social and cultural capital) and precariat, or precarious proletariat (deprived class, scoring low for social and cultural capital).

This classification scheme received widespread publicity, possibly because the research was done in association with the BBC. This aspect, and the fact that the researchers made a number of claims for their scheme in the respected journal *Sociology* (2013), attracted informed and intelligent critical attention. To unpack, and to be able to understand this critical response, we need to look at the arguments Savage et al. (2013) made for doing this research, for how it was done and for the claims they make concerning its contribution to the literature on social class.

Extracts from Savage et al. (2013)	Analysing and mapping questions
Over the past decade, there has been a striking renewal of interest in the analysis of social class inequality, driven by accumulating evidence of escalating social inequalities, notably with respect to wealth and income, but also around numerous social and cultural indicators, such as mortality rates, educational attainment, housing conditions and forms of leisure participation (e.g. Bennett et al., 2008; Dorling, 2011; Hills, 2010; Wilkinson and Pickett, 2008). Theoretically, this interest has been influenced by the deployment of Pierre Bourdieu's conceptual armoury to elaborate a model of class linked not exclusively to employment inequalities, but to the interplay between economic, social and cultural capital (see Bennett et al., 2008; Crompton, 2008; Savage, 2010; Savage et al., 2005). This current of work, sometimes called 'cultural class analysis' (Atkinson, 2010) has cross-fertilised with feminist currents (e.g. Adkins and Skeggs, 2005; Skeggs, 1997) to champion multi-dimensional approaches to the analysis of stratification (Yuval-Davis, 2011).	*Why are the researchers interested in social class?*
	The rationale is stated. The authors claim that there is a growing interest in social class and in particular with, they further claim, escalating social inequalities. The real interest may be with growing inequality and this, the authors claim, is about social class differences.
	Savage et al. (2013) review a selection of sources to place their research into a context. The interesting inclusion in the literature review as justification is Bourdieu and the notion of 'cultural' analysis of social class.
	The authors are recommending a 'new' approach to classifying social differences – but why? The answer is to explain inequalities.
(2013: 2–3)	
The Goldthorpe, class schema, has rightly been of enormous significance, especially in the comparative analysis of social mobility. However, although it is clear that	*What do the researchers believe is wrong with existing social class classification schemes?*

Extracts from Savage et al. (2013)	**Analysing and mapping questions**
for certain purposes it continues to represent a 'gold standard' in the measurement of class, five main lines of criticism can be developed to point to ways, in which its purview is limited.	The 'problem' is defined. Existing and long-standing frames of reference for describing social class are, it is claimed, inadequate. The main target for this inadequacy is the work of Goldthorpe. Anyone studying social class will need to read and properly understand what Goldthorpe and his collaborators intended and why they developed an occupationally based classification scheme. Through a series of points the authors try to show Goldthorpe's class categories, because they are based on occupations, cannot be used to measure and then explain relationships between class and inequality. Savage et al. seem to have misunderstood what Goldthorpe intended and did. Goldthorpe was interested in social mobility and needed reliable and valid sources of data. Employment and income patterns are such sources of the necessary data. Goldthorpe's class categories were practical for measuring changes between the categories. Economic classifications (groupings) are 'proxies' that stand for the detail of information and variables that cannot be directly measured. They allow for measuring changes to the segments of the population that are economically active. Why did Savage et al. not understand this aspect of Goldthorpe's work?
Firstly, as a deductive class schema, the validation of the Goldthorpe, class schema, predominantly focuses on criterion validity that is to say, the extent to which it measures those features of the employment relations, which are held to define class relationships (Evans and Mills, 2000).	
Secondly, it is increasingly apparent that a major appeal of the schema lay as a pragmatic means of placing individuals into social classes using standard nationally representative surveys with a moderate sample size.	
Thirdly, Goldthorpe adopted the standard sociological approach of abstracting class from measures of income and wealth in order to derive class from measures of employment.	
Fourthly, as feminist critics such as Crompton (2008), Skeggs (1997, 2004), and Bradley (1995), have insisted, a focus on occupations as the sole measure of class occludes the more complex ways that class operates symbolically and culturally, through forms of stigmatisation and marking of personhood and value.	
Fifthly, although widely used in comparative studies of social mobility, the validity of the EGP scheme has been challenged. Two formally identical categories, e.g. 'skilled worker' or 'supervisor', may thus refer to clearly different occupational realities in the countries that are compared.	
(2013: 3–5)	
All these factors explain the appeal of developing a new, multi-dimensional way of registering social class differentiation. A highly influential scheme is that developed	*What role does theory play in the researchers' 'new' classification scheme?*

(Continued)

Extracts from Savage et al. (2013)	Analysing and mapping questions
by French sociologist Pierre Bourdieu (1984), which argues that there are three different kinds of capital, each of which conveys certain advantages. He differentiates between (1) economic capital (wealth and income), (2) cultural capital (the ability to appreciate and engage with cultural goods, and credentials institutionalised through educational success), and (3) social capital (contacts and connections that allow people to draw on their social networks).	The solution suggested is based on the critiques of Goldthorpe. The issue is that the critique of Goldthorpe is weak and confused. French social theory is recommended to augment the economic content of class categories. Cultural and social capital are used as variables alongside economic capital to allocate individuals into categories.
This article contributes to this current by elaborating a new model of social class, which shows how measures of economic, cultural and social capital can be combined to provide a powerful way of mapping contemporary class divisions in the UK. We will show that although a large 'rump' of the established middle (or 'service') class, and the traditional working class exists, there are five other classes which fit less easily into this conventional sociological framing, and which reveal the extent of social polarisation and class fragmentation in contemporary Britain.	*What do the authors claim for this study?* A major claim is made about the importance of this study. The problem is – this is not a new or powerful way to map class divisions in the UK. This is because the methodology for measuring is limited to a survey available to anyone on the Internet, supplemented with data from a commercial market research company, analysed using the most basic statistical methods and presented using awful graphs. Plus, there are several other sources that take into account the variables Savage et al. used that are, unlike Savage et al., methodologically sound.

The research and article by Savage et al. (2013) is interesting, and is an example of an attempt to classify a population using a set of variables influenced by French social theory. The resulting seven classes may have some uses but on close reading of the methodology used (see *Sociology*, 2014, 48(3) for intelligent debates about classifying and class), the classes must be treated with caution. For example, the title of Savage et al.'s (2013) article is, *'A new model of social class: Findings from the BBC's Great British Class Survey Experiment'*. The scheme is not a model in the strict sense of the word and no experiment was done. As a researcher, you should, if you intend to use any of the comments made above, go and read this article for yourself. Avoid using secondary critiques without reading the research being critiqued.

The brief discussion of classifications of people shows there are two elements to the argumentative nature of classification in research and different subject disciplines. The first resides in the fact that ideas are not subject to fixed categories. In botany, for example, plants are subject to relatively fixed categories: a species of plant cannot normally belong to more than one class. This does not mean that the classification scheme is fixed. The breeding of some plants can lead to them being placed in different classes. Plants, however, are an example of things normally placed into categories according to a formal classification scheme. Ideas, theories, concepts and arguments are not subject to formal schemes of classification. This is because there is often considerable overlap between categories into which ideas can be placed. For example, where does one place the work of a theorist such as Harold Garfinkel? The problem here is that Garfinkel's work is highly empirical being based on a particular and distinct strategy. Therefore placing his work, say into the category 'qualitative', may be seen as too simplistic, if not naive. Therefore, categories in the social sciences tend to be informal and flexible. The following example from Northcote (2012) shows the iterative nature of concepts when applied to quality criteria (see Table 8.1).

TABLE 8.1   Identifying relevant studies based on categories

Guiding principle	Guiding question	Specific criteria from literature
Contributory in advancing wider knowledge or understanding about policy, practice, theory or a particular substantive field.	Have the findings of this study contributed to our knowledge and understanding of the educational beliefs of university teachers and students? How has being involved in the research benefited the participants?	Significant contribution (Tracy, 2010) Instrumental utility (Eisner, 1991); utility (Garman, 1994, 1996); usability, transferability or applicability; naturalistic generalisability (Stake, 1978; Stake and Trumbull, 1982); extrapolation (Patton, 1990, 2002); retrospective generalisability (Eisner, 1991); fit between the situation studied and others (Schofield, 2002); illuminative fertility (Shank and Villella, 2004) Future focus and contribution to research directions. Ontological and educative authenticity (Guba and Lincoln, 1989) Reciprocity (Patton, 1990, 2002) Importance of the research (Cohen and Crabtree, 2008); worthy topic (Tracy, 2010)
Rigorous in conduct through the systematic and transparent collection, analysis and interpretation of qualitative data.	Are the methods used to gather, analyse, interpret and present the data rigorous, systematic and transparent? – Gathering data – Interpreting and analysing data – Reporting the findings	Openness and clarity (Cohen and Crabtree, 2008) Ethics; carrying out ethical research (Cohen and Crabtree, 2008; Tracy, 2010) Referential adequacy Resonance (Tracy, 2010) Use of multiple sources, multiple voicing (Gergen and Gergen, 2000); fairness (Lincoln and Guba, 2000) Rich rigour (Tracy, 2010); rigour (Cohen and Crabtree, 2008; Flick, 2004; Freshwater et al., 2010; Viney and Nagy, 2011) ... and so on.

Source: Northcote, 2012: 106

Northcote (2012) identified five guiding principles and five related questions to interrogate the literature (only two are shown in Table 8.1). The guiding principles are based on contribution to knowledge, rigour in data collection, defence of research design, credible claims and affective involvement. Each principle has an associated question that both explicates the principle and helps guide in the selection of sources relevant to the principle. Table 8.1 shows some parts of the table Northcote (2012: 106–7) constructed. It shows how she grouped sources according to the principles and questions she was interested in. This kind of table can be a useful tool when beginning to write the review. In the case of Northcote (2012), the sources are now grouped into categories according to criteria (principles) and these can be used as the materials to organise a coherent and logical descriptive review, followed by a recommendation and justification for research.

Summarising the literature

The purpose of using tables (or matrixes as they are sometimes called) is to bring coherence to seemingly individual pieces of research and argument. The use of categories has the essential function of bringing order to the seeming chaos of the individual items and their constituent elements on the 'literature'. Jacob (2004: 518), writing from the standpoint of the profession, whose job it is to understand categories and classification, summarises this point by saying,

> Without the ability to group entities based on perceived similarities, the individual's experience of any one entity would be totally unique and could not be extended to subsequent encounters with similar entities in the environment. Consider a situation, in which each separate entity – each tree, each flower, or each drop of rain – was distinct from all other entities and carried its own unique set of defining characteristics. As Markman (1989) observes, the individual would not be able to handle the variety and complexity of her day-to-day interactions with the environment. By reducing the load on memory and facilitating the efficient storage and retrieval of information, categorisation serves as the fundamental cognitive mechanism that simplifies the individual's experience of the environment.

The concern here, however, is a pragmatic one. It is about reducing large amounts of information using categories and classes. The publications located can be grouped into categories and what we need from each publication (information on methods, assumptions, data and so on) can be made available by analyses using classes (or criteria). Summarising the contents of a given literature can help us manage large amounts of information and cut across disciplinary boundaries. This latter aspect is important, as subject disciplines are categories of knowledge, methodological assumptions and methods that have become formalised. If we can make new categories from publications originating from different subject disciplines, and apply criteria to extract information from them, as a batch, then we will be creating a new 'island of information' (Zerubavel, 1993: 5). This is because the scheme devised to classify information (grids and matrixes devised to summarise and record) is a framework in itself that has the potential to be a unique frame of reference. The framework of categories devised to summarise batches (or categories of literature) takes individual publications out of the context-dependent disciplines in which they were produced and renders them context-independent. By doing this (and it is not always possible) information is produced that may have a use-value across different contexts. Jacob (2004: 519) reminds us that:

> The acquisition and transmission of information are dependent not only on the cognitive ability to create new categories – and thus new information – through the discovery of new patterns of similarity across entities, but also on the ability to capture information about these patterns through the medium of language.

Many seemingly individual pieces of research are related if they are in the same field and address the same or a similar problem. Once located in the search, the relevant studies can be arranged according to different criteria such as chronology, themes, findings, methods and concepts, metaphors and so on. So from a practical standpoint, subject disciplines, as formal categories, can be treated as flexible. There is no compulsion to see them as formal categories. Instead they can be seen as having boundaries that are fuzzy, the contents (individual studies) are able to be cherry-picked for useful methodological insights, and used to synthesise new categories. All of this assumes we have, or are willing to acquire, the cognitive capacity to identify publications from across different subject disciplines, then devise classification schemes to analyse them as batches and create new categories for use in a particular context – the context of our research, directed by our research question.

Care is needed when categorising and classifying things in terms of contrasting labels. One needs to avoid over-simplification and the absurd reductionism that obliterates the detail and complexity of a methodology. Table 8.3 shows the level of detail that Kanekar and Sharma (2007) provided in their review of tobacco prevention interventions with adolescents. This is the level, before developing more detailed notes, as is necessary.

This is because categorising of information is about the process of reducing information into a manageable amount. The detail and complexity, say, of a closely argued monograph may get lost if the category into which it is placed is too general, or if the category itself has too few sub-categories. It is for reasons such as these that we need to take a technical and reflexive attitude to classification; looking to produce a symmetry between organising ideas in the literature with thinking about how we have done that organising.

TABLE 8.2 Minimum necessary details to be included in a grid

Study/grade/age/year	Theory	Intervention	Duration	Major findings
North Karelia Youth Project/ 7grade/13yr/ 1986 (Vartiainen, Pallonen, Mcalister & Pekka Puska, 1986)	No known theory	10 sessions were carried out in 2 schools, which were aimed at teaching children skills necessary to handle social and psychological pressures associated with starting to smoke. The sessions consisted of 3 main topics: making children aware of reasons for not smoking, learning health hazards of smoking, teaching students necessary skills to resist smoking.	2-year intervention	The proportion of children smoking in the reference school increased twice as much as in the intensive-intervention school (30% vs. 20%, p< 0.05). At follow-ups after 2 yrs, the proportion of children smoking were 27% in direct intervention school, 26% in the county-wide intervention school and 37% in the reference schools (p<0.05 and p<0.01 respectively).
Longitudinal smoking prevention program on population-based cohort sample/Grade 6–7/ 12–13 yrs/ Project STAR/1989 (Pentz, et. al.)	Social Learning Theory, transactional and systems theories of environmental change, and communication theories	Comprehensive, continuous school and community based program based on counteracting social influences. Project STAR –10 session school program for resisting and counteracting drug use influence and preventing and prevention practice of homework activities, 31 new clips and commercial talk shows, 39 mass media events and programs, 5-session booster school program	6-year total program	Program effects were significant for all variables at each wave: Percentage smoking in last month, percentage smoking in last week, percentage smoking in last day – for longitudinal program the p-values were 0.0251, 0.0213 and 0.0185 when school of origin was used. The difference in net program effect was negative at 1 year indicating that slightly smaller program effect using school of origin as analyses. At 2-year follow-up it showed a larger program effect-end point.

Study/grade/age/year	Theory	Intervention	Duration	Major findings
Efficacy of mass media and school interventions/(grade 4–6)/10–12yrs/1994 (Flynn et al.)	No known theory	Mass media and school interventions	4-year intervention	The odds ratio for being a smoker in media plus school group was 0.62 indicating reduced risk. The effects persisted 2 yrs after interventions ended.
Model-inspired by 'smoke-free classes' – Danish Council on Smoking and Health/All students (grade 6–9)/12–14yrs/1997–1998	No known theory	32 lessons comprised anti-smoking videos, posters, group sessions with tobacco related subjects, writing articles for local papers, signing of anti-smoking contract	3 years	Overall daily smoking was 80% (p<0.01), lower in Steigen than in control group. 50% fewer cigarettes were smoked by daily smokers in intervention group compared to control.

Source. Extract from Kanekar and Sharma, 2007: 127

Different types of maps

Mapping ideas is about setting out, on paper, the geography of research and thinking that has been done on a topic. At one level, it is about identifying what has been done, when it was done, what methods were used and who did what. At another level, it is about identifying links between what has been done; to show the thinking that has influenced what has been produced. These methods can be used to elicit knowledge about a topic. Diagrams and tables can then be used to represent that knowledge in terms of the relationships between ideas and arguments that you have found in the literature. Mapping can be an effective way of getting an overview of the topic.

A range of methods can be used to classify the materials and ideas from the literature. These range from the relatively simplistic listing of features deemed important to suggesting relationships between features. The following six methods can be adapted for mapping, summarising and then representing the knowledge on any topic.

1. Feature maps
2. The variable matrix
3. Tree constructions
4. Content maps
5. Taxonomic maps
6. Concept maps

Employing a combination of these methods normally results in two kinds of knowledge – *declarative knowledge* and *procedural knowledge*. Mapping the ideas in the literature necessitates that those ideas are organised into some kind of arrangement. This task usually entails that the researcher becomes familiar with the key concepts, theories and methods that have been used by other researchers in that field of study. Therefore, the research student acquires what is called *declarative knowledge* about what the topic is about. The student has knowledge about and is able to describe the different methods of mapping the literature. But they are unable to apply the different methods. In performing classification and placing ideas into categories one becomes familiar with the activity of classification. Therefore, as a research student, you will acquire *procedural knowledge*. This is an understanding about how to apply declarative knowledge about classification (Jonassen et al., 1993). Added to this, you should also begin to acquire procedural knowledge about the relationships between the elements that make up the knowledge on the topic. By looking for relationships between ideas, you will be performing analytical thinking, learning how to see connections and create new and interesting schemes. By mapping out the knowledge on a topic you are thereby *structuring* that knowledge and gaining an understanding of how it has been used: that is, you acquire knowledge of the *content* of that knowledge. The following are some descriptions and illustrations of common methods for mapping the knowledge on any topic.

Feature maps

Feature maps are a method by which the content of many articles can be systematically analysed and recorded in a standardised format. Record the key features of a predetermined aspect of a study to (a) produce summary schemata of the argument proposed by that study and (b) to locate any similarities and differences between other studies on the topic. Tables 8.3 and 8.4 show templates that can be adapted in your own work. Note that an important part of keeping track of individual sheets is to record some basic bibliographical details and even assign a code to each sheet.

The procedure is self-evident. Design the sheet according to what information you need from the articles, books and other materials obtained. The individual sheets can be produced by hand and then word processed later. There is no real advantage of using word processing all of the time, especially if you only have a relatively small number of items. If, however, you have many items, say 30 or more, then some form of computer database can be useful.

TABLE 8.3   Size A3 summary record sheet (reduced)

Author/date	Theory/ standpoint	Argument	Evidence	Core citations	Misc.

TABLE 8.4   Example of a worksheet map

	Author/date	Author/date	Author/date
Key concept			
Characterisation/description			
Antecedents			
Evidence/data			
Consequences (therefore)			
Part of (major category)			

It will allow you to search the records using key words and to produce various combinations from all or part of the records. Many databases will also allow you to change the format; to add another category or to change an existing one. Table 8.5 and Figure 8.1 are extracts taken from Hart (1994) and show the use of a feature map to analyse some of the literature on advertising that has been produced from within a feminist standpoint.

This kind of analysis can also be re-cast into a format that makes visible the assumptions that have been found to influence research. The map postulates the existence of a relationship between how something is viewed (the sexualised image of women) and what Yanni (1990) and Shields (1990) regard as a major contributing force causing it – namely advertising.

It shows in graphical format the kind of argument Yanni (1990) and others are making about how women are objectified in society. The map shows this argument as a correspondence: Yanni (1990) and others believe there to be a correspondence between the natural characteristics of manufactured goods and the artificial characteristics ascribed to women. Hence, their argument is that women are reduced to the status of goods in a capitalist culture dominated by symbolism that is biased towards male views of the world. The map identifies the main declarative and procedural aspects of the argument, to show how the idea of correspondence is used as an argument by Yanni (1990) and others. Many arguments depend implicitly or explicitly on relationships that are believed to exist causing the presence of some phenomenon. Where Table 8.5 shows the common questions in the literature, Figure 8.1 shows the relationship between assumptions and the argument – which are based on the idea of *correspondence*.

You can also use feature maps to isolate and focus on specific aspects in the literature, such as the structure of argument different authors have employed. Table 8.4 is an example, showing a worksheet that can be used for making comparisons between different authors working in the same topic field.

It may be that your research needs to identify evidence for or against a recommendation. Table 8.6 shows a matrix that has been used to harness research to address a practical problem and is a summary of recommendations based on an analysis of a literature. Note that the sources are not cited in the table. We would expect these to be available in the full report. Column five in Table 8.6 indicates the nature of the evidence. The point to note here is the way that the purpose of the review and research questions relates to the recommendation in the table. The question was:

> The purpose of this literature review was to identify what factors, if any, influence both recruitment and retention of rural social workers. There were three primary goals of this literature review: (a) to identify how rural social workers are employed (hired) (b) to identify what leads rural social workers to quit and (c) what are effective strategies to retain rural social workers.

TABLE 8.5 Extract from a feminist analysis of fragrance advertisements

Author/date	Questions/concerns	Materials/ evidence	Argument	Concepts/form of analysis	Main sources
Shields, 1990	How is meaning communicated through visual images, adverts in particular? How do spectators of different sexes find pleasure in images constructed for the male gaze? What are the connections between ways of looking and ways of seeing? How can feminist analysis help in 'reading against the grain'?	Photocopy adverts for cologne, Obsession advert, 2 illustrations, and other studies	Visual images communicate meaning through codes/messages that are produced within the dominant male ideology. Images reflect/reinforce/reproduce dominant cultural sexist, ageist discourse of attractiveness. Looking and seeing are gendered practices. Ads use gendered spectator and definitions of nudity (art) rather than nakedness (porn) to associate commodities with objectified male definitions of female attractiveness/ sexuality. Codes/messages and referent systems can therefore be analysed using visual images to reveal the dominant ideology that specifies the pleasures of looking at, being looked at, and conforming to codes of attractiveness and presentational behaviour of the self.	Feminist/ structural/ semiotics. Male gaze and power of looking. Gendered spectator. Objectified/ commodified female. Nudity and nakedness.	Williamson, 1978 Barthes, 1985 Nichols, 1981 Berger, 1973 Haug, 1987

(Continued)

Author/date	Questions/concerns	Materials/ evidence	Argument	Concepts/form of analysis	Main sources
Yanni, 1990	How do women enter into the 'thing–people relationship' differently to men? How can feminist analysis of ads provide evidence for the power of dominant ideological forms of constraint and suppression of women?	Other studies. No illustrations.	Ad images (visuals/text) continually devalue women while maintaining a priority/privilege to male experience and position of power to define convention codes. Theories of commodities, representation and fetishism have failed to account for the unique position of women and their susceptibility to ad images. The material and symbolic meaning of women is misconceived by ads which misrepresent and objectify women for the sake of associating women's sexuality with commodities, as if their sexuality was a commodity. Women are therefore given material and symbolic value sharing the characteristics of commodity form represented in use value and exchange value. Women are condensed physicality, displaced bodily and symbolized as objects and thereby it is made difficult for them to resist misrepresentations of the fetishised female image. However, women can effect change through education, research and choice of images they view.	Feminist critique. Addresses the nature and function of advertising through (1) the structure of representations (2) the process of commodification (3) the nature of fetishism (4) the power of ads. Gendered ways of seeing: the male gaze. Nude and nakedness codes.	Jhally, 1987 Berger, 1972 Williamson, 1978 Kappeler, 1986

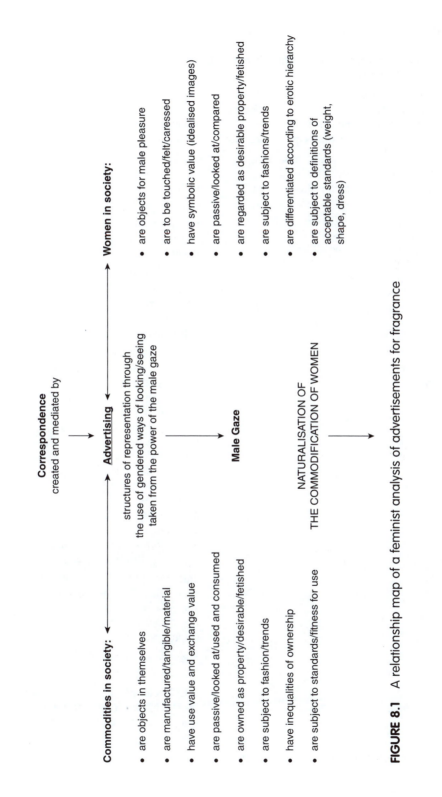

Correspondence
created and mediated by

Commodities in society:

- are objects in themselves
- are manufactured/tangible/material
- have use value and exchange value
- are passive/looked at/used and consumed
- are owned as property/desirable/fetished
- are subject to fashion/trends
- have inequalities of ownership
- are subject to standards/fitness for use

Advertising

structures of representation through
the use of gendered ways of looking/seeing
taken from the power of the male gaze

Male Gaze

NATURALISATION OF
THE COMMODIFICATION OF WOMEN

Women in society:

- are objects for male pleasure
- are to be touched/felt/caressed
- have symbolic value (idealised images)
- are passive/looked at/compared
- are regarded as desirable property/fetished
- are subject to fashions/trends
- are differentiated according to erotic hierarchy
- are subject to definitions of acceptable standards (weight, shape, dress)

FIGURE 8.1 A relationship map of a feminist analysis of advertisements for fragrance

TABLE 8.6 Using the literature to make recommendations

Recommendations from the existing literature: Effective strategies for recruiting and retaining rural social workers

Level of work and cost needed to implement the strategies	Effective for recruitment?	Effective for retention?	Recommended strategies	Cited in more than one report or research study?
Easy to implement/less costly	*Yes/No* – can dissuade potential workers but is more cost effective and time efficient in the long run	Yes	Provide a realistic job preview of working in rural communities DVD (found to be effective in one study) Have job applicant spend a day 'on the job' to attain realistic expectations	Yes (3 studies) – only one was a 'true' intervention testing the effectiveness
Easy to implement/less costly	Yes	Yes	Present a 'strength-based' perspective. This means not only providing the negative factors of working in a rural community as a social worker; social worker educators and workshops need to also address the 'positives'	Yes (2 studies) – both were survey data
Easy to implement/less costly	No – not directly	Yes	Seek 'insider group status' – new professionals should be seen with someone important and trusted in the community Attend local community events	Yes (3 studies) – way to garner trust in the community – self-report surveys
Easy to implement/less costly	No – not directly	Yes	Offer flex time/ change office hours – not always the same	Yes (3 studies) - highly effective in retaining workers

Source: Northern California Training Academy, 2007: 5

The variable matrix

In studies that are based in quantitative methods in which variables are being investigated, a different kind of matrix (or grid) is needed. It may be that you have a behaviour that has been defined as a problem. This could be gambling, smoking, drug use or similar behaviour. Once the literature on the definition and career of the problem has been examined, the time will come when studies investigating variables thought relevant will need to be looked at and compared for research design, sample, variables and other factors such as country. Table 8.7 shows a template for the variable or research design matrix.

Several different grids may be needed to summarise all the necessary information needed to begin comparisons or to identify common findings. This kind of grid tends to need sheets the size of A3.

Tree constructions

In most literature you will find some authors have dealt with general issues, while others have looked at specific aspects of a problem or issue. In order to represent this, you can construct different types of 'subject relevance tree' such as the one shown in Figure 8.2. A subject relevance tree aims to show the different ways in which the major topic has developed sub-themes, raised related questions and how interest in the topic has *branched out*. These kinds of trees can be what you want them to be; showing whatever level of detail you require.

TABLE 8.7   Template for variable matrix

	Study A	Study B
Author Date		
Year published		
Research question or hypothesis		
Dependent variable		
Independent variable		
Sample(s)		
Sample subject features		
Sample selection		
Source of sample		
Period of data collection		
Comments		

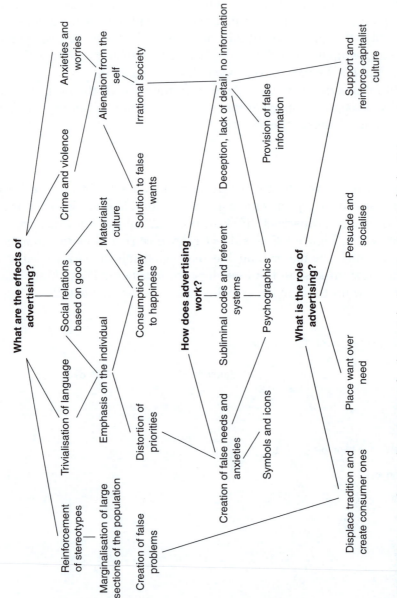

FIGURE 8.2 A subject relevance tree for the social science treatment of advertising

Figure 8.2 shows a *subject relevance tree* based on the general topic of advertising; showing some of the sub-topics within the general literature. Note that only the topics are shown here and not the specific authors that have done work on these topics. The *subject relevance tree* is based on a more detailed one, in which authors and the dates of their publications have been mapped.

The order of a *subject relevance tree* basically follows the kind of arrangement you will find used in libraries, such as, the 'Dewey Decimal Classification,' scheme. It is based on the principle of general-to-particular. At the top of the tree are general ideas and concepts that are sub-divided into further groupings of categories before finally ending in specific studies. This can be an effective way to arrange the literature at the early stage of a review. This is because a subject tree can provide a summative picture of the topic area. This allows the researcher to identify where within the concerns of the topic their research can be placed.

One or more *subject relevance trees* can be used to do further, more detailed analysis. You can use the tree (or multiple trees) to identify the trends in the kinds of data collection techniques that have been used and to make visible the kinds of methodological assumptions of any core paradigm informing work on

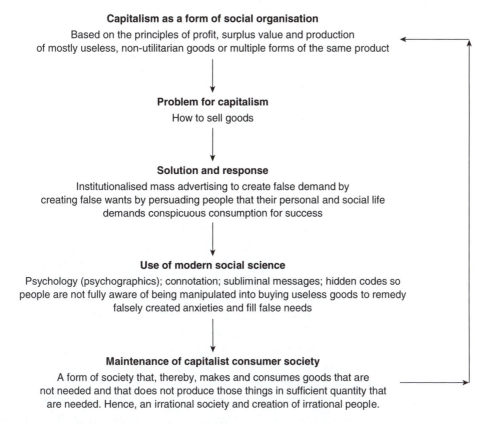

Capitalism as a form of social organisation
Based on the principles of profit, surplus value and production
of mostly useless, non-utilitarian goods or multiple forms of the same product

Problem for capitalism
How to sell goods

Solution and response
Institutionalised mass advertising to create false demand by
creating false wants by persuading people that their personal and social life
demands conspicuous consumption for success

Use of modern social science
Psychology (psychographics); connotation; subliminal messages; hidden codes so
people are not fully aware of being manipulated into buying useless goods to remedy
falsely created anxieties and fill false needs

Maintenance of capitalist consumer society
A form of society that, thereby, makes and consumes goods that are
not needed and that does not produce those things in sufficient quantity that
are needed. Hence, an irrational society and creation of irrational people.

FIGURE 8.3   An example of a linear relationship map: The logic of assumptions about advertising

the topic. A relevance tree can also be constructed to represent stages and trends associated with a phenomenon. For example, stages in the development of a concept such as the concept of community; or stages in the development of a topic area such as geographical information systems or the structure of key-words in the vocabulary of a position within the social sciences such as *Post-structuralism*. A particular kind of 'tree' is applicable to such topics – these are usually called *content maps*. But before looking at content maps we note that we can use one map to construct another map. Figure 8.3 shows, in diagrammatic form, the relationships (or logic) of the content map shown in Figure 8.2. This is the logic of the generic argument and assumptions to be found in the critical approaches to advertising as an institution.

Figure 8.3 shows the ways in which some authors have attempted to make a case for the existence of advertising. The basic argument is that advertising exists to sustain capitalist society. It does this by persuading people to purchase goods and services that are not functional or rational; that is, things people do not need in order to live, such as electric toothbrushes. Notice the linear flow; how the factors that have been identified as causal are arranged to explain several things rather than just one thing. Also note the kinds of assumptions that enable such an explanation; such as the belief that advertising works through hidden structures that people are unaware of; and that create irrational people. The main assumption is that most people cannot see that they are influenced by advertising to purchase goods and services that they do not need. Maps are, of course, just representations of an argument that can be represented in different ways. Importantly, any map is open to different interpretations and critical discussion. We may, for example, want to contend that people do know about what the aims of advertising and are, therefore, not dopes.

Content maps

All areas of knowledge are composed of a content that is structured according to some form of classification scheme such as the 'Dewey Decimal Classification' scheme. The content of a topic can be organised in a hierarchical arrangement. A common arrangement is the top-bottom structure. Starting with the conceptual elements of a topic, you sub-divide the topic into segments and the segments into levels; thus creating a linear flow that can be represented in a diagram and can be the basis of a *writing plan*. It can be used to structure the important elements in the literature into sections for the written review. It also shows what the researcher has selected as the important elements of a topic and the criteria they have used to organise their materials.

The second principle is the selection of attributes or characteristics from the literature and placement of these on the content map. For example, if the topic is the range of methodologies and data collection techniques that have been used to undertake qualitative research, our strategy may be one of locating a sufficient number of studies categorised as qualitative and extract from them the specific qualitative technique employed. We could then list these and begin to map them onto a content chart. Tesch (1990) identifies a number of approaches and techniques to qualitative research that are shown in Figure 8.4.

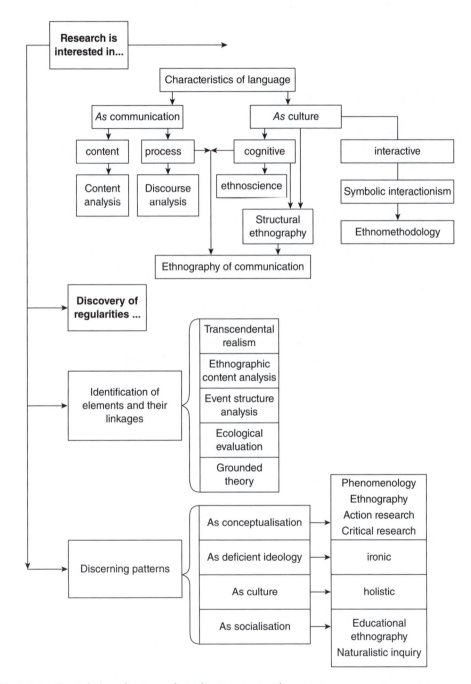

FIGURE 8.4 Partial classification of qualitative research

Source: Adapted from Tesch, 1990

Taxonomic maps

Closely related to content maps are maps that show the ways in which something can be classified. Sometimes called *elaboration* maps, they aim to show how a range of things can be placed into a general class. They also aim to show differences between objects within the general class. Taxonomic maps can be used to produce what are sometimes called *semantic feature maps*.

A paradigm is a pattern

A paradigm is a pattern of something such as behaviours within a given situation. Used by Merton (1938) to reduce and typify responses to a mutually exclusive set of choices or possibilities within a closed system.

The basic principle is the use of a matrix structure to show particular characteristics of items from the taxonomy. There are numerous examples of this in the social sciences, such as Robert K. Merton's (1938) paradigm of possible responses to the value set of a particular social system. This paradigm shown in Figure 8.5 shows Merton's classification, using a rubric, of possible responses to the American Dream of achieving the goal of monetary success. The paradigm shows the different means of achieving the same goals.

Semantic feature maps do not always have to be arranged in a table. Figure 8.6, for example, shows a map of cultural criticism as represented in the text of a book on popular culture (Berger, 1995). These kinds of maps can be developed from

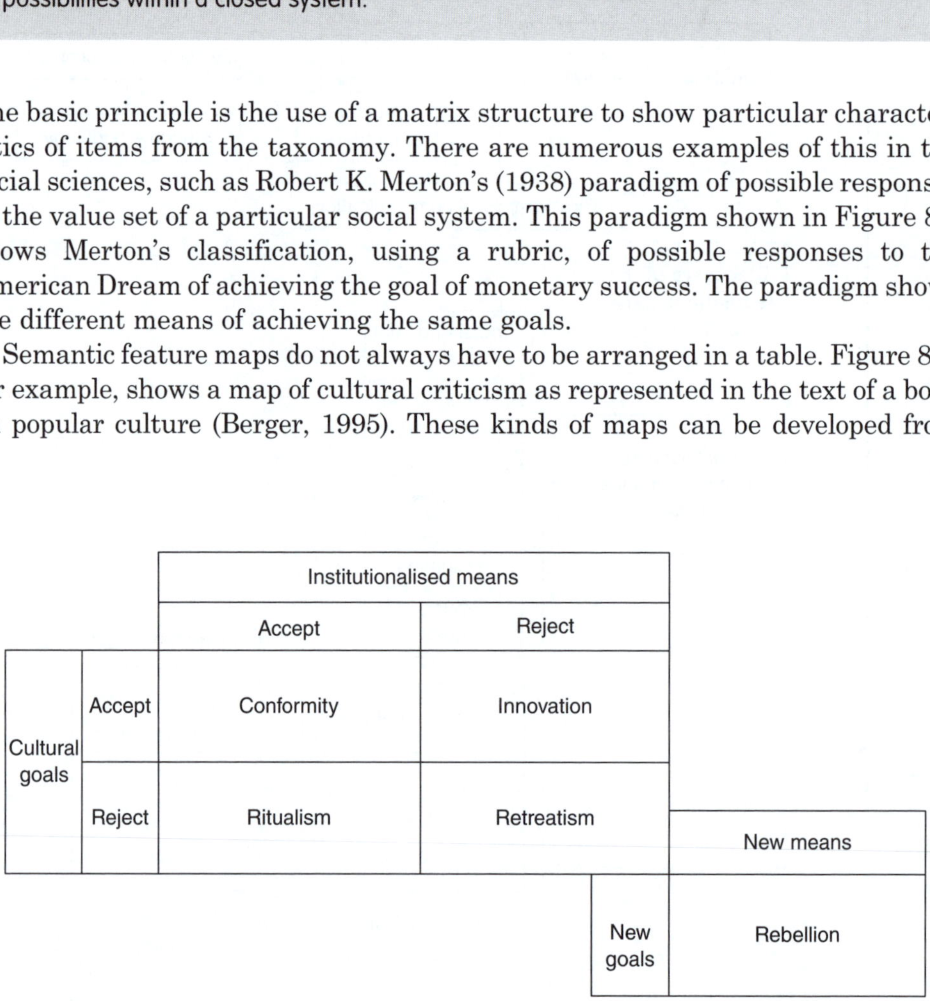

Institutionalised means		
	Accept	Reject
Cultural goals — Accept	Conformity	Innovation
Cultural goals — Reject	Ritualism	Retreatism

New means

	New goals	Rebellion

FIGURE 8.5 Merton's paradigm of possible responses

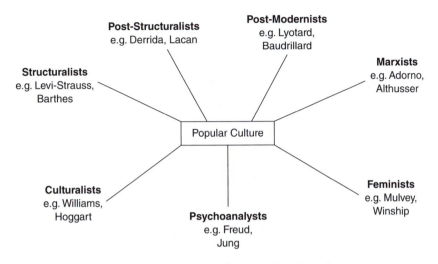

FIGURE 8.6   Semantic map of critical approaches in cultural studies

Source: Based on Berger, 1995

multiple textbooks – using several sources helps avoid taking a parochial perspective. The uses of semantically mapping the different positions different groups of authors have taken within a subject area can help you to make informed choices on which position you should take, or not, as the case may be.

Concept maps

It is often the case that in order to turn declarative knowledge into procedural knowledge you need to know the linkages between concepts and processes. A concept map can be useful because it can be constructed to show the relationships between ideas and practice and include, if necessary, reference to relevant examples. In many ways, a review of the literature is a map of theories and concepts that have potential for your own research. There are many types of concept maps, but what they have in common is the purpose to describe what is going on in a particular situation. In other words, concept maps try to answer the following questions: What kind of things go on when this activity is being done? How are different activities and the context related? What are the core theoretical concepts that can help you understand and possibly explain this activity (or situation)?

Figure 8.7 shows an outline map for the context in which research is done. It shows some of the processes involved in undertaking an analysis of qualitative data. Note how different concepts can be linked in multiple ways, how emphasis can be given to some links and how it would be possible to arrange the relationships hierarchically. An implicit assumption underlying all concept maps is the 'cause and effect' or 'problem and solution' structure that can be plotted within a given context.

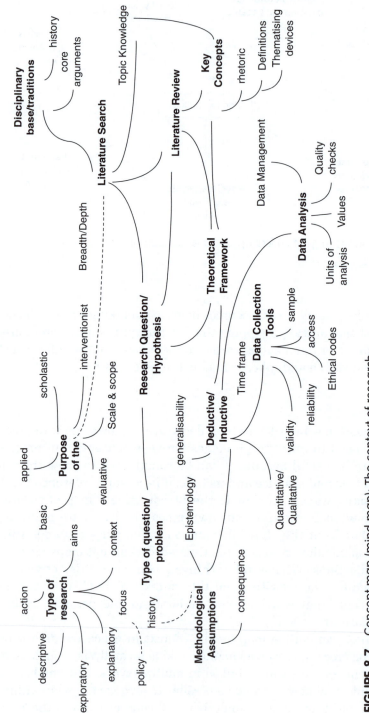

FIGURE 8.7 Concept map (mind map): The context of research

Source: Based on Berger, 1995

Concept mapping can be useful to help you develop your knowledge of a subject and methodology. It is a pictorial method, as Figure 8.7 shows, that represents the main concepts and the relationships between them for a given activity, situation or problem. If matrices, feature maps, content maps and subject relevance trees have been constructed then the materials from any of these can be used to create a structured concept map.

Concept mapping by another name

Concept mapping was first articulated by Novak and Gowin (1984), and has been re-named a number of times. Miles and Huberman (1994) called them *conceptual frameworks, causal networks and event-estate networks*, and Strauss (1987) calls them *integrative diagrams*.

From the materials already generated, you need to use the main research question and then identify useful theories from which you can develop a theoretical and conceptual framework for your own research. An important part of this is to rank or give emphasis to theories and research that show the most promise for your own work. The map should identify the most important contributions first followed by others in a logical order. It is not always the case the publications with the highest citation count will be top of your list. It is the theories, models and their related concepts that are important.

Mapping tools and levels of generality

Mapping tools are not separate from other tools used to analyse a literature. In Chapter 5, we looked at argumentation and mind mapping. Both of these are related to the mapping tools looked at in this chapter. Each has a purpose and role to play. Mind maps aim to gather concepts together that have some kind of association with one another – they enable us to see and think about the domain we are interested in. Concept maps aim to find meaningful relationships between entities – they enable us to identify aspects of a situation and theories for further investigation. Argument maps aim to deconstruct as well as construct structured logical statements about the world – they enable us to make specific inferences and call on detailed sources of evidence in support of our claims. Another way of conceptualising the relationship between these three analytical tools is to think of mind mapping as the most general, argumentation analysis as the most specific and concept mapping in between these two. Mind maps give us an overview of the scene, concept maps help to identify relations between what is in the scene and argument maps help us evaluate the strength of evidence for claims about relationships between concepts and claims.

Analysis as a method of mapping

If mapping ideas in the literature can be used to analyse the literature then analysis can be used to produce maps of the literature. In the two examples that follow, we will look at the role of analysis for understanding the nature of ideas and perspectives in a literature. In the first example, we look at how the *particulars of language use* can be analysed. The technique of *rhetoric analysis* can be used to map the use of language. Analysis can also be used to identify the lines of influence in research on a topic. The *analysis of citations* is used as an example of a technique that can map the history of the developments on a topic.

Rhetorical analysis and mapping

So far, we have made the assumption that much of what is found in a search of the literature will be academic articles and monographs. However, in many topic areas the literature will be much more diverse than articles and books. It will also be made up of non-academic materials such as company reports, trade catalogues, Parliamentary Bills and other official documentation, popular magazines, advertisements and all other kinds of ephemera.

> ### Reading advice: Analysis of rhetoric
>
> There are various sources on how to undertake an analysis of rhetoric. For example, in feminist studies Sara Mills (1995) provides a simple introduction to the analysis of 'text' to show the gendered use of words, phrases and images, while Henderson et al. (1993) contains some useful studies on the language of economic thought and argument.

There are various techniques that can be used to analyse such materials, such as *semiological* analysis and *content* analysis. We will, however, not be looking at these techniques in any detail. This is because these kinds of techniques are more *methodologically* oriented and are not particular to reviewing. Added to this is the abundance of instructional texts on how to do semiological analysis and content analysis. We will focus instead on a technique more particular to reading for reviewing called *rhetorical analysis*.

Items such as advertisements or policy documents contain an element of persuasion. The degree of persuasion may vary from a moderate attempt to influence other people, to a tightly structured argument. Rhetoric is the art of using language to influence and to persuade; it is about the use of style in language. We are, of course, using the term language in a very broad sense to include such things as written text, pictures, objects and diagrams. As such the use of rhetoric is a distinguishing feature of the sciences and the humanities. It is much in evidence in the fields of economics, social policy and political sciences; disciplines known for their *argumentative* character.

Rhetorical analysis is the study of how language has been used to make an argument appear plausible. It involves analysing the elements authors have employed to construct their arguments. In a moment, we will look at an example of rhetorical analysis but first we need to know more about what it is we must look for when reading to analyse rhetoric.

List of rhetorical devices

In his paper, 'How to do a rhetorical analysis, and why', Don McCloskey (1994) provides a list of rhetorical devices for students of economics. The basic ideas are, however, applicable to readers across the humanities and arts.

Ethos is the stance an author takes as a fictional character who has good reason to say what she is saying, i.e. that they can be trusted. An author therefore has to establish his or her credentials by employing a range of techniques such as referring to their experience, or their research, or makes an appeal to morality or politics. The opening statement an author makes is therefore important.

Point of view – the author selects a vantage point from which they will make their argument or tell their story. This may involve using the third- or first-person style. The first-person narrative is more personal and intimate, while the third-person style is more depersonalised. Some authors use both styles: the first person 'I' or collective 'we' when they want to gain or express sympathy and the third person when they want to appear as an objective observer.

Style – most scholars attempt to be modest and this is evident in the style in which they express their ideas. They use such phrases as 'it often appears', 'is likely to be' and 'may be seen as'. These show the use of the passive voice to convey major clauses of an argument. Other authors attempt to appear more objective by using a factual style. They use such phrases as 'it is consistent with the data' and 'observed phenomenon show'.

Gnomic present is a common technique to establish the legitimacy of a statement by connecting it to several other statements. McCloskey gives the following example from David Landes's (1969: 562) book on economic history:

> large scale, mechanised manufacture requires not only machines and buildings ... but ... social capital ... these are costly ... the return on such investment is often long deferred ... [the belief] that the burden has tended to grow ... has become a myth.

In economic terms Landes makes a number of implicit assumptions about the knowledge his readers have. He is challenging the argument that the social costs of manufacturing become more burdensome with time. Thereby, Landes makes a deductive conclusion that the latecomer to manufacturing can be at an advantage because they can reap the outcome of past investment without incurring an equivalent cost to themselves. Landes's conclusion acquires the legitimacy and persuasiveness it has from common acceptance of the previous statements.

Story is the main structure for arranging and for the 'telling' of an event. Academic stories like everyday stories have structure. A common structure is that of stating a past situation, stating what was done and then stating the outcome. The first two parts of the story are the plot line, while the ending is the conclusion. The conclusion is often an interpretation of events and is therefore argumentative. Conversely, one may be dealing with a state of affairs, say an interpretation that is commonly accepted. You may therefore ask for an explanation for that interpretation. In so doing, one is asking for a story that provides a plausible account for assumptions implicitly made on a topic. The story itself can, therefore, be an object for inquiry.

Tropes are figurative phrases like 'the Prime Minister slipped on a banana skin today'. The main tropes are metaphor, synecdoche, metonymy and irony.

- *Metaphor* is the use of something familiar to describe something more complex and not necessarily easily understood. One uses language metaphorically when using the saying, such as 'she is a tigress in debate'. There are numerous metaphors, such as body metaphors when one talks about the 'lifecycle' of a product; environmental metaphors when one talks about the 'decay' of morality; and mechanistic metaphors when one talks about the 'cogs' of bureaucracy.
- *Synecdoche* is figurative speech in which a whole is substituted by a part. For example, The Presidency, one person standing for a country, or 50 head of cattle standing for 50 cows.
- *Metonymy* is similar to a synecdoche in that one thing is substituted to stand for another thing, as in the 'crown' standing for the monarch or the 'bottle' standing for alcohol.
- *Irony* is when one says one thing but means the opposite as in 'and he's so good looking' (meaning, of course, the opposite). Irony is often used to draw attention to some stance or point of view an author has taken. It allows an author to talk about the incongruity of a theory or piece of research in a humorous or mildly sarcastic way. Irony is a common methodological trope in the social sciences. It is often used to compare everyday activities with theoretical accounts to show the incongruity between what is *rationally* expected according to the theory and what actually happened.

Extended example: Rhetorical analysis of a social policy document

Policy documents can be a major source of material as well as evidence for a thesis or application of technique of analysis. The 'toolbox' of rhetorical terms outlined by McCloskey (1994), along with advice on reading plans (Mandelbaum, 1990) and policy analysis (Throgmorton, 1991; Fischer and Forester, 1993), can be useful in identifying the argument authors and organisations propose as policy. The following example is taken from a document produced by a major metropolitan city council in the UK, in pursuit of government funding for a project. The document was part of a competitive bid for substantial funding intended to stimulate the re-generation of areas in economic decline. The objective is to look at the rhetoric used in the bid document to see how the argument for funding was made for a deprived area within a UK city. Two major sections of the document are examined: the vision statement, which briefly states what the programme, if successful, aims to achieve within the five years of its tenure; and the area profile, which identifies the needs and opportunities for the area.

The following is an extract from a bid document called, *A Vision for Newtown South Aston*.

Only 30 years ago there were 35,000 people living in Newtown South Aston where only 12,000 live today. Conditions then were far from ideal but clearance and depopulation have been followed by deprivation, crime, poverty, ill-health and lack of employment, which will not be put right simply by improving the physical fabric of the area (important though that is).

'If I was in charge of millions of pounds for the development of Newtown, I'd put some more radical thinking into the problem than just throwing more good money after bad' (Local resident).

Newtown South Aston is a vital part of the Birmingham inner city. It plays a role providing both a living and working environment, but our vision is to help it do better and to transform it – people, businesses, land and property – into a success story. By taking advantage of the economic opportunities the area offers and by harnessing the potential of its people, we can tackle the issues of social deprivation and environmental blight that have come to characterise the area. This bid has been prepared with the willing support of local business organisations, potential developers, the public and voluntary sectors, and the community itself. These will also be the partners in the Company Limited by Guarantee, which we propose as the delivery mechanism.

We aim to achieve determined and creative progress towards a self-sustaining community. This is the ambition of the people and the businesses of Newtown and with the help of the whole community it is achievable. We must create a climate in which the cycle of poverty, ill health, crime and unemployment is broken. Getting people into work by improving education and creating job-training opportunities is the most important thing we shall do.

So this bid proposes a new deal for Education and Training via a Training Education Zone. Newtown South Aston people will get a first-rate education and training to help them get good jobs in the area, resulting from business growth and relocation, and in the wider Birmingham labour market. Local employers have stated their intention to employ local people who have the right sorts of skills. Overall the bid will result in 2,800 new jobs in the area.

Over the lifetime of City Challenge, the face of Newtown South Aston will be changed. As well as training, education and employment, the following changes will take place. Over 100 acres of land will be developed for business and industry,

(Continued)

housing and community use, serving Newtown South Aston and frequently the wider City. Three key sites Lucas, King Edward's Trust and Newtown Shopping Centre will be brought back into productive use. Existing businesses will be enabled to relocate and expand in the area; prime sites will be provided for new industries within a mile of the City Centre, practically on the national motorway network; and office development will come to Newtown. New private houses and changes in some current management arrangements will help to diversify the housing tenure and increase choice, encouraging people who work in the area, to live there too. A network of community development activities will enable the wider community to play a full part in developing and managing the area. Community enterprise will be supported, particularly to deliver some local services and to tackle problems of tipping rubbish and the fear of crime. Eight innovative and creative ideas will be independently monitored and evaluated, in conjunction with the community, using the City's Higher Academic Institutions where appropriate to assess their success and potential for working elsewhere in the City and nationally.

The bid builds on the unique value of Birmingham Settlement, the South Aston Community project and the work of the Aston Commission. It also recognises the remoteness of the Council's services and proposes the innovator step of devolving the Council's local functions in parallel with the City Challenge structure.

'People who don't live here say it's a deprived area – that annoys me, Newtown has got a hell of a lot going for it, swimming baths, community centre and a far better nursery provision than, shall we say the upper-class areas' (Local resident).

Five years from now Newtown South Aston will be on the way to being busier, cleaner, safer, more prosperous, healthier and more firmly linked to the rest of the City Centre. Its education and training services will be a model for inner city areas to follow and its ugly and blighted vacant sites will have disappeared. Increasingly the local community, including its business and voluntary sector, will be organising and running itself. It will be an inner-city village, in the best sense of the word, in which people want to live or work or both. That ambition is at the heart of all regeneration and we make no apology for giving it priority.

Lastly, it must be said that the commitment of all parties is so strong that it will be unrealistic to imagine that the work will stop on the 22 April 1992 – the date for the Bid submission. We shall carry on putting the machinery in place and developing the proposals in this bid over the coming months so that by the same time we are invited to present those proposals to ministers, the proposals will have been further developed and their framework is likely to be in place. Both of these demonstrate our absolute commitment to improve Newtown South Aston, making the most of the considerable opportunity City Challenge brings.

Source: Adapted from *A Vision for Newtown South Aston*, Birmingham City Council, in Jones, 1997

Ethos

The bid document opens with the following vision statement:

> Only 30 years ago there were 35,000 people living in Newtown South Aston where only 12,000 live today. Conditions then were far from ideal but clearance and depopulation have been followed by deprivation, crime, poverty, ill-health and a lack of employment, which will not be put right simply by improving the physical fabric of the area (important though that is).

The author notes the changing situation of the area, in a way that is reminiscent of the past. The *'only 30 years ago ...'* signifies that the area has undergone change that is relatively recent and therefore dramatic. The impact of change is emphasised as being wholly negative with this string of terms, *'deprivation, crime, poverty, ill-health and lack of employment ...'* As a list these terms characterise the area, functioning as a substitute for the reader. Implicit is the assumption that if the reader of the document were to visit the area, they would also use such terms as deprived to characterise what they see. There is also in the statement the notion that the cultural environment is connected with the physical environment. The problems of the area will not, it is claimed, be put right simply by attending to the physical environment. Therefore, an initial argument is being made for emphasis to be placed on the culture (or community ethos) of the area. This is reinforced by the reference to earlier attempts at improving the area. The word 'clearance' in particular refers to the physical environment, while also conjuring up common images of the conditions created by the high-rise system of buildings of the 1960s and early 1970s. Therefore, this bid is signifying that it will look at the social as well as the physical environment and thereby will be different from what has gone before and will therefore be more likely to be successful. The general ethos of the document may thus be characterised as one of a committed and informed agency.

The next point to note is how the second paragraph answers a number of reader questions. For example, why should public money be spent on this area? The importance of the area is emphasised when the authors claim the area is a 'vital part of the ... inner city ...'. Along with the role of the area the potential and opportunities of the area are emphasised. Given the importance placed on the area, a problem is defined, which needs a solution. If left unattended the problem may have serious consequences for the city. But regeneration will need co-operation and support from local business as well as from residents: does this support exist? Again, references are made to a range of general organisations including developers and charities. The word 'partners' in association with 'company' provides an economic orientation to the bid. It gives the impression of a business-driven approach. Hence, we see the implied reader: a government keen to have a business management approach to the running of public-funded programmes. We can also begin to appreciate the rhetoric the author attributes to the reader. The author uses terms and phrases common to the rhetoric of the reader, a government department. For example, 'economic opportunities', 'land and property', 'success' and 'delivery mechanism' all set the ethos for the argument in terms that will be understood by the organisation that will evaluate the bid.

(Continued)

Finally, if so many organisations are involved or are interested in the area why is it that they cannot regenerate the area without additional funding? The document acknowledges the support of local organisations but makes the point that the problems of the area are too great in scope for local solutions only to be effective. The irony is that local organisations need to be involved but to be effective they need to be co-ordinated by an external agency. Added to this is the implicit criticism of initiatives done in the past by the same organisations. These were responsible for previous attempts at re-generation, and their attempts not only failed but were also extremely costly. Hence, the significance of the anonymous quote. Acknowledgement is given to images of wastage of public finance. Along with the source of the quote the actual author of the bid document remains anonymous. The extensive use of 'we' and reference to the document as 'this bid ...' engenders sympathetic reading. They do this by conveying the impression that the organisations mentioned along with the people of the area and the local authority are the 'we'; as if all were acting as a collective with the shared goals.

Gnomic character

The City Council, being the principal author of the bid document, must also justify why they should be trusted with the programme if the bid is successful. In other words, what makes the local authority an expert capable of managing a major inner-city regeneration scheme? The bid document must, therefore, make a case for the combine headed by the Local Council to be seen as the only one able to manage the regeneration even though previous attempts have failed. An appeal to a knowledge and understanding of the area is used as part of the argument; it functions to provide a story worthy of belief. This is done in various places throughout this extract. But the main device in use is to supply some general images and then to suggest a solution that is both critical and different from what has gone before, and which distances the Local Authority from previous programmes. Among the general assumptions are that the area is very deprived and that no one would choose to live there. Those who could, moved out when it was previously re-built. However, regeneration will attract people back to the area. This is because the old sense of community will be re-established. The story of the once imperfect but populated community and of how it was destroyed is the basis of the argument; it shows self-evaluation along with the willingness to embrace different ideas and practices, especially working with local business.

Metaphor

There are a number of interesting metaphors in this document. The *body metaphor* is used in phrases like the 'life time' of the project and in the argument that the project will be the 'heart of all regeneration'. The use of the *organic metaphor* provides the impression of an area that can be revived, as it were, from a critical state. It also provides arguments for seeing the agency as the 'vital' organ for the resuscitation of the area. The document acts to diagnose the problem by describing the symptoms of the disease (the 'blight') that needs to be treated if it is not to spread or kill the area. The diagnosis is provided along with the prognosis if the treatment is not forthcoming. Hence, the problem and its solution can be more easily viewed. A second metaphor used is the *environmental metaphor*. This is used to describe the processes that will be used to regenerate the area. References to 'climate', 'cycle' and 'self-sustaining' create an argument for the environmental health needed in the area. This is equated with cleansing not only the physical fabric of the area but also its social problems. There is also a mechanistic metaphor. This is used to convey how the regeneration scheme will be managed and what some outcomes will be. The agency will be the 'delivery mechanism' that will enable, by putting the 'machinery in place', the local community to 'organise and run itself'. Underlying these metaphors is another – a *theoretical metaphor* about community. The notion of an 'inner-city village' is very symbolic. It trades on notions about the area as it was and how it may be again; as an area characterised by the quality of social interaction. This notion links firmly with a large literature on community. It is using the traditional paradigm of the rural/urban divide, where life in a rural setting is an idealised construct in which people were somehow happier and more contented than their urban counterparts.

The author of the bid document is using the *metaphor of community* to link various ideas that are current in social policy. One is the idea that if the traditional community can be re-established it will provide a panacea to many social problems, such as crime. This includes people taking responsibility for themselves and for the area in which they live. This implies that people ought not always to look to the State to provide help and support; that they are the best judges of what needs to be done and therefore should initiate actions to solve problems at the local level. This comes out in the bid document in references to local consultation and partnership with residents of the area. The argument of the bid is that it is possible to re-establish community by giving back to local people a sense of responsibility. One of the aims of the project will be just this – to create a self-sustaining community.

In this brief example we have seen how a range of rhetorical devices can be identified and shown to be a part of an argument. Although we have not looked at all the kinds of rhetoric present in this document nor the whole document itself you should be able to appreciate the usefulness of rhetorical analysis. There are several areas that could be expanded from our initial analysis. For example, the use of metaphor is a major device in the bid. The ideas and notions that are the basis of these metaphors have long and interesting histories. In methodological and theoretical terms, the use of community-based metaphors could be a starting point for extended discussion and evaluation. The point is, look not only to analyse but also to map out the origins of rhetorical devices that are used to present a case. In this way, one will be able to make connections between ideas in terms of their history and contemporary use. This will provide the materials and knowledge by which those ideas that have been mapped out can be described and, importantly, subjected to assessment and evaluation.

Citation mapping and analysis

When an author of an article or book refers to the work of another author they have cited a source. The citation along with all the others used in the main body of the text will be listed, using a recognised referencing style such as APA (American Psychological Association) or MLA (Modern Language Association) to provide all the necessary bibliographical details, as a list of references. It is a practice to collate the citations from different publications, from across the different disciplines, into indexes.

The uses of citation analysis

Citation analysis allows the number, frequency and patterns of citations to be identified for a given author and/or publication.

These are based on the simple concept that an author's references (the work they have cited) will indicate subject relationships between their work and the publications they cite. Therefore, the articles, papers, theses, books, reviews, correspondence and all other materials an author references in a published text are collated and published in citation indexes. Regardless of the length of the bibliography, generally the following bibliographic details are recorded: the title, author, when and where the item was published. This information can be a very useful source for investigating the linkages between authors in order to map out the development of an idea, technique or theory.

There are four main sources for finding citations – *Web of Science*, *Scopus*, *Google Scholar* and *PsychINFO*. Others are beginning to appear and may be worth keeping an eye on, such as *Semantic Scholar*. The *Web of Science*, *Scopus*, *Google Scholar* and *PsychINFO* are normally available through an academic library or Athens and their relative features are summarised in Table 8.8.

TABLE 8.8   Four sources for finding citations compared

	Web of Science	Scopus	Google Scholar	PsychINFO
Subjects indexed	Science, technology, social sciences, arts and humanities.	Science, technology, medical, engineering, arts and humanities.	Medical, scientific, technical, business, social sciences, arts and humanities.	Social, behavioural, education, management.

	Web of Science	Scopus	Google Scholar	PsychINFO
Time span	Some records go back to 1900 but most are from the 1970s and 1990s.	Most records go back to the mid-1990s and some back to 1823.	Whatever is available on the visible Internet.	Mostly from the 1800s onwards.
Searching	Form based from basic to advanced searching. Need to select index to search.	One-stop search for records.	Like doing a search of the web.	Form based from basic to advanced searching.
Coverage	Extensive journal coverage, some books, limited number of conference proceedings and some dissertations.	Moderate coverage of journals, books, conference proceedings and dissertations.	Extensive journal coverage, books, conference proceedings and extensive number of dissertations.	Extensive journal coverage in subject areas, limited books, no conference proceedings and limited dissertations.
Graphical representation of findings	Available	Available	Available	Not available

Uses of citation searching and mapping

To build up knowledge of a subject, information on the relationships that exist between different authors, at different times, within and across different disciplines can be useful. Analysis of the citations on a topic can help towards meeting this aim.

Reading advice: Debates on citation analysis

Citation analysis attracts continuing critical debates. See Cho and Neely (2012), Chung and Park (2012), Judge et al. (2007), Smith and Hazelton (2008), and Nosek et al.'s (2010) discussion of citation analysis issues in cognitive science, communications, management, nursing and psychology.

Citation analysis allows a researcher to map the intellectual relationships that exist in the literature on a given topic – they can reveal the otherwise implicit linkages between the origins of an idea, its development and its implementation, and criticisms of it. Citation analysis can also show the decline in popularity of an author, publication and theory. The examples that follow show how citation analysis can be used to:

- map and analyse citation use to provide evidence for an intervention
- list and classify citations to find out how a concept has been applied by different researchers
- map structural relationships of a topic and how it can be employed to verify the history of a discovery
- see how many citations there are of retracted articles.

Citation analysis as evidence for an intervention

Libraries and archives are wonderful places but none can subscribe to every journal or collect every other kind of publication. Different educational institutions tend to have different specialisms such as management, economics, education and so on. When it comes to resources, the library budgets of academic departments need to focus their limited finances on the current and future needs of their researchers, for example, which journals to subscribe to, which books to buy, and which online resources to pay for, need careful consideration. This is because it is impractical to buy everything and different subjects tend to use different types of publications. Researchers in the social sciences, arts and humanities tend to use more book-based publications (Lindholm-Romantschuk and Warner, 1996; Hicks, 1999), while researchers in the natural and biological sciences tend to use more journal-based publications.

Hoffmann and Doucette (2012) provide an interesting and useful research study into the citation research that has been used to inform the management of library resources (called collection management). They argue that, while there is a substantial body of research that reports on the results of citation analysis to inform collection management, there is, they observe (Hoffmann and Doucette, 2012: 322), the following problem:

> the majority of researchers do not provide enough detail in their methodology to reproduce the study, and explanations are generally not provided for decisions related to their study's objectives, scope, and citation retrieval and analysis. Monographs provide information on citation analysis methodologies – but often at a broad level.

Hoffmann and Doucette (2012: 322) recommend that what is needed are some consistent methodological practices that would make possible comparisons between studies. Their approach to this problem was to analyse the methodologies used in 34 citation studies published between 2005 and 2010. To be included in the selection, a study had to fall into one or more of the following classes:

> assess the adequacy of the current library collection; inform collections practices, such as acquisitions and cancellations; or inform collections policies, such as funding distribution, retention policies, and electronic access.

Table 8.9 is an extract from a table of studies reviewed by Hoffmann and Doucette (2012).

TABLE 8.9 Extract of studies reviewed by Hoffmann and Doucette (2012)

Citation analysis study	Variables analysed in study
Brazzeal, Bradley, and Robert Fowler. 'Patterns of Information Use in Graduate Research in Forestry: A Citation Analysis of Master's Theses at Mississippi State University.' *Science & Technology Libraries,* 26 (2005): 91–106.	type, citation age, frequency, holdings, citations per publication, subject area
Burright, Marian A., Trudi B. Hahn, and Margaret J. Antonisse. 'Understanding Information Use in a Multidisciplinary Field: A Local Citation Analysis of Neuroscience Research.' *College & Research Libraries,* 66 (2005): 198–210.	type, citation age, frequency, subject area
Choinski, Elizabeth M. 'Journal Use in Pharmacy.' *Science & Technology Libraries,* 27, no. 3 (2007): 53–64.	type, citation age, frequency, holdings, subject area, publishers
Cox, Janice E. 'Citation Analysis of Graduate Dental Theses References: Implications for Collection Development.' *Collection Management,* 33 (2008): 219–34.	type, citation age, frequency, holdings

Source: Extract from *Appendix A: Citation Analysis Studies Reviewed and Variables Analyzed,* Hoffmann and Doucette, 2012: 328

Table 8.9 provides the necessary bibliographic information of the studies selected and importantly the variables used to classify the studies for inclusion in the analysis. Hoffmann and Doucette's (2012) initial search of the literature identified 194 potential studies. The application of the criteria alongside excluding non-English studies reduced the number to 34. Therefore, Hoffmann and Doucette (2012: 322) explain how they identified potential studies using inclusion and exclusion criteria. Once obtained the individual studies were examined to extract information on, 'how the researchers defined the scope of their study (user group, date range, and types of publications) … as how they retrieved, examined, and then analysed the citations' (2012: 323).

Citation indexes and databases were used to identify potential studies. The indexes and databases used were the disciplinary specific *Library Literature and Library, Information Science and Technology Abstract* (LISTA) and the interdisciplinary database *Scopus*. The search vocabulary (concepts) included, 'citation analysis and collection'. The results covered a number of subject disciplines with most falling into the 'categories of science, medicine or health, social science, or engineering' (2012: 323). When analysing individual publications further indexes and databases were searched including *ProQuest* Digital Dissertations, *Web of Science* citation indexes, *WorldCat*, *Ulrich's Serials Directory*, *CASSI* and *PubMed*. Multiple indexes and databases were, therefore, consulted in order to identify themes, corroborate findings and contextualise each study. It is always recommended to use more than one citation index and/or database.

The practical outcome of Hoffmann and Doucette's (2012) analysis is a guide to using citation analysis methodologies. The guide they produced covers general guidelines, defining the scope of a study, retrieving and refining citations, and analysing citations. While this guide has a pragmatic purpose and has the potential to address the problem identified by Hoffmann and Doucette (2012: 327), in their conclusion they provide a useful piece of advice:

> In all cases, researchers must be deliberate about methodological choices, be selective about what is analysed and presented, and clearly describe their decisions and rationale. These practices will help ensure clarity and comparability, thereby increasing the value of each individual citation analysis study.

Citation analysis to find out how a theory has developed and been applied by different researchers

Occasionally a theory or practice becomes poplar and much is written about it. One such theory is *Relational Frame Theory* (RFT). RFT is a relatively recent behaviour-analytic account of language and cognition. Articles and a book on RFT began to be published in the late 1980s (Hayes and Hayes, 1989). The aim of RFT is to better understand the relationship between language and behaviour.

RFT is not something that can be easily explained. Several authors have provided explanations and examples of RFT (e.g., Barnes, 1994; Hayes and Wilson, 1996; Gross and Fox, 2009). What follows is a summary of the main elements that make up its essential assumptions. The main argument is that language and cognition are related – that humans communicate using language and learn, using their language, about how to relate things, experiences and responses, and to place them into categories. Language is assumed to specify the link between things as well as the strength of the link. Language, therefore, provides information on the appropriate response to a stimulus. The properties of things such as colour, shape, size, texture, use and so on are learnt and are able to be communicated using language. Humans learn that different stimuli can be grouped or placed into specific, context-dependent frames. Humans, unlike other animals, do not automatically respond but can use the context to decide what response would be appropriate. Therefore, the properties of an object and the stimulus it provides are not determining variables for a response. Humans, using language, create relational frames to place the objects and stimulus into context. Understanding how an individual relates and assigns stimuli into frames allows for interventions using language that have the capacity to change the relations that an individual creates. This latter aspect, thereby, gives RFT its therapeutic possibilities.

RFT has an interesting narrative. In 2005, the Association for Contextual Behavioral Science (ACBS) was established. The ACBS has a website that provides access to over 150 articles on RFT. The ACBS focuses on Acceptance and Commitment Therapy (ACT) – the website describes this as a 'unique empirically based psychological intervention that uses acceptance and mindfulness strategies, together with commitment and behaviour change strategies, to increase psychological flexibility.' With thousands of members, across many countries, RFT has, since first appearing in the early 1980s, seen exceptional growth and acceptance among many therapists.

The question is, just what is the empirical basis for RFT? This is the question set by Dymond et al. (2010: 97) when they note that despite the claim to over 70 empirical studies, 'there has been no prior citation analysis of RFT articles.' If RFT and its associated interventionist therapies have an evidence-base, then what does this evidence-base look like, who are the key authors, how much of it is empirically based, how has it developed, and what research methods have been used and are the most common? The rationale for these questions is supplied by Dymond et al. (2010: 98) when, quoting Hayes et al. (2003: 40), they note that, 'RFT is now 18 years old. It has spawned more basic human operant work than almost any theory put forward during that time' and quoting Hayes et al. (2006: 5), 'RFT has become one of the most actively researched basic behavior analytic theories of human behavior, with over 70 empirical studies focused on its tenets.' The point Dymond et al. (2010: 98) want to make is 'no source was provided in support of the statement that RFT had, in the relatively short space of approximately two decades, generated an evidence base of more than 70 empirical studies.' On the basis of their recourse to examples from the RFT literature Dymond et al. (2010: 99) state the purpose of their research as follows:

> The present study, therefore, sought to undertake the first such citation analysis by searching literature databases for articles that cited search terms related to RFT and assigning the subsequent articles to various categories.

The method Dymond et al. (2010: 99) employ is citation analysis. Using the terms 'relational frame theory', 'relational frames', and 'arbitrarily applicable relations', the Web of Science Indexes and PsycINFO database were searched. The different combinations of search terms and phrases were necessary as is often the case in most searches to capture publications that have not been indexed using, say, only 'relational frame theory'. The period for the search was 1981 to 2008. This search resulted in 174 articles; of these 62 were classified as empirical and 112 non-empirical.

In addition, Dymond et al. (2010), through summarising the data, identified the frequency of publications by key authors and collaborations. They found, 'Dermot Barnes-Holmes contributed the highest number of empirical articles (32), followed by Bryan Roche (14) and Steven Hayes (4).' They also noted, 'Other contributors included many of the three editors' former students, such as Yvonne Barnes-Holmes (11), Simon Dymond (9).'

The author of the research we are currently looking at is amongst the contributors to the literature that is the subject of his analysis. Do we then have a case here of an adherent of RFT trying to justify RFT? This issue needs careful consideration but there is, in principle, nothing inherently wrong in a researcher working in a particular field producing a citation analysis of publications that are relevant to themselves and others. This is something all researchers do as part of their research. However, Dymond et al.'s (2010) method and presentation of results have to be, as would any other study, subjected to questioning. This can be done by looking at the account they provide of what they did and at the data they make available. If there is a sufficient level of transparency and if it is possible to replicate the analysis, then their findings can be accepted as valid. In addition, the position of Dymond et al. (2010) within the RFT community can be seen as possibly beneficial. They could be expected to know the intricacies and oddities of the literature in their subject domain better than someone coming to the field anew.

The original article by Dymond et al. (2010) is a research study. As such, we can subject it to the same kind of quality assessment as we would any other research study. In Chapter 3 we looked at design issues and options for a research study and schemes for evaluating a piece of research. Key questions we can use in an evaluation are:

- How credible are the accounts?
- Has the researcher been transparent?
- Are claims substantiated with multiple sources of evidence?
- Are all concepts and variables clearly defined and shown to be measurable?
- Have all of the data been reported?
- Has the research process been fully explained?

Reading and checking some of the citations in Dymond et al. (2010), all of the above questions have been addressed in, space permitting, a positive way. The overall account of the reasons for the research is given and justified by reference to the literature. The researchers have been transparent about their own adherence to the subject domain and have provided all necessary citations and description of the research process. The citations and methods of locating and classifying them are the evidence, and there is sufficient rigour in the attention to detail to say claims are substantiated. The phrases (concepts and categories) used to search the citation indexes and database are explained and graphs show the measures. Sufficient findings are reported. There is no way of knowing from the article if this was all the data. But there is a robust, detailed approach to including as much data, in the form of citations, as could be expected in the space given for an article by a journal. Ultimately, Dymond et al. (2010) have provided enough information, so that this research could be replicated.

The research and analysis by Dymond et al. (2010) show how number, frequency and patterns of citations can be identified for a theory. This kind of study can be a starting point for identifying the key authors and publications within a subject. It also shows that we can distinguish between empirical and non-empirical publications using citation analysis.

Mapping structural relationships and the history of a topic

In his book *Citation Indexing* (1979), Eugene Garfield shows how citation analysis can be used to map structural relationships of a topic and how it can be employed to verify the history of a discovery. Using Isaac Asimov's account of the discovery and verification of the DNA theory of genetic coding, Garfield undertakes an interesting exercise in citation analysis. Garfield had two main aims. The first was to undertake a comparative evaluation of the account given by Asimov (1963) of the development of DNA (which Asimov based on his memory of events) with references from the citation index that also reported developments. The second aim was to see if Asimov (1963) had missed anything from his account that may be important for further developments. Figure 8.8 shows Garfield's stages for the strategy he used.

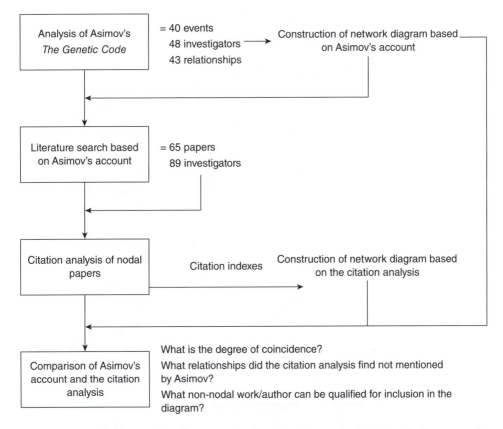

FIGURE 8.8   Garfield's strategy for mapping the development of DNA-code theory and verification

According to Asimov (1963), the development and verification of DNA theory spanned the period 1820 to 1962. Figure 8.9 is a network diagram of DNA development according to Asimov (1963). It involved 40 events and in descriptions of 36 of them, the names of the investigators are noted. Asimov also identified some 43 key relationships between investigators and events that are reproduced in Figure 8.9 as a network diagram. Each node is numbered to identify the investigator credited with the research at that stage, the time the research was undertaken and the type of research. The nodes are grouped by general type along three columns to show the development of the three oldest research areas: protein chemistry; genetics; and nucleic acid chemistry. The separate lines of research evident in the early nineteenth

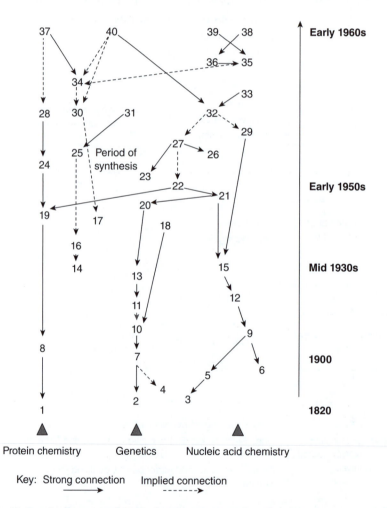

FIGURE 8.9 Network diagram of DNA development and verification according to Asimov, 1963

Source: Adapted from Garfield, 1979: 84

century began to show signs of synthesis by the mid-1950s, combining to form molecular biology.

Having constructed a network diagram from Asimov's account, Garfield then turned to analyse the citation indexes and relevant abstracts. His aim was to see if Asimov's account was correct and find out if he had missed anything. This involved searching the literature based on the names and subjects given in Asimov's book. The main problem Garfield encountered was how to select relevant papers from the literature. After 1945 it became the custom to publish a finding in several journals and in a series, with each stage of a scientific development

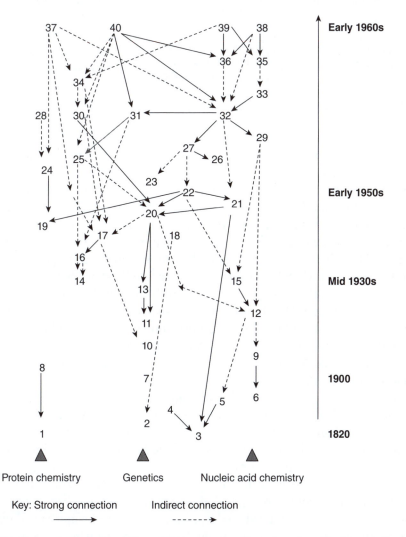

FIGURE 8.10 Network diagram of how DNA was developed and verified according to citation analysis of connections among nodal papers

Source: Adapted from Garfield, 1979: 88

Key to Figures 8.9 and 8.10		
1 Braconnot, 1820	14 Stanley, 1935	27 Watson and Crick, 1953
2 Mendel, 1865	15 Levene and Tipson, 1935	28 DuVigneaud,1953
3 Miescher, 1871	16 Bawden and Pirie, 1936–37	29 Todd, 1955
4 Flemming, 1879	17 Caspersson and Schullz, 1938–39	30 Palade, 1954–56
5 Kossel, 1886		31 Fraenkel-Conrat, 1955–57
6 Fischer and Piloty, 1891	18 Beadle and Tatum, 1941	32 Kornberg, 1956–58
7 DeVries, 1900	19 Martin and Synge, 1943–44	33 Ochoa, 1955–56
8 Fischer, 1907	20 Avery, MacLeod and McCarty, 1944	34 Hoagland, 1957–58
9 Levene and Jacobs, 1909	21 Chargaff, 1947	35 Jacob and Monod, 1960–61
10 Muller, 1926	22 Chargaff, 1950	36 Hurwitz, 1960
11 Griffith, 1920	23 Pauling and Corey, 1950–51	37 Dintzis, 1961
12 Levene with Mori and London, 1929	24 Sanger, 1951–53	38 Novelli, 1961–62
	25 Hershey and Chase, 1952	39 Allfrey and Mirsky, 1962
13 Alloway, 1932	26 Wilkins, 1953	40 Nirenberg and Matthaei, 1961–62

warranting a dedicated paper. Therefore, some developments have produced many papers in a series.

Garfield selected papers on the basis of those identified by Asimov. This tactic had a major benefit. It is often the case that first announcements do not contain extensive bibliographies. It is usual to find that first announcements are brief reports that are followed, at a later stage, with a comprehensive account and long bibliography. Garfield's search located 65 papers that reported the nodal events with 89 researchers being credited with authorship. These papers were then subjected to a citation analysis using the citation indexes.

Using the references to the 65 papers as primary sources the indexes were searched. This identified connections between the papers and enabled another network diagram to be constructed. This is shown in Figure 8.10. The numbering of the nodes is Asimov's but the arrows connecting the nodes are from Garfield's analysis of citations.

The connections in Figure 8.10 represent a small part of the total literature on the nodal events concerning the development of DNA theory. The selection made by Garfield shows the need for criteria to be set and strictly followed when selecting papers to represent the core knowledge on a topic. What we have in Figure 8.10 is the minimum network for representing the connections between papers. Nevertheless 58 relationships are identified. By extending the scope of papers the diagram could be expanded, possibly showing other connections.

If one compares the map produced by Asimov with that constructed by Garfield then a useful comparison can be made. This comparison may be made using a range of criteria such as: the basis of those citations duplicated; the judgements on the relative importance of individual citations; and the identification of the single most important development. If we apply these criteria, we can see a large degree of corroboration between the two accounts. Garfield's analysis shows that Asimov's account is a reliable source on the development of DNA theory. Garfield shows that Asimov did identify many of the significant events and had ranked them in an order of importance that is very similar to the citation indexes. The differences, however, are also interesting. Garfield's analysis of citation reveals 31 references not identified by Asimov. As Garfield's analysis shows, some of these were important to the development of DNA theory.

Garfield's analysis of Asimov's account of the development and proving of DNA theory is a good illustration of the use of citation analysis. It shows how the work of an author like Asimov can be verified. In this case Garfield verified 72% of the events Asimov identified. There is more to simply duplicating the work in the history of science. Garfield's analysis identified new connections and authors not mentioned by Asimov. Four of the authors identified by Garfield and not mentioned by Asimov played a significant role in the development of DNA theory. This shows that even a scientist who had an incredible memory, such as Asimov, can forget to mention some things. Citation analysis can, therefore, add to the accounts that scientists give about the development of a theory or technique: it can show new connections as well as events that appear to have been significant but have no identifiable connection to earlier work. Locating work outside the chronological line is one way of identifying work that may be at the very edges of the paradigm that can reveal something about the nature of originality. Analysis of citations is also a method that can augment traditional historical research into the history of a topic. This is because the compilation of the citation indexes is so thorough that a permanent record is available for continued reference. Added to these points is the nature of constructing citation networks. The diagram, although difficult to construct, can be far superior to a narrative account of the development of a topic. One is able to see the connections between events much more easily than with a textual narrative. By mapping connections in a diagram, the structure of the knowledge is made visible; with the core and the boundaries of work in the field shown making possible the selection of a space for one's own research.

Citation analysis of retracted articles

The three examples discussed above are all positive uses of citation analysis. There is another use of citation analysis that also has a possible use and this is to identify the citation of research that has been retracted. Gabehart (2005) examined the frequency of citations to four articles that had been retracted by the journals in which they had been published. Gabehart's (2005: 11) aims were:

1) to see if retracted articles in the scientific, technical and medical literature are still being cited, and 2) to look at the citations to four retracted papers to get a sense of whether the context of the references is positive or negative.

If an article has been retracted, this means something serious has been found to be wrong with that article. As researchers, we should not cite an article that has been retracted in our literature reviews. The problem arises with printed journals. A retraction statement usually appears after an article has been published. A researcher may cite such an article not knowing it has been retracted. The point here is to take all reasonable care with the search of the literature. If you are finding citations that look useful, especially a paper that reports findings, in another researcher's publication, say a thesis, then check these against the electronic databases to see if they have been retracted.

Gabehart (2005) points out another problem with citing retracted articles. This is when many authors have cited an article that has been retracted. In short, what kind of impact can a retracted article have on subsequent publications? To investigate these questions Gabehart (2005) undertook a search and analysis of MEDLINE that is available through PubMed. Restricting the scope of the search to 1994 to 2000, she looked for articles tagged with 'MeSH Retracted Publication'. Gabehart (2005) restricted her search to the year 2000 to ensure sufficient time had elapsed to allow citations of retracted articles to have been made and recorded in the citation indexes. To supplement MEDLINE, Gabehart (2005: 11) says, 'the *Office of Research Integrity (ORI) Newsletter* and the NIH Guide for Grants and Contracts website were searched for those years to ensure there were none missed by PubMed. Only one additional paper was identified this way.'

Gabehart (2005) found 211 retracted articles. Using PubMed the date of publication and date of retraction were found. Then using the *Science Citation Index* Gabehart (2005) looked for citations post-retraction for each article. From the 211, four articles were selected as case studies for in-depth analysis. These four articles were chosen because of 'a high number of citations to the article after retraction' (2005: 12). After downloading citations for the 211 into Endnote, Gabehart (2005: 13) found that there had been:

a total of 7,937 citations with 2,393 of the citations published after retraction. On average the articles were cited 11.3 times after retraction and 37.6 times in total, which shows that about 30% of the articles' citations were after retraction.

When examining the four papers selected, Gabehart (2005) makes some interesting and important points about retraction. In her first and second case studies, papers (Sparkes et al., 1999a, 1999b) were retracted because of trademark errors. The authors of the two papers had not properly attributed the trademark of chemicals mentioned in their articles. Hence, these two articles had no errors except for using generic words for chemicals that were subject to trademarks. The owners of the trademarks objected and it was the objections that led to the retractions.

In her third case study, Gabehart (2005: 15–16) selected Buchdunger et al. (1995) as an example of a study that had been retracted because 'an aspect of the experiment could not be reproduced or verified.' Gabehart (2005) found that Buchdunger et al. (1995) had been cited 148 times with 100 of these post retraction. Of these citations six of the citations were by Buchdunger citing herself in her subsequent publications.

In her fourth case study, Gabehart (2005) looked at Schön et al. (2000) as an example of an author who had several articles retracted. The Schön case study attracted a lot of attention and further details of this case can be found on the Internet. Gabehart (2005) found 60 citations to Schön et al. (2000), of which 19 were post-retraction. An interesting finding revealed by Gabehart's (2005) analysis was Schön's papers had been cited several times by two other authors. This may mean these two authors were citing work that had been shown to be invalid. The point Gabehart (2005: 18) makes is, 'it is easy in these cases to see how much citations to fraudulent research can taint the results of subsequent papers.'

Conclusion

Mapping the ideas, arguments and concepts from a body of literature is an important part of the review of the literature. The different methods, of which there are many, can be used in whatever way an analyst deems appropriate. Their use will enable them to find their way around the literature, to identify the key landmark studies and concepts and at the same time build, from the bottom up, a picture of the relationships that exist between individual pieces of work. All research is based on some kind of classification scheme. It may be the methodological approach or the phenomena that have been classified. That a classification scheme exists or a new one has been proposed does not mean either has to be accepted. Care needs to be taken when using the schemes of others. This is because the ways in which something is classified often result in a particular interpretation that excludes alternatives. The purpose of mapping the ideas in the literature is to use analytical techniques to critically evaluate the usefulness of ways in which a classification has been used (or assumed) and to develop schemes of your own.

In summary

- We need to map ideas to see how they are related, and to find out what kinds of classifications have been used by others to do their research.
- Even experienced and respected researchers can fudge a scheme of classification – therefore, do not be afraid to challenge any classification.
- Classifying research by type can be a useful guide to the methodological assumptions and research techniques used by different researchers – this means you need to develop a working knowledge of methodological traditions, trying to put aside bias, to fully understand the reasons why a researcher selected to use a particular methodological approach.
- Bibliographic and citation tools can be useful in mapping the literature. It is important to get to know how to use them.

9

Writing the Review

Key questions

- How can the literature review be used to justify the topic?
- What formats are useful for arranging the review of the literature?
- What is meant by criticism and how can you be fair in your critical analysis?
- How do you start to write a literature review?

Core skills

- Manage large, complex amounts of information in preparation for writing
- Plan and draft different documents for different audiences
- Construct valid, systematic and structured arguments for different purposes
- Communicate your ideas and arguments in ways that are clear.

Introduction

The review of the literature is not a separate piece of writing that takes up just one chapter in a dissertation (or report). The literature has a role and purpose throughout the dissertation – it provides evidence for the rationale and research problem, gives the context and history of the topic, supplies a methodological frame of reference and guides selection of data collection methods and, once the data have been collected, provides you with an opportunity to show how your research contributes to the existing literature.

The literature review *as* a piece of writing must be clear, have a logical structure and show that you have acquired a sufficient range of skills and capabilities at an appropriate level. The written dissertation (thesis or report) needs to be viewed as the evidence of your capabilities as a researcher. When you are ready to write up your work, you have to adequately, appropriately and interestingly describe, explain and justify what you have done and found out. The main vehicle for this is the dissertation, so we begin this closing chapter by reformulating the many comments we have made, into the following definitions.

Definition: Dissertation

A dissertation is not just a record of research done. It is a document divided into parts that express, not necessarily in linear form, a coherent argument or investigation. A dissertation should be a holistic demonstration of the skills and intellectual capabilities of the research student. It must show thought and the structures of reason on which the research is based. It must say something that is based on existing knowledge that develops knowledge and does so using argument, evidence, a critical and reflexive stance, and that demonstrates scholarship.

Definition: Evidence-based Report

An evidence-based report presents a comprehensive review of the research literature on a problem, from as many methodological approaches as is feasible. The report is not just a survey of relevant literature. It is a document that is produced to evaluate or make a case for real-world interventions. Therefore, it must be based on a thorough understanding of scholarly standards, with the procedures and methods, including the inclusion and exclusion criteria, clearly explained and described. The criteria for extracting data, including statistical techniques applied, and methods of graphical presentation, must be clear, accurate and evidence a critical and reflexive stance grounded in the transparent provision of all information.

Added to these functions of the evidence-based report as a whole, the literature review should show that all relevant documents, published and unpublished, have been identified and analysed. This means demonstrating that all the main concepts, theories, theorists and methodological approaches relevant to the topic have been identified, understood and critically evaluated. For these reasons, the review is not a continuous piece of writing: it may well have several sections dealing with different reviews, at different levels, at different locations in its structure.

The main challenge is to ensure that all of these demands are met in a review that flows, leading the reader from one set of ideas to the next, and that provides systematic reasoning for the topic you have identified for your own research project.

What we will look at in this chapter are the elements that can be used to construct your review, by showing the role of the review as a proposal for your research and as the means for identifying and justifying your topic.

The review and its use

Through the preceding chapters, we have taken a journey that has shown the reasons for reviewing a literature, the methods that can be used to extract and organise information, and how different ideas can be mapped out so that connections between them can be made. The literature review has no single purpose. Its purpose will be largely dependent upon the type of research that you intend to do. Some of the kinds of research that you can undertake were outlined in Chapter 3. However, the key objective that all reviews share is to provide a clear and balanced picture of current leading concepts, theories and data relevant to the topic or matter that is the subject of study. This basic requirement is not an end in itself but a starting point for thinking about and planning the review. The first thing we will look at, therefore, is the argumentational function of the review, before moving on to look at some technical aspects of the writing process.

The review and the research proposal

One of the main reasons for writing the review is to make a proposal for the research you intend to do. This means that your review of the literature must provide a methodological rationalisation for your research. You need to demonstrate that you understand the history of your topic. The history is the assumptions and definitions other researchers have employed to study the topic.

Literature review of vs literature review for

As you approach writing up your literature review, it is essential to be clear on the intention of your writing. If you need to produce a literature review for a research proposal, remember the distinction made in Chapter 2 between writing a literature review *of* a subject and a review *for* a project.

It is your responsibility to investigate this history in order to provide the story of how the topic was defined, established and developed. We noted in the previous chapter that chronological narrative is the most common arrangement for presenting the methodological story because it is the easiest to use. It follows the kinds of story structure with which many of us are familiar – this happened, then this, then this and so on. However, the story structure needs to be adapted for academic writing, and later in this chapter we will look at some ways in which this can be achieved.

In each part of your methodological story you are aiming to make a recommendation for your research. As a recommendation, your review needs to be a structured argument that in its simplest format achieves the following:

Knowledge-based elements

- a description of previous work on the topic, identifying leading concepts, definitions and theories
- consideration of the ways in which definitions were developed and operationalised as solutions to problems seen in previous work
- identification and description of matters other researchers have considered important.

Argumentational elements

- a description of what you find wrong in previous work on the topic
- a proposal for action that may solve the problem – your research
- an explanation of the benefits that may result from adopting the proposal
- a refutation of possible objections to the proposal.

How and where in your review you place emphasis on each of these is a matter for you to decide. However, you should have sufficient material for the task. The analysis that you will have done when reading the literature should provide sufficient material and understanding of that material, to make a proposal for your own research. From your notes, three kinds of resources you should employ are:

- the relevant vocabulary with alternative definitions of words and concepts
- summaries of the methodological arguments found in key texts
- your assessments of how key definitions and methodological assumptions have been operationalised.

The results of your analysis may also provide you with ideas for the structure of your review. When undertaking argumentational analysis of key texts you will probably have recognised that most authors adopt a generic structure to present their case. This often has the arrangement we have just noted for the argumentational elements. This structure can be used at the end of your review to summarise the analysis that you have made. You can also employ elements of it at different places in your review to provide formulations of what you have said, providing summative signposts of where your argument is leading. As a result, when you provide your conclusions and bring each of your formulations together it is more likely that your argument will be cohesive.

What you are required to do, therefore, is to make a compelling case for your research that it will in some way make a contribution to our understanding of some phenomenon. This can mean a range of things depending on what kind of research you intend to undertake. For example, you may be arguing for the use of a methodological approach that has been used in another discipline. Hence, you will be proposing to undertake a methodologically based piece of research. This may involve providing an illustration of the usefulness of a methodological approach. Alternatively, you may be interested in looking at prior attempts at solving a practical problem. Your interest here may be in identifying factors that have been critical to the success and failure of such prior work. Hence, you will be aiming to do a piece of research based on evaluation. There are many other types of research that you may want to do. The main point at this stage is that all research has a history. It is this history that provides the precedent for further work; it is what forms the starting point for your proposal. The following example from Atkinson (1982) looks at the process of research from the point of using the literature review to identify and justify a topic. Notice how it is a non-linear way in which a research topic is identified and how it goes through a process of redefinition as further information is found in the literature.

Extended example: Justifying your topic

Atkinson and his collaborators had been researching suicide for several years and in *Discovering Suicide* he justifies his work. This may not seem particularly noteworthy but given that by 1927 there were over 4000 works on suicide and by 1961 another 2000 further studies (Atkinson, 1982: 189), anyone studying the topic would need to provide a clear justification for looking once again at what so many had already researched. We want to look in some detail at Atkinson's rationale for studying suicide. This is because he provides a coherent explanation of how he came to choose the topic and how he developed a way of researching it that was different from what had gone before. It may help if the structure of *Discovering Suicide* were outlined before looking at specific sections of it. The full title of the work is *Discovering Suicide: Studies in the Social Organisation of Sudden Death*, and we can gain an understanding of its structure from the list of contents at the front of the book:

(Continued)

PART I: SUICIDE AND SOCIOLOGY

1.   Background and Introduction to the Research
2.   The Suicide Problem in Sociology
3.   Suicide Research and Data Derived from Official Sources
4.   Alternative Sociological Approaches to Suicide Research

PART II: SUICIDE AND THE SOCIAL ORGANISATION OF SUDDEN DEATH

5.   Registering Sudden Deaths: Official Definitions and Procedures
6.   Some Relevant Factors in Imputing Suicide
7.   Common-Sense Theorising about Suicide
8.   Ethnomethodology and the Problem of Categorisation

As we can see, the monograph is divided into two parts. The first part provides the justification for this research into suicide, while the second is mostly the research itself. In giving over nearly half of the 225 pages to justification, Atkinson shows that he is keenly aware of the need to explain the choice of a familiar topic. We are going to look at:

- how he came to choose suicide as a topic for research
- his attitude to criticising works in the literature
- and how he justifies research into what appears to be an over-researched topic and finds a gap for his research.

We can begin with the section Conclusions at the end of Chapter 2. The sociological interest in suicide can, Atkinson argues, best be characterised as:

> fascination from a distance ... For it was the *issues* posed by Durkheim in a book, which just happened to be on suicide itself, rather than the *phenomenon of suicide* itself, which has stimulated most of the sociological interest. (1982: 31)

Atkinson makes part of his claim at the start of Chapter 2. He says that Durkheim chose to study suicide as a topic in order to develop his sociological theories. We can therefore impute that Atkinson is interested in studying suicide as a topic in its own right and this is one thing that makes his work different from that of Durkheim. Atkinson adds to his claim that, although there has been extensive sociological interest in suicide, little research has addressed the problems inherent in empirical research of suicide. He claims that methodological difficulties, which he will deal with, have never been faced because very few people have undertaken an empirical study of suicide. Thus Atkinson is saying that his work is different from that of Durkheim and the several thousand other studies. Working from these claims and the surrounding text, we can extract the reasoning Atkinson employed to construct his argument. We begin with the preface, where Atkinson gives his reader a global summary of his reasons for the topic and its treatment.

An open-minded approach

Very few researchers tell their readers how their topic was chosen. In the preface to his book (which he expands in Chapter 1), Atkinson reflects how he came to study suicide in the way he did. He possibly felt the need to use this preface to justify the topic and also to justify the way he approached and studied suicide. His study is strongly ethnomethodological.

Atkinson tells us that debates over method and methodology posed difficult challenges for empirical research: debate over, for example, the verification and reliability of data, the relationship between data and hypotheses, and competing interpretations and explanations of data. In the spirit of scholarship, he explored these debates, mainly through reading but also through personal contact with some of the main theorists and researchers engaged in the debates. Through reading and talks with others, Atkinson embarked on a journey that took him through most of the major paradigms in the social sciences, exposing him to the main debates and issues concerning the relationship between theory and empirical research. As an empirical researcher, Atkinson says that he reacted against the traditional approaches, finding these to be too far removed from the description of real-world activities.

The structure of his book shows that Atkinson intended to undertake two projects – a review of the literature about suicide and an empirical study of how a death becomes defined as a suicide. Atkinson tells us that the literature review showed that the two projects could not easily be separated in this way. Atkinson says,

> Having got that far ... I found I could no longer distinguish satisfactorily between the two enterprises, as my views on the suicide literature were so closely bound up with a very particular empirical problem, which underpinned so much of the research on suicide by sociologists ... namely the status of the data used in testing hypotheses. (1982: xiii)

His literature review, therefore, provided clarity and intelligibility to the main methodological debates within sociology, for example, disputes between psychology and sociology, and between positivists and non-positivists. The use made of studies like Durkheim's *Suicide*, led Atkinson to his particular approach to the topic. This came out of the literature review. It was through the review that he was able to reassess conventional paradigms to find that these debated suicide rather than studied it. He wanted an approach that enabled him to describe the details of how society, through such agencies as the coroner's court, defines (i.e. accomplish) a death as suicide. None of the existing approaches would give a sufficient purchase to this aim. By being in the right place at the right time (and through reading), Atkinson encountered ethnomethodology. The rigorous detail and descriptive analysis of finely recorded activities in real settings is a major characteristic of ethnomethodology. The ethnomethodological concern with describing empirical activities from within, rather from without, gave Atkinson the approach he needed – it was different, distinct, and with the attraction of being seen as dissenting.

(Continued)

How the topic was chosen

Atkinson came to his topic – as many researchers do – through a course of undergraduate teaching. He was asked to prepare a paper on the question: 'How much deviance is there?' Having looked at the statistics and definitions about deviance, he began to question them.

> On turning to the recommended sources, it struck me as obvious that, to varying degrees, they only told part of the story. It was also obvious sociologists seemed singularly unconcerned by the problematic nature of the figures and were not inhibited about making far-reaching generalisations on the basis of crime rates, suicide rates ... (1982: 3)

Atkinson attempted to make a case for why the question set could not be answered using the numerical data or definitions available. His paper was received, he tells us, with considerable displeasure. He was accused of focusing on mundane problems that were already known about, and which were of no concern to sociologists. This response led Atkinson to pursue his concerns. Although textbooks advocated caution about generalisations and stressed the need for rigour, in practice, sociologists did things differently. They seemed to have little concern for the integrity of data and were too willing to make generalisations in spite of methodological difficulties (1982: 4). Atkinson, therefore, saw this inconsistency between formal theory and subject attitude as a 'discovery'.

Developing the topic by changing the focus

Atkinson tells us that he began by reading the sociology of deviance. His aim was to focus on the problems of rates associated with the data used for talking about suicide as a social phenomenon. However, the literature was far more extensive than he had assumed. He also realised it covered many disciplines and there were many debates between disciplines and within them about suicide rates. His positivist approach was soon dropped in favour of an interactionist approach. After reading works from the symbolic interactionist approach, Atkinson took up pursuit of the labelling approach to deviance. Work of interactionists like Becker (1963) and Lemert (1951) seemed to be more empirically oriented than positivistic studies. His plan now was to undertake an interactionist study of suicide. However, in his journey through the literature he came across a thesis that had done just that. Douglas (1966) had produced a detailed critique of Durkheim's *Suicide* from an interactionist approach, and examined the social construction of suicide statistics. Atkinson's initial reaction was to discontinue with this topic, but realising that someone else was thinking in similar ways to himself encouraged him to continue.

Taking Douglas's work, Atkinson attempted to model the suicide process. Using materials that he had gathered, he played around with a range of research strategies in his attempt to extend the work done by Douglas. Atkinson realised that there were errors in Douglas's work. These centred on Douglas's treatment of how definitions of suicide were treated by officials (e.g., coroners). Douglas had focused on the meaning of suicide to see how rates were socially constructed. He had not looked at how coroners and other officials do defining work to arrive at a category to assign to the corpse. Added to this, Douglas had made no concrete recommendations on how a study of defining work may be done. This led to a thorough critical analysis of Douglas's work. From this, we can see how the general review of the literature can lead to specific reviews that show and debate the main issues and highlight the main problems of previous research.

Atkinson's critical evaluation of Douglas's (1966) work did not indicate what he should do next. Nobody had, it seemed, gone beyond an interactionist treatment of the topic. Atkinson was, therefore, breaking new ground. What had begun as a study within an existing paradigm was turning out to be something new possibly using a very different paradigm. Most of the research was complete by this stage as Atkinson had already done the major parts of the project. The search and review of the literature were done and a large amount of empirical data had been collected (from newspaper cuttings and observations in coroners' courts). His problem was what to do next. This is where opportunity came into play, although Atkinson, in part, made his own opportunity. When looking at labelling theory, he remembered encountering work by a group known as ethnomethodologists.

Atkinson was, therefore, faced with a common problem in research. He had to re-evaluate the work he had done so far. This meant criticising some of his earlier writing on the topic. He had to learn how to be self-evaluative and to acknowledge his own mistakes in interpretation and understanding. But, just as significantly, he had to rewrite his thesis – it was now something very different from what he had originally conceived it to be.

Atkinson's experiences show the non-sequential structure of research. Very few research projects proceed on what may be the recommended structure of reading-research-writing up. Atkinson's went something like this: 'reading-writing-research-writing-research-writing-reading-research-writing' (1982: 6). This structure is more characteristic of most research projects. It indicates something of the processes we actually encounter as researchers, because of thinking things through and not taking things for granted or unquestioningly accepting interpretations other researchers have made. This developmental nature of a topic and self-reflective attitude is shown in the arrangement of Atkinson's book. Atkinson describes this in the following way:

> Thus the topic originally chosen turned out to be one which had been already examined at some length from an interactionist perspective. In examining the various responses to the problem, those of Kitsuse and Cicourel (1963), Cicourel (1968), and Sudnow (1965), had seemed the most useful from the point of view of designing empirical research ... and these writers, it emerged later, were ethnomethodologists and not the simple interactionists they are often presented as being. There were also serious empirical difficulties in the way of doing research along the lines suggested by those who advocated the use of a sequential model (e.g. Becker, 1963), or an exclusive focus on social meanings ... The initial search for an official definition of suicide, coupled with problems which arose out of earlier encounters with coroners, subsequently suggested that the question, 'How do deaths get categorised as suicides?' was the most appropriate way of formulating the research question ... and that question, it was to emerge later, was not unlike the kind of question an

(Continued)

ethnomethodologist may have asked ... Perhaps not surprisingly in view of that, the kinds of results obtained in trying to find an answer ... were later found to be consistent with some of the more important contentions of ethnomethodology. (1982: 7)

Justifying the research by critiquing the literature

Chapter 2 of the study, 'The suicide problem in sociology', is subdivided into the following parts: 2.1 Introduction; 2.2 Deference to Durkheim; 2.3 Positivism; 2.4 Sociologism; 2.5 Functionalism; and 2.6 Conclusions. It is in these sections of his book that Atkinson attempts to justify his research into suicide. We have already indicated the reason for this; but how does he do it? The first thing to notice is the use of the convention of subheadings. He breaks the task down into logical and consistent categories. These may not be the categories everyone would choose but they do fulfil Atkinson's aim – to provide an adequate scholarly warrant for his claim. As you may expect, Atkinson covers the major aspects of the conventional approach to suicide – Durkheim's work, positivism, the functionalist perspective, and the difference between sociology and psychology. However, the main thrust and structure of Atkinson's approach can be seen in how he makes clear that his work is very different from that of Durkheim. So, we will focus our attention on this section.

If Atkinson wants to claim that his study is an original contribution to our knowledge of suicide then he would be expected to show how this is so. This would usually be taken as involving a clear explanation of how his work differs from Durkheim's. One of the things Atkinson, therefore, attends to is the place and role attributed to Durkheim's study of *Suicide*. In Kuhnian terms, Atkinson points out that Durkheim's study of suicide was a paradigm innovation, in that it created a new way of looking at something. Atkinson argues that Durkheim's study provided a clear example of the distinctive possibilities of sociology. Durkheim showed how sociology could be done. It has also been used to illustrate the place of social explanation in contrast to psychological explanation: that even the most seemingly individualistic (or psychological) act has social rather than psychological causes.

Pointing out the place and status conferred on Durkheim's study of *Suicide*, Atkinson attempts to show how subsequent sociological works on suicide have been conducted within the original Durkheimian framework and that these subsequent studies have not come up with anything different. They have used the same kinds of numerical data (suicide rates) and have, therefore, produced confirming evidence. Anyone following Durkheim's example will, Atkinson points out, produce no surprises. They may produce a replicative study, claims Atkinson, but 'may be put off by the prospect of having to compete with someone as eminent as Durkheim, and the internal structural pressures within sociology against embarking on suicide research come to look fairly substantial' (1982: 12–13).

Atkinson, however, focuses the justification for his research on *methodological* grounds. Having shown the general fascination with Durkheim's study, Atkinson looks for reasons for this fascination. Some of these we have just mentioned; the examples it provides and the arguments it makes. But *Suicide* is also a methodological study in that it established a distinctive sociological explanation, based on a range of methodological assumptions. These assumptions included holism and structuralism, which focused attention on the explanation of behaviour by reference to processes occurring in larger social structures.

As a consequence, the enduring interest in *Suicide* has been methodological and theoretical. Subsequent studies have been about refining Durkheim's original research or about debating its strengths and weaknesses. They have not, according to Atkinson (1982: 10), 'been of the phenomenon, which members of a society call suicide'. Therefore, Durkheim was not so much interested in suicide as a topic, but as a resource to demonstrate a methodological and theoretical argument. He used suicide rates to argue for the existence of social facts and that these were to be regarded as concrete things. Properties of social groups, such as cohesiveness, could be measured using numerical indices. Durkheim was thus able to argue that social science, like the natural sciences, looked at facts not in a personal, but in an objective way. Atkinson does not dispute Durkheim's intentions or criticise what he achieved. He does, however, reinforce his main point.

> The extensiveness of the general sociological interest in suicide is of little help to the would-be researcher into suicide. For from whatever stance one approaches the research, one is faced with fundamental and unsolved methodological problems, which appear so obvious that it initially seems strange that they have been given so little attention in the past. That is, whether one's interest is in the relationship between sociological and psychological modes of explanation or in anomie theory, and whether or not one considers oneself a positivist, functionalist, conflict theorist or whatever, important decisions have to be made about the status and adequacy of the data chosen for analysis. Not only is the widespread interest of sociologists in suicide of little help in solving the methodological problems faced by the empirically oriented researcher, but that the character of that interest probably accounts for how it is that such fundamental and obvious problems were ignored for so long. For the difficulties are only likely to emerge as obvious at the point of designing or attempting to do empirical research, and hence to remain hidden from the view of the philosophers, theorists and teachers who use suicide as nothing more than a 'substantive' example in debates about ideas. (1982: 32)

Having read the example, you should note the following points that provide a brief summary of Atkinson's justification:

- Atkinson's preface and review of the literature are a clear justification for his topic
- he employs the basic but very readable narrative approach to his justification
- he provides an introduction, in which the interest in the topic is explained
- he begins to let the reader know about the problems and doubts he had had about the topic and how it had been defined and studied by other researchers
- his analysis of the literature is used to find fault with previous works
- this is then used to make the suggestion that an alternative approach is needed and, most importantly, that he knows what that alternative may look like.

As Atkinson's study shows, with many pieces of research, where you start and where you end up can be two very different things. He started with an idea for a positivist piece of research, but ended up with a qualitative study inspired by ethnomethodological concerns.

(Continued)

This was due partly to the contingent nature of research and partly to his scholarly work. As a researcher, you must expect opportunities to arise; you must therefore be prepared for the unexpected. This means not giving up when you hit a problem. It also means being prepared to follow leads that initially seem obscure and even dissident; that is, not the usual way of doing things. Atkinson in his account of how this work took direction gave an account of all of these happenings.

The structure of scholarship

We have already indicated that there are a number of functions for a literature review, and in Chapter 2 we looked at scholarship in some detail. In this section, we will look at some aspects of scholarship that tend to characterise a good review. This discussion is governed by considerations of what is an appropriate academic style. In the example provided by Atkinson, we were able to show the argumentational nature of some literature reviews, along with his stylistic stance on requesting open-mindedness. In this section, we can follow up what we mean by this attitude when we look at the practice of criticism.

What is criticism?

A major theme of the preceding chapters has been the practice of criticism. Taking a critical stance was advocated when we talked about analysis, understanding arguments and mapping ideas. In terms of your research, whether it is applied or theoretical, the application of a critical attitude should be demonstrated in the thesis. The main points that characterise effective criticism are:

- agreeing with, or defending a position, or confirming its usefulness through an evaluation of its strengths and weaknesses
- conceding that an existing approach or point of view has some merits which can be useful but that others need to be rejected
- focusing on ideas, theories and arguments and not on the author of those arguments, so as to produce a careful, considered and justified evaluation
- being aware of your own critical stance; identifying your reasons for selecting the work you have criticised and recognising the weakness in your critique
- selecting elements from existing arguments and reformulating them to form a synthesis, a new point of view on some subject matter
- finding fault in an argument by identifying fallacies, inadequacies, a lack of evidence or plausibility
- identifying errors in a criticism made by another to provide correction and balanced criticism, thereby advocating the usefulness of the original work and reasons for rejecting the criticism made of it.

When criticising an argument avoid making a number of fallacies. You may remember that fallacies in argument were discussed in Chapter 5. It stated that some positions rely on mistaken beliefs about what is the case or what counts as evidence. When critiquing an argument, it is easy to commit a number of fallacies that will damage the force of your argument. For example, you may strongly disagree with what someone else has said or how they said it. But attacking them personally will not refute what they have to say. Attack their ideas and their argument; do not make the error of name-calling. Related to this is the fallacy of believing you have criticised an argument by attacking the motive of its author. You may wish to point out what the motivation was for someone when they made a claim; but this will not refute what they said. It may even provide added weight to your opponent's position. Finally, if you believe that an argument is bad, it is not sufficient to produce a counter argument that is equally as bad. One poorly constructed argument does not refute an equally fallacious argument.

Criticise fairly and openly

When it comes to writing up your critical evaluation or critical appraisal of the work of others, there is a convention that requires you to treat the work of others with due respect – as you would expect others to treat your work. You may feel that this attitude is not always evident in academic work, but it is good practice, and a good starting point for acquiring good academic standards. Some basic pointers about what makes fair treatment when dealing with the work of others are set out below.

A main requirement is that you summarise the views and arguments that others have made in a way that shows an open-minded and balanced approach. This means not assuming that a reader is familiar with the work with which you are dealing. It also involves acknowledging, where appropriate, what points you agree with in an advocate's work. This is not just about showing how reasonable you can be by projecting a scholarly image for yourself. It may be that you will find some intellectual worth, some pointers, for your own work. Such good practice also demonstrates that you are able to extract what may be useful and possibly that you are able to create a new synthesis. Also avoid a stance that is heavy with statements. Although you will need to state what you have found deficient in an argument, it is not enough simply to provide a list; an explanation is also required. In order for your criticism to be legitimate you need to provide a structured explanation showing what you have found wrong in an argument. This means focusing attention on the major points of the argument and not on minor details. This may mean, as we will shortly see, that you work systematically through the main elements of the argument. This will show that you are able to pick out the major elements of the argument. In doing this, you must avoid unsubstantiated criticisms or using hypothetical examples; if you do, it will only trivialise your analysis.

Structure of criticism

Refuting an argument or series of arguments is therefore not something that can be done lightly; it demands structured thought based on an analytical evaluation. In Chapter 5, we discussed some of the ways in which you can begin to think systematically about analysing and evaluating arguments. In this section, we want to discuss what it means to be systematic when producing a refutation of an argument. The list below gives the structure of an argument developed by Toulmin (1958), as explained in Chapter 5; for each element, criteria are given for the reader to assess the adequacy of its application for the writer. The point to note is that we can work our way systematically through the different elements of an argument that employs this kind of structure. Toulmin's structure, shown in the list below, can act as our guide and at the same time provide us with a structure for our writing.

> Claim – clarity, plausibility, cogency, consequences, practicality
>
> Evidence – amount, relevance, reliability, reproducibility, credibility
>
> Information – details, sources, contacts, time periods
>
> Warrant – robustness, degrees of connection, assumptions, rhetoric
>
> Backing – problem awareness, admissibility, strength, validity
>
> Conclusion – logic, substantiation, consequences, plausibility.

We take as our starting point that we have the following aims: (a) to show the structure of reasoning that someone has employed; (b) find fault with some or all of that reasoning and then (c) show the possibilities of our position. This seemingly simple story structure can be very effective. It will allow you to move in a systematic way through an argument and, if sufficient attention is paid to detail, also allow a coherent position to be established at the end. One way of thinking about this is that you have the task of taking your reader from one position that your *advocate* has stated in his or her argument, to another position, which you are advocating. Working through an argument, we may think about writing our analysis by framing the argument itself. That is, saying what the argument is about and how it is made up. In doing this, we will be framing the position of the argument; and showing what stance he or she has taken on a matter. This may mean working through the claim that is made, the evidence that has been provided, and then examining any warrants that are made, either implicitly or explicitly, before describing the scope of restrictions, if any, that have been imposed. After this you can move on to your critique.

Taking 'the claim' first you can apply a critical assessment by approaching it from a number of different standpoints. People make a number of mistakes when stating a claim which you can look for and then point out if found. First, people tend to be vague about what it is they are claiming. This may be due to a lack of clear definition or mistaken use of a concept. Whatever the reason you can pick out extracts from the argument and show its vague character. Allied to vagueness is overstatement. A trick some advocates use to convince others of the plausibility of their argument is to overstate it. The belief is that if you say something enough times then others will believe it. Show in your critique the number of times the claim has been made in the argument. If a claim is made many times also use extracts to show any differences between the claims, especially if the same evidence is being used for all claims. Also reveal any moral or political claims. These are often the most vague because they are the most difficult to define. Claims based on policy recommendation, value or interpretation can often be shown to be logically absurd (*redictio ad absurdum*); that is, and if taken to their logical conclusions they would result in nonsense. For example, that crime was a manifestation of genetic make-up, therefore people who commit crime cannot help doing so and therefore should not be punished, therefore the only action that can be taken is ... This is what is meant by *redictio ad absurdum*.

Once you have dealt with the claims move on to look at the evidence used to substantiate those claims. The key thing to achieve is to show the evidence is insufficient in some way. This may mean showing that the evidence is insufficient, biased or not relevant. All the evidence that an advocate has used needs to be considered. All the evidence employed needs to be scrutinised. Summarise what an advocate has used and then look at each category and type in detail. The objectives are to show that you understand the nature of the evidence and also how to produce a critique of how others have acquired and employed it. Evidence comes in many forms, such as the following:

Statistics – primary, secondary, descriptive, analytical

Testimony – personal, expert, primary, secondary, historic

Examples – first hand, general, detailed

Hypothetical examples – impossible, abstracted, plausible

Hypothetical scenarios – cause and effect, process oriented

Personal experience – anecdotal, narrative, recent, historic.

If statistics are employed, inquire into their source; find out where they came from and ask for what reasons they were selected. If you find no adequate reasons then focus on the data and analyse them systematically for their relevance to the argument. Look for reasons in the techniques used to collect the statistics and in the specific assumptions of the methodology. Show a willingness to question even those statistics that are generally accepted as true, especially those statistics used to support a definition of a situation. The point to remember is that statistics are an outcome of categorisation and decision making; they are created, and are not natural or universally true. The same point applies to the use of interpretation. All data require an interpretation; no data – especially statistics – speak for themselves. Discuss the interpretation your advocate has given of their evidence: how have they used it to support their claim? Also try to assess the appropriateness of any statistical tests that they have used.

In some cases you may find that you have little argument with the data, but disagree on their meaning. Point out any data that are either inconsistent or trivial, yet which have been used as a central support for the argument. If you can use the same evidence as your advocate and show a different – even opposite – conclusion, you will have produced a strong refutation. This is because you will have pointed out errors, made by your advocate, in their reasoning. This does not have to be long and elaborate. In the example on Marx (see Chapter 3), we saw how, in a few hundred words, Marx turned the tables on a traditional and long-established belief. You will be better able to challenge an advocate's reasoning if you have thoroughly examined what assumptions underlie their argument. Having shown what political, moral or value judgements an author has relied on, you will be able to show how evidence has been used in support of a re-defined position – in other words, how your advocate has actively sought the kinds of evidence that will corroborate a preconceived position. This may also mean looking at the kinds of quotes and extracts your advocate has used in the work. The use of evidence will have been a matter of careful discrimination for your advocate. You can, therefore, discuss what has been selected and show the contradictions and opposing views that exist between experts in the field. This also extends to how others have used the same testimony for different purposes. You can therefore bring in other studies that have used the same experts to show that there is no definitive way to use a concept or study.

Your final element at this stage may be to summarise the strengths of what you have been critiquing. This may be necessary as you may want to use some of the components in the literature to develop your own position. The final stage then consists of showing the problems in the argument you have been dealing with. This may mean showing what the gaps are in the reasoning, use of evidence, the source of evidence, the influence of assumptions, or the logic of what interpretations have been made and the logical consequences of the conclusions. The kind of material and structure to use at this stage is a matter for you to decide. But remember to follow the basic maxims set out by Toulmin, and use the components that he suggests are useful for the analysis of an argument. Here is a summary of some of the main points for sound argument.

Structure – use a reliable structure that is explicit

Definition – define the terms you will use, carefully using clear examples

Reasons – provide the reason for anything you have included as support

Assumptions – substantiate your assumptions (do not leave them as implicit), use only reliable assumptions that are free from value judgements or are based on valid reasoning

Fallacies – avoid fallacies, such as generalisation, abstraction and misplaced concreteness

Evidence – use only reliable documented evidence in the public domain that is legitimate and relevant and not trivial

Authority – avoid appeals to authority, convention and tradition.

Legitimacy and academic style

By using the literature on a topic, you are using the ideas, concepts and theories of other people. It is therefore your responsibility to use the work of other people in a way that is balanced, fair and legal. This involves ensuring that you are citing sources correctly and, where necessary, not infringing copyright or even the Data Protection Act. In this section, we will discuss briefly two areas listed below, which can help you to comply with academic conventions and the law.

Legitimacy – what it means to produce legitimate work

Style – what it means to use conventions in academic writing.

To avoid criticism of your review, you must use your sources properly. You will be expected not to violate the standards and values of academic work. There is a range of actions you may take that could throw your work into question. Here are some of them.

Falsification – misrepresenting the work of others

Fabrication – presenting speculations as if they were facts

Sloppiness – not providing correct citations

Nepotism – citing references of colleagues that are not directly related to your work

Plagiarism – the act of knowingly using another person's work and passing it off as your own.

All of the above can easily be avoided by paying attention to detail. This means being scrupulous in your record keeping and ensuring all details of works used are fully and correctly cited. All of this brings into play the need to be aware of the copyright laws that govern published work and any laws being prepared for work in electronic media such as the Internet.

Copyright
Although the law on copyright is constantly developing and changing, we can summarise the current position as follows. Copyright gives legal protection to the creators of certain kinds of work so that they can control the ways in which their work is used. Copyright protection is automatic; once a work has been

produced it has copyright. There is no need to formally register the work. Therefore, copyright can apply to anything that is presented in such things as books, journals, newspapers, music, photographs, illustrations, diagrams, videos and television broadcasts. Libraries place restrictions on the amount of material that can be copied by a researcher or supplied from a reproduction or copy. Libraries and researchers, however, are allowed certain privileges under copyright. These privileges are called 'fair dealing' and allow a researcher to copy limited amounts from journals, newspapers, books and the like, but only if the copy is for research purposes. This is taken to mean copying for the sake of personal use is acceptable as long as it does not infringe the economic rights of the copyright owner (e.g. copying instead of purchasing the item).

Academic style

In addition to copyright and legitimacy, another important issue is academic style. By style, we are referring to such things as use of tense, voice, and grammatical structure. Although some elements of style tend to be characteristic of a particular discipline, there are certain conventions to which most academics attempt to conform, and the thesis has conventions of its own, which are outlined below.

In terms of tense, the first chapter of most theses is usually written in the present tense with references to literature in the past tense. Chapters that deal with the literature review, methodology and data collection tend to be written in the past tense, as they are about research that has already been done. Chapters on findings, interpretations and conclusions often use a combination of past and present tense. Past tense is used when referring to your research and present tense to your ideas when discussing what your findings mean.

Voice

In terms of using either the active or passive voice, it often helps to have variety in the dissertation. It is usually acceptable to use the active voice (me, I, we) when describing such things as how you came to choose your topic. The active voice can provide a more personal dimension for the reader, aiding understanding of your research and placing the reader in your shoes, as it were. However, there are times when the (impersonal) passive voice ('the research was done', rather than 'I did my research') can be useful. The passive voice can provide not only variety in a long document, but also ensure anonymity for respondents, because you are not referring to them by name, for example, 'It was unclear that...' or 'I was informed that...'.

Appropriate language

Finally, some words and phrases that are common in everyday language are inappropriate for use in a dissertation. For example, 'it is obvious', 'it is welcome', 'it is a fact' and 'everyone can see' are value judgements and should not be used. Also words such as 'very', 'fantastic', 'crucial', 'unique' and 'etc.' should be avoided. This is because words and phrases such as these are unnecessary and imprecise. Remember, too, to use words such as 'normally' carefully, or perhaps avoid them altogether. Bear in mind that you are not writing an opinion column for a popular magazine but a piece of research, a logical convincing argument. Hence, there is no place in such writing for you to use discriminatory language (e.g., sexist) except for the purposes of illustration. Most professional associations, such as the *British Sociological Association*, have published guidelines on the use of language that you are advised to refer to. Here are some examples of discriminatory language followed by suggested alternatives.

Workman   Worker

Ladies   Women, females

Man-hours   Work hours

Laymen   Lay people, general public

Writing your review

There exist many books on general writing techniques that can be of help to the research scholar when writing up their work. What we will do here is to give some basic ideas about the *process of thinking* about writing the review. One way of thinking about the task is to see it as an opportunity to display what you have done and what you have learnt. Think of it as providing information for your readers and your tutor. The benefits that readers will get from your writing will be many. They will see how you have extracted the main points from the literature, undertaken *analysis* and how you have reconstructed the main idea in your own words, producing a *critical synthesis*. Your reader will thereby learn more about the topic than they may have known previously. From your point of view of writing a dissertation, it will most likely take you to the postgraduate level, as your ticket into the academic community of scholars. The satisfaction derived from writing up your research into a coherent piece of text will, we hope, out-weigh some of the natural difficulties that you will experience during the process. Therefore, we would like to emphasise that all writing has difficulties; it is not something that only other people can do. Writing is something most of us can do because we endure and overcome the difficulties and get on with the job. Hence, qualities of determination and endurance will be needed. You may find it helps if you write a little at a time.

Problems and reasons

No one finds writing easy. Most people find writing a coherent piece of text challenging. For some people, the time and effort required can be an excuse to do nothing or very little. The irony about writing is the more you write, the better you get at it and, believe it, the more you enjoy writing and hence the more you want to write. However, we all still have problems about putting our ideas down in writing for others to read. People experience a number of common problems when writing up their work. Table 9.1 shows three of them with some suggestions as to their cause and solution.

There are a number of good guides for students on writing and managing their work and time. Hence, for the remainder of this chapter, we will focus our attention on the processes and stages of organising yourself for writing.

The review is a piece of structured writing that is a formal statement of the results of your analysis. It is therefore a description of current work and issues on the topic. The primary objective is to furnish necessary and sufficient information to demonstrate that you have thought carefully about the knowledge on the topic that is contained in the literature. This objective can be achieved in a range of formats, employing a range of techniques to present information and analysis. For example, text, tables, diagrams and schematics can all be used to convey your analysis. One thing you need to remember is that your thesis is an official record of research. It is therefore a public document and as such is a record of the history of research on the topic. It is therefore probably going to be the only record of your research. One implication of this is that your dissertation may be the only public place in which you are acknowledged as the person

TABLE 9.1 Some problems, reasons and solutions to writing

Problem	Possible cause	Solutions
Lack of time	Especially for part-time mode study. Life makes many demands.	Time management. Re-socialise family and friends to recognise your work is important. Make writing a part of your personal leisure time.
Unfamiliar with different styles, especially academic	Familiar only with style used in the workplace. Lack of academic background.	Reading different styles. Work at understanding different conventions for different situations.
Not used to writing lengthy complex documents	Used to face-to-face communication. Rarely use writing for argument and persuasion, hence not familiar with tenses, the possessive and grammatical conventions.	Reading and learning. Writing short pieces. Sub-divide work up into manageable sections.

who carried out the research. Added to this is the possibility that your thesis may form the basis of further research by another person. It is for such reasons that it is worthwhile investing the effort and time in planning the writing of the thesis. For the review chapter, as with all the other chapters of your dissertation, you will need to plan in advance.

Have a plan

It is important that in the early stages of your work that you develop a pattern to guide your efforts. This pattern begins with your general plan of work. This is the plan for the research as a whole and normally a part of the research proposal. Keep to the plan as far as possible but expect and be prepared to take an opportunity if it arises. That is, things will happen to delay you and these need to be overcome. Sometimes however a *discovery* will be made, often in a completely serendipitous way that is an opportunity to change the research. It may be the availability of some data that you did not know about or expect to be available. Or it may be a sudden appreciation of the worth of an approach not hitherto considered in the area in which you have been looking. You will therefore need to make a decision on what to do; whether to ignore your discovery or use it. In most cases such discoveries are seen as problems that are thought to be a threat to the original plan. The researcher thus experiences a minor crisis that disrupts the flow of their work. Rather than viewing such things as problems, see them as a challenge. Ask yourself what are the advantages of following this unexpected opportunity? Try to think through where this opportunity may lead and what it may bring to our understanding of the topic. In this way, you will continue to work on your research. More importantly, you will be evaluating what you have already read in light of your discovery. Hence, your knowledge and analytical abilities will be moving on even if the writing process has been temporarily delayed.

The thing is, of course, to get your discovery down on paper. This needs to be done as soon as you think that you have grasped the significance of the discovery. This you can do as you think. Notes in the form of rough jottings can be an invaluable way to think and write at the same time. They will also provide you with an indicative structure for writing up your ideas. The point we are making here therefore is that taking time to play around with ideas can be very beneficial. If this is done using pen and paper, then this can be a great aid to the analytical process of systematically identifying relationships between ideas. It is at this stage, when you come to write up your ideas, that a pattern can be useful. That is, if you approach the writing up in much the same way each time, you will soon become familiar with the process and thereby know what to expect. Usually, the writing process has some basic stages (see Figure 9.1), which we will now look at in turn.

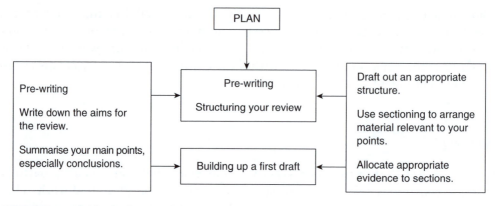

FIGURE 9.1   Thinking about starting to write

Pre-writing: Structuring your review

Having completed your plan, you will need to consider how to structure your review in readiness for writing your first draft. This is the stage at which you will define your purpose and choose an appropriate structure for your argument.

Define your purpose. This is when you will clarify your purpose in terms of what you are aiming to achieve. This needs to be a clear statement that is expressed in no more than a few short sentences. It can help if you write down the aims of the review and include these as a part of the introduction to the chapter itself. The aims are the main reference point for the review. The content of the review should realise those aims in a way that is clear, systematic and direct. To do this, you will need to think about the arrangement of the chapter, and in a moment we will look at three arrangements for a review chapter. At this stage, however, remember that your notes need to be organised in a way that addresses your aims. Try to arrange your materials into three basic blocks (each with as many sub-sections as is deemed necessary) as follows:

1. *Summary of existing work on the topic.* This includes the different ways in which the topic has been studied (methods and methodology) and the issues different authors have high-lighted as a result of their work. Identify the different ways key terms and concepts have been defined or used.
2. *Critical evaluation of previous work.* Assess the methodologies and methods that have been previously employed to study the topic and evaluate the relative strengths and weak-nesses of the literature. The key thing in this block is to make visible the map of methodological assumptions in the literature.
3. *Some general and specific conclusions about work done to date on the topic.* General conclusions can be about the overall direction of work on the topic in relation to earlier more foundational work. Specific conclusions are about identifying gaps, fallacies and failures in previous work in order to show the legitimacy of your own approach.

One thing to remember is that you will not be able to write down everything you have found in the search and review of the literature. This is because you will not have the space. Hence, when arranging your materials for the chapter think carefully about what is strictly necessary to meet your aims. Anything that falls outside this criterion ought to be placed to one side and not included in the review. It may, however, be placed in the general bibliography of works consulted but not cited in the main body of the text.

Choose a structure appropriate for your argument. If you have a structure that you can work with for placing your materials in order then you will also have a starting point to begin writing. There are a number of possible structures that you can use. Table 9.2 shows three of them.

TABLE 9.2   Three structures for making your case

The problem-awareness pattern (summative evaluation)	The cause and effect pattern (analytical evaluation)	The possible solution pattern (formative evaluation)
Describe the nature of the problem.	Establish the existence of the problem (problem awareness).	Consider definitions and solutions already tried.
Give examples of the problem showing its extent.	Propose possible cause of the problem.	Give relevant examples of solutions tried, show why they failed or were inadequate, show factors causing failure, provide evidence of factors.
Offer evidence that the problem exists.	Show the main factors underpinning the proposed causes.	Consider possible alternatives.
Develop a definition of the problem.	Clarify any confusing areas: eliminate any improbable, irrelevant causes/definitions, provide evidence for causes/ definitions eliminated.	Distinguish between alternatives.
Show the relevance of the problem to the reader.	Focus attention on proposed cause/definition.	Provide a summary of the possible effects of alternatives, make a choice from alternatives by elimination, provide evidence for elimination and choice.
Provide specific evidence/ argument of negative effects.	Provide evidence for proposed cause/definition, summarise the argument.	Summarise the problem, solutions tried, why they failed and give recommendations for alternative approaches.
Explain the consequences if nothing is done or if the current state continues.	Suggest course (recommendations) of action to deal with the problem.	
Provide evidence of effects/ current practice.		
Summarise the problem situation.		
Outline the parameters of the problem (definitional argument).		
Outline an approach (recommendations) for tackling the problem situation.		

Elements can be taken from each of these patterns. However, if you are making recommendations, then in all cases you will need to explain the benefits of those recommendations. The following arrangement is the most popular for writing a recommendation:

- describe what is wrong – what the problem is
- make a proposal to solve the problem
- examine the benefits that would result if the proposal were adapted
- acknowledge and refute any possible objections to the proposal.

A recommendation needs to be clear and systematic and using this kind of structure will help you to achieve this. It will also help you to be clear about the potential benefits of the recommendations that you are proposing. This means using evidence from the literature to show the positive aspects of failures that you have identified. There is, therefore, a degree of irony in critical evaluation. When showing the shortcomings of previous research, you are also saying that these failures are good for your research. This is because they will enable you to make a case for your approach to the topic. A major element in this is the use of evidence. This may be quotations from other studies or data from other studies. Whichever is the case, your proposal will rely heavily on other sources, so it is important to use them correctly.

Looking more closely at these three possible structures remember that they are not prescriptive; they are merely suggestions to help you think about what you want to say. The point is to use them as a resource, exploiting them in any way you deem appropriate to your purpose. Before we leave this section, let us look at an example of a structure used by Durkheim (1952/1970[1897]), in his classic *Suicide* (see Table 9.3).

In Chapter 7, we looked at the work of Emile Durkheim on the topic of suicide. We showed that he wanted to define the subject matter for sociology and show how the discipline could be scientific – Durkheim had an argument to make. Using the analytical pattern, we can summarise the main elements in his literature review (see Table 9.3).

TABLE 9.3 The analytical pattern applied to *Suicide*

Elements from the pattern	Elements in *Suicide*
- Propose a possible cause of the problem	Durkheim characterised suicide as a social rather than an individual act thereby challenging conventional perspectives and positions. He argued that it is influenced by the degree of attachment a person has to their community. Hence, a starting point for his argument (his hypo-*thesis*) is that the more strongly a person is attached to their community the less likely they are to commit suicide and vice versa. This is the beginning of his gradual development of a definition.

Elements from the pattern	Elements in *Suicide*
• Describe the nature of the problem	Durkheim introduces statistical data to show the extent and patterns of suicide in some European countries. He further develops his definition through a series of minor formulations of his hypothesis. He did this through a dialogue with himself so odd examples could be accounted for within his definition.
• Show factors underpinning the proposed cause	From the patterns in his data Durkheim begins to identify a number of variables that are connected to his main thesis. He identifies variables such as religious faith, marriage and economic conditions as significant factors in understanding (explaining) patterns in the data.
• Clarify any confusing areas	Durkheim constantly summarises his definition throughout the first part of his argument. This reinforces his position and is often used to strengthen the significance of his evidence and weaken opposing positions.
• Eliminate any alternative proposals for cause	Durkheim systematically eliminates alternative explanations and definitions. He does this through showing that there are no substantial connections between suicide, as recorded, and current explanations.
• Focus attention on proposal cause/ definition	The radical nature of what Durkheim proposed ensured his ideas would get attention. But he constantly keeps his thesis at the forefront of his argument by reiteration and reformulation; using evidence throughout his work to eliminate alternatives. Hence, his deductive approach – stating his thesis at the beginning of his work and then developing it through use of evidence – helps him to make a strong case for the existence of social facts as the subject matter for sociology.

Using structure to present your reasoning

We have emphasised previously (see Chapters 1 and 2) that good academic writing needs to be coherent, systematic and clear. For it to be coherent means that as a whole it talks about a topic in much the same way from beginning to end and that it does not wander from the topic. Different sections may have cohesion but these sections need to have sufficient relationships built into them in order that the whole is coherent. The different sections should be seen as the different parts making up an argument; each having sufficient and necessary information, when combined in an appropriate structure, to make an argument. We have seen this in different examples used throughout this book and in the examples taken from the work of Atkinson and Durkheim. Both looked at suicide however each of them, had to make a case for their particular definition of the topic and give adequate reasons for that definition. They did this, as do most authors, through the use of structured argument and the arrangement of their texts.

In the example of Atkinson, we saw how he communicated his ideas and argument using structured text. This emphasis on the structure and arrangement of text is important. This is because the task of writing forces us, when we are making an argument, to think carefully about what it is we are proposing. To some extent writing down an argument avoids the circumvention often found in spoken language. It also encourages us to pay careful attention to the linear arrangement of our argument; helping us to clarify what we mean and intend that others should understand. If we have a structure to guide the presentation of our argument, then we will be better able to look at what we are proposing and to see where the significant points are, what relationships need to be emphasised, and where reiterations would help the reader follow our argument and help us place this piece of writing within the research as a whole. The three examples of structures (e.g. problem-awareness, cause and effect, possible solution) show us how we can begin to think about arranging our ideas in a systematic way. However, we may also benefit from thinking about the *logical arrangement*, which we may want to use in our writing.

There are a number of arrangements that we may think about using. For example, if we want to show the historical development of work on a topic, we would be interested in using a *chronological arrangement*. In the example (see Chapter 2) on the concept of community, a chronological structure was used as a part of the argument. The different definitions of community were presented in the order of the dates of publication for different studies. The point to note here is that chronology was used as part of the argument; it was not the argument itself. It was used as a method for organising the materials that for a particular audience would have had some familiarity. The writer could have expected her audience to be familiar with most, if not all the works on the list. This leads on to another method that can be used, called *familiar-to-unfamiliar* ordering.

The reader of the material on community was presented with familiar material; the stock of knowledge on the topic and concept. This can be an effective method, especially when introducing a controversial proposal or argument you think will cause difficulty for the reader to understand. By beginning with something already known, analysis and observations were made that may have been new to the reader. Hence, the reader's understanding was enlarged by using knowledge that was already familiar to them. They may, of course, not agree with the kinds of observations that were made about the common methodological policies of community studies. But they will have been given something to think about. You may also have noticed that this example used an *inductive structure*. That is, it went from the particular to the general.

Both chronological and familiar to unfamiliar arrangements can be incorporated into either an *inductive* or *deductive* structure. The example we gave of Durkheim's (1952/1970[1897]) *Suicide* shows the use of a deductive structure. His argument proceeded from the general statement (thesis) to the particular details and illustrations. It is deductive reasoning that is associated with the classical logicians, such as Aristotle and Plato, of Ancient Greece. The classic example of this form of reasoning is this:

1. All humans are mortal [major premise]
2. Jane is human [minor premise]
3. *Therefore,* Jane is mortal [conclusion]

In terms of methodology, we can often see a relationship between the way in which an argument has been written and the methodology used by authors in their work. Tables 9.4 and Figure 9.5 show this relationship.

TABLE 9.4   Deductive writing structure

Deductive procedure for research	Deductive structure for writing
The researcher tests a theory	Introduction: theory and thesis statement
Hypothesis or research questions are derived from the theory	Key questions from the theory and thesis Particular illustrations and examples given to show the reason for the questions
Concepts and variables are operationalised	Definition of key concepts: discussion Elimination of possible alternatives: discussion
An instrument is used to measure the variables in the theory	Data collection technique employed Specifics of data: discussion
Verification of the hypothesis	Findings related to hypothesis and theory: discussion

TABLE 9.5   Inductive writing structure

Inductive procedure for research	Inductive structure for writing
Researcher gathers information and data	Introduction
Questions are asked about the phenomenon	Particular examples given Tentative interpretation on relationships between examples posed as questions
The data are classified and placed into categories	More examples given and classified according to questions. Statements developed and reiterated
Patterns are looked for in the data and potential theories are proposed	More examples given and classified to test degree of fit and usefulness of categories. Statements developed further and reiterated
Theories are tested and developed and patterns compared with other patterns and theories	Main conclusions on patterns and suggestion of plausible theory to account for the relationships in the pattern

Writing a first draft

Whatever else you do during the time you allocate for writing, you must actually do some! It is very easy to get distracted by even the most trivial events – almost anything else can be more attractive than writing. You will need to develop the habit of writing. This may mean doing the obvious, such as setting aside a regular time of the day or evening. Even if you only scribble notes and fiddle about with diagrams you will soon become habituated to the task. Such self-discipline soon leads to the need to spend time writing or thinking about and planning to write. Many research students only realise this once they have completed a piece of work. They miss the need to do work, often finding that they do not know what to do with their time. However, during the writing stage some output is necessary. There are a number of ways to think systematically about the content of your writing. These include the following:

- Think about the needs of the reader: what will they be looking for and expect to read?
- Think about the parts of the chapter: how can sectioning be used?
- Think about the introduction: how can you announce your purpose and topic?

Think about the needs of the reader

This does not mean producing a structure for the entire dissertation. It means taking each part of the dissertation, such as the literature review chapter, and deciding on what kind of structure will be best suited to the material you have decided to put in that chapter. Even at this stage, you are editing your material and at the same time you will be thinking about content. A useful technique to use is to pose a number of questions – what are called the writer's questions. The idea is that if you are aware of who will read your work and what they will need to know then you can work towards producing work that is suited to your reader. The kinds of questions to think about are:

1. How much knowledge can we assume the reader will have?
2. What will the reader want to know?
3. How will they read my dissertation?
4. What kinds of answers to possible questions will I need to provide?

In the first instance, your tutors will read your work. You can assume that they will have some knowledge of your topic and the methodology you employ in your research. However, other tutors may also read your work and you cannot assume that they will be familiar with you or your research. Therefore, ensure that everything is clearly explained and that all concepts are defined. You must also ensure that all your references are correct and that you have cited all those works that you have used.

Your tutors will expect to find a piece of academic writing that meets certain criteria. It will need to be clear, systematic and coherent. The ways in which the work of others was used must be described. The techniques used to analyse ideas need to be explained and justified. Comments and critique need to be balanced and substantiated with argument and evidence. The reader will be assessing your work based on the evidence you provide for the following kinds of criteria:

1. you have worked on the project
2. you have reviewed the literature relevant to the topic with thoroughness and charity
3. you have identified the key ideas, concepts and methodologies from the literature
4. you have taken a cross-disciplinary approach
5. you have recorded your sources accurately and consistently
6. your analysis is systematic, comprehensive and relevant.

Think about the parts of the chapter

It can be useful to break up a chapter in sections using side headings. Once you have a general idea of what needs to go into the chapter as a whole, think about how you will take the reader from one piece of information and analysis to another, in a way that is logical. You may have descriptive information at the beginning of the chapter followed by analysis and finally have as a conclusion some form of positive or evaluative critique. Thus you will have three broad parts, each of which could be further sub-sectioned. You will, of course, need an introduction (we will look at introductions later). Once you have an indicative structure, begin filling in the sub-sections with your materials. There is no need to do this sequentially unless it suits your particular way of working. Most writers work on different sections at different times. There are a couple of reasons for this. Firstly, it provides a way of managing what often seems a large task. Rather than trying to work though the task from beginning to end, breaking it up and working on different sections in a random way can make that task seem less daunting. Secondly, some writers find that this way of working helps them to continuously review the content; this method encourages them to move back and forward over what they have written and thereby re-drafting becomes a part of the process. Finally, once you have written something do not go over it in an endless way trying to make it perfect. Some re-working and corrections are nearly always necessary. Proof reading is a necessary stage. If someone else does this for you take criticisms in a positive way. The objective is, to put it crudely, to get your work down on paper and not to write a classic.

Writing an introduction

Trying to write an introduction is by far the most common problem most writers have when it comes to communicating their ideas. Many people tend to leave the introduction until the main body of their text has already been drafted. In this way, they have a better idea of what it is they want to say to their readers about what they will be reading. However, before you begin to write, you need to know the purpose of what you will be writing. For this reason, a draft introduction can be a useful guide for the main body of text. A good place to start is with the objectives of your review. Write down what it is you want to achieve with your review and why. Throughout this book, we have provided lists and explanations of the kinds of objectives that a review should fulfil; use these in whatever way you deem appropriate to your own work.

When planning the introduction think about the review as a whole. In operational terms, your review has two dimensions. One is to provide *information* and the other is to *persuade* your reader that you have a case; that case being that you have identified a gap in existing research that you can fill through your own research. The introduction should also employ these two aims. There are certain things you can do to achieve both of these. To persuade others that you have a case worth considering, choose an argumentative structure that is appropriate for your purpose and materials. Different structures were discussed in an earlier part of this chapter. To meet the information needs of your reader think about the following questions:

1. How much information does the reader need?
2. How much do they already have?
3. How do I want them to use the information?

Consideration of these questions will help you to select the amount and kind of information that will be sufficient and necessary for the task of writing the introduction. Remember it is not necessary to include a reference to every piece of material that you have located; selection and editing are part of the process as much as reviewing. Your reader will have more respect for you if you only present relevant information. Therefore, it is often more effective to plan the main body of the text first, breaking it up into sub-sections with appropriate side headings before writing the introduction. Through this method the introduction is one of the last things that is written.

As you sort your material into sections, begin to think about the support that will be adequate for the information. There are two kinds of support you can provide to help your reader understand what it is you are saying: *information* support and *interest* support. Information support is the pieces of information that you are providing while interest support helps keep the attention of your reader. This does not mean your writing has to be entertaining. Table 9.6 summarises elements of both types of support.

You can employ both informative and interest devices in your introduction. This makes an introduction a difficult section to write because you will have to include in your introduction the five main components shown in Table 9.7.

TABLE 9.6 Information and interest support

Information	Interest
Facts – statements and statistics	Anecdotes – stories and personal experience
Expert testimony – quotes and extracts	Visual aids – diagrams; charts
Examples: cases – instances and illustrations	Listings – lists of points
Explanation – discussion	Rhetorical questions – prompts to make the reader consider

TABLE 9.7 Five main components of an introduction

Aim	Means
To announce the topic of your review	A clear and careful statement
To state the purpose of your review	A careful explanation of what you aim to achieve
To explain the relevance of the topic	An indication of the importance in the literature
To establish your credibility	Information on why you should be seen as competent to write about this topic
To preview the main points that you will make in the main body of the text	Advance notice of the structure of your text, possibly including your thesis statement

Added to these is another job for your introduction. You may be looking at a topic that has a long history and assume that your reader will think nothing new could possibly be written. In your introduction you therefore need to show otherwise by grabbing the attention of your reader from the beginning. This can be done in a number of ways. For example, you may make a bold statement that contradicts preconceived expectations about the topic or you may give a startling statistic. Whatever device you use, it needs to be highly relevant to the topic and to focus attention on the information that follows.

Re-working the draft

The first draft should be just that: a first, tentative outline of what you want to say based on a structure. Never attempt to do all of this in one go. Every writer goes through a series of drafts, gradually working towards something that they are satisfied with. Therefore, once you have something that has content and some structure begin to reflect on it. At this stage, you will need to analyse this in terms of its clarity, structure and coherence. Look for disjunctions between the main ideas. Ask yourself if the argument is logical and expressed in a way that is clear and easy to follow. Be aware that clarity can vary throughout a piece of writing. Look to see which parts are clear and which are not, and re-write those parts that need more explanation. Check your use of evidence and rhetoric. Have you made any claims that are not backed up with appropriate evidence?

Editing is a necessary task that will improve what you have written, and help to make it clearer, simple and consistent. The following may help you edit your writing:

1. identify unclear or excessively long sentences and re-write into shorter sentences
2. examine each paragraph to ensure it covers only one topic
3. see if any important paragraphs can be re-written to be more effective
4. list the topics for each paragraph to ensure the links between them are sequential
5. replace jargon with either an everyday word or explain the meaning of the jargon
6. check that the verbs are active and not passive
7. look for unnecessary adjectives and delete qualifications such as 'very'
8. look at the metaphors you have used and check they are appropriate
9. look for pompous and polysyllabic words and replace them with simpler more sensible words.

Some of these points we have looked at under writer's style. In terms of *coherence*, see if the introduction is sufficiently linked to the conclusion and main body of the text. This demands that you reflect on the overall structure. You can do this by summarising the points made in each paragraph. Check whether each point has a logical link, that each develops on the previous point in some way. Therefore, edit out anything that is not strictly needed for the argument. You are looking at the arrangement and sequence of sub-clauses in your work and at what kind of evidence you have to support those clauses. There are a number of presentational devices that may help, and some that you should avoid, in order to give more coherence to your work. Indications of things to remember are shown in the list below.

Sentences	Express one idea in a sentence. Ensure all your sentences have a subject, a verb and an object.
Paragraphs	Group sentences that express and develop one topic. When another topic or aspect of the topic is introduced use a new paragraph.
Consistent grammar	Use sentences and paragraphs with appropriate use of commas, colons and semi-colons.
Transition words	Use words that link paragraphs and show contrast and development in your argument, such as 'hence', 'therefore', 'as a result', 'but', and 'thus'.

Analysing your own work is not easy, but it is necessary. Using what we have shown in this section should help you to be *reflexive* and *analytical*, and lead to the improvement of your writing. But remember that one of the most effective ways of understanding how to write is to read as widely as possible. Look for examples of good and bad writing. Try to identify ways in which other authors have structured their arguments and used various methods and techniques to express ideas. Things like the use of structure and style have no copyright on them. Hence, you can borrow and adopt ideas for your own work as other people will borrow and adopt your ideas.

Conclusion

This chapter has provided advice and guidance on how to write a review of the literature. In many ways, we have tried to link this advice with the themes and arguments in this book as a whole. You should be aware that all types of research benefit from a competent review of the literature. Many different techniques for analysing ideas and arguments have been shown. In themselves these techniques, such as mapping ideas, do not constitute a review of the literature. They are some of the means for understanding what the literature is about and what different authors intended to produce in their research. Hence, we have emphasised the role of thinking about ideas, reflecting on the reasons an author had when undertaking their research and how this activity requires a particular attitude. We have considered the importance of tolerance, understanding and open-mindedness when interpreting and evaluating research. In short, when you come to do your literature review you need to check that the review:

1. shows a clear understanding of the topic
2. includes all key landmark studies
3. develops, through gradual refinement, a clear research problem
4. states clear conclusions about previous research using appropriate evidence
5. shows the variety of definitions and approaches to the topic area
6. reaches sound recommendations using a coherent argument that is based on evidence
7. shows a gap in existing knowledge.

In summary

- The literature review plays a number of roles within a research project, regardless of the reasons for that project or the methodological tradition being used.
- The researcher(s) need to be fully knowledgeable of the role of the different types of literature in a project.

(Continued)

- All literature reviews are unique because no research question is the same and over time contexts change.
- There are different ways of arranging and structuring a literature review. Familiarise yourself with these and develop your own structure to suit your own work.
- You do not have to be a brilliant writer to write a literature review. You need, however, to understand what the role of the review is, and how to arrange your materials, in a logical order, to serve your purpose.

References

Afolabi, M. (1992). 'The review of related literature in research'. *International Journal of Information and Library Research*, 4(1): 59–66.

American Education Research Association (2006). 'Standards for reporting on empirical social science research in AERA publications'. *Educational Researcher,* 35(6): 33–40.

Anderson, R.J., Hughes, J.A. and Sharrock, W.W. (1985). *The Sociology Game: An Introduction to Sociological Reasoning*. London: Longman.

Archer, M. (1995). *Realist Social Theory*. Cambridge: Cambridge University Press.

Asimov, I. (1963). *The Genetic Code*. New York: New American Library.

Atkinson, J.M. (1982). *Discovering Suicide: Studies in the Social Organisation of Sudden Death*. *London*: Macmillan Press.

Ayer, A.J. (1946[1936]). *Language, Truth and Logic*. London: Victor Gollancz.

Barnes, D. (1994). 'Stimulus equivalence and Relational Frame Theory'. *The Psychological Record*, 44: 91–124.

Barnett-Page, E. and Thomas, J. (2009). *Methods for the Synthesis of Qualitative Research: A Critical Review*, NCRM Working Paper Series Number (01/09). London: EPPI. Available at: http://eppi.ioe.ac.uk/cms/Default.aspx?tabid=188.

Barthes, R. (1967). *Elements of Semiology*. London: Jonathan Cape.

Becker, H. (1963). *Outsiders: Studies in the Sociology of Deviance*. New York: Free Press.

Becker, H.S. (1986). *Writing for Social Scientists: How to Start and Finish your Thesis, Book, or Article*. Chicago: University of Chicago Press.

Beloff, H. (ed.) (1980). 'A balance sheet on Burt'. Supplement to *The British Psychological Society*, 33.

Berger, A.A. (1972). *Ways of Seeing*. London: BBC and Penguin Books.

Berger, A.A. (1995). *Cultural Criticism: A Primer of Key Concepts*. London: Sage.

Bhaskar, R. (1978). *A Realist Theory of Science*. London: Verso.

Blunkett, D. (2000). *Influence or Irrelevance: Can Social Science Improve Government?* Swindon/London: UK Economic and Social Research Council/ Department for Education and Employment.

Boaz, A., Ashby, D. and Young, K. (2002). *Systematic Reviews: What Have They Got to Offer Evidence Based Policy and Practice?*, Working Paper 2. London: ESRC UK Centre for Evidence Based Policy and Practice.

Bodanis, D. (2000). *E=mc²: A Biography of the World's Most Famous Equation*. London: Macmillan.

Boote, D.N. and Beile, P. (2005). 'Scholars before researchers: On the centrality of the dissertation literature review in research preparation'. *Educational Researcher*, 34(6): 3–15.

Brewer, J. *and* Hunter, A. *(2005)*. *Foundations of Multimethod Research*. Thousand Oaks, CA: Sage. Campbell Collaboration. Available at: http://campbell.gse.upenn.edu.

Brockman, J. (2013). *This Explains Everything: Deep, Beautiful, and Elegant Theories of How the World Works*. New York: HarperCollins World.

Buchdunger, E., Zimmermann, J., Mett, H., Meyer, T., Müller, M., Regenass, U. and Lydon, N.B. (1995). 'Selective inhibition of the platelet-derived growth factor signal transduction pathway by a protein-tyrosine kinase inhibitor of the 2-Phenylaminopyrimidine Class'. *Proceedings of the National Academy of Sciences*, 92(7): 2558–62.

Button, G. (ed.) (1991). *Ethnomethodology and the Human Sciences*. Cambridge: Cambridge University Press.

Buzan, T. (1995). *The Mind Map Book*. London: BBC Books.

Cakir, M. (2008). 'Constructivist approaches to learning in science and their implications for science pedagogy: A literature review'. *International Journal of Environmental and Science Education*, 3(4): 193–206.

Calvillo, E.R. and Flaskerud, J.H. (1993). 'The adequacy and scope of Roy's adaptation model to guide cross-cultural pain research'. *Nursing Science Quarterly*, 6: 118–29.

Carnap, R., Hahn, H. and Neurath, O. (1973[1929]). 'The scientific conception of the world'. In M. Neurath and R.S. Cohen (eds), *Empiricism and Sociology*. Dordrecht: Reidel.

Carr, S., Lhussier, M., Forster, N., Geddes, L., Deane, K., Pennington, M., Visram, S., White, M., Michie, S., Donaldson, C. and Hildreth, A. (2011). 'An evidence synthesis of qualitative and quantitative research on component intervention techniques, effectiveness, cost-effectiveness, equity and acceptability of different versions of health-related lifestyle advisor role in improving health [Briefing paper]'. *Health Technology Assessment*, 15 (9): 1–284.

Catt, H. (2005). 'Now or never – electoral participation literature review'. Paper delivered at *Citizenship: Learning by Doing. Children and Young People as Citizens: Participation, Provision and Protection*, Sixth child and family policy conference, University of Otago, Dunedin. Available at: http://www.elections.org.nz/sites/default/files/plain-page/attachments/Youth%20Participation.pdf.

Cha, K.Y. and Wirth, D.P. (2001). 'Does prayer influence the success of in vitro fertilization–embryo transfer?'. *Journal of Reproductive Medicine*, 46: 781–7.

Chen, D. (2003). 'A classification system for metaphors about teaching'. *Journal of Physical Education, Recreation & Dance*, 74(2): 24–31.

Cho, K.W. and Neely, J.H. (2012). 'Is Hirsch's H the best predictor of the number of a researcher's extremely highly cited articles?' *Measurement*, 10: 157–60.

Chung, C.J. and Park, H.W. (2012). 'Web visibility of scholars in media and communication journals'. *Scientometrics*, 93(1): 207–15.

Ciapponi, A. (2011). *Systematic Review of the Link Between Tobacco and Poverty*', work conducted for WHO by the Institute for Clinical Effectiveness and Health Policy (Instituto de Efectividad Clínica y Sanitaria – IECS), Argentine Cochrane Centre IECS, Iberoamerican Cochrane Network. Available at: http://www.cochrane.org.

Cohen, L.J. (1986). *The Claims of Reason*. Oxford: Oxford University Press.

Coleman, E.G. (2010). 'Ethnographic approaches to digital media'. *Annual Review of Anthropology*, 39(1): 487–505.

Connelly, J., Duaso, M. and Butler, G. (2007). 'A systematic review of controlled trials of interventions to prevent childhood obesity and overweight: A realistic synthesis of the evidence'. *Public Health*, 121: 510–17.

Cooper, H. and Hedges, L.V. (1993). *The Handbook of Research Synthesis*. New York: Russell Sage Foundation.

Cooper, H.M. (1988). 'Organising knowledge synthesis: Taxonomy of literature reviews'. *Knowledge in Society*, 1: 104–26.

Cooper, H.M. (1984). *The Integrative Research Review: A Systematic Approach*, Applied Social Research Methods Series (Vol. 2). Beverly Hills, CA: Sage.

Cooper, J. (2007). *Cognitive Dissonance: 50 Years of a Classic Theory*. London: Sage.

Cornelissen, J.P., Oswick, C., Christensen, L.T. and Phillips, N. (2008). 'Metaphor in organizational research: Context, modalities and implications for research'. *Organization Science*, 29(1): 7–22.

Cuff, E.C. and Payne, G.C.F. (1984). *Perspectives in Sociology*, 2nd edn. London: Allen & Unwin.

Davies, H.T.O. and Nutley, S.M. (2000). 'Healthcare: Evidence to the fore'. In H.T.O. Davies, S.M. Nutley and P.C. Smith (eds), *What Works? Evidence-based Policy and Practice in Public Services*. Bristol: Policy Press.

Daykin, N., Evans, D., Petsoulas, C. and Sayers, A. (2007). 'Evaluating the impact of patient and public involvement initiatives on UK health services: A systematic review'. *Evidence & Policy,* 3(1): 47–65.

De Guerrero, M.C. and Villamil, O.S. (2001). 'Metaphor analysis in second foreign language instruction: A sociocultural perspective'. Revised version of paper presented at the Annual Meeting of the American Association of Applied Linguistics, St. Louis, MO, 24-27 February.

Design-based Research Collective (2003). 'Design-based research: An emerging paradigm for educational inquiry'. *Educational Researcher*, 32(1): 5–8.

Dicks, B., Mason, B., Coffey, A. and Atkinson, P. (2005). *Qualitative Research and Hypermedia: Ethnography for the Digital Age*. London: Sage.

Douglas, J. (1966). 'The sociological analysis of the social meaning of suicide'. *European Journal of Sociology*, 7: 249–98.

Dowden, C. and Andrews, D.A. (1999). 'What works for female offenders: A meta-analytic review'. *Crime and Delinquency*, 45(4): 438–52.

Durkheim, E. (1984 [1893]). *The Division of Labour in Society*. London: Macmillan.

Durkheim, E. (1952/1970 [1897]). *Suicide: A Study in Sociology*. London: Routledge.

Dymond, S., May, R.J., Munnelly, A. and Hoon, A.E. (2010). 'Evaluating the evidence base for Relational Frame Theory: A citation analysis'. *The Behavior Analyst*, 33(1): 97–117.

Erikson, K.T. (1966). *Wayward Puritans*. New York: Wiley.

Evans-Pritchard, E. (1937). *Witchcraft and Oracles among the Azande*. Oxford: Oxford University Press.

Fawcett, J. (1990). 'Preparation for caesarean childbirth: Derivation of a nursing intervention from the Roy adaptation model'. *Journal of Advanced Nursing,* 15: 1418–25.

Fischer, F. and Forester, J. (eds) (1993). *The Argumentative Turn in Policy Analysis and Planning*. Durham: Duke University Press.

Fisher, A. (1993). *The Logic of Real Arguments*. Cambridge: Cambridge University Press.

Fishman, J.A. (1956). 'An examination of the process and function of social stereotyping'. *Journal of Social Psychology*, 43: 1.

Fitt, M.H., Walker, A.E. and Leary, H.M. (2009). 'Assessing the quality of doctoral dissertation literature reviews in instructional technology'. Paper presented at the Annual Meeting of the American Educational Research Association, San Diego, CA, April.

Flint, K. (1993). *The Woman Reader, 1837–1914*. Oxford: Oxford University Press.

Fossey, E., Harvey, C., McDermott, F. and Davidson, L. (2002). *Understanding and Evaluating Qualitative Research*. Australasian Society for Psychiatric Research and the Research Board of the Royal Australian and New Zealand College of Psychiatrists. Available at: http://pathways.bangor.ac.uk/fossey-et-al-evaluating-qual-research.pdf.

Francis, D. (1986). 'Advertising and structuralism: The myth of formality'. *International Journal of Advertising*, 5: 197–214.

Francis, D. (1987). 'The great transformation'. In R.J. Anderson and W.W. Sharrock (eds), *Great Debates in Sociology*. London: Allan Unwin.

Francis, J.R.D. (1976). 'Supervision and examination of higher degree students'. *Bulletin of the University of London,* 31: 3–6.

Frankel, S. and West, R. (1993). *Rationing in the National Health Service*. Basingstoke: Macmillan.

Frankfort, H. (2005). *On Bullshit*. Princeton: Princeton University Press.

Gabehart, M.E. (2005). 'An analysis of citations to retracted articles in the scientific literature'. Unpublished Master's Paper, School of Information and Library Science, University of North Carolina at Chapel Hill.

Gall, M.D., Borg, W.R. and Gall, J.P. (1996). *Educational Research: An Introduction*. London: Longman.

Garfield, E. (1979). *Citation Indexing, its Theory and Application in Science, Technology, and Humanities*. Philadelphia: ISI Press.

Garfinkel, H. (1991). 'Respecification: Evidence for locally produced, naturally accountable phenomena of order, logic, reason, meaning, method, etc. in and as of the essential haecceity of immortal ordinary society (I) – an announcement of studies'. In G. Button (ed.), *Ethnomethodology and the Human Sciences*. Cambridge: Cambridge University Press.

Gaventa, J. and Barrett, G. (2010). *So What Difference does it Make? Mapping the Outcomes of Citizen Engagement*. Brighton: IDS.

Geertz, C. (1980). 'Blurred genres: Refiguration of social thought'. *The American Scholar* (Spring).

Gentner, D. (1982). 'Are scientific analogies metaphors?' In D.S. Miall (ed.), *Metaphor: Problems and Perspectives*. Hemel Hempstead: Harvester.

Giltrow, J. (1995). *Academic Writing*. Cardiff: Broadway Press.

Goldman, L. (1964). *The Hidden God*. London: Routledge & Kegan Paul.

Gould, S.J. (2003). *The Hedgehog, the Fox, and the Magister's Pox*. New York: Harmony Books.

Grahame-Smith, D. (1998). 'Evidence-based medicine: Challenging the orthodoxy'. *Journal of The Royal Society of Medicine Supplement*, 91(35): 7–11.

Gray, J.A.M. (2001). *Evidence-based Healthcare: How to Make Health Policy and Management Decisions*, 2nd edn. London: Churchill Livingstone.

Greenberg, D.N. (1995). 'Blue versus gray: A metaphor constraining sensemaking around a restructuring'. *Group Organization Management,* 20(2): 183–209.

Gross, A. and Fox, E.J. (2009). 'Relational Frame Theory: An overview of the controversy'. *The Analysis of Verbal Behavior,* 25: 87–98.

Guba, E. and Lincoln, Y. (1994). 'Competing paradigms in qualitative research'. In N. Denzin and Y. Lincoln (eds), *Handbook of Qualitative Research.* Thousand Oaks, CA: Sage.

Hammersley, M. (2002). 'Systematic or unsystematic, is that the question? Some reflections on the science, art, and politics of reviewing research evidence'. Text of a talk given to the Public Health Evidence Steering Group of the Health Development Agency. Available at: www.nice.org.uk/download.aspx?o=508244.

Hanson, S. and Jones, A. (2015). 'Is there evidence that walking groups have health benefits? A systematic review and meta-analysis'. *British Journal of Sports Medicine,* 49: 710–15

Hart, C. (1993). 'The social production of an advertisement'. Unpublished PhD Thesis, Manchester Metropolitan University.

Hart, C. (1994). 'By gum pet you smell gorgeous: Representations of sexuality in perfume advertisements'. British Sociological Association Annual Conference: Sexualities in Social Context, University of Central Lancashire, 28-31 March.

Hart, C. (2001). *Doing a Literature Search: A Comprehensive Guide for the Social Sciences.* London: Sage.

Hart, C. (2005). *Doing your Masters Dissertation: Realising your Potential as a Social Scientist.* London: Sage.

Haug, W.F. (1987). *Commodity Aesthetics, Ideology and Culture.* Paris: International General.

Hayes, S.C. and Hayes, L.J. (1989). 'The verbal action of the listener as the basis for rule governance'. In S.C. Hayes (ed.), *Rule Governed Behavior: Cognition, Contingencies and Instructional Control.* New York: Plenum.

Hayes, S.C. and Wilson, K.G. (1996). 'Criticisms of Relational Frame Theory: Implications for a behavior analytic account of derived stimulus relations'. *The Psychological Record,* 46: 221–36.

Hayes, S.C., Barnes-Holmes, D. and Roche, B. (2003). 'Behavior analysis, Relational Frame Theory, and the challenge of human language and cognition: A reply to the commentaries on Relational Frame Theory: A Post-Skinnerian Account of Human Language and Cognition'. *The Analysis of Verbal Behavior,* 19: 39–54.

Hayes, S.C., Bunting, K., Herbst, S., Bond, F.W. and Barnes-Holmes, D. (2006). 'Expanding the scope of organizational behavior management: Relational frame theory and the experimental analysis of complex human behavior'. *Journal of Organizational Behavior Management,* 26: 1–23.

Hempel, C.G. (1965). *Aspects of Explanation.* New York: Free Press.

Henderson, W., Dudley-Evans, T. and Blackhouse, R. (eds) (1993). *Economics and Language.* London: Routledge.

Hicks, D. (1999). 'The difficulty of achieving full coverage of international social science literature and the bibliometric consequences'. *Scientometrics,* 44(2): 193–215.

Higgins, J.P.T. and Green, S. (eds) (2011). *Cochrane Handbook for Systematic Reviews of Interventions.* Version 5.1.0 [updated March 2011]. The Cochrane Collaboration. Available at: www.cochrane-handbook.org.

Hinderer, D.E. (1992). *Building Arguments*. California: Wadsworth Publishing Company.

Hoffmann, K. and Doucette, L. (2012). 'A review of citation analysis methodologies for collection management'. *College and Research Libraries*, July: 321–35.

Hospers, J. (1988). *An Introduction to Philosophical Analysis*. London: Routledge.

Huedo-Medina, T., Sanchez-Meca, J., Marin-Martinez, F. and Botella, J. (2006). 'Assessing heterogeneity in meta-analysis: Q statistic or I2 index?' *CHIP Documents*, Paper 19. Available at: http://digitalcommons.uconn.edu/chip_docs/19.

Hyman, R.T. (1973). 'Leadership and metaphors in teaching'. *Notre Dame Journal of Education*, 4: 80–8.

Jackson, L., Langille, L., Lyons, R., Hughes, J., Martin, D. and Winstanley, V. (2009). 'Does moving from a high poverty to lower poverty neighborhood improve mental health? A Realist review of "Moving to Opportunity"'. *Health & Place*, 15: 961–70.

Jacob, E.K. (2004). 'Classification and categorization: A difference that makes a difference'. *Library Trends*, 52(3): 515–40.

Jacobs, K., Kemeny, J. and Manzi, T. (1999). 'The struggle to define homelessness: A constructivist approach'. In S. Hutson and D. Clapham (eds), *Homelessness: Public Policies and Private Troubles*. London: Cassell.

Jadad, A.R., Moore, R.A., Carroll, D., Jenkinson, C., Reynolds, J.M., Gavaghan, D.J. and McQuay, H.J. (1996). 'Assessing the quality of reports of randomized clinical trials: Is blinding necessary?'. *Controlled Clinical Trials*, 17: 1–12.

Jhally, S. (1987). *The Codes of Advertising*. London: Francis Pinter Ltd.

Johnson, D.E. (1980). 'The behavioral system model for nursing'. In J.P. Riehl and C. Roy (eds), *Conceptual Models for Nursing Practice*, 2nd edn. New York: Appleton-Century-Crofts.

Jonassen, D.H., Beissner, K. and Yacci, M. (1993) *Structural Knowledge: Techniques for Representing, Conveying, and Acquiring Structural Knowledge*. New Jersey: Lawrence Erlbaum.

Jones, K. (1997). 'Community as a documentary reality'. Unpublished PhD, UCE, Birmingham.

Judge, T.A., Cable, D.M., Colbert, A.E. and Rynes, S.L. (2007). 'What causes a management article to be cited – article, author, or journal?' *Academy of Management Journal*, 50(3): 491–506.

Justus, R. (2009). 'A guide to writing the dissertation literature review'. *Practical Assessment, Research & Evaluation*, 14(13). Available at: http://pareonline.net/getvn.asp?v=14&n=13.

Kanekar, A. and Sharma, M. (2007). 'Tobacco prevention interventions in adolescents'. *Californian Journal of Health Promotion*, 5(3): 120–30.

Kantar, L. (2014). 'Incorporation of constructivist assumptions into problem-based instruction: A literature review'. *Nurse Education in Practice*, 14(3): 233–41.

Kappeler, S. (1985). *The Pornography of Representation* (Feminist Perspectives). Bristol: Polity Press.

Kimball, R. (2008). *Tenured Radicals: How Politics has Corrupted our Higher Education*. New York: HarperCollins.

Kruszewski, A.Z. (1999). 'Psychosocial adaptation to termination of pregnancy for fetal anomaly'. *Dissertation Abstracts International*, 61: 194B.

Kuhn, T. (1970). *The Structure of Scientific Revolutions*. Chicago: University of Chicago Press.

Kumar, M. (2014). *Quantum: Einstein, Bohr and the Great Debate about the Nature of Reality*. London: Icon Books.

Landes, D. (1969). *The Unbound Prometheus: Technological Change and Industrial Development in Western Europe from 1750 to the Present*. Cambridge: Cambridge University Press.

Law, J. and Lodge, P. (1984). *Science for Social Scientists*. London: Macmillan Press.

Lemert, E.M. (1951). *Social Psychology*. New York: McGraw Hill.

Levine, G. (2010). *Dying to Know: Scientific Epistemology and Narrative in Victorian England*. Chicago: University of Chicago Press.

Levine, M.E. (1991). 'The conservation principles: A model for health'. In K.M. Schaefer and J.B. Pond (eds), *Levine's Conservation Model: A Framework for Nursing Practice*. Philadelphia: F.A. Davis.

Levi-Strauss, C. (1958/1963). *Structural Anthropology*. New York: Basic Books.

Levi-Strauss, C. (1964–1972). *Mythologies*, 3 vols. Paris.

Lindholm-Romantschuk, Y. and Warner, J. (1996). 'The role of monographs in scholarly communication: An empirical study of philosophy, sociology and economics'. *Journal of Documentation*, 52(4): 389–404.

Lipmann, W. (1922). *Public Opinion*. New York: Harcourt Brace.

Lock, S. and Wells, F. (eds) (1997). *Fraud and Misconduct in Medical Research*, 2nd edn. London: BMJ Books.

Lodenstein, E., Dieleman, M., Gerretsen, B. and Broerse, J.E.W. (2013). 'A realist synthesis of the effect of social accountability interventions on health service providers' and policymakers' responsiveness'. *Systematic Reviews*, 2: 98. Available at: www.systematicreviewsjournal.com/content/2/1/98.

Magenta Book (2003). *The Magenta Book: Guidance Notes for Policy Evaluation and Analysis*. Background paper 2: What do we Already Know? Harnessing Existing Research (updated October 2007). London: Government Social Research Unit, HM Treasury.

Malinowski, B. (1922). *Argonauts of the Western Pacific*. No. 65 in the series of Monographs by writers connected with the London School of Economics and Political Science. Available at: https://archive.org/stream/argonautsofthewe032976mbp/argonautsofthewe032976mbp_djvu.txt.

Malinowski, B. (1989 [1967]). *A Diary in the Strict Sense of the Term*. Stanford: Stanford University Press.

Mandelbaum, S.J. (1990). 'Reading plans'. *APA Journal*, Summer: 350–8.

Masters, K.S., Spielmans, G.I. and Goodson, J.T. (2006). 'Are there demonstrable effects of distant intercessory prayer? A meta-analytic review'. *The Society of Behavioral Medicine*, 30(21): 609–10.

Marx, K. (1950 [1898]). 'Value, prices and profit'. In K. Marx and F. Engels, *Selected Works in Two Volumes*. London: Lawrence and Wishart.

Mayo, E. (1933). *The Human Problems of Industrial Civilisation*. New York: Macmillan.

McCloskey, D.N. (1994). 'How to do rhetorical analysis, and why'. In R.E. Blackhouse (ed.), *New Directions in Economic Methodology*. London: Routledge.

McFarlane, A. (1979). *The Origins of Modern English Individualism*. Cambridge: Cambridge University Press.

McGlone, M.S. (2007). 'What is the explanatory value of a conceptual metaphor?' *Language & Communication*, 27: 109–26.

McLellan, A. (2010). 'A systematic review of the corticosteroid regime for pediatric patients with steroid-responsive nephrotic syndrome'. *Health Sciences Library*, 20 October, McMaster University.

McMahon, T. and Ward, P. (2012). 'HIV among immigrants living in high-income countries: A realist review of evidence to guide targeted approaches to behavioural HIV prevention'. *Systematic Reviews*, 1: 56.

Merton, R.K. (1938). 'Social structure and anomie'. *American Sociological Review*, 8: 672–82.

Merton, R.K. (1957). 'The role-set: Problems in sociological theory'. *British Journal of Sociology*, 8: 106–20.

Merton, R.K. (1967). 'On sociological theories of the middle-range'. In R.K. Merton, *On Theoretical Sociology: Five Essays Old and New*. New York: Free Press.

Miles, M. and Huberman, M. (1994). *Qualitative Data Analysis: An Expanded Sourcebook*. Thousand Oaks, CA: Sage Publications.

Mills, J., Bonner, A. and Francis, K. (2006). 'The development of constructivist grounded theory'. *International Journal of Qualitative Methods*, 5(1): Article 3. Available at: www.ualberta.ca/~iiqm/backissues/5_1/html/mills.htm.

Mills, S. (1995). *Feminist Stylistics*. London: Routledge.

Mills, S.L., Pumarino, J., Clark, N., Carroll, S., Dennis, S., Koehn, S., Yu, T., Davis, C. and Fong, M. (2014). 'Understanding how self-management interventions work for disadvantaged populations living with chronic conditions: Protocol for a realist synthesis'. *BMJ Open,* 4: e005822. doi:10.1136/bmjopen-2014-005822.

Moodie, C., Stead, M., Bauld, L., McNeill, A., Angus, K., Hinds, K., Kwan, I., Thoma, J., Hastings, G. and O'Mara-Eves, A. (2012). 'Plain tobacco packaging: A systematic review'. Evidence for Policy and Practice, Information and Co-ordinating Centre. Available at: http://eppi.ioe.ac.uk.

Morgan, G. (1980). 'Paradigms, metaphors, and puzzle solving in organization theory'. *Administrative Science Quarterly*, 25(4): 605–22.

Morgan, G. (2006). *Images of Organization*, 4th edn. London: Sage Publications.

Moustakas, C. (1994). *Phenomenological Research Methods*. Thousand Oaks, CA: Sage Publications.

Neuman, W.L. (1994). *Social Research Methods: Qualitative and Quantitative Approaches*. Boston, MA: Allyn and Bacon.

Nichols, W. (1981). *Ideology and the Image*. Bloomington, IN: Indiana University Press.

Nikitina, L. and Furuoka, F. (2008). '"A language teacher is like...". Examining Malaysian students' perceptions of language teachers through metaphor analysis'. *Electronic Journal of Foreign Language Teaching*, 5(2): 192–205.

Northcote, M. (2012). 'Selecting criteria to evaluate qualitative research'. In M. Kiley (ed.), *Narratives of Transition: Perspectives of Research Leaders, Educators & Postgraduates*. Proceedings from the 10th Quality in Postgraduate Research Conference. Adelaide: The Centre for Higher Education, Learning and Teaching, The Australian National University.

Northern California Training Academy (2007). 'Recruitment and retention of child welfare social workers in rural communities – literature review'. Northern California Training Academy: The Center for Human Services Recruitment.

Nosek, B.A., Graham, J., Linder, N.M., Kesebir, S., Hawkins, C.B., Hahn, C., Schmidt, K., Motyl, M., Joy-Gaba, J.A., Frazier, R. and Tenney, E.R. (2010). 'Cumulative and career-stage citation impact of social-personality psychology programs and their members'. *Personality and Social Psychology Bulletin*, 36(10): 1283–300.

Novak, J.D. and Gowin, D.B. (1984). *Learning How to Learn*. New York, NY: Cambridge University Press.

Noyes, J., Popay, J., Pearson, A., Hannes, K. and Booth, A. (2013). *Qualitative and Implementation Evidence and Cochrane Reviews*. Available at: http://methods. cochrane.org/sites/methods.cochrane.org.qi/files/public/uploads/Handbook52_QQ_ Qualitative_web%20update%20Oct%202015.pdf.

Oakes, P.J., Haslam, S.A. and Turner, J.C. (1994). *Stereotyping and Social Reality*. London: Blackwell.

Ogawa, R.T. and Malen, B. (1991). 'Towards rigor in reviews of multivocal literature: Applying the exploratory case method'. *Review of Educational Research*, 61: 265–86.

Otte-Trojel, T., de Bont, A., Rundall, T.G. and van de Klundert, J. (2014). 'How outcomes are achieved through patient portals: A realist review'. *Journal of the American Medical Informatics Association*, 21: 751–7.

Oxford, R., Tomlinson, S., Barcelos, A., Harrington, C., Lavine, R.Z., Saleh, A. and Longhini, A. (1998). 'Clashing metaphors about classroom teachers: Toward a systematic typology for the language teaching field'. *System*, 26(1): 3–50.

Parsons, T. (1951). *The Social System*. London: Routledge.

Pattern, M. (1990). *Qualitative Evaluation Methods*. London: Sage.

Pawson, R. (2006). *Evidence-based Policy: A Realist Perspective*. London: Sage.

Pawson, R. (2013). *The Science of Evaluation: A Realist Manifesto*. London: Sage.

Pawson, R. and Tilley, N. (1997). *Realistic Evaluation*. London: Sage.

Pawson, R. and Tilley, N. (2004). *Realist Evaluation*. London: British Cabinet Office.

Pawson, R., Greenhalgh, T., Harvey, G. and Walshe, K. (2005). 'Realist review: A new method of systematic review designed for complex policy interventions'. *Journal of Health Service and Research Policy*, 10 Suppl(1): 21–34.

Payne, G. (1993). 'The community revisited: Some reflections on the community study as a method'. British Sociological Association Annual Conference, Essex, 5–8 April.

Phillips, E. and Pugh, D.S. (1994). *How to Get a PhD: A Handbook for Students and Supervisors*, 2nd edn. Buckingham: Open University.

Piaget, J. and Inhelder, B. (1955). *The Growth of Logical Thinking from Childhood to Adolescence*. London: Routledge & Kegan Paul.

Pollock, S.E. (1993). 'Adaptation to chronic illness: A program of research for testing nursing theory'. *Nursing Science Quarterly*, 6: 86–92.

Popper, K. (1959 [1934]). *The Logic of Scientific Discovery*. London: Hutchinson.

Prewitt, K., Schwandt, T.A. and Straf, M.L. (2012). *Using Science as Evidence in Public Policy*. Washington: National Academic Press.

Putman, H. (1981). *Reason, Truth and History*. Cambridge: Cambridge University Press.

Radcliffe-Brown, A.R. (1952). *Structure and Function in Primitive Society*. London: Cohen and West.

Rainbow Framework (2014). *Better Evaluation*. Available from: http://betterevaluation. org/sites/default/files/Rainbow%20Framework%20-20compact%20version.pdf.

Richardson, R., Trépel, D., Perry, A., Ali, S., Duffy, S. and Gabe, R. (2015). 'Screening for psychological and mental health difficulties in young people who offend: A systematic review and decision model'. *Health Technology Assessment*, 19(1).

Ried, K. (2006). 'Interpreting and understanding meta-analysis graphs: A practical guide'. *Australian Family Physician,* 35(8): 635–8.

Roy, C. (1976). *Introduction to Nursing: An Adaptation Model.* Englewood Cliffs, NJ: Prentice-Hall.

Roy, C. (1988). 'An explication of the philosophical assumptions of the Roy Adaptation Model'. *Nursing Science Quarterly,* 1: 26–34.

Russell, C.A. (1983). *Science and Social Change: 1700–1900.* London: Macmillan.

Ryle, G. (1949). *The Concept of Mind.* Harmondsworth: Penguin.

Sapir, E. (1985). *Selected Writings of Edward Sapir in Language, Culture and Personality* (D.G. Mandelbaum, ed.). Berkeley, CA: University of California Press.

Saussure de, F. (1966). *Course in General Linguistics.* New York: McGraw-Hill.

Savage, M., Devine, F., Cunningham, N., Taylor, M., Li, Y., Hjellbrekke, J., Le Roux, B., Friedman, S. and Miles, A. (2013). 'A new model of social class: Findings from the BBC's Great British class survey experiment'. *Sociology,* 47(2): 219–50.

Schlick, M. (1974[1918]). *General Theory of Knowledge: Introduction.* Vienna, (A.E. Blumberg, trans.). New York: Springer.

Schön, J.H., Kloc, C. and Batlogg, B. (2000). 'A light-emitting field-effect transistor'. *Science,* 290(5493): 963–6.

Schutz, A. (1967). *Collected Papers. Vol 1. The Problem of Social Reality.* The Hague: Martinus Nijhoff.

SCONUL (2011). *The SCONUL Seven Pillars of Information Literacy: A Research Lens for Higher Education.* Available at: www.sconul.ac.uk/sites/default/files/documents/coremodel.pdf.

Seale, C. (1994). 'Quality in qualitative research'. In N. Denzin and Y. Lincoln (eds), *Turning Points in Qualitative Research: Tying Knots in a Handkerchief.* Walnut Creek: AltaMira Press.

Shapin, S. and Schaffer, S. (1985). *Leviathan and the Air Pump: Hobbes, Boyle and the Experimental Life.* Princeton: Princeton University Press.

Shields, V.R. (1990). 'Advertising visual images: Gendered ways of seeing and looking'. *Journal of Communication Inquiry,* 14(2): 25–39.

Simon, H.A. (1957) *Models of Man.* New York: Wiley.

Smith, D.R. and Hazelton, M. (2008). 'Bibliometrics, citation indexing, and the Journals of Nursing'. *Nursing & Health Sciences,* 10(4): 260–5.

Snow, C.P. (1963 [1960]). *The Two Cultures.* Cambridge: Cambridge University Press.

Sokal, A.D. (1996). 'Transgressing the boundaries: Towards a transformative hermeneutics of quantum gravity'. *Social Text,* 46/47: 217–52.

Sokal, A.D. (1997). 'Response to Vincent Fleury and Yun Sun Limet'. *Times Literary Supplement,* 17 October: 17.

Sokal, A.D. and Bricmont, J. (1997). *Impostures Intellectuelles.* Paris: Editions Odile Jacob.

Sparks, L.E., Guo, Z., Chang, J.C. and Tichenor, B A. (1999a). 'Volatile organic compound emissions from Latex Paint – Part 1. Chamber experiments and source model development'. *Indoor Air,* 9(1): 10–17.

Sparks, L.E., Guo, Z., Chang, J.C. and Tichenor, B.A. (1999b). 'Volatile organic compound emissions from Latex Paint – Part 2. Test house studies and indoor air quality (Iaq) modelling'. *Indoor Air,* 9(1):18–25.

Spencer, H. (1969 [1884]). *The Man Versus the State*. London: Penguin.

Spencer, L., Ritchie, J., Lewis, J. and Dillon, L. (2003). *Quality in Qualitative Evaluation: A Framework for Assessing Research Evidence*. London: Government Chief Social Researcher's Office.

Squire, C. (2008). 'Approaches to narrative research'. Unpublished Discussion Paper, The National Centre for Research Methods (NCRM). Available at: www.ncrm.ac.uk/.

Stein, M., Rees, G., Hicks, L. and Gorin, S. (2009). *Neglected Adolescents – Literature Review*. London: DCSF.

Strauss, A. (1987). *Qualitative Analysis for Social Scientists*. Cambridge: Cambridge University Press.

Sweet, M. and Moynihan, R. (2007). *Improving Population Health: The Uses of Systematic Reviews*. Atlanta, GA/New York: Milbank Memorial Fund and Centers for Disease Control and Prevention.

Tesch, R. (1990). *Qualitative Research: Analysis, Types and Software Tools*. London: Falmer Press.

Thouless, R.H. and Thouless, C.R. (1990). *Straight and Crooked Thinking*, 4th edn. Sevenoaks: Hodder and Stoughton.

Throgmorton, J.A. (1991). 'The rhetoric of policy analysis'. *Policy Science*, 24: 153–79.

Tonnies, F. (1957 [1887]). *Community and Society*. London: Routledge & Kegan Paul; East Lancing, MI: University Press.

Toulmin, S. (1958). *The Uses of Argument*. Cambridge: Cambridge University Press.

Treadwell, J.R., Singh, S., Talati, R., McPheeters, M.L. and Reston, J.T. (2011). *A Framework for 'Best Evidence' Approaches in Systematic Reviews*. Rockville, MD: Agency for Healthcare Research and Quality. Available at: www.ncbi.nlm.nih.gov/books/NBK56660/.

Trigg, R. (1993). *Rationality and Science*. London: Blackwell.

Trowler, V. (2010). 'Student engagement literature review'. *The Higher Education Academy*. Available from: www.heacademy.ac.uk.

Tsai, P-F. (2003). 'A middle-range theory of caregiver stress'. *Nursing Science Quarterly*, 16: 137–45.

Tulman, L. and Fawcett, J. (2003). *Women's Health During and After Pregnancy: A Theory-based Study of Adaptation to Change*. New York: Springer.

Turnbull, C. (1971). *The Mountain People*. London: Jonathan Cape.

Turner, B.S. (1984). 'Orientalism and the problem of civil society'. In A. Hussain (ed.), *Orientalism, Islam and Islamists*. Brattleboro, VT: Amana Press.

Victor, L. (2008). 'Systematic reviewing'. *Social Research Update*, Issue 54, University of Surrey. Available at: www.soc.surrey.ac.uk/sru/.

Walkup, L.E. (1967). 'Creativity in science through visualisation'. *Journal of Creative Behavior*, 1(3): 283–90.

Wallas, G. (1926). *Art of Thought*. New York: Harcourt, Brace & Company.

Weber, M. (1965a [1930]). *The Theory of Social and Economic Organisation*. Oxford: Oxford University Press.

Weber, M. (1965b). *The Protestant Ethic and the Spirit of Capitalism*. London: Allen & Unwin.

Whittemore, R. and Roy, C. (2002). 'Adapting to diabetes mellitus: A theory synthesis'. *Nursing Science Quarterly,* 15: 311–17.

Williams, R. (1980). 'Advertising: The magic system'. In R. Williams, *Problems in Materialism and Culture*. London: Verso.

Williamson, J. (1979). *Decoding Advertisements*. London: Marion Boyears.

Wittgenstein, L. (1953). *Philosophical Investigations*. Oxford: Blackwell.

Wittgenstein, L. (1972 [1921]). *Tractatus Logico-philosophicus*. London: Routledge.

Wong, G., Westhrop, G., Pawson, R. and Greenhalgh, T. (2013). *Realist Synthesis*, RAMESES training materials. London: National Institute for Health Research Health Services and Delivery Research Program (NIHR HS&DR).

Wright-Mills, C. (1978 [1959]). *The Sociological Imagination*. Oxford: Oxford University Press.

Yanni, D.A. (1990). 'The social construction of women as mediated by advertising'. *Journal of Communication Inquiry*, 14(1): 71–81.

Zerubavel, E. (1993). *The Fine Line: Making Distinctions in Everyday Life*. Chicago: University of Chicago Press.

Ziebland, S. and Wyke, S. (2012). 'Health and illness in a connected world: How might sharing experience on the Internet affect people's health?'. *Milbank Quarterly*, 90(2): 219–49.

Index

Figures and Tables are indicated by page numbers in bold print.